T0318900

small arms survey
2015

----

weapons and the world

small
arms
survey

THE GRADUATE INSTITUTE | GENEVA

INSTITUT DE HAUTES ÉTUDES
INTERNATIONALES ET DU DÉVELOPPEMENT

GRADUATE INSTITUTE OF INTERNATIONAL
AND DEVELOPMENT STUDIES

Shaftesbury Road, Cambridge CB2 8EA, United Kingdom

One Liberty Plaza, 20th Floor, New York, NY 10006, USA

477 Williamstown Road, Port Melbourne, VIC 3207, Australia

314–321, 3rd Floor, Plot 3, Splendor Forum, Jasola District Centre, New Delhi – 110025, India

103 Penang Road, #05–06/07, Visioncrest Commercial, Singapore 238467

Cambridge University Press is part of Cambridge University Press & Assessment,
a department of the University of Cambridge.

We share the University's mission to contribute to society through the pursuit of
education, learning and research at the highest international levels of excellence.

www.cambridge.org
Information on this title: www.cambridge.org/9781107690677

© Small Arms Survey, Graduate Institute of International and Development Studies, Geneva 2015

This publication is in copyright. Subject to statutory exception and to the provisions
of relevant collective licensing agreements, no reproduction of any part may take
place without the written permission of Cambridge University Press & Assessment.

First published 2015
Reprinted 2021

A catalogue record for this publication is available from the British Library

ISBN   978-1-107-04198-1   Hardback
ISBN   978-1-107-69067-7   Paperback

Cambridge University Press & Assessment has no responsibility for the persistence
or accuracy of URLs for external or third-party internet websites referred to in this
publication and does not guarantee that any content on such websites is, or will
remain, accurate or appropriate.

FOREWORD

Today's wildlife crime threatens the survival of endangered and vulnerable species in many African countries. Evidence documented by WildlifeDirect—a Kenyan NGO founded in 2004—shows that legal penalties designed to deter such crimes have had little impact on poachers and traffickers; worse, poor law enforcement and corruption among government officials and security forces facilitate wildlife crime and trafficking.

In a chapter on the poaching of elephants and rhinos, the *Small Arms Survey 2015: Weapons and the World* offers valuable analysis of the relative roles of different actors, including non-state armed groups, criminal networks, and commercial poachers, in wildlife crime. The research reveals that while poachers are becoming increasingly militarized, law enforcement units have yet to adopt a systematic approach to recording and tracing firearms and ammunition found at poaching sites—steps that increase the likelihood of identifying poachers, the sources of their guns, and broader trafficking networks. These findings are especially valuable to broader efforts to tackle the illegal killing of wildlife.

The volume's chapter on armed violence around resource extraction sites is also pertinent to our work. As the *Survey* observes, the establishment of mining sites tends to be accompanied by the rapid urbanization of adjacent communities, growing inequalities, and shortfalls in service delivery—all of which attract a variety of armed actors and increase the pressure on natural habitats and wildlife.

I commend the *Small Arms Survey 2015: Weapons and the World* for the many insights it offers into the relationship between firearms and wildlife crime, as well as other pertinent small arms issues. I have little doubt that this volume will be of great interest to those working to protect our natural heritage, as well as others involved in arms control and the promotion of peace and security.

—Paula Kahumbu
Executive Director, WildlifeDirect

CONTENTS

Chapter 6. Expanding Arsenals: Insurgent Arms in Northern Mali

Chapter 7. Waning Cohesion: The Rise and Fall of the FDLR-FOCA

Chapter 8. Stockpiles at Sea: Floating Armouries in the Indian Ocean

Chapter 9. Unprotected: Young People in Post-conflict Burundi

Index

ABOUT THE SMALL ARMS SURVEY

The Small Arms Survey is a global centre of excellence whose mandate is to generate impartial, evidence-based, and policy-relevant knowledge on all aspects of small arms and armed violence. It is the principal international source of expertise, information, and analysis on small arms and armed violence issues, and acts as a resource for governments, policy-makers, researchers, and other stakeholders. It is located in Geneva, Switzerland, at the Graduate Institute of International and Development Studies.

Established in 1999, the Survey is supported by the Swiss Federal Department of Foreign Affairs and current or recent contributions from the Governments of Australia, Belgium, Denmark, Finland, France, Germany, the Netherlands, New Zealand, Norway, the United Kingdom, and the United States, as well as from the European Union. The centre is grateful for past support received from the Governments of Canada, Spain, and Sweden, as well as from foundations and many bodies within the UN system.

The Survey has an international staff with expertise in security studies, political science, law, economics, development studies, sociology, and criminology, and collaborates with a network of researchers, partner institutions, non-governmental organizations, and governments in more than 50 countries.

NOTES TO READERS

Abbreviations: Lists of abbreviations can be found at the end of each chapter.

Chapter cross-referencing: Chapter cross-references are fully capitalized in brackets throughout the book. One example appears in Chapter 7: 'As a result, commanders who controlled areas with natural resources—especially gold and cassiterite (tin ore)—tended to become the wealthiest (VIOLENCE AND RESOURCE EXTRACTION).'

Exchange rates: All monetary values are expressed in current US dollars (USD). When other currencies are also cited, unless otherwise indicated, they are converted to USD using the 365-day average exchange rate for the period 1 September 2013 to 31 August 2014.

Small Arms Survey: The plain text—Small Arms Survey—is used to indicate the organization and its activities, while the italicized version—*Small Arms Survey*—refers to the publication. The *Survey*, appearing italicized, relates generally to past and future editions.

Small Arms Survey
Graduate Institute of International and Development Studies
Maison de la Paix, Chemin Eugène-Rigot 2E
1202 Geneva
Switzerland

t +41 22 908 5777
f +41 22 732 2738
e sas@smallarmssurvey.org
w www.smallarmssurvey.org

ACKNOWLEDGEMENTS

This is the 15th edition of the *Small Arms Survey*. Like previous editions, it is a collective product of the staff of the Small Arms Survey, a centre of excellence on small arms and armed violence based at the Graduate Institute of International and Development Studies in Geneva, Switzerland. Numerous researchers in Geneva and around the world have contributed to this volume, and it has benefited from the input and advice of government officials, advocates, experts, and colleagues from the small arms research community and beyond. Several people who supported research for this edition of the yearbook asked to remain anonymous; we are grateful for their contributions, including some of the photographs used in this volume.

The principal chapter authors were assisted by in-house and external contributors, who are acknowledged in the relevant chapters. In addition, chapter reviews were provided by: Julian Blanc, Mark Bromley, Deborah Bryceson, Ledio Cakaj, Gilles Carbonnier, Prasenjit Chaudhuri, Chris Chew, Vincent Choffat, Julie Claveau, Mohammad Hassan Faizee, Gary Fleetwood, Gillian Goh, Claudio Gramizzi, Yvan Guichaoua, Etienne Huber, N.R. Jenzen-Jones, Evert Kets, Gaspard Kisoki Sumaili, Carolin Liss, Daniel Mack, Nic Marsh, Blaž Mihelič, Laura Nicolson, David Niyonzima, Rebecca Peters, Daniël Prins, Ellen Regeling, Dilys Roe, Conor Seyle, Delaney Simon, Jonathan Somer, Jason Stearns, Rachel Stohl, Savannah de Tessières, David Towndrow, Michael Ungar, Peter Uvin, Christoph Vogel, Michael Wessells, and Adrian Wilkinson.

Anna Alvazzi del Frate, Eric G. Berman, Keith Krause, Emile LeBrun, and Glenn McDonald were responsible for the overall planning and organization of this edition. Alessandra Allen and Estelle Jobson managed its production. Tania Inowlocki copy-edited the book; Jillian Luff produced the maps; Rick Jones provided the design and the layout; Donald Strachan undertook the proofreading; and Indexing Specialists (UK) Ltd compiled the index. John Haslam and Carrie Parkinson of Cambridge University Press provided support throughout the production process. Natacha Cornaz, Elli Kytömäki, Salome Lienert, Irene Pavesi, Stéphanie Perazzone, and Michael Stinnett fact-checked the chapters. Olivia Denonville conducted photo research. Cédric Blattner and Elise Lebret Agneray provided administrative support under the direction of Carole Touraine, who is responsible for the Small Arms Survey's financial oversight.

The organization also benefited from the support of the Graduate Institute of International and Development Studies.

We are extremely grateful to the Swiss government—especially the Federal Department of Foreign Affairs and the Swiss Agency for Development Cooperation—for its generous financial and overall support of the Small Arms Survey. In particular, we extend our appreciation to Tiziano Balmelli, Erwin Bollinger, Prasenjit Chaudhuri, Vincent Choffat, Sabrina Dallafior Matter, Thomas Greminger, Jasna Lazarevic, Urs Schmid, Paul Seger, Frédéric Tissot-Daguette, and Claude Wild.

The Small Arms Survey further benefits from the support of international agencies, including the Bureau for Policy and Programme Support of the UN Development Programme, the UN Mine Action Service, the UN Institute for Disarmament Research, the UN Office for Disarmament Affairs, the UN Office on Drugs and Crime, and the World Health Organization.

In Geneva, the centre has benefited from the expertise of Michael Biontino, Silvia Cattaneo, Silvia Mercogliano, Elsa Mouelhi-Rondeau, Namdi Payne, and Jarmo Sareva.

Beyond Geneva, we also receive support from a number of colleagues. In addition to those mentioned above and in specific chapters, we would like to thank Philip Alpers, James Bevan, Steve Costner, Tarmo Dix, Thomas Goebel, Marianne Hille, Aurélie Lamazière, Jonah Leff, Myriam Marcuello, Hideki Matsuno, Frank Meeussen, Sho Morimoto, Cédric Poitevin, Jorge Restrepo, Damien Spleeters, Zahir Tanin, and Nicola Williams.

Our sincere thanks go out to many other individuals (who remain unnamed) for their continuing support of the Small Arms Survey. Our apologies to anyone we have failed to mention.

—**Keith Krause**, Programme Director
Eric G. Berman, Managing Director
Anna Alvazzi del Frate, Research Director

Small Arms Survey 2015

Editors	Glenn McDonald, Emile LeBrun, Anna Alvazzi del Frate, Eric G. Berman, and Keith Krause
Coordinator	Glenn McDonald
Publication Managers	Alessandra Allen and Estelle Jobson
Designer	Rick Jones, StudioExile
Cartographer	Jillian Luff, MAP*grafix*
Copy-editor	Tania Inowlocki
Proofreader	Donald Strachan

Principal chapter authors

Introduction	Emile LeBrun and Glenn McDonald
Chapter 1	Khristopher Carlson, Joanna Wright, and Hannah Dönges
Chapter 2	Oliver Jütersonke and Hannah Dönges
Chapter 3	Glenn McDonald
Chapter 4	Paul Holtom and Christelle Rigual
Chapter 5	Pierre Gobinet and Jovana Carapic
Chapter 6	Holger Anders
Chapter 7	Raymond Debelle and Nicolas Florquin
Chapter 8	Ioannis Chapsos and Paul Holtom
Chapter 9	Claudia Seymour

A ranger from the Lewa Wildlife Conservancy searches for poachers while on patrol, near Meru, Kenya April 2013. © Tom Pilston/Panos Pictures

Introduction

We tend to approach the issues of small arms proliferation and armed violence in terms of people and the relations between them: perpetrators and victims, buyers and sellers, groups in conflict with one another. This people-centred approach is understandable because our ultimate aims are to reduce human suffering and improve human security. But if the focus is too narrow, it can obscure the broader picture.

This year, the *Small Arms Survey 2015: Weapons and the World* aims to provide several pieces of that broader picture, examining small arms and armed violence from contrasting, but complementary angles. Its first section explores two specific aspects of an emerging issue area, namely the environment and small arms. A second section, titled 'weapons, markets, and measures', looks at small arms markets and control challenges. The final section of the 2015 *Survey* focuses on armed actors.

THE ENVIRONMENT AND SMALL ARMS

This is not the first time the Small Arms Survey has stepped back from the specifics of arms markets and armed violence to examine broader socio-economic, political, and cultural influences. The connections between small arms and the natural world, however, remain largely unexplored, even though in some cases they are lying in plain sight. Many of the world's battlefields, for example, are scarred with the physical by-products of ammunition use, in the form of lead and, in some cases, depleted uranium.

On a much broader scale, the many ways in which environmental factors can trigger, sustain, and shape armed conflicts are gaining increasing attention. Resource constraints have provoked violence throughout history. In the 21st century, overpopulation, increasing urbanization, resource depletion, and climate-linked change, including drought-induced privation, are adding fuel to the fire.

Global climate change is now seen as the most pressing of all environmental problems. The year 2014 was the warmest ever recorded (NASA, 2015), and there are concerns regarding the impact of climate change on human interactions—including on underlying causes of armed conflict, as well as on actual fighting. In tropical conflict areas, for example, fighting traditionally stops during the rainy season, only to resume when the soil hardens enough for vehicles to navigate unpaved roads. Terrain influences—even determines—battle tactics. In some parts of the world, rainy seasons are now shifting in time and intensity. As global warming alters temperature, rainfall, and sea levels, as many expect it will, it is almost certain to affect armed violence and armed conflict in ways that for now are unpredictable.

Two chapters in the *Small Arms Survey 2015* take up environmental themes. In addition to causing environmental degradation, the extraction of natural resources can transform remote outposts into urban hubs virtually overnight; it can also spur insecurity and violence as different groups compete over spoils and as local communities protest perceived wrongs (VIOLENCE AND RESOURCE EXTRACTION). At the same time, poachers' use of weapons, including military-style firearms, has led to a marked reduction—and, in some cases, the near elimination—of protected elephant and rhino populations in Africa. While national anti-poaching forces and organized poaching groups are becoming increasingly militarized, poaching rates continue to outpace natural population replacement rates in many parts of the continent (POACHING IN AFRICA).

WEAPONS, MARKETS, AND MEASURES

The second section of the *Survey* looks at small arms markets and the various attempts under way, at the national, regional, and global levels, to strengthen small arms control and prevent legal weapons from becoming illicit. This section begins with a review of the latest steps agreed at the global level, specifically at the Fifth Biennial Meeting of States on the UN Programme of Action (UN UPDATE). It ends with an examination of possible ways forward for Southeast Europe as countries there, in partnership with other governments and regional organizations, struggle with their often-excessive weapons and ammunitions stockpiles (STOCKPILE MANAGEMENT). In between, the Trade Update chapter presents some of the latest trends in international small arms transfers, with a specific focus on transfers to selected countries in the Middle East and North Africa region, before and after the 'Arab Spring'.

This last chapter underlines the magnitude of the control challenges that still lie ahead. There is little evidence that the Arab uprisings have had much impact on the policies of significant exporters of small arms to the region, notwithstanding the clear risks of diversion and misuse in the cases examined in the chapter (TRADE UPDATE). Meanwhile, the UN small arms process faces a challenge in translating diplomatic discussions of the past several years into more concrete prescriptions for action at the Second Open-ended Meeting of Governmental Experts. UN member states have known for some time that weapons marking, record-keeping, and tracing are made more difficult by certain recent developments in small arms manufacturing, technology, and design (UN UPDATE). But they have yet to decide what to do about it.

Overall, the weapons, markets, and measures section of the 2015 *Survey* highlights a patchwork of action, as well as inaction, with respect to the critical control challenges of the day—challenges that are not likely to dissipate any time soon, neither in the Middle East and North Africa, nor elsewhere.

ARMED ACTORS

Moving from the tools of armed violence to those who wield them, the last four chapters in the 2015 *Survey* highlight special challenges concerning armed actors, ranging from insurgents in northern Mali to maritime security guards operating against pirates in and around the Indian Ocean.

Two chapters document the somewhat contrasting fortunes of insurgent forces. In northern Mali, jihadists remain a pervasive threat. Their aggressive campaign for Islamic rule is hindering reconciliation between other rebels and the government, while their use of roadside bombs and suicide attacks will likely pose a threat to peacekeepers and government security forces for the foreseeable future (NORTHERN MALI). In the eastern Democratic Republic of the Congo, government military operations and two separate disarmament, demobilization, and reintegration campaigns have sapped the internal cohesion and overall strength of the insurgent group, the Forces Démocratiques de Libération du Rwanda–Forces Combattantes Abacunzi. While this is good news, the group's remaining members have dispersed into the jungle with their weapons, where they can still threaten civilians (FDLR–FOCA).

Definitions

The Small Arms Survey uses the term 'small arms and light weapons' to cover both military-style small arms and light weapons, as well as commercial firearms (handguns and long guns). Except where noted otherwise, it follows the definition used in the *Report of the UN Panel of Governmental Experts on Small Arms* (UNGA, 1997):

Small arms: revolvers and self-loading pistols, rifles and carbines, sub-machine guns, assault rifles, and light machine guns.

Light weapons: heavy machine guns, grenade launchers, portable anti-tank and anti-aircraft guns, recoilless rifles, portable anti-tank missile and rocket launchers, portable anti-aircraft missile launchers, and mortars of less than 100 mm calibre.

The term 'small arms' is used in this volume to refer to small arms, light weapons, and their ammunition (as in 'the small arms industry') unless the context indicates otherwise, whereas the terms 'light weapons' and 'ammunition' refer specifically to those items.

'Armed violence' is defined as 'the use or threatened use of weapons to inflict injury, death or psychosocial harm' (OECD, 2011, p. ii).

Private security companies appear to be fulfilling their role of security provision in and around the Indian Ocean, an area that has seen a sharp decline in the number of Somali pirate attacks in recent years, correlating with the deployment of private armed guards on board vessels transiting the area. Yet, in the absence of common rules and regulations, there are concerns over the security of the arms and ammunition that these guards store on board the 'floating armouries' that operate in these waters (FLOATING ARMOURIES).

The *Small Arms Survey 2015* concludes with a consideration of youths in Burundi. Currently, despite their aspirations to lead normal lives, many young people, already made vulnerable by years of armed conflict and poverty, have few options but to join political parties that have a history of manipulating and mobilizing their members for violence. As the chapter relates, including in the words of Burundian youths, whether the country's future is peaceful or conflict-ridden depends largely on whether young Burundians will be offered better alternatives (YOUNG PEOPLE IN BURUNDI).

CHAPTER HIGHLIGHTS

The environment and small arms

Chapter 1 (Poaching in Africa). From the Central African Republic to South Africa, Africa's elephant and rhino populations are under threat from poachers. Armed militias, rogue military officers, commercial poachers, and local hunters are some of the perpetrators involved. They use a variety of instruments and methods to kill protected wildlife, including military-style weapons and high-calibre hunting rifles. This chapter investigates both the weapons types and methods used by poachers and the responses by governments, conservancy groups, and local communities. As international demand for ivory and rhino horn remains high, poachers and anti-poaching forces have increasingly adopted military tactics and weaponry, leading to lethal encounters between poachers, wildlife rangers, and civilians.

Chapter 2 (Violence and Resource Extraction). This chapter focuses on violence related to the rapid urbanization of areas surrounding resource extraction sites. Extraction—particularly of oil, gas, and minerals—tends to attract a variety of armed actors, including security forces and predatory groups. Resource extraction frontiers tend to be characterized by insufficient public service provision, including of security, which is often outsourced to non-state providers. The violence in these urbanized frontiers involves not only conflict over the resources themselves, but also unrest related to precarious socio-economic and environmental conditions, post-extraction decline, and state-induced urban clean-up.

Weapons, markets, and measures

Chapter 3 (UN Update). The Fifth Biennial Meeting of States (BMS5), the latest meeting on the UN Programme of Action (PoA), was held in June 2014. But to what end? This year's UN Update chapter recaps the key features of the meeting and assesses the BMS5 outcome document against pre-existing PoA-meeting text. The chapter also anticipates the next meeting on the PoA calendar, the Second Open-ended Meeting of Governmental Experts (MGE2), scheduled for June 2015. It reviews the control challenges posed by new developments in small arms manufacturing, technology, and design and charts possible ways forward at MGE2. MGE1 helped alert states to some of the new developments. It will be up to MGE2 to engage with the associated challenges and indicate how to respond.

Chapter 4 (Trade Update). This chapter examines small arms flows to Egypt, Libya, and Syria, both before and after the 'Arab Spring'. As a rule, significant exporters of small arms to the Middle East and North Africa have not introduced restrictive policies in response to the increased armed violence and political instability in the region since 2011. States have also authorized the export of small arms to non-state armed groups inclined to fight extremist groups in the region, despite the risk of diversion and misuse. In line with previous Trade Updates, the chapter presents updated information on the main actors of the global authorized trade, including top exporters and importers (those with annual exports and imports of at least USD 100 million) in 2012. In advance of the presentation of a revised Transparency Barometer in the 2016 *Survey*, it also assesses the extent to which regional reporting instruments have promoted transparency in small arms transfers.

Chapter 5 (Stockpile Management). While most countries in South-east Europe face the challenge of managing operational, excess, and ageing weapons and ammunition, few have the capacity to administer their stockpiles in a comprehensive manner, thus increasing the risks of diversion and accidental explosions. Since 2009, the Regional Approach to Stockpile Reduction initiative has fostered stockpile management synergies in the region. This chapter describes the rationale behind the initiative and reviews surplus stockpile, disposal, and storage data provided by participating states for the years 2009–14. The research highlights the constraints hindering regional cooperation in terms of surplus ammunition transport and demilitarization, and points to opportunities for the building of sustained capacity for stockpile management in South-east Europe.

Armed actors

Chapter 6 (Northern Mali). This chapter reviews the types and sources of arms and ammunition used by insurgents in northern Mali in 2014, comparing these findings to a similar study conducted in 2005. It shows that these arsenals are expanding in this restive region. Having overcome shortages of light weapons and ammunition, insurgents now possess larger-calibre weapons not previously documented in northern Mali. Much of the newer materiel appears to come from looted Malian stockpiles as well as from Libya and, to a lesser extent, other sources in the region.

Chapter 7 (FDLR–FOCA). The Forces Démocratiques de Libération du Rwanda–Forces Combattantes Abacunzi (FDLR–FOCA) was long considered one of the most enduring and destabilizing armed groups operating in the eastern Democratic Republic of the Congo. Yet its membership has dwindled in recent years, from an estimated 12,000 combatants in 2002 to just 1,500 in 2014. The chapter examines the origins, evolution, and small arms holdings of the group. It documents some of the 'state-like' mechanisms that FDLR–FOCA put in place to ensure group cohesion, and how these eroded over time. Importantly, the chapter analyses the factors that contributed to the group's decline, including targeted military operations and demobilization programmes implemented by regional and international actors.

Chapter 8 (Floating Armouries). Maritime private security companies that protect merchant vessels against piracy in the high-risk area in and around the Indian Ocean face legal restrictions regarding the transfer of arms and ammunition between coastal states. Their solution has been the use of 'floating armouries'—maritime vessels that store company arms and ammunition in international waters. Research presented in this chapter indicates that security and storage practices varied significantly among the approximately 30 floating armouries operating in the high-risk area in 2013, with some violating the terms of arms export licensing provisions. Key stakeholders, however, have not developed common minimum standards for the safety and security of floating armouries and show no signs of preparing to do so.

Chapter 9 (Young People in Burundi). Young people's experiences and means of coping with armed violence are important for both security and development in post-conflict contexts—factors that are often overlooked by policy-makers. This chapter focuses on Burundi, a country where civil war ended more than a decade ago but where insecurity persists. Based on original narrative data collected between 2012 and 2014, the chapter shows how a history of violent conflict affects the lives of young people and their families, and how the conditions of poverty, unemployment, and lack of access to basic social services prompt many young people to adopt high-risk coping strategies, including ones that lead to violence. It points to the need for increased consideration of young people's capacities for resilience.

CONCLUSION

In an earlier era, the biological sciences placed an organism and its environment in separate domains of study. Subsequent research has shown that they cannot be separated so easily. Our understanding of complex human behaviours, such as armed violence, is moving in the same direction. Increasingly, all aspects of human life—including armed violence—appear entwined with broader environmental factors.

This edition of the *Small Arms Survey* contributes to the emerging research agenda on the environment and small arms in the specific, but related areas of wildlife poaching and resource extraction. It also broadens and deepens our understanding of the tools of violence and those who wield them, including for purposes of environmental predation. The poaching of elephants in West and Central Africa, for example, has significantly cut numbers, with some herds now close to extinction. The causes of this debacle include weak governance, ongoing armed conflicts, substantial firearms proliferation, and the presence of criminal groups.

The same afflictions are threatening the security of people and countries in other parts of the world. Some of the news, including the persistence of small arms transfers to a volatile Middle East, is dire. But there are also sources of hope: modest, but significant steps forward in the fight against small arms proliferation and misuse. While the broader small arms picture is complex and often troubling, the 2015 *Survey* details many practical means of grappling with today's current challenges—at the level of the individual, her community, and the planet as a whole. ☛

—Emile LeBrun and Glenn McDonald

BIBLIOGRAPHY

NASA (National Aeronautics and Space Administration). 2015. 'NASA, NOAA Find 2014 Warmest Year in Modern Record.' Press release. 16 January. <http://www.nasa.gov/press/2015/january/nasa-determines-2014-warmest-year-in-modern-record>

OECD (Organisation for Economic Co-operation and Development). 2011. 'Breaking Cycles of Violence: Key Issues in Armed Violence Reduction.' Paris: OECD. <http://www.oecd.org/governance/governance-peace/conflictandfragility/docs/48913388.pdf>

UNGA (United Nations General Assembly). 1997. *Report of the Panel of Governmental Experts on Small Arms.* A/52/298 of 27 August (annexe).

Kenya Wildlife Service officials display elephant tusks seized from poachers, Nairobi, January 2013
© Noor Khamis/Reuters

In the Line of Fire

ELEPHANT AND RHINO POACHING IN AFRICA

1

INTRODUCTION

In June 2014, armed poachers entered the Ol Jogi sanctuary in Kenya and killed four rhinos in one evening. The Kenya Wildlife Service (KWS) described the attack as the worst perpetrated against rhinos since the 1988 killing of five rhinos in Meru National Park (Jorgic, 2014). A month prior to the rhino attack at Ol Jogi, KWS rangers found themselves caught between two gangs of armed poachers. When the shootout ended, 25-year-old KWS ranger Paul Harrison Lelesepei was dead from gunshot wounds (Heath, 2014). The two recent incidents underscore the danger armed poachers pose to wildlife and rangers alike, not only in Kenya, but across African range states where poachers target elephants and rhinos for their ivory and horn, fuelling a thriving international illicit trade.

In Africa, elephant populations on the whole are in decline and the illicit killing of rhinos has escalated sharply over recent years. The actors involved in poaching these animals include armed militias, rogue military officers, commercial poachers, and bush meat and subsistence hunters. Poachers are making widespread use of military-style weapons and high-calibre hunting rifles in their pursuit of elephants and rhinos, complicating the efforts of wildlife rangers to stop them.

This chapter draws on interviews with leading wildlife conservation experts and open-source material to examine the challenges facing and strategies adopted by anti-poaching forces and wildlife management agencies in African range states with elephant and rhino populations. Based on original field research conducted in Kenya, the chapter also offers insight provided by rangers, conservationists, and others affected by poaching in the country. The main findings are that:

- Poachers use multiple means to kill elephants and rhinos, including firearms and non-firearm methods.
- As demand for ivory and rhino horn remains high, some poachers and anti-poaching forces are becoming increasingly militarized, using military-style weapons and adopting more aggressive tactics.
- Firearms and ammunition found at poaching sites are not systematically identified, recorded, or traced despite the potential use of such techniques in identifying the sources and trafficking routes of poacher weapons.
- Armed groups have been responsible for major cases of large-scale elephant poaching, yet poaching allegations have also been levelled against some government military forces.
- Small groups of poachers also target elephant herds and rhinos, killing significant numbers of animals over time, particularly in rangeland where elephant and rhino populations are dense.
- Without a substantial reduction in the demand for ivory and rhino horn, efforts to deter poachers through armed interventions may disrupt poaching, but not stop it.

The chapter begins with an overview of poaching in Africa, covering trends and drivers in elephant and rhino poaching. It then discusses armed groups involved in poaching, highlighting the cases of groups operating primarily in Central African states. Next, it provides insight into the different types of weapons used in poaching, including military-style weapons, hunting rifles, and craft firearms, as well as traditional weapons and methods, such as spears, arrows, and poison. The final section reviews national responses to poaching and the roles of law enforcement, the military, and local communities.

OVERVIEW OF POACHING IN AFRICA

Poaching is the illegal killing of wildlife in contravention of national or international law. Since 2010, the illegal killing of elephants in Africa has outpaced natural population replacement rates (Wittemyer et al., 2014); meanwhile, conservationists estimate that rates of rhino poaching could surpass birth rates by 2018 (Save the Rhino, n.d.). The 1970s and 1980s witnessed earlier escalations in the illegal killing of elephants and rhinos (Blanc et al., 2007; Okello et al., 2008; UNEP et al., 2013).

The Convention on International Trade in Endangered Species of Wild Fauna and Flora (CITES) was adopted in 1973 and entered into force for states parties in 1975 (CITES, 1973). CITES regulates the international trade in wildlife

Map 1.1 **Elephant rangeland in Africa**

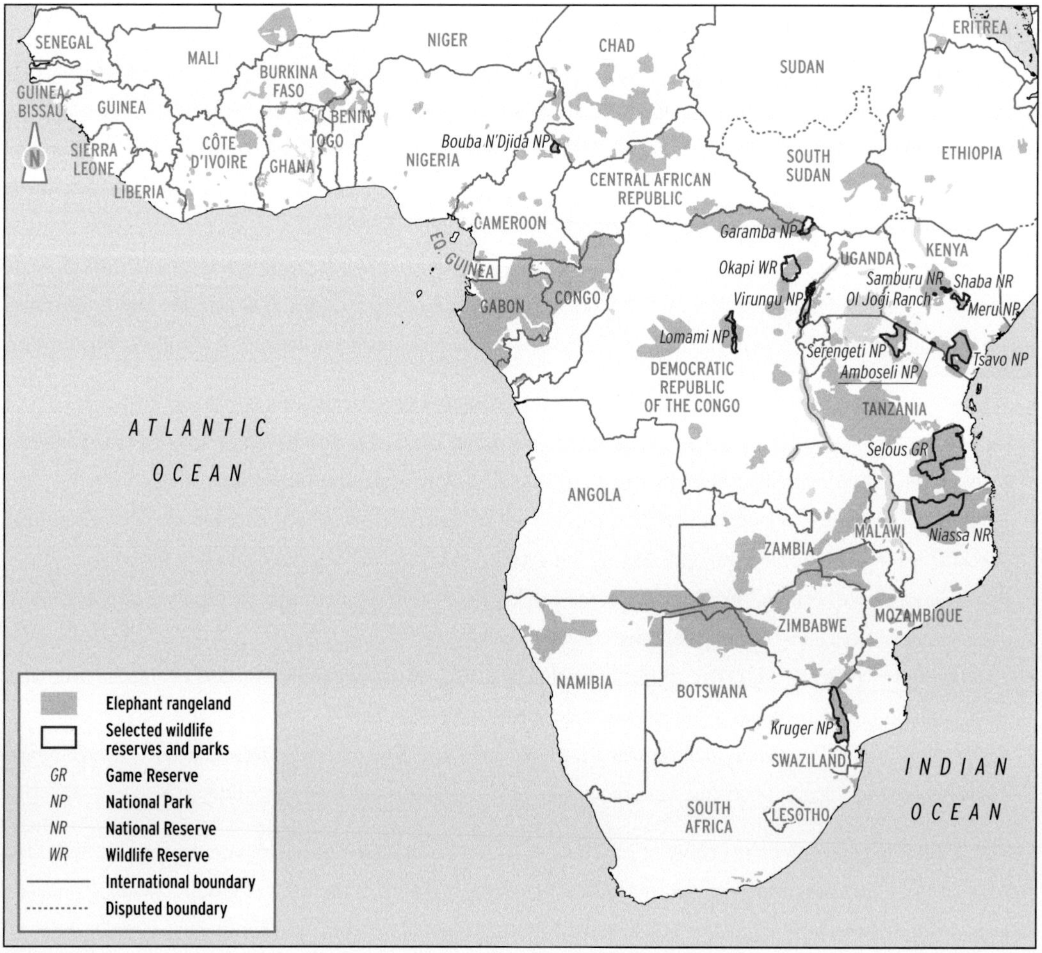

Source: IUCN (n.d.)

species that it classifies as threatened or endangered. In 1989, a CITES vote listed elephants on Appendix I—a classification given to the most endangered species—in essence prohibiting all trade, with a few exceptions, including scientific research. In 1990, the trade ban came into force in CITES countries and territories. In 1997, the elephant populations of Botswana, Namibia, and Zimbabwe were relisted to Appendix II, which comprises 'species that are not necessarily threatened with extinction but that may become so unless trade is closely controlled' (CITES, 1973). White and black rhinos are on CITES Appendix I, with the exception of southern white populations in South Africa and Swaziland, which are listed on Appendix II for acceptable trade in live animals and hunting trophies.

Sport hunting of elephants is permitted under a quota in a number of countries, subject to domestic legislation; CITES also allows the export of hunting trophies (such as ivory) collected by hunters as long as it is for non-commercial use (FWS, 2013). Wildlife services are also allowed to carry out the controlled killing of animals that pose a danger to the public.

Poaching of various types takes place across African range states (see Maps 1.1–1.2). In Central Africa, where some elephant populations have decreased significantly, poachers include armed militias, rogue law enforcement officers,

Map 1.2 **Rhino rangeland in Africa**

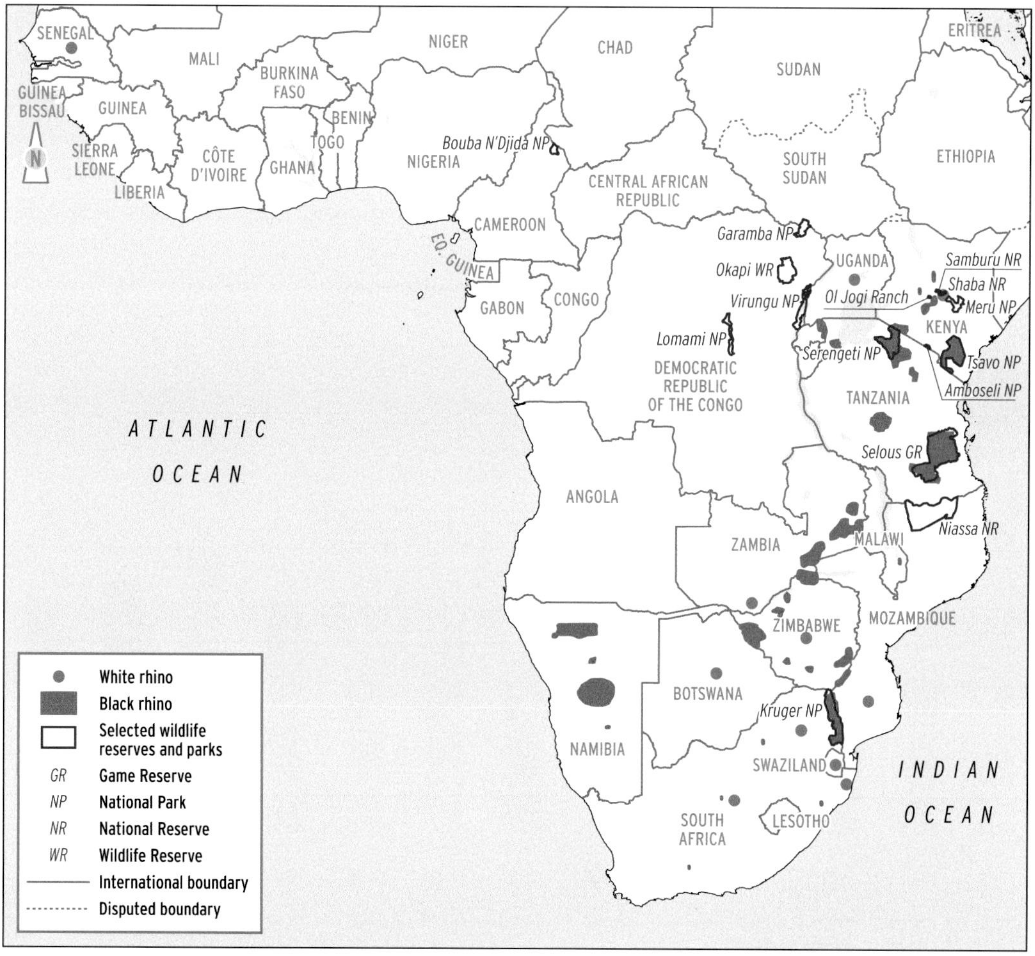

Sources: San Diego Zoo and International Rhino Foundation (n.d.); Rookmaaker and Antoine (2013)

commercial poachers, and subsistence hunters. The potential threat that armed groups pose to governments and wildlife alike has prompted the UN Security Council to identify poaching in Central Africa as a regional security threat requiring urgent action (UNSC, 2014a; 2014c).

As discussed in this chapter, the problem of poaching extends well beyond Central Africa. The CITES Secretariat has recommended that a number of African states parties to the Convention, including Angola, Cameroon, the Democratic Republic of the Congo (DRC), Gabon, Kenya, Mozambique, Nigeria, Tanzania, and Uganda, develop national action plans to combat ivory poaching and trafficking, and monitor progress in their implementation (CITES Secretariat, 2014b).

Poaching trends

The latest population estimates of elephants in Africa range from 419,000 to 650,000 (UNEP et al., 2013, p. 22). Established under CITES and operational since 2002, a monitoring system known by its acronym, MIKE—Monitoring the Illegal Killing of Elephants—is used to estimate poaching rates. MIKE determines the cause of an elephant's death, making distinctions between illegally killed elephants, non-intentional elephant deaths (such as death due to natural causes), and intentional but legal killings, such as those resulting from sport hunting or the control of problem animals. Elephant kills can involve an array of weapons, including firearms, spears, machetes, and poisons, and can result from commercial poaching, bush meat hunting, or human–elephant conflict. Data collected from kill site investigations is used to establish the proportion of illegally killed elephants (PIKE). PIKE is the total number of illegally killed elephants discovered, divided by the total number of carcasses encountered per year for each site investigated (UNEP et al., 2013).

In 2011, PIKE rates were at their highest levels following a steady upward trend that began in 2006 (see Figure 1.1). Data shows a slight decline in overall PIKE rates after 2011; yet, despite this decline, aggregate levels are probably unsustainable. PIKE rates from 2013 show that the illegal killing of elephants across Africa accounted for almost two-thirds of all discovered elephant carcasses that year (CITES Secretariat, 2014a).

Figure 1.1 **PIKE trends in Africa, 2002–13**

ESTIMATED PIKE

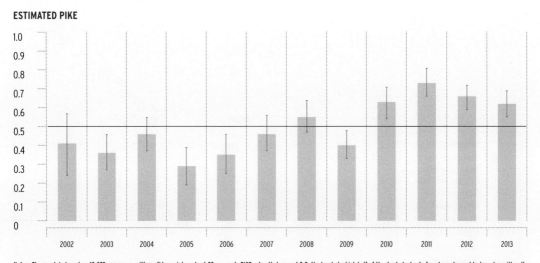

Notes: The graph is based on 12,073 carcasses, with confidence intervals at 95 per cent. PIKE rates that exceed 0.5–the level at which half of the dead elephants found are deemed to have been illegally killed (marked by a red line)–are likely to be unsustainable.

Source: CITES Secretariat (2014a, p. 18)

At the *global* level, demand for illegal ivory is a strong predictor of poaching trends. The strongest *national-level* factor influencing PIKE rates is poor governance, which enables both poaching and ivory trafficking 'through ineffective law enforcement or active aiding and abetting by unscrupulous officials' (CITES Secretariat, 2014a, pp. 19, 21). Ineffective law enforcement may involve the poor collection of evidence at poaching sites or poor security with regard to seized weapons, which occasionally re-enter the illicit weapons market. In fact, many areas of wildlife rangeland are in remote areas where control over state weapons may be poor, whether due to a lack of ranger training or professionalism or inadequate storage facilities. Poverty is the most significant *local* factor associated with high PIKE levels (CITES Secretariat, 2014a, p. 19).

Central Africa, which exhibits the highest regional poaching levels in Africa, suffers from weak governance and poverty—as well as widespread insecurity and the presence of armed groups. In parts of the region where private and public investment is low and job opportunities are limited, poaching may offer an attractive, alternative livelihood.[1] Yet as elephant populations in Central Africa decline, conservationists fear that ivory trafficking may increase in East and Southern Africa (CITES Secretariat, 2014a, p. 32).

> Well-organized criminal networks are involved in rhino poaching and horn trafficking.

In West Africa, where elephant populations are fragmented, limited PIKE data precludes the identification of poaching trends. While PIKE levels in Southern Africa are the lowest in Africa, East African levels were approximately 50 per cent higher from 2010 to 2013 than during preceding years, and the highest average rates since 2002 for that region (CITES Secretariat, 2014a, p. 19).

Compared to elephant protection efforts in East and Southern Africa, those in West and Central Africa face challenges related to weak governance, ongoing armed conflicts, substantial firearms proliferation, and the presence of criminal groups. Elephant populations in these areas are now low, with some groups nearing extinction (UNEP et al., 2013, p. 51).

Regional and international networks and trade

A variety of civil society actors involved in the fight against ivory poaching have initiated joint data collection activities on various aspects of the trade. The Elephant Trade Information System (ETIS), for example, is maintained by TRAFFIC, a joint International Union for Conservation of Nature and World Wildlife Fund programme, on behalf of CITES.

The linking of longitudinal data concerning different seizures can yield tentative inferences about ivory poaching and trafficking networks. The evidence shows that a large number of facilitators—including illicit mineral transporters, freight forwarding companies, shipping agents, and politicians—make up the complex networks (Vira, Ewing, and Miller, 2014, p. 31). Container ports in East Africa currently appear to be the primary export points for ivory to international markets (UNODC, 2013). Since 2009, all large-scale (≥500 kg) ivory seizures recorded by ETIS have taken place on routes between Africa and Asia (CITES Secretariat, 2014a, p. 29).

The involvement of well-organized criminal networks is also evident in the case of rhino poaching and horn trafficking (see Box 1.1). Many rhino populations in Africa have become locally extinct or are in decline. The two rhino species in Africa—the black (*Diceros bicornis*) and white rhino (*Ceratotherium simum*)[2]—are distributed across Southern and East Africa, with the majority living in South Africa, where, in absolute terms, the most poaching also takes place. At the end of 2012, estimates placed rhino populations at 20,954 in South Africa, 2,274 in Namibia, and 1,025 in Kenya (CITES Secretariat, 2013).

South Africa's rhino population has been the most heavily affected in terms of numbers killed, with 1,004 poached in 2013 and 1,215 in 2014. Taken as a percentage of the 2012 population estimate, those 2,219 killed rhinos represent

Box 1.1 Rhino poaching in South Africa

Rhino horn trafficking differs substantially from ivory trafficking. While ivory is often containerized in large quantities, rhino horns–which are significantly more valuable pound-for-pound (Vira, Ewing, and Miller, 2014, p. 28), less bulky, and lighter–are often transported in small amounts, commonly by aircraft, to final destinations in Asia.[3]

The illegal rhino horn trade threatens all African species of rhino. Despite some successful efforts to reintroduce rhinos to protected areas in South Africa, which is home to 80 per cent of all African rhinos, the rate of poaching continues to accelerate (WWF International et al., 2014, p. 27).

South Africa's Kruger National Park is the most densely populated rhino region in the world. It is also where poaching is at its most concentrated (Lunstrum, 2014, p. 816); from 2012 to 2014 more than 60 per cent of all rhino poaching in South Africa took place in the park (WESSA, 2014; see Figure 1.2).

Most poaching gangs in Kruger National Park are small groups who enter via the Great Limpopo Transfrontier Park in Mozambique, often on a daily basis. The economic incentives driving rhino horn poaching are great. Prices for rhino horn in 2012 were estimated at more than USD 60,000 per kilogram (IUCN, 2012). Mozambican poaching syndicates support and equip the heavily armed poaching gangs, and operations to hunt and kill rhinos and extract their horns often unfold rapidly. Indeed, poachers can extract rhino horns in a matter of minutes; having done so, they quickly move across the border into Mozambique and transfer the horn to 'consolidation points'. From there, the contraband begins its journey across the Indian Ocean to Asia (Vira, Ewing, and Miller, 2014, p. 16). Yet arrests of South African poachers indicate that the problem of rhino poaching is not restricted to Mozambican nationals.

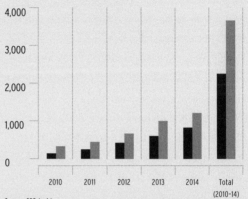

Figure 1.2 **Rhino poaching in Kruger National Park and all of South Africa, 2010-14**

Source: SRP (n.d.)

The tactics and equipment used–by both poachers and anti-poaching units–are increasingly sophisticated, with the term 'rhino wars' reflecting the trend towards the militarization of poaching and anti-poaching efforts (Humphreys and Smith, 2014, p. 795). As discussed elsewhere in this chapter, the involvement of national armed forces and the growing emphasis on the arrest of poachers are part of the strategy to curb increasing rates of rhino poaching. Poachers have responded by adopting a wide range of methods to target rhinos. While the majority of rhinos are shot dead–sometimes with firearms equipped with sound suppressors–some rhinos are immobilized with veterinary tranquilizers before their horns are hacked off (Milliken and Shaw, 2012, p. 75).

10 per cent of the South African population (SRP, n.d.). In Kenya, 59 rhinos—or nearly 6 per cent of the national herd—were poached in 2013 (KWS, 2014). A leading Kenyan conservationist stressed that the poaching rate is not sustainable, and that recovery will grow more difficult as populations decline.[4]

Unlike elephants, many of which migrate beyond reserve and park boundaries, rhinos in the central region of Kenya typically remain within secured conservancies. As these areas are designed to offer protection, the 2014 incident that claimed four rhinos at Ol Jogi is unusual. To find rhinos, poachers tend to recruit game industry insiders to assist them in locating rhinos and security patrols (Milliken and Shaw, 2012, p. 66). Since 2009, increasing prices for rhino horn have encouraged poachers to enter conservancies in central Kenya. Poaching gangs are usually made up of two or three people, some with weapons and some without; they generally strike at dusk and escape under cover of darkness. They wait inside the conservancy, tracking a target animal, and only strike at a moment that they deem will give them a good chance of escaping rangers, who will have been alerted by a gunshot. As security teams often patrol fence lines at scheduled times, poachers aim to avoid these times when entering the conservancies,[5] an illustration of the importance of insider information to poachers.

Drivers of elephant poaching

As noted above, ivory demand drives poaching (CITES Secretariat, 2014a, p. 23). The impact of this demand has been seen at monitored sites where poaching increased markedly after 2008, in step with increases in the price of ivory locally and in China (Wittemyer et al., 2014, p. 2; Save the Elephants, 2014).

Ivory is highly sought after in Asia, and particularly in China, where intricate carving is an established industry. Economic growth and increased consumer purchasing power in China have significantly expanded the market for ivory; some of the trade is legal, such as the trade in ivory purchased from the CITES-approved sales, but poor enforcement of the legislation fuels a flourishing trade in illegal ivory in the country (Martin and Vigne, 2011). There are other significant markets for ivory in Asia, but not all are growing. Japan was a major ivory importer, but strict regulation of the trade after the CITES ban, a decline in consumer demand, and an economic recession have suppressed this market (Martin and Vigne, 2010, pp. 45, 51).

News of rising ivory prices can spread quickly, prompting spikes in poaching levels and attracting greater numbers of would-be poachers. Among Maasai communities in Kenya, information about high prices paid for ivory can come from radio broadcasts or via Internet news sources. Since 2011, more local people have engaged in poaching although the Maasai have traditionally shunned the killing of elephants.[6] In some regions, the killing of elephants provides not

Seized ivory figurines and sculptures are displayed before being crushed at an event attended by US government officials and leading conservationists, Denver, Colorado, November 2013. © Kate Brooks/Redux

only large sums of money from ivory, but also meat and other products of value to poachers, as evidenced in a number of Central African countries (Stiles, 2011, p. 86).

Types of poaching

Large-scale poaching

Firearms, large quantities of ammunition, and even military helicopters are used in large-scale poaching.

Large-scale poaching is the targeting and illegal killing of a concentrated population of elephants in a short period of time. Documented cases have involved the use of firearms, large quantities of ammunition, and even military helicopters. By one account, large-scale poaching is facilitated by automatic weapons such as Kalashnikov-pattern rifles, particularly if elephants gather into groups as a defensive mechanism, such as when they sense danger (Crone, 2014). Yet large-scale poaching does not always involve firearms, as illustrated by a mass poisoning event that reportedly killed hundreds of elephants in Zimbabwe over several months in 2013 (Thornycroft and Laing, 2013).

A conservationist interviewed for this chapter identified two major types of groups involved in large-scale poaching. The first type is non-state armed groups, such as former 'janjaweed' members from Sudan and Mai Mai militias of Congolese origin; they are heavily armed with military-style weapons and carry out large-scale poaching in groups of more than ten members. The degree of organization of their ivory sales varies across groups. The second type of group engaged in large-scale poaching is rogue military units that also use military-style weapons. Operating on the orders of specific officers, these groups usually take a highly organized approach to selling ivory, as discussed below.[7]

Evidence of large-scale poaching can be found by comparing DNA taken from seized ivory with DNA samples of mapped elephant populations. Between 2002 and 2006, DNA testing was conducted on samples from more than 20 tons of ivory seized from a number of container consignments in Asia. Findings showed that the samples had been drawn from a small number of elephant populations belonging to related elephant herds (Wasser et al., 2008), suggesting that the poachers may have targeted particular geographic areas.

Shipping containers loaded with multi-ton ivory consignments are the product of hundreds of elephants' ivory and point to the involvement of organized criminal networks in the storage and preparation of these shipments. Nevertheless, containerized ivory consignments are not necessarily linked to large-scale incidents, as they could also result from leakage from government stockpiles or traffickers' consolidation of ivory over a period of time or broad geographic region.

Two major poaching incidents in Cameroon and Chad provide some sense of the magnitude of large-scale poaching and its impact on herds. In Cameroon's Bouba N'Djida National Park, between 300 and 600 elephants were allegedly killed by armed raiders in 2012 (UNEP et al., 2013, p. 58). A year later, 89 elephants were poached in southern Chad, with dozens of pregnant females and 15 calves among those killed (WWF New Zealand, 2013).

Following the incident in Cameroon, the secretary-general of CITES warned that the attack was reflective of a growing trend across African range states, where armed poachers with military-style weapons were decimating elephant populations (CITES Secretariat, 2012). Most national parks were—and, in some cases, still are—ill-equipped to defend against such large-scale poaching.

Small-scale poaching

Small-scale poaching is the targeting of an individual elephant or rhino, or small numbers of them, for profit. In contrast to large-scale poaching, which involves the concentrated killing of a herd in a short period of time, small-scale poaching tends to be conducted over a significant period of time. The poachers make use of firearms and non-firearm methods to kill animals. Like large-scale poaching, small-scale activities are mainly driven by profit from illegal ivory.

The groups involved in small-scale poaching vary considerably. In some areas, small groups of local people with knowledge of the bush may target animals to supply a known dealer. This type of poaching has been documented in the Samburu area of Kenya and typically involves the use of firearms (see Box 1.4). Local people who target nearby elephants and rhinos often operate with a low degree of organization and unsophisticated weapons, such as snares, spears, artisanal weapons, or poison.[8] These types of weapon may benefit poachers in areas where security patrols are active, as rangers will not be alerted by a gunshot.

Outsiders may also travel to elephant and rhino rangeland to poach small numbers of animals. Such poachers tend to be well organized, with groups consisting of 2–12 hunters and porters. Using hunting rifles or military-style firearms, they may carry out poaching to order or be self-financed; their sale of ivory or rhino horn also tends to be well structured. Military and law enforcement personnel are known to have engaged in small-scale poaching—sometimes opportunistic, sometimes planned; their activities normally involve the use of military-style firearms.[9]

While a single elephant kill may not garner news headlines in the same way larger raids in places such as Cameroon and Chad have, PIKE levels in East Africa, where large-scale poaching incidents have not recently been reported publicly, exceeded 40 per cent from 2010 to 2013 (CITES Secretariat, 2014a, p. 19).

Rhinos are not as numerous as elephants, nor do they gather in large herds or migrate. For these reasons, they are most often poached individually and cases of several rhinos being killed together are rare. As a consequence, rhino horn is trafficked in smaller quantities than ivory, although this distinction also reflects the fact that its selling price is much higher than that of ivory.

ARMED GROUPS

Armed groups involved in poaching encompass a variety of actors and include pro-government militias and armed opposition forces, as well as economically motivated bands of former or current state military. As these groups can potentially operate in large numbers and possess considerable firepower, they can pose unique challenges to rangers and others charged with protecting wildlife.

Over the past decade, armed groups from Darfur have allegedly killed elephants in Chad and Cameroon (Gettleman, 2012a); meanwhile, multiple non-state groups and military forces have been blamed for the killing of elephants in the DRC (UNSC, 2014c). The Lord's Resistance Army (LRA), active since 1986, is among the groups that have reportedly killed elephants in the DRC (Agger and Hutson, 2013; see Box 1.2). Despite the efforts of national wildlife agencies, security providers, conservancy organizations, and UN bodies to combat illegal poaching, armed groups continue to kill elephants for their ivory.

> ### Box 1.2 The Lord's Resistance Army
>
> In a 2013 report, the UN Security Council called upon UN member states and regional partners to combat illicit trade networks operating in Central Africa, citing in particular the LRA and its involvement in poaching (UNSC, 2013a). Consisting of an estimated 200 fighters, plus abducted civilians, the LRA reportedly poaches elephant tusks to trade for food, weapons, ammunition, and other supplies, including radios (Resolve, Enough Project, and Invisible Children, 2014).[10] While it lacks the logistical capacity to move large quantities of ivory, the group can reportedly access trafficking routes, including Sudanese ones, to move what it manages to poach (Poffenberger, 2013; Ronan, 2014).
>
> The LRA's poaching activity is not as significant as that of other armed groups operating in the DRC, however. This has led some conservation experts and researchers to express concern that media interest in the LRA, including its elephant poaching, has deflected attention away from the more serious regional threats that elephants face (Duffy and St. John, 2013). These include national armed forces, or elements of those forces, and non-state armed groups other than the LRA, such as Séléka fighters in the Central African Republic, Mai Mai militias in the DRC, and the Forces démocratiques de libération du Rwanda (Democratic Forces for the Liberation of Rwanda, or FDLR) (Titeca, 2013).[11]

Poaching by national armed forces

The Forces Armées de la République Démocratique du Congo (Armed Forces of the Democratic Republic of the Congo, FARDC) have been identified by independent observers as among the most ruthless ivory poachers in the DRC, where the state military is reportedly responsible for 75 per cent of all poaching in nine of 11 investigated areas with elephant populations in the country (Kakala, 2013). FARDC soldiers, who are often deployed into elephant range areas in eastern DRC, allegedly control large criminal poaching networks and trading routes that move ivory out of the region and into foreign markets (Vira and Ewing, 2014, p. 38). In 2004, the FARDC apparently moved 17 tons of ivory out of the Okapi Wildlife Reserve in six months (Apobo, 2004)—evidence of the sophisticated logistical arrangements in place and the intense pace at which elephant poaching can be conducted.

Allegations have also been made against high-ranking officers in the FARDC concerning collusion with rebel groups and other poachers. In 2012, a UN report accused FARDC Gen. Gabriel Amisi of trading weapons and ammunition in exchange for poached ivory (UNSC, 2012). President Kabila suspended Amisi soon after the UN accusations, but in August 2014 he was cleared of all charges, reinstated, and promoted in the military (RFI, 2014).

Armed groups operating in Central Africa have the most significant impact on elephant herds.

There are also accusations that soldiers from other countries' militaries have poached elephants in the DRC. In a 2012 poaching incident in Garamba National Park, 22 elephants were killed and stripped of their tusks. Fifteen of those elephants were shot through the top of their heads, suggesting they were shot from above. In fact, witnesses claim that a helicopter—later identified as an Mi-17MD transport helicopter registered with the Uganda People's Defence Force (UPDF)—was flying above the area at the time the elephants were killed (Gettleman, 2012a). In addition, there are allegations that poached ivory from Virunga National Park was smuggled into Uganda with the assistance of an armed escort provided by a former senior UPDF officer (UNSC, 2014b, para. 234).

During Sudan's civil war (1983–2005), the main agents of the ivory trade in Sudan were reportedly members of the national armed forces who poached elephants in what was then southern Sudan, as well as in the Central African Republic (CAR) and the DRC (UNEP, 2007). Observers assert that since the independence of South Sudan, its military has poached elephants in Garamba National Park and engaged in shootouts with park rangers (Gettleman, 2012a).

Non-state armed groups in Central Africa

Among armed groups in Africa, those operating in Central Africa have had the most significant impact on elephant herds; their poaching activity in the region has been condemned by international bodies, including the UN Security Council and CITES.

Poaching and other forms of illicit trading in resources—such as minerals and timber—enable these groups to purchase weapons and ammunition with which to challenge local and national authorities, such as the military and the police, as well as security forces affiliated with UN missions (Agger, 2014; UNSC, 2014a). International reports on poaching by armed groups in Central Africa highlight the transnational nature of their activities; these groups move across international borders to poach wildlife, to exploit trafficking routes that furnish them with weapons and ammunition, and to supply distant markets with ivory (ICG, 2014; UNEP et al., 2013). Most poachers operating in CAR are believed to originate in neighbouring states, particularly Chad and Sudan, although Séléka fighters (insurgents) in CAR are also engaged in poaching (Agger, 2014; ICG, 2014). Local bands of armed poachers in CAR and in Cameroon have reportedly transported ivory westward to Nigeria (Lombard, 2012).

Independent observers claim that some armed groups entering CAR from Sudan receive funding from prominent Sudanese businessmen, including several based in the Nyala area in Darfur, who equip them with firearms, night-vision goggles, and satellite phones (Agger, 2014; ICG, 2014). The continued presence of armed groups in remote areas of CAR, coupled with weak governance and corruption, suggests that law enforcement and government officials are either absent or colluding with the poachers (ICG, 2014, p. 14).

Poaching by armed groups in Central Africa is not new. In what are today CAR and Sudan, Sudanese groups have been killing elephants for their ivory for centuries, supplying Khartoum, one of the world's oldest ivory carving centres (UNEP, 2007). More recently, in 2013, it was reported that bands of Khartoum-supported fighters, including 'janjaweed' members, poached more than 3,000 elephants in Chad and Cameroon (Gettleman, 2012a). In 2010, UPDF soldiers searching for LRA camps inside CAR encountered what they described as a 'janjaweed caravan', alleging that the group counted more than 400 members and was well armed. The encounter resulted in the deaths of ten Ugandan soldiers (Gettleman, 2012a).

Across the border from CAR in the DRC, many armed groups have poached elephants, including Mai Mai militias, the Allied Democratic Forces–National Army for the Liberation of Uganda, the Congolese March 23 Movement (until its recent demise), and the Forces démocratiques de libération du Rwanda (Democratic Forces for the Liberation of Rwanda, FDLR) (FDLR–FOCA). Some of these groups reportedly attacked ranger patrols and poached wildlife in national parks such as Garamba, Lomami, and Virunga, as well as in the Okapi Wildlife Reserve (Vira and Ewing, 2014, p. 37).

In the DRC and elsewhere, armed groups are believed to assist each other in the collective pursuit of ivory and other resources. Mai Mai fighters supply ivory in exchange for material provisions and support from other groups (Vira and Ewing, 2014, p. 41). The Katanga and Gedeon Mai Mai militias, with 8,000 fighters or more, are believed to acquire most of their revenue from poaching (IRIN, 2013).

The revenues that some groups can generate from illicit trading, including dealing in ivory, are high. One report estimates that the FDLR previously generated as much as USD 71 million per year from a combination of illicit tax collection and trading, including in ivory (AllAfrica, 2014a). There are indications that some armed groups involved in poaching are now disarming, with large numbers of FDLR fighters having done so already (Mwai, 2014; FDLR–FOCA); it is still too early to determine whether such disarmament campaigns will lead to any significant reductions in poaching in Central Africa.

> Weapons range from hunting rifles and Kalashnikov-pattern rifles to craft muzzle-loading firearms.

POACHERS' WEAPONS

The weapons used by armed groups and other poachers, both commercial and subsistence, vary considerably, ranging from hunting rifles and Kalashnikov-pattern rifles to craft muzzle-loading firearms. In addition to firearms, pastoralists and subsistence poachers also use traditional weapons and methods to kill wildlife, such as spears and poisons. The complicity of some government officials reportedly facilitates the supply of firearms and ammunition to armed groups involved in poaching in Central Africa (ICG, 2014, p. 14; see Box 1.3). To a certain extent, it appears this is also true of commercial poaching networks operating independently of armed groups in the sub-region (Stiles, 2011).

Firearms and ammunition

In Central Africa, illicit weapons reportedly originate from multiple sources, including Libya (UNODC, 2013; UNSC, 2013b). Individual poachers and poaching groups across Africa have sourced other weapons from conflict zones in countries including Angola, Burundi, Mozambique, South Sudan, and Sudan. Some armed groups, such as those in

Box 1.3 Firearms and ammunition data collection

Although information on weapons and ammunition used by poachers could provide insight into the networks that support and conduct poaching, including weapons sources and supply lines, it is not systematically collected or analysed. The form used to gather MIKE data at elephant kill sites includes a section for the type of weapons used, but this information is provided on a voluntary basis.[12]

Richard Leakey, the director of the Kenya Wildlife Service from 1989 to 1994,[13] implemented a system to recover components of fired cartridges–typically projectiles and cartridge cases. As a result, his agency was able to trace several poaching incidents back to a small number of firearms registered with the Kenyan police. These guns, it appears, were being hired out to multiple poachers.[14] Yet a lack of firearm registration data from neighbouring countries, where many of the weapons his rangers seized were thought to originate, prevented investigations into the origins of many other firearms.

While it is possible to trace firearms used by poachers that bear certain markings, such as the country of manufacture or country of last legal import, many anti-poaching forces have not been trained to do so. Moreover, wildlife rangers rarely have the opportunity to seize weapons used by poachers. Fired cartridge cases are sometimes found at poaching sites and bullets–if not fragmented–can be recovered from the remains of dead animals, but ballistics checks are only exceptionally run on these items, despite their potential value in identifying poachers, their guns, and broader arms trafficking networks.[15]

the DRC, are believed to be so flush with weapons that they have little need to acquire more (UNODC, 2013).

Kalashnikov-pattern rifles are prominent among the military-style weapons used for poaching in Central Africa, while 12-gauge shotguns, sometimes loaded with craft bullets, are also reported to be in use (*Independent*, 2013; Stiles, 2011, p. 13). A report on weapons and ammunition use among hunters in four Central African countries finds hunting rifles to be less common than automatic military rifles and shotguns, possibly due to the high price of hunting rifles (USD 1,365–2,200) and hunting ammunition (Stiles, 2011, p. 48).

Firearms commonly used to hunt elephants and other big game can be classified into three groups: hunting rifles of various calibres; automatic military-style small arms, including assault rifles and light machine guns; and shotguns (Stiles, 2011). Large-calibre rifles are considered ideal for hunting large game, with the .375 calibre bullet[16] representing the minimum calibre needed to kill either an elephant or a rhino with one shot (McAdams, 2014). The larger .458 calibre bullet, also commonly used for hunting big game, has a firing range of more than two miles (more than 3.2 km). Automatic military small arms, including Kalashnikov-pattern rifles, are chambered for smaller-calibre cartridges (such as 7.62 × 39 mm) and, in comparison with most hunting rifles, have decreased range and stopping power, making them less suitable than hunting rifles for poaching big game.

Many firearms reach poachers, including armed groups, after having been diverted from government security forces, particularly in situations where ethnic and political alliances trump national security interests (UNODC, 2013, p. 98). A 2014 report links ammunition found at elephant kill sites in Cameroon, CAR, Chad, and the DRC to ammunition in Sudanese government stores (Vira and Ewing, 2014). It is unclear whether the ammunition was transferred deliberately, or instead leaked accidentally from Sudanese stockpiles.

It is common for smaller poaching groups to be supplied by middlemen and financiers, who supply them with guns, ammunition, food, and medical supplies (Stiles, 2011). Poachers often use hunting rifles to kill elephants or rhinos, given their greater range and accuracy, but assault rifles better equip them to confront armed rangers or other armed anti-poaching units.

Which guns elephant poachers use may depend on the resources or external support they can access to finance poaching activity. A study of cartridges in several Central African states finds that the cost of cartridges for hunting rifles ranged from USD 18 to USD 34 each, while those for automatic rifles, including Kalashnikov-pattern rifles, cost as little as USD 0.17 a piece (Stiles, 2011, pp. 49–50). The same study concludes that bush meat hunters in the Republic of Congo use between 18 and 60 pieces of 7.62 × 39 mm cartridges to kill an elephant, while in Cameroon hunters typically use between three and five .458 calibre cartridges for this purpose. This translates to a total cost per animal of USD 90–170 in the Cameroon case, versus USD 3.60–42.00 in that of the Republic of Congo (Stiles, 2011, p. 50).

Some poachers have used homemade sound suppressors in rhino conservancies in central Kenya. Ammunition produced by the former Royal Ordnance Factories facility at Radway Green in the UK[17]—both 5.56 × 45 mm and 7.62 × 39 mm—has reportedly been found in rhino conservancies in Kenya. Conservancy security officers posit that the ammunition, manufactured for the British Armed Forces, has been picked up from British firing ranges following training exercises.[18]

As seen in countries such as South Africa, some poaching groups carry different types of weapons for different purposes. Most rhino poaching groups entering Kruger National Park are composed of three poachers; roughly a dozen such groups are inside the park at any given time (Ramsey, 2014). Mozambican poaching groups commonly employ a designated shooter. While the shooter wields a hunting rifle, the other members of the group tend to use military-style rifles to provide a protective perimeter during the tracking of animals and the extraction of horns or ivory (Vira and Ewing, 2014, p. 73).

Arms and ammunition seized from poachers by the Kenya Wildlife Services, Nairobi, June 2012. © Tony Karumba/AFP Photo

The fight against poaching may be able to benefit from civilian firearm controls. Mozambique has passed a new bill—to be enacted in 2015—that increases the fines for poaching with illegal firearms, regardless of whether the poacher in possession of the firearm kills wildlife (AllAfrica, 2014b). Neighbouring South Africa already has stringent laws against the use of illegal firearms in hunting, with poachers and permit-carrying hunters alike subject to fines and/or imprisonment for the use of prohibited weapons (Library of Congress, 2014).

To kill rhinos, Mozambican poachers appear to prefer hunting rifles over other firearms available to them. There is evidence that Czech CZ 550 bolt-action rifles have become more popular with poachers in recent years (MacLeod and Valoi, 2013). While obtaining a rifle through official channels in Mozambique can take up to six months, there is a brisk trade in illicit hunting rifles, as evidenced by some recent seizures of hunting rifles affixed with sound suppressors, including a Winchester Magnum rifle chambered for .458 ammunition (Bloch, 2012; MacLeod and Valoi, 2013). While it is possible to suppress the sound of a .458 Winchester Magnum rifle by using a reduced-power subsonic cartridge,[19] doing so requires significant technical expertise on the part of users.

In several cases, firearms seized by Mozambican police and rangers have been traced to multiple poaching incidents (Vira and Ewing, 2014, p. 71), indicating that security forces and ranger patrols were negligent in storing seized weapons or were resupplying criminals, or both. In fact, poachers arrested or killed in Mozambique have included active

Box 1.4 Poaching in Samburu, Kenya

Firearms play an important role in poaching in the Samburu-Laikipia area of the North Rift region of Kenya. A recent analysis of KWS data covering the first six months of 2012 demonstrates that 85 per cent of the elephants killed in the area died from gunshot wounds (Vira and Ewing, 2014, p. 60). Historically, the Samburu have experienced conflict with Somali ethnic groups to the east and Pokot and Turkana groups to the west. They began arming themselves in the late 1990s, following the emergence of conflict with Somali ethnic groups, and firearms have been a common means of poaching elephants in the area for the past 15 years.[20]

Poaching inside Samburu National Reserve is rare as the area is well patrolled by rangers and experiences heavy tourist traffic. Most illegally killed elephants are poached outside the reserve boundaries. Not all reserves in the region are safe for elephants, however. Conservationists who have visited nearby Shaba National Reserve, an area without the same law enforcement presence as the Samburu reserve, report that elephants there have become fearful of vehicles and visitors after having been targeted by poachers.[21]

Poachers in the area are from four different ethnic groups and sometimes work together to hunt wildlife. They are familiar with the terrain and skilled in animal tracking. While they try to avoid park rangers, 'they will shoot back if they are shot at and they shoot first sometimes'.[22]

Criminal ivory trafficking networks are reportedly well established in the Samburu region, enabling quick movement of tusks from the area to ports. Independent observers say poaching kingpins facilitate ivory smuggling from their homes in the Kenyan town of Archer's Post, a trading centre on the edge of Samburu National Reserve, and Shaba National Reserve (Koross, 2013). Criminal syndicates in the region reportedly benefit from police corruption and political protection. Indeed, as KWS rangers observe, vehicles suspected of transporting ivory have on occasion passed freely through manned police checkpoints (Koross, 2013).

With the support of NGOs, such as the Northern Rangelands Trust, communities and ethnic groups in northern Kenya are participating in efforts to curb poaching. The Trust has helped to establish community committees that are led by locally chosen elders and act to discourage poaching and support livelihood initiatives, with an emphasis on the local management of resources, including wildlife conservancies (NRT, 2009). Communities also work with Trust rangers to recover stolen livestock, reduce banditry, and identify those involved in illegal activity, including poaching (King, 2011).

It appears that the programmes have been largely successful in turning the communities against poaching, although some members, especially young men, continue to poach wildlife. The latter often enjoy a measure of protection from other community members, in part because they are seen as potential defenders of the community, specifically in conflicts with other groups.[23]

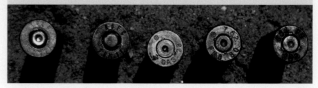

Ammunition casings recovered in the Samburu area, Kenya, August 2014. © Joanna Wright

and former members of the army, border guards, and police (Vira and Ewing, 2014). Active and former state security providers who are involved in poaching may have insider access to state-held firearms. Moreover, they are often professionally trained in the use of such weapons. Depending on their experience and former duties, poachers with military backgrounds may also have knowledge of bush combat tactics and possess skills that can be adapted to wildlife tracking.

Given the high price of rhino horn and elephant tusks, the financial rewards from poaching are considerable. There is evidence that increasing numbers of 'non-professionals' are getting involved in poaching, with kill-site investigations in Tanzania identifying the use of 'spray and pray' methods that involve shooting an animal with many more bullets than are strictly needed to kill it.[24]

Similarly, in Kenya, some rhino killings have reportedly involved the use of large numbers of bullets. This may largely be determined by the types of weapons or ammunition available to the poacher. As noted above, a poacher will need more bullets to kill a rhino with an automatic rifle than with a hunting rifle. Limited financial resources may force some poachers to use a Kalashnikov-pattern rifle, in part because compatible cartridges are much less expensive than some hunting rifle ammunition.

Traditional and craft weapons

As noted above, poachers do not always use firearms to kill wildlife. In Tsavo National Park, in Kenya's Coast province, the percentage of elephants killed by gunshot is much lower (34 per cent) than in the North Rift region of the country (85 per cent) (Vira, Ewing, and Miller, 2014). Instead of relying on firearms to kill animals, poachers in the Tsavo area use trusted methods that often involve traditional weapons that have the advantage of not drawing the attention of rangers—unlike a discharged firearm.[25]

Poachers do not always use firearms to kill wildlife.

According to a member of the African Elephant Specialist Group of the International Union for Conservation of Nature, traditional weapons—including poison-tipped spears and arrows—are commonly used for poaching in Tsavo.[26] These 'silent' methods often kill animals more slowly than a high-calibre gunshot, but the poachers are patient, avoiding detection and tracking the animal over many hours as they wait for it to die. One such case is that of Satao, a giant tusker killed with a poisoned arrow in Kenya in 2014 (Tsavo Trust, 2014).

Some members of the Maasai use poison-tipped traditional spears. Data collected by the NGO Big Life in a Maasai area outside Amboseli National Park indicates that of the 42 elephants poached in 2011–13, more than three-quarters (32) were killed with poisoned spears. Of the remaining ones whose means of death could be identified, five elephants died from gunshot wounds, one was killed by a snare, another by poison, and a one by arrows.[27]

Poisoning is used in many locations in East, Central, and Southern Africa. In some areas, conservationists find that poisoning is increasing (Ogada, 2014). Although the reasons for the increase are unclear, it could be linked to hunters' growing use of silent methods of killing to avoid detection by anti-poaching patrols. Poisons are easy to transport and widely accessible, as they can be made from local flora or commercial ingredients that are available in trading centres and towns. Plant-based poisons are typically used on spears or arrows, whereas shop-bought poisons tend to be used on bait foods, such as pumpkins, watermelons, and pineapples, which are left near watering holes or crops and eaten by elephants.[28]

Craft firearms and ammunition offer an inexpensive alternative when factory-made materiel is beyond poachers' means. Commonly used by subsistence and small-scale local poachers, they are principally made by hand in relatively small quantities (Berman, 2011). Blacksmiths are known to make cheap and effective shotguns, as well as firearms constructed from car steering columns that are loaded with melted-down gunshot to make single, pointed bullets (Chappaz, 2006).

NATIONAL RESPONSES TO POACHING

Across African range states that have elephant and rhino populations, anti-poaching initiatives take many different forms. In some
cases, they involve a combination of state and private rangers, government soldiers, and locally based organizations working jointly to
combat poaching through the use of force or through grassroots work
aimed at influencing local behaviour and attitudes. Anti-poaching
rangers and units form the first line of defence against poaching,
along with supporting law enforcement structures. While holding
poachers accountable for poaching is important, so is the arrest and
conviction of the people running the criminal syndicates that sponsor
and facilitate the trafficking of ivory and rhino horn. To be effective,
initiatives against poaching must be able to rely on cooperative efforts
by government agencies (including judiciaries), local conservation
organizations, and national and international organizations and conservation groups.

The limits of law enforcement

South Africa has sought to curb poaching by boosting ranger patrols
and army presence in parks, reserves, and other wildlife habitats. In
Kruger National Park, increased funding for anti-poaching efforts has
accompanied a steady increase in annual arrests of poachers over
the past five years, from 67 arrests in 2010 to 147 in 2014 (Save the
Rhino, n.d.). Yet, despite these gains, the number of rhinos poached
in Kruger National Park increased at an even higher rate than the
arrests. During the same period, the total number of poached rhinos
in the park quintupled, from 146 in 2010 to at least 827 in 2014 (SRP,
n.d.; see Figure 1.2). According to one conservation expert, this
trend reflects the relatively low likelihood of being detected, arrested,
and convicted in South Africa (Stiles, 2011). Figure 1.3 shows the total
number of rhinos poached and arrests made in South Africa from 2010
to 2014.

When South African courts do convict poachers, they are increasingly opting for stiffer penalties. In 2014, a convicted poacher was
sentenced to 77 years in prison for his involvement in a 2011 incident
during which three rhinos were killed. He was convicted on charges
of illegal hunting, rhino horn theft, illegal possession of firearms and
ammunition, and, notably, the killing of his poaching accomplice, who
was shot by South African anti-poaching forces. The court determined

A park ranger holding an FAL-type rifle searches from a helicopter for a poacher on the run in Kruger National Park, South Africa, November 2014.
© James Oatway/Sunday Times/Gallo Images/Getty Images

that he bore responsibility for the death of his fellow poacher because—by virtue of entering the park illegally with intent to poach—he was responsible for the well-being, and eventual death, of his companion (Torchia, 2014).

In neighbouring Zimbabwe, a recent evaluation shows that penalties—including jail sentences and fines—led to a reduction in the number of small-scale and subsistence poachers but had little impact on professional poachers who were financed by criminal networks (Duffy, 2014).

A review of 743 wildlife crimes committed between 2008 and 2013 in Kenya finds that only 4 per cent of the cases resulted in jail sentences. Of the ones that involved elephant or rhino poaching, just 7 per cent ended with

Figure 1.3 **Total number of rhinos killed and arrests made in South Africa**

■ Poaching arrests ■ Rhinos killed

NUMBER OF RHINOS POACHED/ARRESTS MADE

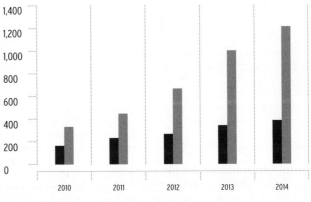

Source: Save the Rhino (n.d.)

the incarceration of offenders. Further, 91 per cent of all fines imposed on convicted elephant poachers were below the maximum fine of KES 40,000 (USD 440). Charges relating to firearms were brought in only 12 of the cases, resulting in three convictions for illegal ammunition possession (Kahumbu et al., 2014).

Kenya's Wildlife Act provides for the imposition of relatively harsh fines on convicted poachers (Kenya, 2013). In practice, however, the act potentially discourages the conviction of poachers charged with minor offences as the penalties may be seen as disproportionate.[29] Nevertheless, the law has given teeth to Kenyan authorities, who had previously shown little enthusiasm for the prosecution of major players who enable illicit wildlife trafficking in the country. A lack of political will has also been a problem in Tanzania, where state corruption allegedly enables some poaching syndicates to operate with impunity, with members of parliament accusing a former donor of the ruling Chama Cha Mapinduzi party (Party of the Revolution) of using land allocated for legal hunting for the purpose of illegal poaching (*Economist*, 2014). As of late 2014, the donor had not been formally charged with any crime.

Even when suspects are apprehended and charged with poaching-related offences, prosecutions are often poorly handled, with insufficient evidence offered to prove guilt in many cases (Ross, 2013). The International Criminal Police Organization (INTERPOL) has sought to assist East African countries in addressing legislative and law enforcement shortfalls and in strengthening their capacity to carry out investigations (INTERPOL, 2014). It has established a Nairobi-based office to support its Project Wisdom, which combats the illicit wildlife trade. The special investigative team collaborates with national law enforcement agencies under a specific mandate that targets ivory and rhino horn trafficking.

In October 2014, Kenyan police requested INTERPOL's assistance in arresting a suspected poaching 'boss', Feizal Ali Mohammed, accused of trafficking large quantities of ivory (Akwiri, 2014). The warrant for his arrest, part of a global round-up and arrest effort, is one of many targeting the most wanted fugitives for serious environmental crimes (UN News Service, 2014). On 22 December 2014, Mohammed was arrested in Dar es Salaam and extradited to Kenya, where he was charged in a Mombasa court for dealing in elephant trophies (Onsarigo, 2014). While the targeting of prominent individuals involved in poaching in Kenya and elsewhere represents important progress, challenges remain at the national and local levels.

A 2012 study from Tanzania estimates that within 45 km of the western boundary of Serengeti National Park, between 52,000 and 60,000 people have engaged in poaching, with 86 per cent of them involved due to poverty and an income shortfall (Knapp, 2012). A majority of these poachers are not ivory or rhino horn poachers, but rather bush meat hunters. Whatever the reason for their poaching—whether male initiation rites or small-scale or commercial poaching—the rewards for poaching consistently outweighed the risks involved. The study finds that a poacher's likelihood of being injured while poaching was 0.02 per cent for each day spent on the hunt, with most injuries the result of aggressive wildlife, not encounters with park rangers. The study also infers that, on average, poachers faced a 0.07 per cent chance of being caught each time they set out to hunt wildlife. The report concludes that, as long as the rewards for poaching in the Serengeti outweigh the financial, physical, and psychological risks, it is unlikely to decrease (Knapp, 2012).

A memorial to rangers killed in the line of duty, Kenya Wildlife Service headquarters, Nairobi, Kenya, August 2014.
© Joanna Wright

The military option

In view of the fact that arrests, fines, and the threat of injury are not enough to deter poachers, a former Israeli special forces operator and current anti-poaching consultant, Nir Kalron, has argued for military sweeps of targeted areas; he proposes that infantry and special forces should operate under 'carte blanche' arrangements and be financially supported by NGOs (Kalron, 2013, p. 165). While many feel there is an urgent need to 'stop the bleeding' of poaching,[30] evidence shows that militarization strategies can have unintended consequences (Stiles, 2013; see Box 1.5).

Botswana, Cameroon, Kenya, South Africa, and Zimbabwe are among the countries that have recently increased military involvement and the use of military techniques and technology in anti-poaching efforts. These states have emphasized the military training of rangers, established special anti-poaching task forces, and enhanced intelligence capabilities with helicopters, satellite imagery, and, in some countries, drone usage.

The adoption of more aggressive, militarized anti-poaching strategies is not new. In the 1980s and 1990s governments of what are today the DRC, Kenya, and Zimbabwe provided rangers with extensive military training and permission to use deadly force when confronting poachers (Lunstrum, 2014). Nowadays African states continue to employ anti-poaching strategies involving shoot-on-sight policies and sweeps of villages and parks to forcibly remove

---

Box 1.5 Militarization of anti-poaching: the case of Botswana

Research has identified the incursion of armed poachers from neighbouring states into the game reserves of Botswana as one of that country's biggest illicit firearms challenges (Thwala, 2004). In 2014, poaching remained a problem for Botswana, but had become even thornier.

From inside Botswana's borders, organized criminal networks seek ivory and rhino horn by funding militias that comprise former guerrilla fighters, are equipped with military-style weapons, and are skilled in bush warfare. These militias either cross into or live in Botswana. The Botswana Defence Force claims that poaching is becoming increasingly militarized, with poaching groups commanded by people with military backgrounds. Further, poachers have reportedly used sound suppressors on their weapons to avoid detection by rangers.

The situation prompted the national anti-poaching coordinator to call poaching a national security threat and to argue for the adoption of shoot-to-kill policies and the deployment of the armed forces into high-risk areas (*Sunday Standard*, 2013). Botswana's environment, wildlife, and tourism minister has also argued that shoot-to-kill policies are the only effective means of stopping poachers (Ontebetse, 2013).

The case of Botswana points to an emerging trend in many sub-Saharan African range states, as increasingly well-armed poachers confront ever more militarized anti-poaching units. It is not clear, however, that poaching has a military solution. Those who oppose the militarization of anti-poaching initiatives cite, in particular, the increased risk to innocent civilians as weapons become more prevalent and tactics more aggressive, bringing with them a heightened risk of violent encounters between civilians and poachers (Pflanz, 2014).

poachers. In Uganda, for example, President Yoweri Museveni has given the UPDF the authority to shoot anyone suspected of being a poacher inside the country's national parks (Tentena, 2014). In some cases, however, local subsistence hunters are being caught in this net.

In Swaziland, King Mswati III has given the head of the national parks service and its rangers complete immunity in the shooting deaths of suspected poachers under the country's Game Act (Dube and Magagula, 2007). But this has led to the shooting deaths of several subsistence poachers of small game, who were killed while trying to trap warthogs (Rooney, 2014).

In October 2013, Tanzania's minister for natural resources and tourism, Khamis Kagasheki, oversaw an anti-poaching strategy that included shoot-to-kill orders (Saramba, 2013). More than 2,300 security personnel from multiple security units, including the People's Defence Force, local police, anti-poaching militias, and wildlife rangers, were sent to enforce the country's ban on rhino and elephant poaching. Two months later, 'Operesheni Tokomeza' (Operation Destroy), as it was called, was abandoned and Kagasheki was dismissed from government following allegations that anti-poaching units were raping, murdering, and torturing civilians (Ng'wanakilala, 2013). The units were subsequently accused of crimes such as the theft of thousands of domesticated animals and other property, including money (Makoye, 2014).

Data supporting military anti-poaching policies is inconclusive. One study that investigated the effectiveness of shoot-to-kill policies adopted in Kenya and Zimbabwe in the 1980s observed that elephant populations began steady increases in both countries after the policies were implemented. Nevertheless, the study's author acknowledges that it did not take into account many factors that may have influenced poaching rates in those countries, including fluctuations in the price paid to poachers, the raw ivory price, government expenditures on anti-poaching efforts, firearms legislation and enforcement, and the impact of development programmes (Messer, 2010).

The militarization of anti-poaching units and programmes is also difficult to fund and maintain. Between 1989 and 1994, when Richard Leakey was head of the Kenya Wildlife Service, he successfully raised more than USD 153 million to operate the Service, which included such measures as arming anti-poaching units with helicopters, vehicles, and better firearms. Yet, by 1998, a lack of funding was preventing the upkeep of the air-support equipment and vehicles.

Some observers have also posited that shoot-to-kill policies probably put rangers and other anti-poaching units at greater risk of death than those operating in areas without such policies (Messer, 2000, p. 55).

Despite such drawbacks, some claim that certain shoot-to-kill policies have reduced the rate of poaching. After the cessation of 'Operation Destroy' in Tanzania, for example, illegal elephant kill rates quickly rose, with 60 such kills reported in the two months immediately following the operation's end. This figure stands in sharp contrast to only two reported illegal elephant kills during the operation's one-month duration (AFP, 2014). With more than 950 suspected poachers arrested, 104 tusks seized, and 31 illegal firearms and 1,458 rounds of ammunition confiscated, the Tanzanian government has argued that the initiative merits further evaluation and possible future retooling (Jopson, 2013; Kiishweko, 2013). Yet whatever successes it might claim, Operation Tokomeza must also be weighed against the abuses government security forces reportedly committed against civilians. Conservation experts have argued that increased levels of military-style enforcement risk alienating local communities and, as a result, undermining overall anti-poaching efforts (Duffy and St. John, 2013).

Community-based initiatives

In 2014 the UK government hosted an international conference on the illegal wildlife trade, including in ivory and rhino horn. It concluded that, in addition to increased law enforcement and the reduction of global demand, engagement with local communities was key to combating trafficking (UK, 2014).

In Africa, poaching dynamics can vary significantly across as well as within countries. Differences in terrain, the location of rangeland, economic factors, the nature of land ownership (state vs. private), the degree of government control over territory, and the local capacity to manage land all influence where and how poaching takes place. Proponents of community-based conservation initiatives argue that involving local communities in anti-poaching efforts can bolster formal law enforcement in a way that responds to local conditions (Roe et al., 2014).

Numerous organizations are running community-based initiatives and providing training to local people to better protect wildlife and prevent poaching. Conservation NGOs, training colleges, and academies, along with grassroots groups, operate across African range states. While some organizations train and equip local people to serve as (non-governmental) scouts in conservancies and wildlife reserves, other organizations offer specialized training, including in the use of GPS systems, weapons, and tracking skills. Educating local communities in the value of conservation is an important component of many of these programmes, including those run by Space for Giants, an elephant conservation group in Kenya (Pflanz, 2014).

To access elephants and rhinos, poachers must often pass through communities, whose assistance they must solicit in caching weapons, transporting supplies, and carrying ivory. Cooperation with local leadership—who generally serve as gatekeepers through whom communities can be engaged more broadly—is often critical. In 2012, one of Kenya's most notorious elephant hunters converted from poacher to ranger after village elders intervened and convinced him to stop (Gettleman, 2012b). In Tanzania, a programme focused on wildlife in Serengeti National Park helps local committees recruit village scouts to monitor poaching activity. The work of the scouts has resulted in the capture of poachers and their sentencing—not to prison time, but rather to community service and village development work (Shetler, 2007, p. 226). In Uganda, traditional chiefs in Nebbi district collected more than 500 weapons from game poachers there (Ocowun, 2010). While most of those weapons were not firearms, the elders' ability to collect them underscored their importance in coordinating anti-poaching and weapons collection initiatives. In Kenya, some elders have reportedly offered to assist the KWS by using magic to make poachers fall asleep (Mwadime, 2014).

Poaching dynamics can vary significantly across as well as within countries.

The Tsavo Trust, a Kenyan NGO, emphasizes the physical security of communities, as well as wildlife, in its anti-poaching efforts. It supports the local recruitment of professionally trained anti-poaching units that are mandated to identify and apprehend poachers residing or working out of the same communities. The Tsavo Trust works in partnership with the KWS, as well as other private conservancy groups, and serves as a link between government agencies and local people in collating elephant data and supporting cooperative efforts to combat poaching. By coordinating aerial and ground teams, the Tsavo Trust can identify where poaching incidents have taken place and assist in the tracking and apprehension of poachers (Tsavo Trust, 2014).

Community-based initiatives to combat poaching ultimately depend on the achievement of basic levels of security.

Farther south, in Tanzania, the PAMS Foundation, another NGO, uses a similar approach in engaging communities and helping them to play a leading role in wildlife protection. The aims of the Ruvuma Elephant Project (REP) are to improve the status of elephant conservation in the 2-million-hectare area covered by the Selous Game Reserve in Tanzania and the Niassa National Reserve in Mozambique. Among its objectives, the REP seeks to prevent elephant poaching through interventions that include the training of local game scouts and support for community-driven conservation and development initiatives (PAMS Foundation, n.d.). Village scouts are trained in field data collection, satellite GPS use, community rights, and anti-poaching techniques.[31]

Most REP scouts are from local communities and, unlike some government park rangers and members of other anti-poaching units, they are highly familiar with the environment in which they work and the communities with whom they engage—communities that are also home to many poachers. The REP scouting teams typically involve members from several different agencies, including police, wildlife rangers, and other conservancy organizations. According to the PAMS chairman, the inter-agency composition of these anti-poaching teams can reduce corruption by promoting operational transparency. Further, most PAMS scouts are not armed; those who are carry only single-shot rifles. Since 2009, they have confiscated more than 800 firearms, including .375 and .458 hunting rifles, Kalashnikov-pattern rifles, and vast quantities of craft firearms and ammunition. Most importantly, elephant populations within the REP project area are reportedly increasing.[32]

In Namibia, elephant population numbers have been increasing at a steady pace over the past 15 years, in part because of the establishment of community-managed conservancies (Elephant Database, 2013). Committees formed of local people manage each conservancy. They develop a management plan that includes the designation of locally selected wildlife scouts. These scouts report poaching incidents to their respective committees and incidents are posted publicly at conservancy offices in order to facilitate responses to them (FZS, 2010). The conservancies promote the inclusion of women as decision-makers and committee members, ensuring the involvement of a broad range of local people in community-led management of wildlife and lands (ODI, 2011).

Ultimately, however, community-based initiatives to combat poaching, such as those described above, depend on the achievement of basic levels of security. The large-scale elephant massacres in the CAR and Cameroon underscore the need to control and reduce rates of armed violence in areas where armed groups poach *before* local populations can safely support and engage in wildlife protection initiatives.

CONCLUSION

Poaching has multiple drivers, including the international demand for ivory and rhino horn, the illegal bush meat trade, and subsistence hunting. The main actors involved in poaching elephants and rhinos in Africa are non-state armed groups, rogue military officers, commercial poachers, and subsistence hunters. Together, these actors are sharply reducing the numbers of elephants and rhinos present in many habitats, even pushing herds in some areas towards extinction.

The widespread availability of firearms complicates the fight against elephant and rhino poaching. The illicit trade in weapons and ammunition, including diversion from state stockpiles, is giving poachers relatively easy access to military-style weapons and hunting rifles. Further, conviction rates in many countries are relatively low and weapons confiscated from poachers occasionally find their way back to the black market (and back into the hands of poachers). Perhaps most critically, it appears that some government officials, including members of national armed forces, are facilitating, or even conducting, poaching activities.

The militarization of anti-poaching efforts in some states has had both positive and negative consequences. While there are indications that aggressive anti-poaching policies have resulted in high numbers of arrests and seizures of ivory, weapons, and ammunition, in some cases civilians have faced increased threats from firearms and violence related to anti-poaching activity.

The collection of relevant firearms data could be improved. More data could be gleaned from elephant kill sites, which often contain evidence, such as ammunition casings, that could shed light on the sources of poacher weapons and ammunition, as well as associated trafficking networks. The use of law enforcement tools, such as INTERPOL's firearms tracing system, remains low, despite their potential utility in helping national law enforcement agencies fight environmental crime.

Governments, NGOs, and conservancy organizations are increasingly recognizing and acting to harness the support of local communities in anti-poaching efforts. Community involvement in the management of conservancy areas and the monitoring of elephant and rhino poaching can complement law enforcement efforts focused on the arrest and conviction of poachers. Just as poaching has different causes and takes diverse forms, actions to combat poaching will need to be multidimensional, but also context-sensitive, if the threat currently facing African elephant and rhino populations is to be lifted. ◪

LIST OF ABBREVIATIONS

CAR	Central African Republic
CITES	Convention on International Trade in Endangered Species of Wild Fauna and Flora
DRC	Democratic Republic of the Congo
ETIS	Elephant Trade Information System
FARDC	Forces armées de la République démocratique du Congo (Armed Forces of the Democratic Republic of Congo)
FDLR	Forces démocratiques de libération du Rwanda (Democratic Forces for the Liberation of Rwanda)
INTERPOL	International Criminal Police Organization
IUCN SSC	International Union for Conservation of Nature Species Survival Commission
KWS	Kenya Wildlife Service
LRA	Lord's Resistance Army
MIKE	Monitoring the Illegal Killing of Elephants
PIKE	Proportion of illegally killed elephants
REP	Ruvuma Elephant Project
UPDF	Uganda People's Defence Force

ENDNOTES

1   Author interview with Colman O'Criodain, policy analyst, World Wildlife Fund International, Geneva, 24 September 2014.

2   The last remaining three northern white rhinos (*Ceratotherium simum cottoni*) are located in a conservancy in Kenya.

3   Author interview with Colman O'Criodain, policy analyst, World Wildlife Fund International, Geneva, 24 September 2014.

4   Author interview with Richard Leakey, conservationist, Nairobi, Kenya, August 2014.

5   Author interviews with security managers at several conservancies in central Kenya, August 2014.

6   Author interview with a wildlife ranger, south-east Kenya, August 2014.

7   Author correspondence with Daniel Stiles, member, International Union for Conservation of Nature Species Survival Commission (IUCN SSC) African Elephant Specialist Group, 7 November 2014.

8   Author correspondence with Daniel Stiles, member, IUCN SSC African Elephant Specialist Group, 7 November 2014.

9   Author correspondence with Daniel Stiles, member, IUCN SSC African Elephant Specialist Group, 7 November 2014.

10   Author telephone interview with Paul Ronan, project director, the Resolve LRA Crisis Initiative, 28 August 2014.

11   Correspondance with Daniel Stiles, member, IUCN SSC African Elephant Specialist Group, 7 November 2014.

12   Author interview with Julian Blanc, coordinator, CITES Monitoring of Illegally Killed Elephants, Nairobi, August 2014.

13   The Kenya Wildlife Service was called the Wildlife Conservation and Management Department until 1990.

14   Author interview with Richard Leakey, conservationist, Nairobi, August 2014.

15   Author interview with Iain Douglas Hamilton, conservationist and founder of Save the Elephants, Samburu, Kenya, August 2014.

16   The width of a bullet cartridge is its calibre. A bullet size beginning with a decimal, such as the .375 calibre hunting bullet, is measured in inches. A bullet size starting with a number, such as the 7.62 AK-47 bullet, is measured in millimetres.

17   The facility is now operated by BAE Systems Global Combat Systems Munitions.

18   Author interviews with security managers in central Kenya, August 2014.

19   Author correspondence with N.R. Jenzen-Jones, military arms and munitions specialist, 13 December 2014.

20   Author interview with Iain Douglas Hamilton, conservationist and founder of Save the Elephants, Samburu, Kenya, August 2014.

21   Author interviews with conservationists, Kenya, August 2014.

22   Author interview with Iain Douglas Hamilton, conservationist and founder of Save the Elephants, Samburu, Kenya, August 2014.

23   Author interview with Iain Douglas Hamilton, conservationist and founder of Save the Elephants, Samburu, Kenya, August 2014.

24   Author telephone interview with Keith Roberts, conservationist, 24 August 2014.

25   Author telephone interview with Daniel Stiles, member, IUCN SSC African Elephant Specialist Group, 19 August 2014.

26   Author telephone interview with Daniel Stiles, member, IUCN SSC African Elephant Specialist Group, 19 August 2014.

27   Data collected by the NGO Big Life from poaching sites in its local area and shared with the author.

28   Author interview with a wildlife ranger, south-east Kenya, August 2014.

29   Author interview with Richard Leakey, conservationist, Nairobi, August 2014.

30   Author telephone interview with Keith Roberts, conservationist, 24 August 2014.

31   Author telephone interview with Wayne Lotter, chair, PAMS Foundation, 20 August 2014.

32   Author telephone interview with Wayne Lotter, chair, PAMS Foundation, 20 August 2014.

BIBLIOGRAPHY

AFP (Agence France-Presse). 2014. 'Tanzania Elephant Population Plummets.' 11 January.
   <http://www.enca.com/africa/tanzania-elephant-population-plummets>

Agger, Casper. 2014. 'Behind the Headlines: Drivers of Violence in the Central African Republic.' Washington, DC: Enough Project. May.
   <http://www.enoughproject.org/files/CAR%20Report%20-%20Behind%20the%20Headlines%205.1.14.pdf>

— and Jonathan Hutson. 2013. *Kony's Ivory: How Elephant Poaching in Congo Helps Support the Lord's Resistance Army.* Washington, DC: Enough Project. June. <http://www.enoughproject.org/files/KonysIvory.pdf>

Akwiri, Joseph. 2014. 'Interpol Joins Hunt for Kenyan Poaching Suspect.' Reuters. 16 October.
   <http://www.reuters.com/article/2014/10/16/us-kenya-wildlife-poaching-idUSKCN0I524820141016>

AllAfrica. 2014a. 'Rwanda: FDLR Generating U.S. $71 Million from Businesses with Wives of DRC Officers.' 28 August.
    <http://allafrica.com/stories/201408290133.html>

—. 2014b. 'Mozambique: Agreement on Fight against Wildlife Crime.' 31 October. <http://allafrica.com/stories/201410311377.html>

Apobo, Amboya. 2004. 'Rapport sur le braconnage d'éléphant et sur le commerce de l'ivoire dans et à la périphérie de la Réserve de Faune à Okapis
    (RFO) Ituri, RDC.' Kinshasa: Institut Congolais pour la Conservation de la Nature/Wildlife Conservancy Society.

Berman, Eric. 2011. 'Craft Production of Small Arms.' Research Note No. 3. Geneva: Small Arms Survey. March.
    <http://www.smallarmssurvey.org/fileadmin/docs/H-Research_Notes/SAS-Research-Note-3.pdf>

Blanc, Julian, et al. 2007. 'African Elephant Status Report 2007: An Update from the African Elephant Database.' SSC Occasional Paper Series 33. Gland,
    Switzerland: International Union for Conservation of Nature. <https://portals.iucn.org/library/efiles/documents/SSC-OP-033.pdf>

Bloch, Simon. 2012. 'Unarmed Farm Manager Gives Rhino Poachers a Bloody Nose for Christmas.' *Africa Geographic*. 28 December.
    <http://africageographic.com/blog/unarmed-farm-manager-gives-rhino-poachers-a-bloody-nose-for-christmas/>

Chappaz, Nicolas. 2006. 'How Poachers Kill Elephants in Banyang-Mbo Wildlife Sanctuary, Cameroon.' Open Earth Project. 9 June.
    <http://www.open-earth.org/document/natureR_main.php?natureId=283>

CITES (Convention on International Trade in Endangered Species of Wild Fauna and Flora). 1973. Adopted 3 March. Entered into force 1 July 1975.
    <http://www.cites.org/eng/disc/text.php>

— Secretariat. 2012. 'CITES Secretary-General Expresses Grave Concern over Reports of Mass Elephant Killings in Cameroon.' Media statement. 28 February.
    <http://www.cites.org/eng/news/pr/2012/20120228_elephant_cameroon.php>

—. 2013. 'African Rhinoceroses: Latest Trends in Rhino Numbers and Poaching.' CoP16 Inf. 51.
    <http://www.cites.org/sites/default/files/eng/cop/16/inf/E-CoP16i-51.pdf>

—. 2014a. 'Elephant Conservation, Illegal Killing and Ivory Trade.' SC65 Doc. 42.1. Geneva: CITES Standing Committee.
    <http://www.cites.org/sites/default/files/eng/com/sc/65/E-SC65-42-01_2.pdf>

—. 2014b. 'Interpretation and Implementation of the Convention—Species Trade and Conservation: Elephants.' SC65 Doc. 42.2.
    <http://www.cites.org/sites/default/files/eng/com/sc/65/E-SC65-42-02.pdf>

Crone, Anton. 2014. 'Beyond the Infinity Pool: Running a Park at the Sharp End of Conservation.' *Africa Geography Magazine*. 3 October.
    <http://magazine.africageographic.com/weekly/issue-14/zakouma-chad-african-parks-safari-adventure>

DEA (Department of Environmental Affairs). 2014. 'South Africans Urged to Work together to Curb Rhino Poaching.' Pretoria: Government of South Africa.
    11 September. <https://www.environment.gov.za/mediarelease/southafricans_workingtogether_rhinopoaching>

Dube, Buhle and Alfred Magagula. 2007. 'The Law and Legal Research in Swaziland.' New York: Hauser Global Law School Program, New York University
    School of Law. <http://www.nyulawglobal.org/globalex/Swaziland.htm>

Duffy, Rosaleen. 2014. 'Waging a War to Save Biodiversity: The Rise of Militarized Conservation.' *International Affairs*, Vol. 90, No. 4, pp. 819–34.

— and Freya St. John. 2013. *Poverty, Poaching and Trafficking: What Are the Links?* Evidence on Demand. June.
    <http://eprints.soas.ac.uk/17836/1/EoD_HD059_Jun2013_Poverty_Poaching.pdf>

Economist. 2014. 'Tanzania's Dwindling Elephants: Big Game Poachers.' 8 November.
    <http://www.economist.com/news/middle-east-and-africa/21631202-claims-links-between-politicians-and-poachers-merit-further-investigation-big>

Elephant Database. 2013. 'Namibia, 2012 ("2013 Africa" Analysis).'
    <http://www.elephantdatabase.org/preview_report/2013_africa/Loxodonta_africana/2012/Africa/Southern_Africa/Namibia>

FWS (United States Fish and Wildlife Service). 2013. 'CITES and Elephants: What Is the "Global Ban" on Ivory Trade?' November.
    <http://www.fws.gov/le/pdf/CITES-and-Elephant-Conservation.pdf>

FZS (Frankfurt Zoological Society). 2010. 'Experience Sharing Visit to Namibia: September 10–20, 2010.' Draft. September.
    <http://www.macaulay.ac.uk/CAMP/Namibia-Report-Sep10.pdf>

Gettleman, Jeffrey. 2012a. 'Elephants Dying in Epic Frenzy as Ivory Fuels Wars and Profits.' *The New York Times*. 3 September.
    <http://www.nytimes.com/2012/09/04/world/africa/africas-elephants-are-being-slaughtered-in-poaching-frenzy.html?pagewanted=all&_r=2&>

—. 2012b. 'Notorious Poacher Now Leads a Fight to Save Africa's Elephant.' *Sydney Morning Herald*. 31 December.
    <http://www.smh.com.au/world/notorious-poacher-now-leads-a-fight-to-save-africas-elephants-20121230-2c1ix.html>

Heath, Kevin. 2014. 'KWS Ranger Killed by Poachers.' *Wildlife News*. 4 June. <http://wildlifenews.co.uk/2014/06/kws-ranger-killed-by-poachers/>

Humphreys, Jasper and M.L.R. Smith. 2014. 'The "Rhinofication" of South African Security.' *International Affairs*, Vol. 90, No. 4, pp. 795–818.

Independent (United Kingdom). 2013. '10 Things You Need to Know about Elephant Poaching.' 4 December.
    <http://www.independent.co.uk/voices/iv-drip/10-things-you-need-to-know-about-elephant-poaching-8983276.html>

ICG (International Crisis Group). 2014. *The Central African Crisis: From Predation to Stabilization.* Africa Report No. 219. Brussels: ICG. 17 June.
   <http://www.crisisgroup.org/~/media/Files/africa/central-africa/central-african-republic/219-la-crise-centrafricaine-de-la-predation-a-la-stabilisation-english.pdf>

INTERPOL (International Criminal Police Organization). 2014. 'Elephant Poaching and Ivory Trafficking in East Africa: Assessment for an Effective Law
   Enforcement Response.' Lyon: INTERPOL. February. <http://www.interpol.int/News-and-media/News/2014/N2014-029>

IRIN. 2013. 'Conflict Cuts off Civilians in DRC's Katanga.' 2 May.
   <http://www.irinnews.org/report/97963/conflict-cuts-off-civilians-in-drc-s-katanga>

IUCN (International Union for Conservation of Nature). 2012. 'Facts and Fiction: The Rhino Horn Trade.' 16 November.
   <http://cmsdata.iucn.org/downloads/factsheet_rhino_poaching.pdf>

—. n.d. 'Loxodonta Africana: African Elephant.' <http://maps.iucnredlist.org/map.html?id=12392>

Jopson, Tyson. 2013. 'Tanzania's Controversial Anti-poaching Campaign to Continue.' *Getaway.* 12 November.
   <http://www.getaway.co.za/travel-news/tanzania-operation-terminate-anti-poaching-drive/>

Jorgic, Drazen. 2014. 'Four Rangers Killed in Kenya's Worst Poaching Attack in Years.' Reuters. 11 July.
   <http://in.reuters.com/article/2014/07/11/kenya-rhinos-idINKBN0FG1HD20140711>

Kahumbu, Paula, et al. 2014. *Scoping Study on the Prosecution of Wildlife Related Crimes in Kenya Courts: January 2008 to June 2013.* Wildlifedirect.org.
   <http://baraza.wildlifedirect.org/files/2014/01/WILDLIFEDIRECT-court-study-26.1.14.pdf>

Kakala, Taylor Toeka. 2013. 'Soldiers Trade in Illegal Ivory.' Inter Press Service. 25 July.
   <http://www.ipsnews.net/2013/07/soldiers-trade-in-illegal-ivory/>

Kalron, Nir. 2013. 'Neo-conservation: A Commentary on the Future Security of Africa's Wildlife.' *African Security Review,* Vol. 22, No. 3. September,
   pp. 160–66. <http://www.tandfonline.com/doi/pdf/10.1080/10246029.2013.823795>

Kenya. 2013. 'The Wildlife Conservation and Management Act.' No. 47 of 2013. 27 December.
   <http://www.kws.org/export/sites/kws/info/publications/acts_policies/The_wildlife_conservation_and_management_bill_2013.pdf>

Kiishweko, Orton. 2013. 'Tanzania: 952 Arrested in "Tokomeza" Operation.' AllAfrica.com. 31 October. <http://allafrica.com/stories/201310310131.html>

King, Juliet. 2011. 'Northern Rangelands Trust Report 2010: Development of a Joint Conservancy Anti-poaching Team to Protect African Elephants in
   Northern Kenya.' March. <http://www.elephantconservation.org/northern-rangelands-trust-report-2010/>

Knapp, Eli. 2012. 'Why Poaching Pays: A Summary of Risks and Benefits Illegal Hunters Face in Western Serengeti, Tanzania.' *Journal of Tropical
   Conservation Science,* Vol. 5, No. 4, pp. 434–45.
   <http://tropicalconservationscience.mongabay.com/content/v5/TCS-2012_Vol_5%284%29_434-445_Knapp.pdf>

Koross, Kibiwott. 2013. 'Untouchable Lords of Poaching in Samburu.' *Star* (Kenya). 29 January.
   <http://www.the-star.co.ke/news/article-104884/untouchable-lords-poaching-samburu>

KWS (Kenya Wildlife Service). 2014. 'Kenya Airways, Born Free back War against Rhino Poaching.' 5 December.
   <http://www.kws.org/info/news/2014/5dec2014kenyaairways.html>

Library of Congress (United States). 2014. 'Wildlife Trafficking and Poaching: South Africa.' Last updated 11 March.
   <http://www.loc.gov/law/help/wildlife-poaching/southafrica.php>

Lombard, Louisa. 2012. 'Dying for Ivory.' *The New York Times.* 20 September.
   <http://www.nytimes.com/2012/09/21/opinion/elephants-dying-for-ivory.html?_r=0>

Lunstrum, Elizabeth. 2014. 'Green Militarization: Anti-poaching Efforts and the Spatial Contours of Kruger National Park.' *Annals of the Association of
   American Geographers,* Vol. 104, No. 4, pp. 816–32. <http://www.tandfonline.com/doi/abs/10.1080/00045608.2014.912545#.VCQjC1OAqD>

MacLeod, Fiona and Estacio Valoi. 2013. 'Rhino Trafficking: Down the Rabbit Hole at the Kruger Park.' *Daily Maverick.* 8 July.
   <http://www.dailymaverick.co.za/article/2013-07-08-rhino-trafficking-down-the-rabbit-hole-at-the-kruger-park/#.VDJ4zFOApDx>

Makoye, Kizito. 2014. 'Anti-poaching Operation Spreads Terror in Tanzania.' Inter Press Service. 6 January.
   <http://www.ipsnews.net/2014/01/anti-poaching-operation-spread-terror-tanzania/>

Martin, Esmond and Lucy Vigne. 2010. 'Consumer Demand for Ivory in Japan Declines.' *Pachyderm Journal,* No. 47, January–June.
   <http://pachydermjournal.org/index.php/pachy/article/viewFile/173/109>

—. 2011. 'The Ivory Dynasty: A Report on the Soaring Demand for Elephant and Mammoth Ivory in Southern China.' London: Elephant Family, Aspinall
   Foundation, and Columbus Zoo and Aquarium. <http://www.elephantfamily.org/uploads/copy/EF_Ivory_Report_2011_web.pdf>

McAdams, John. 2014. 'The Five Best Cartridges for Hunting Africa.' 17 August.
   <http://www.wideopenspaces.com/5-best-cartridges-for-hunting-africa/>

Messer, Kent. 2000. 'The Poacher's Dilemma: The Economics of Poaching and Enforcement.' *Endangered Species Update*, Vol. 17, No. 3.
   <http://www.leedr.cornell.edu/kdm22/docs/Poacher%27s%20Dilemma%20-%20Messer%202000.pdf>

—. 2010. 'Protecting Endangered Species: When Are Shoot-on-Sight Policies the Only Viable Option to Stop Poaching?' *Ecological Economics*, Vol. 69,
   No. 12, pp. 2334–40.

Milliken, Tom and Jo Shaw. 2012. 'The South Africa–Viet Nam Rhino Horn Trade Nexus: A Deadly Combination of Institutional Lapses, Corrupt Wildlife
   Industry Professionals and Asian Crime Syndicates.' Johannesburg: TRAFFIC.
   <http://www.traffic.org/species-reports/traffic_species_mammals66.pdf>

Mwadime, Raphael. 2014. 'Kenya: Magic Can Catch Poachers—Elders.' *Star* (Kenya). 16 August. <http://allafrica.com/stories/201408180714.html>

Mwai, Collins. 2014. 'Disarm Unconditionally, Regional Leaders Tell FDLR.' *New Times* (Rwanda). 24 September.
   <http://www.newtimes.co.rw/section/article/2014-09-24/181239/>

Ng'wanakilala, Fumbuka. 2013. 'Tanzanian President Sacks Four Ministers over Poaching Abuses.' Reuters. 21 December.
   <http://www.reuters.com/article/2013/12/21/us-tanzania-politics-idUSBRE9BK04X20131221>

NRT (Northern Rangelands Trust). 2009. 'Planned Grazing to Reduce Conflict.' 18 April.
   <http://northernrangelands.wildlifedirect.org/2009/04/18/planned-grazing-to-reduce-conflict/>

Ocowun, Chris. 2010. 'Nebbi Chiefs Disarm Poachers.' *New Vision* (Uganda). 22 August.
   <http://www.newvision.co.ug/news/612717-Via-Kalikwani-held-in-South-Africa.html>

ODI (Overseas Development Institute). 2011. *Sustainable Natural Resource Management in Namibia: Successful Community-based Wildlife Conservation.*
   London: ODI. <http://www.developmentprogress.org/sites/developmentprogress.org/files/namibia_report_-_master_0.pdf>

Ogada, Darcy. 2014. 'Poisons and Poaching: A Deadly Mix Requiring Urgent Action.' National Geographic. 17 August.
   <http://newswatch.nationalgeographic.com/2014/08/17/poisons-and-poaching-a-deadly-mix-requiring-urgent-action/>

Okello, John, et al. 2008. 'Population Genetic Structure of Savannah Elephants in Kenya: Conservation and Management Implications.' *Journal of Heredity*,
   Vol. 99, No. 5, pp. 443–52.

Onsarigo, Calvin. 2014. 'Interpol Arrests Poaching Kingpin in Tanzania.' *Star* (Kenya). 24 December.
   <http://www.the-star.co.ke/news/interpol-arrests-poaching-kingpin-tanzania>

Ontebetse, Khonani. 2013. '"Execute Elephant Poachers on the Spot"—Khama.' *Sunday Standard* (Botswana). 9 December.
   <http://www.sundaystandard.info/article.php?NewsID=18626&GroupID=1>

PAMS Foundation. n.d. 'Ruvuma Elephant Project.' <http://pamsfoundation.org/our-initiatives/ruvuma-elephant-project/>

Pflanz, Mike. 2014. 'The Ivory Police.' *Christian Science Monitor.* 2 March. <http://www.csmonitor.com/World/Africa/2014/0302/The-ivory-police>

Poffenberger, Michael. 2013. '5 Questions on Kony and Poaching.' Inside the LRA blog. 29 July.
   <http://www.theresolve.org/2013/07/5-questions-on-kony-and-poaching/>

RFI (Radio France International). 2014. 'RDC: réoganisation des FARDC et retour en grâce du général Amisi.' 20 September.
   <http://www.rfi.fr/afrique/20140920-rdc-fardc-reorganisation-general-amisi-kifwa/>

Ramsey, Scott. 2014. 'Interview with Kruger's Anti-poaching Chief.' *Africa Geographic.* 19 August.
   <http://africageographic.com/blog/interview-with-krugers-anti-poaching-chief/>

Resolve, The, Enough Project, and Invisible Children. 2014. 'Kony to LRA: Bring Me Ivory, Gold, and Diamonds.' Press release. 19 November.
   <http://www.enoughproject.org/files/publications/LRA-Trafficking-Presser-Enough-TheResolve-InvisibleChildren-Nov2014.pdf>

Roe, Dilys, et al. 2014. 'The Elephant in the Room: Sustainable Use in the Illegal Wildlife Trade Debate.' Briefing. London: International Institute for
   Environment and Development. February. <http://pubs.iied.org/pdfs/17205IIED.pdf>

Ronan, Paul. 2014. 'Crisis Tracker: Is Kony Using the Chaos in CAR as a Lifeline?' Inside the LRA blog. 11 February.
   <http://www.theresolve.org/2014/02/crisis-tracker-is-kony-using-the-chaos-in-car-as-a-lifeline/>

Rookmaaker, L.C. and Pierre-Olivier Antoine. 2013. 'White Rhino Range Map.' Cambridge, UK: Rhino Resource Center. <http://www.rhinoresourcecenter.
   com/images/White-Rhino-Range-Map_i1362661062.php?type=search&keywords=map&sort_order=desc&sort_key=score>

Rooney, Richard. 2014. 'King Lets Game Rangers Shoot-to-Kill.' Swazi Media Commentary Blog. 20 January.
   <http://swazimedia.blogspot.ch/2014/01/king-lets-game-rangers-shoot-to-kill.html>

Ross, Philip, 2013. 'Kenya to Microchip All Rhinos, Chips Will Provide "Crucial Evidence" to Prosecute Poachers.' *International Business Times.* 16 October.
   <http://www.ibtimes.com/kenya-microchip-all-rhinos-chips-will-provide-crucial-evidence-prosecute-poachers-1428774>

San Diego Zoo and International Rhino Foundation. n.d. 'Black Rhino: Historic & Present Distribution.'
   <http://library.sandiegozoo.org/factsheets/black_rhino/map.htm>

Saramba, Peter. 2013. 'Gov't Issues Shoot-to-Kill Order in Attempt to Tackle Poaching.' *Citizen* (Tanzania). 5 October.

    <http://www.thecitizen.co.tz/News/Govt-issues-shoot-to-kill-order-in-attempt-to-tackle-poaching/-/1840392/2019478/-/p9b30/-/index.html>

Save the Elephants. 2014. 'Price of Ivory in China Triples in Four Years, with Grave Implications for Elephants in Africa.' Press release. 2 July.

    <http://savetheelephants.org/press-releases/price-of-ivory-in-china-triples-in-four-years-with-grave-implications-for-elephants-in-africa/>

Save the Rhino. n.d. 'Poaching: The Statistics.' Accessed January 2015. <http://www.savetherhino.org/rhino_info/poaching_statistics>

Shetler, Jan Bender. 2007. *Imagining Serengeti: A History of Landscape Memory in Tanzania from Earliest Times to the Present*. Ohio: Ohio University Press.

Stiles, Daniel. 2011. *Elephant Meat Trade in Central Africa: Summary Report*. Gland, Switzerland: International Union for Conservation of Nature.

    <https://portals.iucn.org/library/efiles/documents/ssc-op-045.pdf>

—. 2013. 'The Ivory War: Militarized Tactics Won't Work.' *Conversation*. 9 November.

    <http://theconversation.com/the-ivory-war-militarised-tactics-wont-work-19164>

SRP (Stop Rhino Poaching). n.d. 'Rhino Poaching and Population Statistics.' Accessed January 2015. <http://www.stoprhinopoaching.com/statistics.aspx>

Sunday Standard (Botswana). 2013. 'Inside Botswana's Cocktail of Poaching Militias, Security Moles and Chinese Handlers.' 14 February.

    <http://www.sundaystandard.info/article.php?NewsID=16163&GroupID=1>

Tentena, Paul. 2014. 'Shoot Poachers on Sight—Museveni.' *East African Business Week*. 3 March.

    <http://www.busiweek.com/index1.php?Ctp=2&pI=678&pLv=3&srI=%2057&spI=&cI=1>

Thornycroft, Peta and Aislinn Laing. 2013. 'Poachers Kill 300 Zimbabwe Elephants with Cyanide.' *Telegraph* (United Kingdom). 20 October.

    <http://www.telegraph.co.uk/news/worldnews/africaandindianocean/zimbabwe/10390634/Poachers-kill-300-Zimbabwe-elephants-with-cyanide.html>

Thwala, Phumelele. 2004. 'Country Study: Botswana.' In Chandré Gould and Guy Lamb, eds. *Hide and Seek: Taking Account of Small Arms in Southern Africa*. Pretoria: Institute for Security Studies, pp. 22–46.

Titeca, Kristof. 2013. 'Ivory beyond the LRA: Why a Broader Focus Is Needed in Studying Poaching.' *African Arguments*. 17 September.

    <http://africanarguments.org/2013/09/17/ivory-beyond-the-lra-why-a-broader-focus-is-needed-in-studying-poaching-by-kristof-titeca/>

Torchia, Christopher. 2014. 'South Africa Rhino Poacher Jailed for 77 Years.' *Independent* (United Kingdom). 23 July.

    <http://www.independent.co.uk/news/world/africa/south-africa-rhino-poacher-jailed-for-77-years-9623177.html>

Tsavo Trust. 2014. 'Kwaheri Satao: Saying Goodbye to a Tsavo Icon.' 13 June.

    <http://tsavotrust.org/news/2014/6/13/kwaheri-satao-saying-goodbye-to-a-tsavo-icon>

UK (United Kingdom). 2014. 'London Conference on the Illegal Wildlife Trade 2014.'

    <https://www.gov.uk/government/topical-events/illegal-wildlife-trade-2014/about>

UNEP (United Nations Environment Programme). 2007. 'Sudan: Post-conflict Environmental Assessment.' Nairobi: UNEP. June.

    <http://postconflict.unep.ch/publications/UNEP_Sudan.pdf>

— et al. 2013. 'Elephants in the Dust—The African Elephant Crisis: A Rapid Response Assessment.' Arendal, Norway: UNEP et al.

    <http://www.unep.org/pdf/RRAivory_draft7.pdf>

UN (United Nations) News Service. 2014. 'UN-backed Treaty, INTERPOL Operation Targets "Most Wanted" Environmental Fugitives.' 17 November.

    <http://www.un.org/apps/news/story.asp?NewsID=49361#.VHxK5YeLac8>

UNODC (United Nations Office on Drugs and Crime). 2013. *Transnational Organized Crime in Eastern Africa: A Threat Assessment*. Vienna: UNODC.

    <http://www.unodc.org/documents/data-and-analysis/Studies/TOC_East_Africa_2013.pdf>

UNSC (United Nations Security Council). 2012. 'Letter Dated 12 October 2012 from the Group of Experts on the Democratic Republic of Congo Addressed to the Chair of the Security Council Committee Established Pursuant to Resolution 1533 (2004) Concerning the Democratic Republic of Congo.' S/2012/843 of 15 November.

    <http://www.securitycouncilreport.org/atf/cf/%7B65BFCF9B-6D27-4E9C-8CD3-CF6E4FF96FF9%7D/s_2012_843.pdf>

—. 2013a. *Report of the Secretary-General on the Activities of the United Nations Regional Office for Central Africa and on the Lord's Resistance Army-affected Areas*. S/2013/671 of 14 November. <http://www.un.org/en/ga/search/view_doc.asp?symbol=S/2013/671>

—. 2013b. *Report of the Secretary-General on the Activities of the United Nations Regional Office for Central Africa and on the Lord's Resistance Army-affected Areas*. S/2013/297 of 20 May. <http://www.un.org/en/ga/search/view_doc.asp?symbol=S/2013/297>

—. 2014a. Resolution 2134. S/RES/2134 of 28 January. <http://www.un.org/ga/search/view_doc.asp?symbol=S/RES/2134%20%282014%29>

—. 2014b. 'Final Report of the Group of Experts on the Democratic Republic of the Congo.' S/2014/42 of 23 January.

    <http://www.securitycouncilreport.org/atf/cf/%7B65BFCF9B-6D27-4E9C-8CD3-CF6E4FF96FF9%7D/s_2014_42.pdf>

—. 2014c. Resolution 2136. S/RES/2136 of 30 January. <http://www.un.org/en/ga/search/view_doc.asp?symbol=S/RES/2136(2014)&referer=http://www.un.org/en/sc/documents/resolutions/2014.shtml&Lang=E>

Vira, Varun and Thomas Ewing. 2014. 'Ivory's Curse: The Militarization and Professionalization of Poaching in Africa.' Born Free USA and C4ADS. April.
<http://www.all-creatures.org/articles/ar-Ivorys-Curse-2014.pdf>

—, and Jackson Miller. 2014. *Out of Africa: Mapping the Global Trade in Illicit Elephant Ivory*. Hong Kong: C4ADS and Born Free.
<http://www.c4ads.org/#!project-highlights/c21l1>

Wasser, Samuel, et al. 2008. 'Combatting the Illegal Trade in African Ivory with DNA Forensics.' *Conservation Biology*, Vol. 22, No. 4, pp. 1065–71.
<http://stephenslab.uchicago.edu/MSpapers/Wasser2008.pdf>

WESSA (Wildlife and Environment Society of South Africa). 2014. 'Current Rhino Poaching Stats.' 23 November.
<http://wessa.org.za/get-involved/rhino-initiative/current-rhino-poaching-stats.htm>

Wittemyer, George, et al. 2014. 'Illegal Killing for Ivory Drives Global Decline in African Elephants.' *Proceedings of the National Academy of Sciences*, Vol. 111, No. 36. 9 September. <www.pnas.org/cgi/doi/10.1073/pnas.1403984111>

WWF (World Wildlife Fund) International et al. 2014. *Living Planet Report 2014: Species and Spaces, People and Places*.
<http://wwf.panda.org/about_our_earth/all_publications/living_planet_report/>

WWF (World Wildlife Fund) New Zealand. 2013. 'Poachers Kill at Least 89 Elephants in Chad.' 21 March.
<http://www.wwf.org.nz/?10521/Poachers-kill-at-least-89-elephants-in-Chad>

ACKNOWLEDGEMENTS

Principal authors

Khristopher Carlson, Joanna Wright, and Hannah Dönges

Contributor

Daniel Stiles

786   TONGA SOA!
SIDDEEK GEM PALACE
MANOMBO BE
MIVIDY VATO   AMBONY PRIX

The hub of Madagascar's sapphire region, Ilakaka, September 2008.
© Roberto Schmidt/AFP Photo

Digging for Trouble
VIOLENCE AND FRONTIER URBANIZATION

2

INTRODUCTION

In 2008, Redeyef, a phosphate mining town in Tunisia's Gafsa mining basin, experienced months of protest and security force violence that claimed three lives and injured dozens (Chouikha and Geisser, 2010). The protests had emerged in response to a lack of work opportunities and unaccountable and unfair application procedures for mining jobs. For despite the significant wealth generated by phosphate extraction, the Gafsa mining basin remains one of the poorest regions of Tunisia. By 2008, youth unemployment was almost 40 per cent in some of the mining towns (Vann, 2008), partly due to new extraction procedures that had cut personnel requirements by 75 per cent since 1980 (Gobe, 2010, pp. 4–5).

In Madagascar, the establishment in 2008 of a new nickel and cobalt mine completely transformed the formerly small urban area of Moramanga. Following an influx of foreign workers, local labourers, and private security personnel, most of the town inhabitants have been living in informal housing without access to basic services. Violence in the form of armed break-ins and robberies—often organized and involving former members of the armed forces—has increased, as has sexual and gender-based violence (Razafindrazaka, 2014). In contrast, the oil boom that brought jobs to the remote creek community of Oloibiri in the Niger Delta, Nigeria, has long passed. For 20 years following the discovery of oil in 1956, the area prospered. But oil production ended in the mid-1970s (Akpan, 2005, p. 139), and the population has since dropped to 10 per cent of its boom levels. In the shell of the former town, youth violence is routine (Watts and Ibaba, 2011, pp. 1–3).

This chapter focuses on violence related to one specific form of urbanization prevalent in the global South—*frontier urbanization*—here defined as the rapid growth of previously marginalized, underdeveloped regions and hinterlands into urban areas that service resource extraction, particularly of oil, gas, and minerals. Little is known about the spatial and institutional dynamics and competing interests of the extractive sector, state and non-state security providers, and populations in such settings. Is there a link between frontier urbanization and specific types of violence? What are the security effects when the extractive boom recedes?

The main findings of this chapter are as follows:

- The extraction of oil, gas, and strategic or precious minerals is typically accompanied by significant urbanization of the adjoining area, with often-dramatic socio-economic repercussions.
- The effort to control and secure resources that are being extracted can attract a variety of armed actors, including security forces and predatory groups, not only to the mining sites themselves, but also to the rapidly expanding urban service areas.
- The sudden urbanization around extraction sites is rarely accompanied by sufficient public service provision, including security. As a result, these services are increasingly outsourced to non-state providers, such as private security companies or protection squads.

- Frontier urbanization can lead to conflict over the control of the land and its extractable resources; insecurity and social unrest related to precarious socio-economic and environmental conditions; and tensions, sometimes expressed violently, around post-extraction decline or state-led urban clean-up and rejuvenation plans.
- While the intersection of extractive industries and frontier urbanization is associated with various types of violence, key information, including rates of violence and small arms proliferation, remains elusive.

Following a brief introduction that conceptualizes frontier urbanization and identifies what is known about the links between urbanization and extraction-related armed violence, the main part of this chapter is divided into three sections that describe interrelated sources of violence and insecurity in such areas. The first discusses armed actors' protective and predatory responses to resource extraction. The second highlights the political, societal, and ecological challenges posed by unserviced and impoverished (and often informal) urban areas that can arise in response to extraction activities. This section also touches on urban protest and social unrest in the face of perceived injustice and environmental damage related to resource extraction. The third discusses the extent to which frontier areas can cope with demise and decline. A final section reflects on the scenarios presented and offers possible directions for further research.

URBAN VIOLENCE ON THE RESOURCE EXTRACTION FRONTIER

This chapter draws on three bodies of literature to grasp the dynamics of urban violence on the resource extraction frontier. The first relates the political economy of resource extraction, particularly oil, gas, and minerals, to global urbanization trends. This is a fledgling field that is just beginning to examine the ways in which the onset of extraction activities—whether large-scale industrial endeavours led by multinational corporations (MNCs) or artisanal or small-scale mining—generates urbanization of the adjoining area. The second relates the political economy of resource extraction to armed violence. This is a more established field that explores the ways in which the presence of resources can fuel the onset, conduct, and longevity of insurgency and conflict. The third, more novel perspective seeks to describe the forms and patterns of violence in urban areas on the resource extraction frontier, a field of research that remains largely unexplored.

Urbanization around extractive sites

Discussions of urbanization often focus on the increasing number of megacities, each boasting tens of millions of inhabitants, many of whom are living in poverty and squalor, and working in informal (and at times exploitative and unsafe) labour conditions. Yet a significant portion of the world's urbanization occurs on a much smaller scale, involving the penetration of rural areas by 'urban-like forms of production, infrastructure, and administration', and offering 'new possibilities for dispersed economic growth and new patterns of spatial and social mobility' (Hackenberg, 1980, p. 391). This chapter adopts a broad definition of urban settlements as:

> *populations of 10,000 people or above which are ethnically diverse, engaged in varied specialised economic activities rather than depending primarily on agriculture, and stratified by class in terms of different levels of income earning, asset holding and political power* (Bryceson and MacKinnon, 2012, p. 517).

Resource extraction activities are an important component of urbanization trends, and the topic is beginning to receive more attention (Büscher, Cuvelier, and Mushobekwa, 2014; Bryceson and MacKinnon, 2013).[1] Artisanal and small-scale mining (particularly of gold, diamonds, and precious stones) is common across many parts of South America, Africa, and Asia. Much of this mining is informal—up to 90 per cent of all gold production and export in the Democratic Republic of the Congo (DRC), according to Geenen (2012, p. 322); it frequently involves large numbers of people in each mining area, which is reflected in population movements and local settlement patterns. At the same time, relatively steady world demand and high world prices for hydrocarbon products (petroleum and natural gas) have led many governments, in collaboration with MNCs, to dig and drill in places that had not previously been considered economically viable. These activities draw a significant influx of capital and labour to the extraction site, increasing the size of existing towns or helping to establish new towns altogether.

The term 'frontier urbanization' (Browder and Godfrey, 1990) is useful for making sense of these dynamics. Echoing the experiences of the American Frontier in the 17th, 18th, and 19th centuries (Turner, [1893] 1961; Webb, 1964), 'frontier' captures the boom-and-bust nature of the settlements that spring up around extractive sites. The frontier is a setting where groups with varying cultural and economic backgrounds—as well as differing ecological convictions—begin to interact with one another by means of cooperation, coercion, and conflict (Osterhammel, 2009, pp. 471, 513–14; Richards, 2003). The notion of the frontier implies a judgement about centrality and marginality (Woodworth, 2012, p. 76; Pullan, 2011), in that a certain set of socio-economic interests and technologies are introduced to empty hinterlands with the supposed aim of accessing and extracting available resources. In this context, the arrival of pioneer 'intruders' can produce new forms of social order and new institutions (Kopytoff, 1989), the culmination of which is

A soldier from the Forces Populaires du Congo watches artisanal miners at work, DRC, November 2013. © James Oatway/Panos Pictures

the establishment of frontier towns by 'urban pioneers' (Billington, 1967, p. 7). The result is a web of urban areas rang-ing from those in the immediate vicinity of the extractive sites, to new local and ultimately regional urban service centres.

By using the terminology of 'frontier urbanization', this chapter tries to capture the volatility of urban growth and decline in areas affected by extraction activities. Such urbanization is not a uniform phenomenon and is dependent on the type of resource extracted as well as the way this extraction proceeds. The labour-intensive artisanal mining of alluvial diamond fields, for instance, may produce a form of population mobility and urban growth quite different from that generated by a capital-intensive MNC-led exploitation of a coalmine or an oilfield. Often, artisanal and more large-scale forms of extraction activities occur simultaneously. As one observer notes with reference to Sierra Leone's diamond-rich Kono district:

> both formal company mining and informal indigenous extraction have stimulated temporary and permanent migration, the emergence of new towns and the expansion of existing ones, and a strong element of season-ality with populations moving between mining and farming activities over the course of the year (Maconachie, 2012, p. 707).

'Frontier urbanization' captures the volatility of urban growth and decline in areas affected by extraction activities.

There is no clear correlation between capital generated by extractive activities and the growth or decline of related settlements. Oil and mining wealth is seldom invested on site, but rather in other parts of the country or abroad, indirectly contributing to urban growth in other locations. This is especially true of smaller-scale and possibly illegal mining activities, where the incentive to take the money and run is much higher (Gough and Yankson, 2012, p. 665). Yet even larger transnational extraction companies, which generally have an incentive to invest in mining towns (albeit selectively), may spark urban growth elsewhere—either in the regional metropolitan area or in the national capital. A good example of the former is Port Harcourt in the Niger Delta. An example of the latter is Harare, which became the headquarters for both national and foreign mining companies operating in Zimbabwe. As a result, many employ-ment opportunities there are related to mining in some way, even though the actual extraction activities occur in other parts of the country (Kamete, 2012).

Natural resources and armed conflict

Many environmental and development analysts argue that an over-reliance on the extractive sector is detrimental to a country's economic growth rates and societal stability, and that the sudden extractive revenues tend to slow down or even reverse democratization processes, consolidating authoritarian, unaccountable, and often corrupt regimes (Collier, 2010). Moreover, resource wealth is said to correlate with the likelihood and longevity of armed conflict (Ross, 2004), in part because armed groups are likely to pursue economic opportunities (due to greed) rather than political or ideological grievances alone (Berdal and Malone, 2000; Weinstein, 2007).

But the evidence base in support of these claims is weak, tends to be based on national-level data, ignores the local level, and 'hardly pays any attention to the position and role of populations living in those conflict areas' (Cuvelier, Vlassenroot, and Olin, 2014, pp. 344, 348). Researchers insist that micro-level case studies are needed to complement broader understandings of conflict dynamics to identify local and regional patterns, and to 'trace more precisely the channels through which rent seeking and relative deprivation associated with extractive activities translate into armed violence' (Carbonnier and Wagner, 2015, p. 130). In addition to a lack of local-level victimization data, empirical infor-mation on the use of small arms and light weapons in such settings is quite patchy.

In the absence of good data, Korf's work on the micro-dynamics of conflict is a useful starting point: it focuses on the entanglement of both greed and grievance and tries to capture 'the intricate links of violence with contentious politics, coercion, consent, avoidance, resistance and vulnerability' (Korf, 2011, p. 748). Similarly, this chapter seeks to uncover the complex relationships between urbanization and violence on the resource extraction frontier. It begins with the observation that, in general, the sudden influx of capital and labour into a region creates urban areas marked by severe social inequalities and spatial segregation, as well as potential conflict over control of the extracted resources themselves. State and municipal authorities thus find themselves caught in the tensions between private property and public control; between the rights of local populations to their land and its resources; and between the interests of the domestic and foreign market players as well as armed groups seeking to gain from the extraction activity.

Urban violence on the extraction frontier

There is a growing body of literature dealing with the ways in which urban life may produce particular forms of inter-personal and collective violence (Rodgers, 2010; Moncada, 2013; Jütersonke, Muggah, and Krause, 2007). Analysts have tended to stress the rate of urbanization, rather than urbanism itself, as a risk factor for violence in both the public and private spheres. They find that the likelihood of violence tends to increase when urban population growth vastly outpaces the speed at which state and municipal institutions can provide basic community services, particularly law and order (Brennan-Galvin, 2002, pp. 133–34; Fox and Beall, 2012, p. 974).

> Frontier urbanization is not by definition harmful to collective and individual socio-economic well-being.

When the capacities of public authorities are over-stretched, people increasingly rely on informal and non-state forms of service provision, ranging from commercial forms offered by the private sector and unpaid community service, to more illicit, black-market services (Kartas and Jütersonke, 2012). In the security sphere, such non-state service provision ranges from private military and security companies to self-defence and vigilante units, some of which may have ties with organized crime (Koonings and Kruijt, 2004). Violence in rapidly urbanizing spaces is thus conceived as both a dependent and independent variable: a specific institutional setting generates particular forms of violence, which in turn create new structural conditions that themselves reinforce the dynamics of violence.

The following sections draw together what is known about violence and urbanization under the specific conditions generated by resource extraction. Such extraction is frequently accompanied by an influx of people and thus an urbanization of adjoining areas; yet once the extractive boom has passed, de-urbanization may occur. Extraction also presents the potential to fuel armed conflict and social unrest. This raises the question: what is known about the micro-dynamics of violence in urban areas related to such resource extraction?

The chapter does not suggest that frontier urbanization is by definition harmful to collective and individual socio-economic well-being. In fact, the extractive industries can be a catalyst for stability, economic growth, job creation, and knowledge transfer—including the promotion of less environmentally damaging extraction technologies. Nevertheless, the boom-and-bust nature of these settlements on the resource extraction frontier has generated significant societal conflict and various forms of armed violence in numerous cases, as discussed in the following sections.

Because a robust evidence base on this issue does not yet exist, this chapter offers a provisional typology of violence based on insight obtained from fieldwork and extensive desk research. The cases studied in this chapter suggest that a variety of armed actors are drawn not only to the mining sites themselves, but also to the rapidly expanding service areas with the aim of controlling the extracted resources. These areas appear to generate a variety of policing frameworks involving transnational companies, global and local private security companies (PSCs), and different state security forces; they also attract militias, protection squads, and sometimes-violent protest groups (Johnston, 1999; Kempa et al., 1999). Ultimately, the outsourcing of security to non-state providers turns PSCs or protection squads into *de facto* urban police—pointing to the need for a greater focus on frontier urbanization when it comes to regulatory guidelines for MNCs in the extractive sector (see Box 2.1).

Box 2.1   MNC governance and frontier urbanization

International initiatives such as the Extractive Industry Transparency Initiative or the Publish What You Pay campaign seek to promote openness and accountability in the extractive sector (EITI, n.d.; PWYP, n.d.). The first is a coalition of governments, extraction companies, and civil society groups; the second is a global network of more than 800 civil society organizations. Understandably, their work has been focused on generating a more equitable and sustainable regime of resource wealth management; meanwhile, spatial dynamics and urbanization trends that accompany the extraction of oil, gas, and minerals have received only limited attention in the formulation of such governance guidelines (Obeng-Odoom, 2014, p. 23).

More generally, the same is true of the UN Guiding Principles on Business and Human Rights, produced by the team of the UN Special Representative of the Secretary-General, John Ruggie, in 2011 (UN, 2011). Corporate social responsibility (CSR) activities pursued by the extractive industry focus predominantly on workers' rights and conditions within the extractive sites themselves. Different development agencies have thus called for the establishment of certification processes for workers' rights in artisanal and small-scale mining, yet these often neglect significant administrative hurdles or precarious security situations that may prevent local workers from forming effective coalitions for the promotion of their rights as miners (Hütz-Adams and Müller, 2012, p. 5). Such advocacy is part of an urban politics in mining regions that goes well beyond the notion of the 'local community' commonly referenced in CSR standards and guidelines.

Security and safety concerns are a particularly crucial component of extractive industry regulation, and the Voluntary Principles on Security and Human Rights, established in 2000 as specific human rights guidelines for extractive sector companies, are a promising initiative in this regard (VPSHR, 2000). The accountability of private security companies, which are frequently contracted by local and multinational mining firms, is a delicate issue, and the Government of Switzerland has recently championed an International Code of Conduct for Private Security Providers that seeks to establish an external and independent oversight mechanism for PSCs (FDFA, 2010). Yet the presence of private and other non-state security providers in urban areas dominated by the extractive industry continues to be an underexplored phenomenon, and there is a need for further comparative, local-level studies on the forms of collaborative policing generated by state, corporate, and community interests on the resource extraction frontier.

Three broad, interrelated types of urban violence on the extractive resource frontier can be delineated. The first involves security providers tasked with controlling the resources themselves, as well as armed actors trying to pry them away from their declared owners. The second arises from the political, societal, and ecological challenges facing the unserviced and impoverished informal urban areas themselves. The third type occurs at the 'bust' end of urbanization, when violence can accompany post-extraction decline or when state authorities implement urban clean-up and rejuvenation plans. These three types are discussed in turn, building on insight gleaned from a number of cases.

PROTECTION AND PREDATION

In the face of high global prices for oil, gas, and minerals, the extraction of these resources is potentially lucrative for the business sector, the state, party-political elites seeking to finance their campaigns, and armed actors ranging from rebels to organized criminal groups. The practicalities of extracting, transporting, and selling what comes out of the earth depends to a large extent on the nature of the raw materials themselves, and the type of machinery and equipment required to extract and transport them. Security concerns, however, appear to be a fundamental aspect of all extraction endeavours—fuelled by protective measures on the one hand, and the resort to violent, predatory behaviour on the other.

Historically, the extractive industries have always sought to protect their investment, and the influx of all sorts of security providers—and armed bandits—has long been one of the defining characteristics of many towns on the resource extraction frontier. Already in colonial times, mining companies, usually subsidiaries of colonial governments, sought to contain illegal mining activities by establishing their own vigilante militias. At that time, uniformed police forces were a rarity, expensive to set up and maintain, and generally confined to policing the 'European' neighbourhoods of central colonial cities (Jütersonke and Kartas, 2015). Companies such as the Sierra Leone Selection Trust,

Box 2.2   Out of control: armed groups and illegal mining in Segovia and Remedios

Segovia and Remedios are two municipalities in Colombia's mineral-rich north-western department of Antioquia. Founded in the mid-19th century as a consequence of British capital invested in the Frontino Gold Mines and Mineros de Antioquia mining companies, their history has been directly influenced by mineral extraction that began in the days of the Spanish colony, when Antioquia became one of the biggest gold and silver providers for the Kingdom of Granada (Correa Restrepo, 2011). Over the past decades, and in the context of Colombia's ongoing conflict, the two towns have suffered the presence of various guerrilla, paramilitary, and armed criminal groups–all of which swiftly recognized that gold was easier to produce and more profitable to sell than cocaine (Hoyos, 2012). Since the 1970s, rural insecurity as a result of the conflict, and the mining boom itself, have resulted in the rapid expansion of both urban areas through voluntary and forced displacement (Trujillo, 2014).

In 1985, the Fuerzas Armadas Revolucionarias de Colombia (Revolutionary Armed Forces of Colombia, FARC) began to participate in local and regional politics through the Unión Patriótica (UP), founded by the Communist Party. The UP aimed to represent the mining labour unions in the country, including those in Segovia and Remedios. As early as 1983, nascent paramilitary groups–Muerte a Secuestradores (Death to Kidnappers) and Muerte a Revolucionarios del Nordeste (Death to Revolutionaries of the North-east)– engaged in targeted assassinations of political leaders who were connected to the mining unions and the UP. By 1997, the number of victims had exceeded 300, more than one-quarter of whom had lost their lives in a series of massacres that were only recently documented (GMH, 2011).

Facing significant financial difficulties, the Frontino Gold Mines and Mineros de Antioquia mining companies were both sold to Gran Colombia Gold in 2010, a Canadian company, registered in Panama, operating in Colombia, and obtaining capital from Venezuelan and Australian stakeholders. The aim of the new owners was to increase productivity of the mines and reduce costs. In Segovia, the results were mass lay-offs and the introduction of new technical procedures that boosted the use of water (to 4.4 million litres of water per day in 2011) and the amount of solid waste produced (Trujillo, 2012; 2014). The social and environmental impacts continue to be a significant source of tension and resentment in both towns.

The arrival of Gran Colombia Gold and large-scale foreign investment has also sealed the fate of artisanal miners, whose operations have either been declared illegal, or who were co-opted by armed groups. Both regular and irregular armed forces now seek to prevent their access to the mines– either by claiming that they lack the relevant land titles or government paperwork, or by forcing the miners to pay for mine access (Trujillo, 2014). Moreover, artisanal miners are now caught between the competing interests of two regrouped paramilitary factions, the Rastrojos and the Urabeños, and two guerrilla groups, the FARC and the Ejército de Liberación Nacional (National Liberation Army), while the region has become both a transit hub and a final destination for a significant number of the three million illegal firearms circulating in the country (Aguirre, 2011). Between 2011 and 2013, targeted assassinations connected with the mining business reached a high of eight murders per day and led to a wave of population displacement (Verdad Abierta, 2013; SAT, 2012, p. 13). With 100 illegal digging machines now in operation, and in the face of severely elevated levels of mercury and cyanide in the water supplies of both towns, the local government has acknowledged that the situation is 'out of control' (*El Espectador*, 2013).

A view of Segovia municipality, May 2014. © Raul Arboleda/AFP Photo

established in 1934, deployed its own security forces in the Kono district, supplemented with the arrival of the Sierra Leone Police Force in the early 1950s. There, they faced protection squads of well-organized gangs of illegal diamond diggers, who also fought violent battles among themselves (Machonachie, 2012, pp. 710–11).

Similar violent contestation continues today in places such as the Colombian mining towns of Segovia and Remedios, which have already suffered the loss of hundreds of lives, mainly through firearm homicide (see Box 2.2). The extractive activity there has also provoked severe environmental consequences, with cyanide and mercury waste, both in the rivers as well as in the air, reaching levels much higher than what the World Health Organization deems tolerable thresholds (*Semana*, 2013).

Extractive industry activities are increasingly marked by the presence of private, corporate security.

While Colombia is a special case in some ways because of its long history of conflict, extractive industry activities in less extreme settings are increasingly marked by the presence of private, corporate security. The result is a variety of collaborative partnerships between public and private, formal and informal types of security provision, in a complex network of actors and practices that Abrahamsen and Williams (2010) call 'security assemblages'. By complementing the often-insufficient capacities of state security forces, private security companies play a rather ambivalent role. On the one hand, they enhance the coercive power of the state by providing material and technical capacities. On the other, when PSCs adhere to international guiding principles, they may reduce the likelihood of violence (Abrahamsen and Williams, 2010, pp. 147–48). More systematic research is needed to establish whether PSC presence actually mitigates or exacerbates levels of violence related to the extractive sector.

Spatially, large-scale extraction with a PSC presence can produce enclaves in which entire urban areas are sealed off for security reasons, effectively turning boom towns into huge gated communities. A case in point is the diamond town of Orapa in Botswana, owned and run by De Beers (Gwebu, 2012). Having emerged to serve one of the largest open-pit diamond mines in the world, this town soon expanded to house a population approaching 10,000. Completely fenced in, the town allows access only to residents with permit cards, via one of two gates. Yet such arrangements can also cater to the interests of PSCs that oversell the security risks to retain their lucrative business and prolong their presence, as has occurred in eastern DRC (Schouten, 2013, p. 11).

In contrast to these large-scale corporate security methods, protective measures often come in the form of bodyguard service for at-risk individuals. The town of Ilakaka, the hub of Madagascar's sapphire region, provides a good example. When the extent of the available sapphire wealth became known in the late 1990s, Ilakaka was still a sleepy village of a few hundred residents, a pit stop on the long and arduous Route Nationale 7 from the capital Antananarivo to the port city of Tulear. Since then, an estimated 50,000 people have flocked to the town to participate in the sapphire rush. Fieldwork suggests that armed violence has become routine, involving a range of weapons, from industrially manufactured pistols and assault rifles (predominantly AK-pattern rifles) to locally produced craft small arms. Wealthy foreign investors and traders, predominantly from South and South-east Asia, are frequently the targets of attacks, and bodyguard protection for these individuals has become financially rewarding for PSCs across the island (Razafindrazaka, 2014).

The lines between private and public security provision are not always clear, limiting the control large-scale extraction companies exert over their security operations, and potentially slowing efforts to establish liability for the misuse of force (Umlas, 2011, p. 135). In Ilakaka, for example, members of the Malagasy military, gendarmerie, and police offer their services as bodyguards to wealthy individuals in exchange for housing, board, and around MGA 150,000 (USD 60) per month.

In Turkana county, where the Kenyan government has signed an agreement with Tullow Oil for large-scale oil extraction, the main security provider, employed directly by the oil company, is the Kenya Police Reserve (KPR). Armed by the state, the KPR is an auxiliary force detached from the main police and made up of volunteers operating in their own localities (Mkutu and Wandera, 2013, p. 11). The KPR, however, has a 'reputation as an ill-disciplined and troublesome force, with the media reporting regular cases of firearms misuse, banditry, renting of state-issued weapons, and livestock raiding' (pp. 19–20). Recent fieldwork observations in Turkana suggest a gradual move towards a more community-based approach to security provision.

Turkana county is an example of what happens when frontier urbanization besets a remote rural area even before extraction has begun. Oil was only discovered there in 2012, and Tullow has announced that extraction will start by 2017 (Mutegi, 2014). Since oil finds need to be exported to generate a return to the country, Kenya relaunched the USD 25.5 billion Lamu Port–South Sudan–Ethiopia Transport project in 2012; this major initiative, originally conceived in the mid-1970s, seeks to connect East Africa via a system of highways, railway lines, airports, and oil pipelines (see Map 2.1).

Map 2.1 **Oil development and frontier urbanization in East Africa**

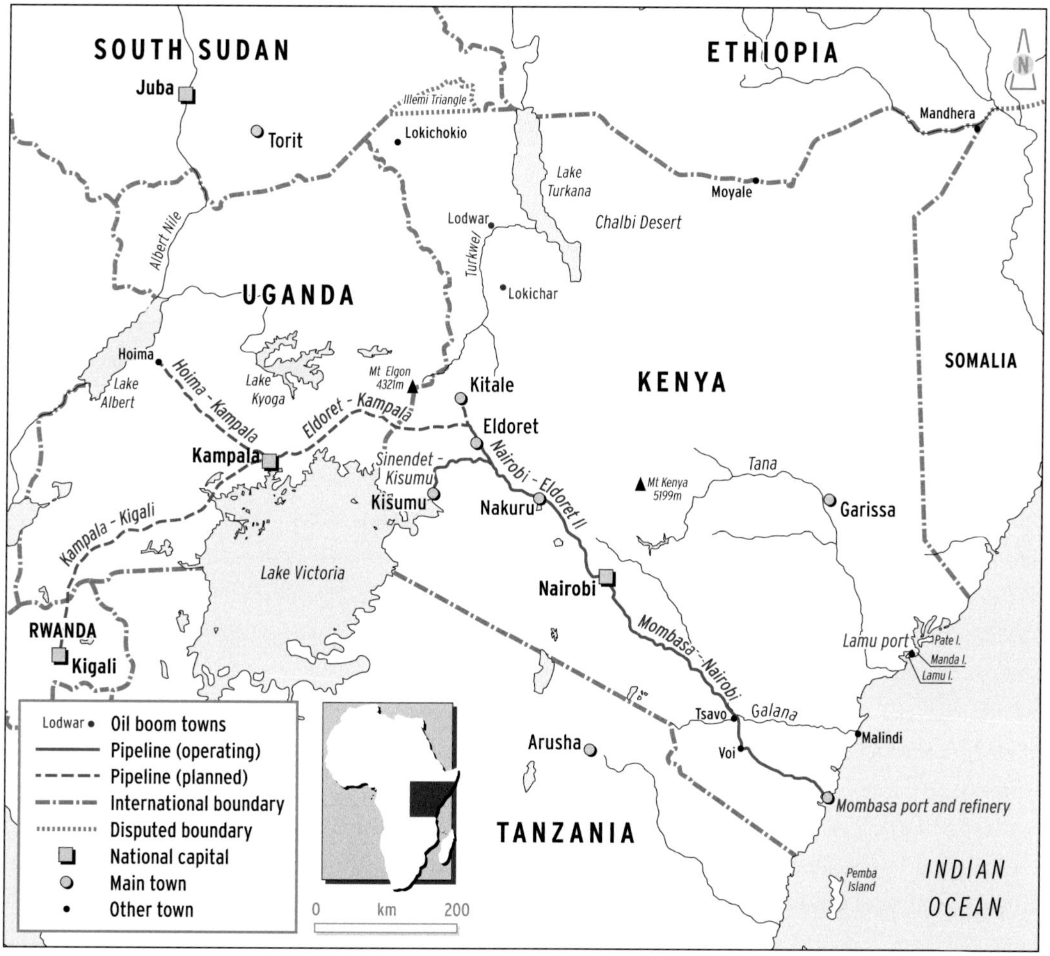

Sources: EIA (n.d.); Tullow Oil (n.d.)

A striking side effect of these activities is the rapid urbanization of the area. South Lokichar, where oil was discovered, has been converted from a remote, dusty community into a buzzing oil town, with new bars and guesthouses. Turkana's regional capital, Lodwar, is being fitted with a new road network and its first five-star hotel (Vasquez, 2014b). The KPR forces are also being 'urbanized' in the process, transforming from unpaid volunteers in remote rural areas into a significant, yet undertrained, possibly ill-disciplined, and largely unaccountable urban security provider (Mkutu and Wandera, 2013, p. 31).

POVERTY AND PROTEST

Mining boom towns are among the poorest urban areas on earth. In many places, digging and pumping proceed without violent disputes over control of the resources, or major security operations. Yet localized conflicts may arise over land disputes, indigenous rights, environmental degradation, and socio-economic inequalities, often fuelled by 'old, unresolved grievances and a history of marginalization of the affected groups' (Vasquez, 2014a, p. 6). Even the remote and sparsely populated Turkana region has recently experienced public protests over a perceived lack of job opportunities in the oil sector for local inhabitants (Lutta, 2013). As noted above, however, the relationship between such local conflicts and frontier urbanization remains understudied. One recent survey suggests that in some parts of Latin America, the oil-induced urbanization of indigenous populations and ethnic minorities has reduced the likelihood of armed rebellion (Wei, 2014), but a more finely grained analysis of the urban micro-dynamics of violence related to resource extraction is needed.

State institutions, particularly at the local level, sometimes lack either the capacity or the political will to react to the rapid growth of mining boom towns. As a result, these towns are among the poorest urban areas on earth, featuring high unemployment, a lack of social fabric, and dire living conditions because of air, water, and soil pollution. These processes of social and psychological dislocation have been termed the 'Gillette syndrome', following the experiences of a mining town of the same name in the US state of Wyoming (Kohrs, 1974). Preliminary evidence suggests that it often manifests itself in 'high rates of crime, drug and alcohol abuse, material break down, mental issues and a reduced sense of community' (Bryceson and MacKinnon, 2012, p. 515), as well as in an exacerbation of gender-based violence (Cane, Terbish, and Bymbasuren, 2014). Further research is required to understand the specific risk factors and how they interact.

Resource-rich sub-Saharan Africa provides some striking examples of the characteristics described by the Gillette syndrome. The second- and third-largest cities of the DRC, Lubumbashi and Mbuji-Mayi, the provincial capitals of Katanga and Kasaï Oriental, are expected to grow by roughly 50 per cent between 2010 and 2020 (UN-Habitat, 2010, p. 200). By 2025, the populations of both cities are expected to reach about 2.7 million (UN-Habitat, 2013, p. 157). The two cities, founded by the Belgian colonial authorities in 1910 and 1918, are essentially the product of mining activities. Their original urban plans involved three distinct areas: an indigenous town (*la cité indigène*), the European colonial town, and separate labour camps directly administered by the mining authorities. Despite having been exposed to very different mining and urbanization dynamics, both cities feature vast informal settlements, extreme social and economic inequalities, environmental degradation, and the emergence of a variety of 'self-help' mechanisms and service provision in 'self-built' neighbourhoods beyond any formal control of the public authorities (Perazzone, 2014). Fieldwork conducted for this chapter suggests that much of this urbanization and related insecurity is linked to mining activities in the adjoining areas, although a more accurate appraisal of these complex dynamics is still needed—not least because rural–urban migration in the region is also related to the activities of rebel groups, which are themselves intricately linked to resource extraction.

Waterfront settlements in Port Harcourt, Nigeria, July 2010. © Akintunde Akinleye/Reuters

Nigeria's Port Harcourt is roughly the same size as Lubumbashi and Mbuji-Mayi, having grown from a small operational base for the multinational oil industry in the 1950s into a sprawling city of more than 800,000 inhabitants in 2006 (see Figure 2.1). The city has all but cast off the British 'garden city concept'— the original urban design that surrounded a central business district with residential areas and suburbs, as well as ample open spaces and parks (UN-Habitat, 2009, pp. 8–9). As the city grew, it began to absorb many surrounding rural communities in an unplanned manner. What makes Port Harcourt a special case is that much of the urban growth has taken the form of squatter settlements at the waterfronts of the adjoining rivers, achieved

Figure 2.1 **Population growth of Port Harcourt, Nigeria, 1931-2006**

POPULATION (THOUSANDS)

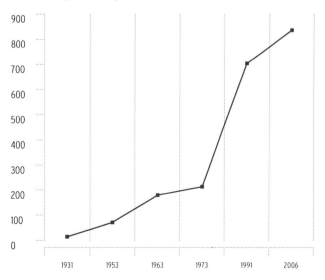

Source: UN-Habitat (2009, p. 9)

by progressively adding stabilizing materials into the swamps. None of this was foreseen by the city's 1975 urban plan (Obinna, Owei, and Mark, 2010, p. 224; UN-Habitat, 2009, p. vi). Over subsequent decades, and coupled with increasingly violent armed confrontation between the Nigerian army and militias in the Niger Delta, Port Harcourt became one of the most volatile, impoverished, and violent cities in the region (AOAV and NWGAV, 2013; Sheeriñ, 2007).

In Moramanga, nearly 65 per cent of the town's residents live in precarious informal housing.

Many of these dynamics are seen on a smaller scale in the town of Moramanga, Madagascar. A small urban area on the road between the capital Antananarivo and the main port city of Toamasina, Moramanga was one of the main areas of nationalist insurrection in 1947, as well as the scene of bloody repression by French colonial forces (Razafindrazaka, 2014). Sixty years later, in 2008, the government agreed to the establishment of a new nickel and cobalt mine on its outskirts. The Ambatovy Joint Venture, a partnership headed by Sherritt International of Canada and involving other Canadian, Japanese, and Korean investors, has an annual design capacity of 60,000 tonnes of nickel and 5,600 tonnes of cobalt (Ambatovy, 2012). Soon, Moramanga witnessed the influx of foreign workers—predominantly miners from the Philippines (Ambatovy, 2012, p. 29)—as well as private security personnel, Malagasy labourers from other parts of the country hoping for a share of the supposed riches, and the displacement of rural residents when the open-pit mine encroached on their villages. According to interviews conducted with the mayor's office, Moramanga's population jumped from some 37,000 in 2006 to at least 50,000 in 2014 (Razafindrazaka, 2014)—although accurate figures are unknown, even to the authorities.

In the absence of an urban plan, nearly 65 per cent of the town's residents live in precarious informal housing without building permits or access to basic services, such as clean water, electricity, or sanitation (UN-Habitat, 2012). Small arms, ranging from old assault rifles from military and gendarmerie stockpiles to craft production, are reportedly in wide circulation (Jütersonke and Kartas, 2011); moreover, the number of armed break-ins and acts of robbery is on the rise, particularly in the richer neighbourhoods of the mining management (Razafindrazaka, 2014). Fieldwork conducted for this chapter revealed that armed robbers are increasingly organized and sometimes include former soldiers—a phenomenon that may be a continuation of the events of 2002, when both presidential candidates supplied their supporters with military weapons in a six-month stalemate that placed Madagascar on the brink of civil war (Jütersonke and Kartas, 2011). The situation in Moramanga, which has also seen rising levels of prostitution, notably involving children, as well as child pornography and gang rape (Radasimalala, 2011; UN-Habitat, 2012, p. 11), has deteriorated to the point where the mayor's office and the police services admit an inability to provide public order. The gendarmerie is reportedly considering adding Moramanga to its list of 'red zones'—large swaths of the island where they are unable to provide effective security (Razafindrazaka, 2014). Residents have created a protest group to denounce the way in which Sherritt's presence fails to benefit the town and people of Moramanga (Rakotomalala, 2013).

The scene in Moramanga is comparable to that in Cajamarca, northern Peru. The city is the local service hub of Yanacocha, the world's second largest open-pit gold mine (AIDA, 2011). This gigantic mine has engulfed more than 26,000 hectares of land, displacing hundreds of rural families in the process. Most resettled in Cajamarca's poor urban periphery, in the hopes of securing one of the thousands of jobs the mining company had promised to generate (Trujillo, 2014). Yet many of these jobs are temporary or require qualifications that these workers do not possess. As a result, socio-economic cleavages and societal tensions in Cajamarca, which has more than doubled in size since the early 1990s, have been exacerbated (Bury, 2007; 2008; Trujillo, 2014).

Pollution—such as the spill of 151 kg of mercury in 2000 (Arana-Zegarra, 2009, p. 113)—complicates matters, as did plans to extend exploration to the sacred mountain of Cerro Quilish in 2004, over which 50,000 demonstrators protested (Lambrigger, 2007). After weeks of violent clashes with police, the plans were eventually dropped (Bebbington

Box 2.3 **Trouble in paradise**

Most of the nickel currently being extracted on the planet comes from nickel laterite ore deposits found in the earth's mantle of ultramafic rock. Only 1 per cent of the earth's land surface is made up of such rock, but on the main island of the New Caledonian archipelago in the Western Pacific, it covers almost a third of the surface, or around 5,600 km² (Lison, 2013). As a result, nickel (along with cobalt) is the territory's primary export commodity, and the mining industry is the main economic driver and its principal employer.

Since 2006, the chief business actor has been the Brazilian mining giant Vale, which bought the Goro-Nickel mine company operating in the south of the island (previously owned by Inco), close to the capital, Nouméa, and invested USD 6 billion into a new metallurgical plant that began its operations in 2009 (Levacher, 2012; Lefort and Burton, 2014). The mining and metallurgy project has, from the beginning, raised tensions with the indigenous Kanak population, which not only fears the destruction of its traditional livelihoods and natural habitat (much of which is under UNESCO protection), but resents the lack of economic opportunities offered to the local population by a mining sector that relies increasingly on foreign labour. Some 15,000 workers hail from the Philippines, according to Kanak NGOs (Graff, 2014), although some media reports cite lower figures (Les Nouvelles Calédoniennes, 2002). The result has been an increasingly disgruntled youth population in the ever-expanding metropolitan area of Greater Nouméa (Rivoilan and Broustet, 2011).

In 2006, local Kanak NGOs and traditional leaders blocked the entrance to the construction site of the metallurgical plant (Graff, 2014). The gendarmerie reacted by shooting live ammunition at demonstrators and dropping tear gas on them from helicopters. In 2005, the gendarmerie even mobilized several dozen combat divers to disperse a group of Kanak youths who had staged a sit-in of the mining harbour. The authorities' increasingly militarized response to protests thus became the subject of debate during a session of the UN's Working Group on Indigenous Populations (Graff, 2014). According to public statements made during that session, the gendarmerie had deployed a permanent contingent of 100 officers to protect the mining zone, and the MNC had begun to recruit PSCs employing US mercenaries.

The standoff has continued between the French authorities and Kanak youths from the tribes around Nouméa's expanding peri-urban areas. Successive mining-related accidents have exacerbated the tension: between 1,000 and 5,000 litres of sulphuric acid were spilled into adjoining rivers in 2009 (Les Nouvelles Calédoniennes, 2009). On 7 May 2014, a further spill from the Goro-Nickel plant caused more than 100,000 litres of hydrochloric acid to enter the creek of the northern bay of the UNESCO-protected lagoon (Souche, 2014). A new wave of protests and violence following this latest environmental disaster forced the plant to close for a few weeks. According to a variety of often-conflicting media reports, the plant suffered mining property damage to the tune of USD 20–30 million, including the destruction of one-third of the company's truck fleet (Lefort and Burton, 2014).

Residents of Mont-Dore protest following an acid spill from the Goro-Nickel plant, Nouméa, New Caledonia, May 2014. © Fred Payet/AFP Photo

et al., 2008; AIDA, 2011), although the idea has recently been revived (Emery, 2014). Protests and violent responses, which again erupted over the construction of the Rio Azufre dam in 2006, have become almost routine in Cajamarca, with demonstrators facing police crackdowns and self-defence forces (*rondas urbanas* and *rondas campesinas*) that had originally been established in the 1970s to help resist terrorist attacks from the Sendero Luminoso (Shining Path) and other militia groups. In collaboration with mining interests, these forces have recently turned on rural migrants and environmental activists. In 2013, the *rondas* also began taking action against vandalism and prostitution in the ever-expanding informal neighbourhoods on the outskirts of the city (Trujillo, 2014).

Being neither unique to Cajamarca nor the Andean region, social unrest between demonstrators and security providers recently occurred in far-flung New Caledonia in the Pacific Islands (see Box 2.3). Protests tend to revolve around working conditions, disputes over the land and its resources with property owners or indigenous groups, and environmental issues related to pollution and the destruction of natural habitat. Sometimes the demonstrations (and violent responses) happen at the mining sites themselves, such as occurred in South Africa's Marikana massacre, or the violent removal of protest camps at the Letpadaung copper mine in Myanmar, both in 2012 (BBC News, 2012; HRW, 2012). But often the protests are organized in the urban area of the service hub. This was the case in the city of Soma, Turkey, following a mining accident that claimed the lives of at least 282 people in May 2014; following the incident, protest-related violence also spread to the capital, Ankara (BBC News, 2014). Similar scenes have taken place in parts of Europe and North America over fracking (Jackson, 2014; Lukacs, 2013).

> **Extractive towns may experience a mass exodus of residents once the mining boom is over.**

THE BUST AFTER THE BOOM

What happens to the new urban environment when digging and pumping for non-renewable resources slows down or ceases altogether? Ferguson (1999) describes a paradigmatic case of de-urbanization in Zambia's Copperbelt in the 1980s. He emphasizes the complex nature of rural–urban mobility and settlement patterns, highlighting that an incoming wave of migrant labour does not necessarily lead to permanent urbanization. Instead, workers coming to the mining towns continue to maintain complicated (and at times conflicted) relationships with the rural communities from which they come, and many, if not most, return to their families upon retirement or with the onset of unemployment. In times of decline, economic despair can turn into collective anger and violence, as was the case in the Copperbelt food riots in December 1986, which left six people dead (AP, 1986; Ferguson, 1999, p. 264; Mukela, 1988). Frontier urbanization is far from being a linear path to prosperity, instead ebbing and flowing with changing fortunes in the industry.[2]

In light of significant labour mobility, extractive towns in the global South may experience the mass exodus of residents once the mining boom is over. An example is Oloibiri, a small and remote creek community in the Niger Delta, Nigeria. Oil was discovered there in 1956, and soon a camp with prefabricated housing, electricity, water, and a new road were built for incoming workers. Over the next 20 years, Shell-BP extracted more than 20 million barrels of crude oil from the field, which was connected with Nigeria's first crude oil pipeline to Port Harcourt. In the 1960s, Oloibiri had a population of 10,000. Oil production ended in the mid-1970s, and today the town has barely 1,000 inhabitants and is characterized by youth violence, 'scorched earth, and capped wellheads' (Watts and Ibaba, 2011, pp. 1–3; Akpan, 2005, p. 139).

In Sierra Leone, by contrast, mining towns in diamond-rich Kono district received a new lease of life—but also renewed insecurity—with the end of the civil war in 2002. Earlier, rebel forces had taken control of the minefields and

An aerial view from 2001 of the diamond mines of Koidu, abandoned after rebel forces took control of the minefields and surrounding areas, Kono district, Sierra Leone. © Rob Huibers/Panos Pictures

surrounding areas, forcing many residents and mine workers to flee, predominantly to the capital, Freetown. After the war, some fighters flocked to the towns of Kono district, in what has been called the region's 'second diamond rush' (Maconachie, 2012, p. 716). Many had not gone through disarmament, demobilization, and reintegration, but immediately became artisanal miners. Cities such as Koidu have turned into some of the most ethnically diverse urban areas of the country, but they also suffer from severe impoverishment, interpersonal violence, and ethnic tensions between Kono locals and incoming youth populations (Maconachie, 2012, p. 716).

Dilapidated mining towns can also become havens for those fleeing political violence and state repression, as has recently been the case in Zimbabwe (Kamete, 2012). The first wave of newcomers arrived in these towns in response to the official 'fast-track' land resettlement programme of 2000, which allowed the government to acquire (with compensation) any land settled by colonists, including their mining operations (Matondi, 2012). According to Hartnack (2005, p. 173), the programme forcibly displaced more than one million farm labourers and their families—half of the entire farm population—with many ending up in the country's empty chromite mining towns that had been hit by falling mineral prices in the 1980s. The second wave of newcomers to these areas arrived in 2005, following the government's countrywide urban clean-up campaign, called 'Operation Murambatsvina' or 'Restore Order'. The campaign allegedly involved the army, police, and youth militia, which:

> demolished illegal residential and business structures in informal settlements and low-income residential areas;
> [. . .] forcibly and violently evicted vagrants, street children and vendors operating in undesignated places; and
> [. . .] arrested, detained and/or forcibly relocated [residents] to 'transit camps' or 'holding centres' (Kamete, 2012, pp. 599–600).

Overall, the campaign displaced around 700,000 urban dwellers, many of whom had been the victims of the land resettlement programme five years earlier.

With Zimbabwe's mining towns turning into squatter-type informal settlements—urban centres in which municipal planning and public service provision are all but absent—the government then launched Operation Chikorokosa Chapera ('finished with illegal gold mining') in 2006. The operation officially targeted environmental degradation but was possibly motivated more by the state's perceived loss of income through uncontrolled and untaxed gold smuggling (Spiegel, 2009). In any event, over the space of only a few months more than 31,500 miners were arrested and many settlements were bulldozed (*Herald*, 2007; Spiegel, 2009, p. 42).

Some urban areas servicing extractive activities are too large to become true ghost towns. In such larger areas, state authorities tend to apply long-term approaches to persistent, informal, 'ungovernable' neighbourhoods (Obafemi and Odubo, 2013, p. 7). Their methods are often violent and violence-inducing. Over the past two decades, the government of Nigeria's Rivers state has attempted to implement a series of urban planning initiatives to tackle the volatility and persistent insecurity of Port Harcourt. Many of these efforts focused on the waterfront settlements that house more than 200,000 of the city's residents, many of whom came to the city in hopes of benefiting from the petroleum boom (Theis et al., 2009). The question of ownership of the land and its resources has long caused tensions in the city, often leading to violence between local (armed) groups, Niger Delta armed groups, and the government, or between residents of informal settlements and government forces (AOAV and NWGAV, 2013, pp. 73–74).

In 1988, the Rivers state government introduced a policy to 'improve [the] overall quality of life' in the squatter settlements through redevelopment projects in the Aggrey Road, Marine Base, and Ndoki waterfronts. But since new housing was only provided for less than 30 per cent of the residents, the initiative effectively only relocated the problem, rather than alleviating it (Obinna, Owei, and Mark, 2010, pp. 224–25). Nearly two decades later, in August 2007—following weeks of violent clashes that culminated in running street battles between the military and armed fighters on motorbikes, as well as the deployment of attack helicopters—the government announced plans to demolish slums in Port Harcourt's waterfront areas (IRIN, 2007). In 2009, finally, the authorities launched an 'urban regeneration programme' in the form of the Greater Port Harcourt Master Plan (Theis et al., 2009). As part of the programme, the Njemanze informal settlement, where an estimated 13,800–19,000 people lived, was demolished on 28 August 2009. The subsequent demolition of the Bundu waterfront community, on 12 October 2009, saw troops of the Joint Task Force and the police use firearms to disperse the crowds; at least 12 people were shot and seriously injured, and eyewitnesses saw six corpses being carried away (AI, 2010).

CONCLUSION

Historically, the accessibility of raw materials has been an important factor in determining human settlement patterns. Today, more than ever, extraction activities bring to urbanization trends complex dynamics of population movements and migratory patterns, as well as sheer numbers. Not all of this urbanization is necessarily detrimental to collective and individual socio-economic well-being. The extractive industries can be a catalyst for stability, economic growth, job creation, and knowledge transfer. Moreover, they can be instrumental in promoting less environmentally damaging extraction technologies. Increasingly, transnational mining corporations have been embracing the so-called 'Ghanaian open model' of having mine workers live in the adjoining urban area, rather than in camps or compounds. This approach potentially generates greater population stability and welfare, as miners have more of an incentive to move to the urban area with their families. In the process, mining companies also invest significantly in the local infrastructure (Bryceson and MacKinnon, 2012, p. 529).

But there remain far too many instances where extractive activities—both industrial and artisanal—exacerbate poverty levels, destroy indigenous livelihoods and natural habitats (from deforestation to unfishable coastlines), and emit dangerous waste products into surrounding areas. This chapter's review of a number of cases suggests that the intersection of the extractive industries and frontier urbanization is associated with a range of types of violence. These include violent conflict over the control of the land and its extractable resources; insecurity and social unrest related to the precarious socio-economic and environmental conditions; and violent tensions around post-extraction decline or state-led urban clean-up and rejuvenation plans. But the frontier urbanization aspect of extraction, and its potential for generating interpersonal and collective armed violence, remain understudied. Further, while urban armed violence has been moving to the forefront of conflict and fragility analyses (Beall, Goodfellow, and Rodgers, 2013), little is known about the societal conditions under which such violence occurs.

Among the challenges to moving from a case study approach to a more comprehensive analysis is the lack of key data points, such as rates of violence and small arms proliferation in frontier urbanization compared to other urbanized areas. Research on the different facets of frontier urbanization and security provision across actors and communities is needed to better understand violence trends. Only then can promising policies and legal frameworks be developed to mitigate violence and improve security. ◼

LIST OF ABBREVIATIONS

CSR	Corporate social responsibility
DRC	Democratic Republic of the Congo
ELN	Ejército de Liberación Nacional
FARC	Fuerzas Armadas Revolucionarias de Colombia
MGA	Malagasy ariary
MNC	Multinational corporation
PSC	Private security company
UP	Unión Patriótica

ENDNOTES

1   For instance, the Centre for Social Responsibility in Mining at the University of Queensland in Australia has studied in detail urbanization related to Mongolia's current coal mining boom; see, for example, McKenna (2013). The rapid expansion of this extractive activity has raised fears that the capital, Ulaanbaatar, may soon be short of water (ADB, 2014).

2   Echoing Ferguson, Walsh (2012) depicts a similar picture of urban decline in the Malagasy sapphire mining and trading town of Ambondromifehy.

BIBLIOGRAPHY

Abrahamsen, Rita and Michael Williams. 2010. *Security Beyond the State: Private Security in International Politics*. Cambridge: Cambridge University Press.

ADB (Asian Development Bank). 2014. *Demand in the Desert: Mongolia's Water–Energy–Mining Nexus*. Manila: ADB.

Aguirre, Katherine. 2011. 'El tráfico de armas en Colombia: una revisión desde los orígenes a los destinos.' *URVIO, Revista Latinoamericana de Seguridad Ciudadana*, No. 10. November, pp. 36–59.

AI (Amnesty International). 2010. *Nigeria—Port Harcourt Demolitions: Excessive Use of Force against Demonstrators*. London: AI. 11 October.
    <http://www.amnesty.org/en/library/asset/AFR44/022/2010/en/cf8ec406-13ef-45d3-928b-f97b3fc4f293/afr440222010en.pdf>

AIDA (Asociación Interamericana para la Defensa del Ambiente). 2011. 'Agotamiento de agua dulce: La mina de Yanacocha, Peru.'
    <http://www.aida-americas.org/sites/default/files/YANACOCHA%20SPANISH%20FINAL%2011-05-27%20LN.pdf>

Akpan, Wilson. 2005. 'Putting Oil First? Some Ethnographic Aspects of Petroleum-related Land Use Controversies in Nigeria.' *African Sociological Review*,
    Vol. 9, No. 2, pp. 134–52.

Ambatovy. 2012. *2012 Sustainability Report*. <http://www.ambatovy.com/docs/wp-content/uploads/GRI2012-ENG.pdf>

AOAV (Action on Armed Violence) and NWGAV (National Working Group on Armed Violence–Nigeria). 2013. 'The Violent Road: Nigeria's South South.'
    12 December. <https://aoav.org.uk/2013/the-violent-road-nigeria-south-south/>

AP (Associated Press). 1986. 'Six Dead, 1,000 Arrested, in Zambian Food Riots.' 10 December.
    <http://www.apnewsarchive.com/1986/Six-Dead-1-000-Arrested-in-Zambian-Food-Riots/id-e165610b1aa7e554b5ffed4d1ff551df>

Arana-Zegarra, Marco. 2009. 'El caso del derrame de mercurio en Choropampa y los daños a la salud en la población rural expuesta.' *Revista Peruana
    de Medicina Experimental y Salud Pública*, Vol. 26, No. 1, pp. 113–18.

BBC News. 2012. 'South Africa's Marikana Mine Closed by "Intimidation".' 27 August. <http://www.bbc.com/news/world-africa-19388584>

—. 2014. 'Turkish Mine Disaster: Unions Hold Protest Strike.' 15 May. <http://www.bbc.com/news/world-europe-27415822>

Beall, Jo, Tom Goodfellow, and Dennis Rodgers. 2013. 'Cities and Conflict in Fragile States in the Developing World.' *Urban Studies*, Vol. 50, No. 15,
    pp. 3065–83.

Bebbington, Anthony, et al. 2008. 'Mining and Social Movements: Struggles over Livelihood and Rural Territorial Development in the Andes'. *World
    Development*, Vol. 36, No. 12, pp. 2888–905.

Berdal, Mats and David Malone, eds. 2000. *Greed and Grievance: Economic Agendas in Civil Wars*. Boulder, CO and London: Lynne Rienner Publishers.

Billington, Ray Allen. 1967. *Westward Expansion: A History of the American Frontier*, 3rd edn. New York: Macmillan.

Brennan-Galvin, Ellen. 2002. 'Crime and Violence in an Urbanizing World.' *Journal of International Affairs*, Vol. 56, No. 1, pp. 123–45.

Browder, John and Brian Godfrey. 1990. 'Frontier Urbanization in the Brazilian Amazon: A Theoretical Framework for Urban Transition.' *Yearbook:
    Conference of Latin Americanist Geographers*, Vol. 16, pp. 56–66.

Bryceson, Deborah and Daniel MacKinnon. 2012. 'Eureka and Beyond: Mining's Impact on African Urbanization.' *Journal of Contemporary African
    Studies*, Vol. 30, No. 4, pp. 513–37.

—, eds. 2013. *Mining and African Urbanisation: Population, Settlement and Welfare Trajectories*. London: Routledge.

Büscher, Karen, Jeroen Cuvelier, and Franck Mushobekwa. 2014. 'La dimension politique de "l'urbanisation minière" dans un contexte fragile de conflit
    armé: Le cas de Nyabibwe.' In Filip Reyntjens, Stef Vandeginste, and Marijke Verpoorten, eds. *L'Afrique des grands lacs: annuaire 2013–2014*.
    Paris: L'Harmattan, pp. 243–68.

Bury, Jeffrey. 2007. 'Mining Migrants: Transnational Mining and Migration Patterns in the Peruvian Andes.' *Professional Geographer*, Vol. 59, No. 3.
    August, pp. 378–89.

—. 2008. 'Transnational Corporations and Livelihood Transformations in the Peruvian Andes: An Actor-Oriented Political Ecology.' *Human Organization*,
    Vol. 67, No. 3, pp. 307–21. <http://people.ucsc.edu/~jbury/.../BuryFinalHumanOrganization2008.pdf>

Cane, Isabel, Amgalan Terbish, and Onon Bymbasuren. 2014. *Mapping Gender Based Violence and Mining Infrastructure in Mongolian Mining
    Communities*. Perth: International Mining for Development Centre.

Carbonnier, Gilles and Natascha Wagner. 2015. 'Resource Dependence and Armed Violence: Impact on Sustainability in Developing Countries.'
    Defence and Peace Economics, Vol. 26, No. 1, pp. 115–32. <http://www.tandfonline.com/doi/pdf/10.1080/10242694.2013.848580>

Chouikha, Larbi and Vincent Geisser. 2010. 'Retour sur la révolte du bassin minier: Les cinq leçons politiques d'un conflit social inédit.' *L'Année du
    Maghreb*, No. VI, pp. 415–26. <http://anneemaghreb.revues.org/pdf/923>

Collier, Paul. 2010. 'The Political Economy of Natural Resources.' *Social Research*, Vol. 77, No. 4, pp. 1105–32.

Correa Restrepo, Juan Santiago. 2011. '1830–1928, Un siglo crítico: el esfuerzo empresarial colombiano.' *Credencial Historia*, No. 254. February.
    <http://www.banrepcultural.org/blaavirtual/revistas/credencial/febrero2011/un-siglo-critico-empresarial>

Cuvelier, Jeroen, Koen Vlassenroot, and Nathaniel Olin. 2014. 'Resources, Conflict and Governance: A Critical Review.' *The Extractive Industries and
    Society*, Vol. 1, No. 2, pp. 340–50. <http://www.sciencedirect.com/science/article/pii/S2214790X14000537>

EIA (United States Oil and Gas Sector). n.d. 'Kenyan Oil and Gas Sector.' Map. Updated 23 May 2013.
    <http://www.eia.gov/countries/regions-topics.cfm?fips=eeae>

EITI (Extractive Industries Transparency Initiative). n.d. 'What Is the EITI?' <https://eiti.org/eiti>

El Espectador (Colombia). 2013. 'El monstruo dormido de Segovia.' 8 May.
    <http://www.elespectador.com/noticias/actualidad/vivir/el-monstruo-dormido-de-segovia-articulo-421016>

Emery, Alex. 2014. 'Yanacocha May Still Develop Cerro Quilish, Says Buenaventura CEO.' Business News Americas. 18 March.
    <http://www.bnamericas.com/news/mining/yanacocha-may-still-develop-cerro-quilish-says-buenaventura-ceo>

FDFA (Swiss Federal Department of Foreign Affairs). 2010. International Code of Conduct for Private Security Providers.
    <http://www.news.admin.ch/NSBSubscriber/message/attachments/21143.pdf>

Ferguson, James. 1999. *Expectations of Modernity: Myths and Meaning of Urban Life on the Zambian Copperbelt*. Berkeley and Los Angeles: University
    of California Press.

Fox, Sean and Jo Beall. 2012. 'Mitigating Conflict and Violence in African Cities.' *Environment and Planning C: Government and Policy*, Vol. 30, pp. 968–81.

Geenen, Sara. 2012. 'A Dangerous Bet: The Challenges of Formalizing Artisanal Mining in the Democratic Republic of Congo.' *Resources Policy*,
    Vol. 37, No. 3. September, pp. 322–30. <http://www.sciencedirect.com/science/article/pii/S0301420712000104>

GMH (Grupo de Memoria Histórica de la Comisión Nacional de Reparación y Reconciliación). 2010. *Silenciar la democracia: Las masacres de
    Remedios y Segovia, 1982–1997*. Bogotá: GMH and Ediciones Semana.
    <http://www.banrepcultural.org/sites/default/files/silenciar-la-democracia_1.pdf>

Gobe, Eric. 2010. 'The Gafsa Mining Basin between Riots and a Social Movement: Meaning and Significance of a Protest Movement in Ben Ali's Tunisia.'
    Working Paper. <https://halshs.archives-ouvertes.fr/halshs-00557826>

Gough, Katherine and Paul Yankson. 2012. 'Exploring the Connections: Mining and Urbanisation in Ghana.' *Journal of Contemporary African Studies*,
    Vol. 30, No. 4, pp. 651–68.

Graff, Stéphanie. 2014. 'Le nickel de Nouvelle-Calédonie: richesse ou malédiction? Aperçu des conflits et des enjeux autour de l'usine de Vale.'
    Unpublished background paper. Geneva: Small Arms Survey.

Gwebu, Thando. 2012. 'Botswana's Mining Path to Urbanisation and Poverty Alleviation.' *Journal of Contemporary African Studies*, Vol. 30, No. 4, pp. 611–30.

Hackenberg, Robert. 1980. 'New Patterns of Urbanization in Southeast Asia: An Assessment.' *Population and Development Review*, Vol. 6, No. 3.
    September, pp. 391–419.

Hartnack, Andrew. 2005. '"My Life Got Lost": Farm Workers and Displacement in Zimbabwe.' *Journal of Contemporary African Studies*, Vol. 23,
    No. 2, pp. 173–92.

Herald (Harare). 2007. 'Nhara Arrested over Diamonds.' 3 March. <http://allafrica.com/stories/200703030116.html>

Hoyos, Juan José. 2012. 'Dios y el diablo en la tierra del oro.' *Revista Semana* (Colombia). 25 August.
    <http://www.semana.com/edicion-30-anos/articulo/dios-diablo-tierra-del-oro/263448-3>

HRW (Human Rights Watch). 2012. 'Burma: Investigate Violent Crackdown on Mine Protesters.' 1 December.
    <http://www.hrw.org/news/2012/12/01/burma-investigate-violent-crackdown-mine-protesters>

Hütz-Adams, Friedel and Marie Müller, eds. 2012. 'Auf der Suche nach dem sauberen Gold: Kleinbergbau von Gold in Peru und DR Kongo.' Brief 46.
    Bonn: Bonn International Center for Conversion. <http://www.bicc.de/uploads/tx_bicctools/BICC_brief_46_d.pdf>

IRIN. 2007. 'Nigeria: Demolition Plans Bring New Ethnic Twist to Port Harcourt Conflict.' 28 August.
    <http://www.irinnews.org/report/73978/nigeria-demolition-plans-bring-new-ethnic-twist-to-port-harcourt-conflict>

Jackson, Will. 2014. 'Police Violence at Anti-fracking Protests Is about Order, Not Law.' The Conversation. 7 May.
    <http://theconversation.com/police-violence-at-anti-fracking-protests-is-about-order-not-law-25518>

Johnston, Lee. 1999. 'Private Policing in Context'. *European Journal on Criminal Policy and Research*, Vol. 7, No. 2, pp. 175–96.

Jütersonke, Oliver and Moncef Kartas. 2011. 'Ethos of Exploitation: Insecurity and Predation in Madagascar.' In Small Arms Survey. *Small Arms Survey 2011:
    States of Security*. Cambridge: Cambridge University Press, pp. 166–91.

—. 2015. 'The State as Urban Myth: Governance without Government in the Global South.' In Robert Schuett and Peter M. Stirk, eds. *The Concept of
    the State in International Relations: Philosophy, Sovereignty, and Cosmopolitanism*. Edinburgh: Edinburgh University Press, pp. 108–34.

Jütersonke, Oliver, Robert Muggah, and Keith Krause. 2007. 'Guns in the City: Urban Landscapes of Armed Violence.' In Small Arms Survey. *Small Arms
    Survey 2007: Guns and the City*. Cambridge: Cambridge University Press, pp. 160–95.

Kamete, Amin. 2012. 'Of Prosperity, Ghost Towns and Havens: Mining and Urbanisaton in Zimbabwe.' *Journal of Contemporary African Studies*, Vol. 30,
    No. 4, pp. 589–609.

Kartas, Moncef and Oliver Jütersonke. 2012. 'Urban Resilience in Situations of Chronic Violence: Case of Kigali, Rwanda.' URCV Research Report.
    Cambridge, MA: MIT Center for International Studies. May. <http://www.urcvproject.org/Research.html>

Kempa, Michael, et al. 1999. 'Reflections on the Evolving Concept of "Private Policing".' *European Journal on Criminal Policy and Research*, Vol. 7,
    No. 2, pp. 197–223.

Kohrs, ElDean. 1974. 'Social Consequences of Boom Growth in Wyoming.' Paper presented at the Annual Meeting of the Rocky Mountain American
    Association for the Advancement of Science in Laramie, Wyoming.

Koonings, Kees and Dirk Kruijt. 2004. 'Armed Actors, Organized Violence and State Failure in Latin America: A Survey of Issues and Arguments.'
    In Kees Koonings and Dirk Kruijt, eds. *Armed Actors: Organised Violence and State Failure in Latin America*. London: Zed Books, pp. 5–15.

Kopytoff, Igor. 1989. 'The Internal African Frontier: The Making of African Political Culture'. In Igor Kopytoff, ed. *The African Frontier: The Reproduction
    of Traditional African Societies*. Bloomington and Indianapolis: Indiana University Press, pp. 3–84.

Korf, Benedikt. 2011. 'Resources, Violence and the Telluric Geographies of Small Wars.' *Progress in Human Geography*, Vol. 35, No. 6. December,
    pp. 733–56. <http://phg.sagepub.com/content/35/6/733>

Lambrigger, Jonas. 2007. *Transformación de Estrategias de Vida de Familias Campesinas en Cajamarca, Perú como Consecuencia de las Actividades Mineras Auríferas de la Empresa Transnacional Newmont Mining Corporation (Minera Yanacocha S. R. L.): Movimientos Sociales y Contribución al Desarrollo Sostenible con Enfoque a los Actores*. University of Bern: Centre for Development and Environment, Institute of Geography. July.

Lefort, Cecile and Melanie Burton. 2014. 'Protesters Burn Vehicles, Buildings at New Caledonia Nickel Mine.' Reuters. 26 May.
<http://www.reuters.com/article/2014/05/27/us-vale-sa-newcaledonia-spill-idUSBREA4Q00P20140527>

Les Nouvelles Calédoniennes. 2002. 'Recrutement des Philippins: une sélection très pointue.' 26 November.
<http://www.lnc.nc/article/mines/recrutement-des-philippins-une-selection-tres-pointue>

—. 2009. 'Pollution chimique à l'usine Vale Inco.' 3 April. <http://www.lnc.nc/article/mines/pollution-chimique-a-lusine-vale-inco>

Levacher, Claire. 2012. 'Kanaky/Nouvelle-Calédonie: Mine de Goro.' Groupe International de Travail pour les Peuples Autochtones. January.
<http://www.gitpa.org/web/KANAKY-NC%20Mine%20de%20Goro%20doc.pdf>

Lison, Céline. 2013. 'Ravagée par les exploitations de nickel, la Nouvelle-Calédonie soigne sa nature.' *National Geographic*. 21 June.
<http://www.nationalgeographic.fr/2812-nouvelle-caledonie-nickel-nature/>

Lukacs, Martin. 2013. 'New Brunswick Fracking Protests Are the Frontline of a Democratic Fight.' *Guardian*. 21 October.
<http://www.theguardian.com/environment/2013/oct/21/new-brunswick-fracking-protests>

Lutta, Sammy. 2013. 'Oil Drilling Halted after Row.' *Daily Nation* (Nairobi). 27 October.
<http://mobile.nation.co.ke/News/Tullow-halts-drilling-over-job-protests-/-/1950946/2049540/-/format/xhtml/-/c6y30fz/-/index.html>

Maconachie, Roy. 2012. 'Diamond Mining, Urbanisation and Social Transformation in Sierra Leone.' *Journal of Contemporary African Studies*, Vol. 30, No. 4, pp. 705–23.

Matondi, Prosper. 2012. *Zimbabwe's Fast-track Land Reform*. London: Zed Books.

McKenna, Phill. 2013. 'Mongolia Research Hub: Landsat Time Series Sharyngol Coal Mine 1989–2013.' Video. St. Lucia, Australia: Centre for Social Responsibility in Mining, Sustainable Minerals Institute, University of Queensland. December. <https://www.youtube.com/watch?v=rOboFQ17GdU>

Mkutu, Kennedy and Gerald Wandera. 2013. *Policing the Periphery: Opportunities and Challenges for Kenya Police Reserves*. Working Paper No. 15. Geneva: Small Arms Survey. March.

Moncada, Eduardo. 2013. 'The Politics of Urban Violence: Challenges for Development in the Global South.' *Studies in Comparative International Development*, Vol. 48, No. 3. September, pp. 217–39.

Mukela, John. 1988. 'Food and Flames'. *New Internationalist*, Iss. 189. November. <http://newint.org/features/1988/11/05/food/>

Mutegi, Mugambi. 2014. 'Tullow Sets 2017 Date to Start Commercial Oil Production.' *Business Daily* (Nairobi). 27 June.
<http://www.businessdailyafrica.com/Corporate-News/Tullow-sets-2017-for-Kenya-crude-oil-output-/-/539550/2363134/-/txq8vj/-/index.html>

Obafemi, Andrew and Tonye Odubo. 2013. 'Waterfronts Redevelopments in Port Harcourt Metropolis: Issues and Socio-Economic Implications for Urban Environmental Management.' *International Journal of Engineering and Science*, Vol. 2, No. 12, pp. 1–14.
<http://www.theijes.com/papers/v2-i12/Version-1/A021201001014.pdfY>

Obeng-Odoom, Franklin. 2014. *Oiling the Urban Economy: Land, Labour, Capital, and the State in Sekondi-Takoradi, Ghana*. London: Routledge.

Obinna, Victor, Opuene Owei, and E.O. Mark. 2010. 'Informal Settlements of Port Harcourt and Potentials for Planned City Expansion.' *Environmental Research Journal*, Vol. 4, No. 3, pp. 222–28. <http://www.medwelljournals.com/fulltext/?doi=erj.2010.222.228>

Osterhammel, Jürgen. 2009. *Die Verwandlung der Welt: Eine Geschichte des 19. Jahrhunderts*. Munich: C.H. Beck.

Perazzone, Stéphanie. 2014. 'Mbuji-Mayi and Lubumbashi: The Urban Offspring of the "Resource Curse"?' Unpublished background paper. Geneva: Small Arms Survey.

Pullan, Wendy. 2011. 'Frontier Urbanism: The Periphery at the Centre of Contested Cities.' *Journal of Architecture*, Vol. 16, No. 1, pp. 15–35.

PWYP (Publish What You Pay). n.d. 'Extractive Industries Transparency Initiative (EITI).'
<http://www.publishwhatyoupay.org/activities/advocacy/extractive-industries-transparency-initiative>

Radasimalala, Vonjy. 2011. 'Moramanga: lutte contre la prostitution juvénile.' *L'Express de Madagascar*. 16 February.
<http://www.cci.mg/index.php?p=journaux&id=17&id_det=2047>

Rakotomalala, Mahefa. 2013. 'Ultimatum et revendications: Ambatovy monte au créneau.' *L'Express de Madagascar*. 27 April.
<http://fr.allafrica.com/stories/201304270480.html>

Razafindrazaka, Désiré. 2014. 'Urban Insecurity in Ilakaka and Moramanga, Madagascar.' Unpublished background paper. Geneva: Small Arms Survey.

Richards, John. 2003. *The Unending Frontier: An Environmental History of the Early Modern World*. Berkeley, CA: University of California Press.

Rivoilan, Pascal and David Broustet. 2011. 'Recensement de la population 2009.' *Synthèse No. 19*. Nouméa, New Caledonia: Institut de la statistique et des études économiques. <http://www.insee.fr/fr/themes/document.asp?ref_id=ip1338>

Rodgers, Dennis. 2010. 'Urban Violence Is Not (Necessarily) a Way of Life: Towards a Political Economy of Conflict in Cities.' WIDER Working Paper No. 20. Helsinki: United Nations University–World Institute for Development Economics Research. March.

Ross, Michael. 2004. 'How Do Natural Resources Influence Civil War? Evidence from Thirteen Cases.' *International Organization*, Vol. 58, No. 1, pp. 35–67.

SAT (Sistema de Alertas Tempranas). 2012. *Informe de riesgo N° 002-12A.I: Antioquia, Remedios, Segovia y Zaragoza*. Bogotá: SAT, Defensoría del Pueblo. 3 April.

Schouten, Peer. 2013. 'Brewing Security? Heineken's Engagement with Commercial Conflict-dependent Actors in the Eastern DRC.' Commercial Conflict Dependent Actors Project Report. <http://www.ccda.se/wp-content/uploads/CCDA-Report-Heineken-DRC.pdf>

Semana (Colombia). 2013. 'Minería ilegal: entre el oro y el crimen.' 29 March.
<http://www.semana.com/nacion/articulo/oro-crimen-mineria-ilegal/338107-3>

Sheerin, Jude. 2007. 'Lawlessness Plagues Oil Rich City.' *BBC News*. 5 July. <http://news.bbc.co.uk/2/hi/africa/6274416.stm>

Souche, Angélique. 2014. 'Fuite d'acide chlorhydrique à VALE NC: une erreur humaine?' Nouvelle Calédonie. 8 May.
<http://nouvellecaledonie.la1ere.fr/2014/05/08/fuite-d-acide-chlorydrique-vale-nc-une-erreur-humaine-150005.html>

Spiegel, Samuel. 2009. 'Resource Policies and Small-Scale Gold Mining in Zimbabwe.' *Resources Policy*, Vol. 34, Nos. 1–2, pp. 39–44.

Theis, Michael, et al. 2009. *Port Harcourt Waterfront Urban Regeneration: Scoping Study*. London: MLC Press, Max Lock Centre, University of Westminster.

Trujillo, Luisa Fernanda. 2012. 'Gran minería: biografía documentada de un predador veloz.' *Razón Pública*. 11 June.
<http://www.razonpublica.com/index.php/econom-y-sociedad-temas-29/3019-gran-mineria-biografia-documentada-de-un-depredador-veloz.html>

—. 2014. 'Digging for Trouble: Insights from Colombia and Peru.' Unpublished background paper. Geneva: Small Arms Survey.

Turner, Frederick Jackson. [1893] 1961. 'The Significance of the Frontier in American History.' In Ray Allen Billington, ed. *Frontier and Section: Selected Essays*. Englewood Cliffs, NJ: Prentice-Hall, pp. 37–62.

Tullow Oil. n.d. 'Tullow Oil Kenya.' Map. Updated 19 November 2014. <http://www.tullowoil.com/index.asp?pageid=433>

Umlas, Elizabeth. 2011. 'Protected but Exposed: Multinationals and Private Security.' In Small Arms Survey. *Small Arms Survey 2011: States of Security*. Cambridge: Cambridge University Press, pp. 135–65.

UN (United Nations). 2011. *Guiding Principles on Business and Human Rights: Implementing the United Nations 'Protect, Respect and Remedy' Framework*. New York and Geneva: UN. <http://www.ohchr.org/Documents/Publications/G\uidingPrinciplesBusinessHR_EN.pdf>

UN-Habitat. 2009. *Evictions and Demolitions in Port Harcourt: Report of Fact-Finding Mission to Port Harcourt City, Federal Republic of Nigeria, 12–16 March 2009*. Abuja and Nairobi: UN-HABITAT. August.
<http://www.stakeholderdemocracy.org/uploads/Other%20publications/2009%2008%2022%20Port%20Harcourt%20Report%20FINAL.pdf>

—. 2010. *The State of African Cities 2010: Governance, Inequality and Urban Land Market*. Nairobi: UN-Habitat. November.

—. 2012. *Madagascar: profile urbain de Moramanga*. Nairobi: UN-Habitat.
<http://unhabitat.org/publications/moramanga-urban-profile-madagascar-french-language-version/>

—. 2013. *State of the World's Cities 2012/2013: Prosperity of Cities*. Nairobi: UN-Habitat.

Vann, Carole. 2008. 'En Tunisie, la révolte à huis clos du peuple des mines.' Swissinfo. 17 October.
<http://www.swissinfo.ch/fre/en-tunisie--la-r%C3%A9volte-%C3%A0-huis-clos-du-peuple-des-mines/6981004>

Vasquez, Patricia I. 2014a. *Oil Sparks in the Amazon: Local Conflicts, Indigenous Populations, and Natural Resources*. Athens, GA: University of Georgia Press.

—. 2014b. 'Turkana: Challenges around the Development of Oil.' Unpublished background paper. Geneva: Small Arms Survey.

Verdad Abierta. 2013. 'Segovia y Remedios, siguen en medio de la guerra.' 2 May.
<http://www.verdadabierta.com/component/content/article/50-victimarios/rearmados/rearmados/4569-segovia-y-remedios-escenario-de-guerra>

VPSHR (Voluntary Principles on Security and Human Rights). 2000. <http://www.voluntaryprinciples.org/what-are-the-voluntary-principles/>

Walsh, Andrew. 2012. 'After the Rush: Living with Uncertainty in a Malagasy Mining Town.' *Africa*, Vol. 82, No. 2, pp. 235–51.

Watts, Michael J. and Ibaba Samuel Ibaba. 2011. 'Turbulent Oil: Conflict and Insecurity in the Niger Delta.' *African Security*, Vol. 4, No. 1, pp. 1–19.

Webb, Walter Prescott. 1964. *The Great Frontier*. Austin, TX: University of Texas Press.

Wei, Chi-hung. 2014. 'Oil, Urbanization and "Pacted" Ethnic Politics: Indigenous Movements in Latin America.' *International Political Science Review*. 26 September, pp. 1–16.

Weinstein, Jeremy. 2007. *Inside Rebellion: The Politics of Insurgent Violence*. Cambridge: Cambridge University Press.

Woodworth, Max. 2012. 'Frontier Boomtown Urbanism in Ordos, Inner Mongolia Autonomous Region.' *Cross-Currents: East Asian History and Culture Review*, Vol. 1, No. 1. May, pp. 74–101. <http://muse.jhu.edu/journals/cross_currents_east_asian_history_and_culture_review/v001/1.1.woodworth.pdf>

ACKNOWLEDGEMENTS

Principal authors

Oliver Jütersonke and Hannah Dönges

Contributors

Stéphanie Graff, Stéphanie Perazzone, Désiré Razafindrazaka, Luisa Fernanda Trujillo, and Patricia I. Vasquez

Members of IANSA meet with the chair of BMS5, Ambassador Zahir Tanin, UN headquarters, New York, 17 June 2014. © International Action Network on Small Arms (IANSA)

One Meeting after Another

UN PROCESS UPDATE

3

INTRODUCTION

Nine rounds of informal consultations before the meeting. Multiple formal and informal sessions at the meeting itself. Seven draft outcome documents. The final outcome of the Fifth Biennial Meeting of States (BMS5),[1] the latest in a series of meetings on the UN Programme of Action (PoA),[2] was the product of months of work and intense diplomatic effort. But was it worth it?

This chapter, drawing on official documents and the author's own observations of the meeting, including its preparatory phase, seeks to answer this question. In addition to conducting a retrospective analysis of BMS5, centred on an examination of the meeting outcome document, the chapter also looks ahead to the next meeting on the PoA calendar, the Second Open-ended Meeting of Governmental Experts (MGE2), scheduled for June 2015. As explained in the chapter, BMS5 fits within a broader framework that includes the PoA, its follow-up meetings, and practical follow-up on the outcomes of those meetings.

The chapter's main conclusions include the following:

- Following months of intense diplomatic activity, the BMS5 process produced an outcome document featuring practical implementation measures in the areas that states discussed (stockpile management; marking, record-keeping, and tracing; and international cooperation and assistance).

- The BMS5 outcome builds on previous PoA meeting outcomes by, for example, promoting women's participation in PoA-related processes, highlighting the importance of stockpile security and weapons tracing in conflict and post-conflict situations, and emphasizing training in building sustainable capacity for PoA implementation.

- The BMS5 text also encourages the exchange of tracing results and other information, as well as robust stockpile management, for purposes of reducing diversion risks.

- Modular weapons design complicates the task of unique identification, which is essential for tracing. Policy responses include the identification of a 'control component' for these weapons.

- Unlike metal firearms, polymer guns are difficult to mark durably, as the International Tracing Instrument (ITI)[3] prescribes. Policy guidance is needed on issues such as the marking methods applicable to polymer firearm parts and the depth and placement of such markings.

- Current norms, both national and international, are largely adequate for the control of 3D-printed firearms, but their application is more difficult. Governments, moreover, have a clear interest in preparing for the day when fully functional 3D-printed firearms can be produced easily and economically.

- Certain new technologies could improve weapons marking, record-keeping, and tracing, strengthen stockpile security, and prevent unauthorized use, but critical barriers to their adoption and diffusion must first be overcome.

This chapter begins by placing BMS5 in the broader context of the UN small arms process and recounts the steps taken on the road to the adoption of the outcome document. It then focuses on that outcome, identifying sources of value added in the three substantive sections of the BMS5 text—stockpile management; marking, record-keeping, and tracing; and international cooperation and assistance—as well as its follow-up section. BMS5 successfully dealt with one important element of follow-up, namely defining the mandate for MGE2. The chapter also examines, issue-by-issue, some of the new developments and technologies, both adopted and prospective, that are up for discussion at MGE2 and that challenge key premises of small arms control, specifically as articulated in the PoA and ITI.

JOURNEY OF A THOUSAND MEETINGS: THE BMS5 PROCESS

The mandate for BMS5 originally stems from the PoA and, more immediately, from the PoA's Second Review Conference and the UN General Assembly resolutions that gave effect to the meeting schedule agreed at the Conference.[4] While the same resolutions indicated that BMS5 was 'to consider the full and effective implementation of the Programme of Action' (UNGA, 2012b, para. 5; 2013b, para. 5), as described below, this formal, but somewhat open-ended, mandate was less important than the practice that had shaped both the process and substance of PoA meetings since 2008.

By the time of the PoA's Second Review Conference (2012), three distinct types of meeting had emerged (see Figure 3.1). Review conferences, also mentioned in the PoA (UNGA, 2001b, para. IV.1.a), were relatively high-level diplomatic events, important for setting priorities for future PoA and ITI implementation, including the question of future meetings.[5] Open-ended meetings of governmental experts, the first of which was held in May 2011, were, as the name indicates, expert-led—involving police officials responsible for tracing, for example—and focused on the exchange of information concerning 'implementation challenges and opportunities', rather than the negotiation of agreed meeting text (UNGA, 2008b, para. 13).[6]

Figure 3.1 **Timeline of PoA meetings**

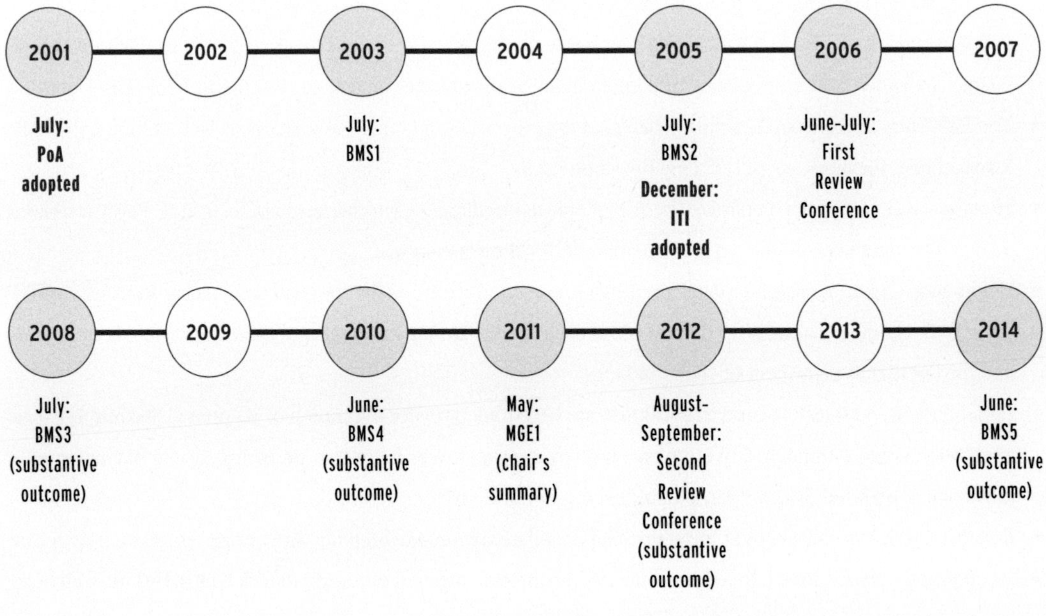

BMSs, in essence, fell between review conferences and MGEs; while they were diplomat- rather than expert-driven, they were less focused on broad agenda-setting, and more concerned with practical implementation in specific substantive areas. The first two BMSs, convened in July 2003 and July 2005, were lacklustre affairs that covered all aspects of the PoA, largely through the prism of one-way national statements, and that yielded no collective agreement on future action; neither BMS1 or BMS2 produced agreed substantive outcomes. Under the chairmanship of Ambassador Dalius Čekuolis of Lithuania, BMS3, convened in July 2008, took a new, more focused approach that led to an agreed outcome document (see Box 3.1). The same method of work was applied for BMS4, in 2010, which again resulted in a substantive outcome.

Like BMS3 and BMS4, BMS5 got off to an early start, with the nomination of the chair-designate, Ambassador Zahir Tanin of Afghanistan, in August 2013—some ten

Box 3.1 **New twists to the old method**

The method of work Ambassador Dalius Čekuolis of Lithuania employed for BMS3 comprised various elements designed to keep the meeting 'focused and [to] avoid the politicization of technical issues' (Čekuolis, 2008, p. 23).[7] In preparing for BMS5 and in conducting the meeting itself, Ambassador Zahir Tanin of Afghanistan used most of the same elements. They included '[e]xtensive consultation'; limiting the number of topics for discussion and 'deepening discussion on those'; posting national statements on the UN website, while encouraging delegations to read condensed versions of their statements at the meeting itself; and '[d]ispensing with the general exchange of views', instead moving directly to the discussion of substantive meeting themes (p. 23).

Breaking with the approach taken at BMS3, BMS4, and the Second Review Conference, Ambassador Tanin did not use facilitators–except for the discussions on the ITI, which, in keeping with past practice, were shepherded by an ITI moderator, Anthony Simpson of New Zealand.[8] This was made possible by the reduced number of substantive topics at BMS5–three, as opposed to four for both BMS3 and BMS4–and, as noted elsewhere in the chapter, by the extensive preparatory work Ambassador Tanin had undertaken, such as securing early agreement on a provisional meeting agenda (UNGA, 2014b) and conducting five rounds of informal consultations devoted to consideration of his draft meeting text (fifth to ninth consultations). While the chairs of BMS3 and BMS4 had also submitted draft outcome text in advance of each biennial meeting, Ambassador Tanin embarked on the task much earlier–in this regard, following the example of the PoA's Second Review Conference, rather than the preceding BMSs.

months prior to BMS5.[9] Ambassador Tanin held his first round of open-ended consultations[10] on BMS5 at UN headquarters in New York on 25 October 2013. The initial consultations focused on reaching provisional agreement on the BMS5 agenda, in particular the substantive meeting themes. The topics of ITI implementation and international cooperation and assistance were given, having been agreed previously.[11] 'Stockpile management, including physical security measures of small arms and light weapons', was added to the list.[12]

In late 2013 and early 2014, states turned their attention to the identification of focus areas within the agreed agenda items and, as of March 2014, to the consideration of draft text produced by the chair-designate.[13] Ambassador Tanin put forward five draft versions of the BMS5 outcome document in advance of the meeting itself. While the 'zero draft' that he issued on 5 March was limited to a list of 'proposed topics' and a draft structure for the BMS5 outcome (Afghanistan, 2014b), subsequent drafts, beginning with the 'Draft 1' he produced on 7 May (Afghanistan, 2014c), put substantial flesh on this skeleton. All told, Ambassador Tanin convened nine rounds of informal consultations, eight in New York and one in Geneva—a flurry of diplomatic activity that surpassed, by a fair margin, that which had accompanied BMS3 and BMS4, themselves no slouches in this regard.

On the eve of BMS5, the chair's draft outcome document ('Draft 4') (Afghanistan, 2014d; UNGA, 2014d) was relatively close to the final version in its general structure and content. Although specific language would change significantly, Draft 4 included almost all of the issues that would figure in the final outcome document.

BMS5, held at UN headquarters in New York from 16 to 20 June 2014, followed two parallel paths. The first, defined by the formal meeting agenda and 'programme of work' (UNGA, 2014b; 2014c), comprised formal statements on the various meeting topics—mostly from states, but also, on 19 June, from representatives of civil society and international organizations (see Box 3.2). The second track, which to some extent overshadowed the first,[14] consisted of a series of informal meetings or 'consultations' that were restricted to states and designed to narrow differences on the draft outcome document.

As at previous PoA meetings, several contentious issues, such as ammunition, Security Council work, and the relative strength of commitments for international assistance, would take a significant share of meeting time. New bones of contention also arose—in par-

---

Box 3.2   Survivor: IANSA at BMS5

There was speculation about how effective the NGO umbrella group, the International Action Network on Small Arms (IANSA), would be at BMS5 as it had lost its international secretariat due to funding shortfalls. Expectations for the meeting were low among some IANSA-affiliated NGOs, one of which announced its intention to skip the meeting (Mack, 2014).

In the event, IANSA's contribution to BMS5 was significant. As at previous PoA meetings, NGOs and research institutes, in collaboration with states and international organizations, organized a series of 'side events' that highlighted various small arms- and armed violence-related issues.[15] NGOs also took to the floor on the morning of 19 June to give prepared statements in plenary session.[16] Later the same day, during consultations on the draft outcome document, several states cited the IANSA presentations of the morning and other civil society inputs,[17] as they stressed the importance of a meaningful meeting outcome. Behind the scenes at BMS5, as during the negotiations on the Arms Trade Treaty (UNGA, 2013a), NGOs also liaised with national delegations, alerting them to perceived weaknesses in the draft outcome document and proposing fixes that, in some cases, found their way into the final meeting text.

While the debate among IANSA-affiliated NGOs about the value of BMS5, and the UN small arms process generally, has yet to subside,[18] these groups made their presence, and even absence, felt at BMS5.

---

ticular, the relationship between the PoA and the Arms Trade Treaty (ATT), the latter having been adopted, in April 2013, after the last PoA meeting, in August–September 2012 (Second Review Conference).

Early on 19 June, on the basis of inputs received at the meeting, Ambassador Tanin issued a new version of the draft outcome document ('Draft 5') (Afghanistan, 2014e), which was discussed that same day. On the morning of the final day of the meeting, 20 June, the chair issued another revised text (UNGA, 2014e). That afternoon, after a few last fixes to this text,[19] UN member states adopted the BMS5 outcome document, along with the meeting report, by consensus (UNGA, 2014g; 2014f).

ANATOMY OF AN OUTCOME: THE BMS5 TEXT

The BMS5 outcome document comprises a five-paragraph introductory part, three sections covering the main meeting themes (stockpile management, the ITI, and international cooperation and assistance), a section on meeting follow-up, and a final, brief[20] 'other issues' section. As described in greater detail below, certain subjects figure in two or more sections of the document. They include:

- the application of the PoA and ITI to conflict and post-conflict situations;
- the participation of women in small arms control efforts;
- diversion; and
- recent developments in small arms manufacturing, technology, and design.

A few topics that figure prominently in the section on international cooperation and assistance, including the transfer of technology and equipment, capacity building, and research and training, are also echoed in other parts of the BMS5 outcome. The following sections assess the contents of the outcome document, including the question of whether the text adds value to pre-existing PoA-related documentation.

Stockpile management

The subject of stockpile management had been addressed quite comprehensively at BMS3.[21] For BMS5, the challenge was to build on this earlier discussion.

Application to conflict and post-conflict situations. In the first instance, the BMS5 outcome document underlines the importance of stockpile management 'in settings of armed violence, transnational organized crime and conflict and post-conflict situations' (UNGA, 2014g, para. 6), a somewhat broader set of reference points than is typically found in PoA-related documentation relating to stockpile management. In several places, however, the document emphasizes the application of stockpile management to 'conflict and post-conflict situations', citing, in this regard, disarmament, demobilization, and reintegration (DDR) programmes, UN peacekeeping, and 'other relevant national programmes' (paras. 7–8, 17b).[22] The PoA does not explicitly link stockpile security and UN peacekeeping.[23] The fact that this connection is 'noted' in the BMS5 outcome (para. 7) represents something of a step forward—although earlier draft versions of the BMS5 outcome contained additional references to UN peacekeeping and related Security Council work.[24]

Weapons and ammunition stored in a disused factory in Lubumbashi, Katanga province, DRC, February, 2009. © Gwenn Dubourthoumieu/MAG

Life-cycle management. Although the BMS5 outcome makes few explicit references to the identification and disposal of surplus small arms, an issue BMS3 dealt with in some detail,[25] it arguably broaches the subject in a more holistic way by referring to 'life-cycle management procedures' (UNGA, 2014g, paras. 11, 17e). While this term is typically used in relation to ammunition,[26] it would normally include design, procurement, storage, and use—in addition to final disposal. The BMS5 text, however, does not explain the term.

Guidelines for stockpile management. Like the BMS3 outcome, the BMS5 text makes a reference to 'guidelines' for stockpile management;[27] but it is unclear how these differ from the 'standards and procedures' that the PoA refers to in its core provision on stockpile management (UNGA, 2001b, para. II.17). Moreover, BMS5 language referring to 'standards', 'procedures', and 'guidelines' is heavily qualified,[28] in contrast to the PoA, which anchors its exception to the norm of 'adequate and detailed standards and procedures' in a narrower reference to the 'constitutional and legal systems of States' (para. II.17).

The key norms on stockpile management remain those found in the PoA.

Other provisions. The stockpile management section also includes language encouraging the sharing of information and good practices on stockpile management (UNGA, 2014g, paras. 12, 16, 17f) and the sharing of 'experience and research in the area of diversion' (para. 13). In line with the outcome of the PoA's Second Review Conference and the UN's broader agenda concerning women, peace, and security,[29] it also promotes the 'meaningful participation and representation' of women in PoA-related 'policymaking, planning and implementation processes', including in the areas of stockpile management, and awareness-raising and education (para. 17d)—building on an equivalent provision in the Review Conference outcome.[30] Finally, international cooperation and assistance, addressed in a general way in section III of the BMS5 text, is also approached through a stockpile management lens, with a focus on training and, to some extent, technology transfer (paras. 14–17, 38c).

These provisions, in conjunction with those cited earlier in this section, and like those contained in the BMS3 outcome,[31] offer national governments and other stakeholders detailed guidance on the implementation of PoA provisions on stockpile management, including in conflict and post-conflict situations. They do not, however, constitute a normative shift in the area of stockpile management. The key norms remain those found in the PoA.[32]

The International Tracing Instrument

Although it is a separate instrument, the ITI, devoted to weapons marking, record-keeping, and tracing, was developed within the framework of the PoA. BMS5 was the third time the UN membership took up the ITI in the context of a BMS. While the first such meeting, BMS3, had seen UN member states engage with the new instrument in a relatively 'practical and focused' way,[33] BMS4 saw them in a holding pattern, with the meeting outcome on the ITI offering little value added over its predecessor.[34] In fact, the BMS5 outcome on the ITI takes its cue not from the BMS3 and BMS4 texts, but from the outcome document of the PoA's Second Review Conference—and, before it, the 2011 MGE (MGE1). The gains in the BMS5 text are modest, but it does give more concrete expression to several issues that the Review Conference document only sketched out in rough form.

Conflict tracing. The first of these issues is the tracing of small arms and light weapons in conflict and post-conflict situations ('conflict tracing'), an application of the ITI that, while embedded in the instrument itself, was not given much attention before the Second Review Conference.[35] The tracing of weapons in countries suffering or emerging from armed conflict can serve to detect violations of applicable arms embargoes, spot attempts to rearm, and expose weaknesses in stockpile management (the diversion of weapons from government or peacekeeping force stockpiles).[36]

Paragraph 21 of the BMS5 text highlights, in a general way, the utility of exchanging tracing information relating to conflict and post-conflict situations, as well as crime, while paragraph 27g calls for 'the enhanced exchange' of tracing information 'between relevant United Nations entities'. Both paragraphs cite the potential application of conflict tracing to 'the planning and imple-

A shell casing is placed under a microscope to identify markings scored on it when fired from a handgun during a demonstration by the New York State Police, Albany, 2008.
© Mike Groll/AP Photo

mentation of [DDR] programmes and other relevant national programmes'. Paragraph 27f, meanwhile, encourages the provision of support for tracing to governments that host UN peacekeeping missions. Building on general language contained in the outcome of the Second Review Conference,[37] UN member states are, in effect, starting to work out some of the practical modalities for the tracing of small arms in conflict and post-conflict situations. In conjunction with related efforts by the UN Security Council,[38] conflict tracing is now taking a more tangible form at the UN.

Exchanging tracing results and preventing diversion. A second step forward on ITI-related matters at the Second Review Conference, building on discussions at MGE1, was to promote the exchange of tracing results, both within governments and with other states.[39] Among other things, this can raise awareness of significant diversion risks among relevant governmental agencies, including export licensing departments. The ITI section of the BMS5 outcome document similarly emphasizes the importance of exchanging tracing information in order to prevent diversion,[40] but also stresses its utility generally.[41] In fact, the diversion of small arms from legal to illicit spheres is a concern that cuts across the ITI and stockpile management sections. The BMS5 text frequently cites the exchange of tracing results and other information, as well as robust stockpile management and security, as important means of reducing diversion risks.[42]

New technologies. The ITI section of the BMS5 outcome takes up a further issue, one that was introduced at MGE1 and given more concrete expression at the Second Review Conference, namely the 'implications of recent developments in small arms and light weapons manufacturing, technology and design for effective marking, record-keeping and tracing' (UNGA, 2012a, annexe II, para. 3g).[43] The Second Review Conference had requested that the UN Secretary-General report on these issues (para. 3g), and the resulting document was published shortly before BMS5 (UNGA, 2014a). At BMS5, states did not really grapple with the contents of the report, preferring instead to refer to these developments in general terms, including the challenges and opportunities they present for ITI implementation (UNGA, 2014g, paras. 19–20). The UN membership did indicate that it would consider the implications of these developments for the ITI, including 'practical steps to ensure the continued and enhanced effectiveness of national marking, record-keeping and tracing systems' (para. 27d), but it basically kicked the topic farther down the road, proposing it for discussion at the PoA's Second MGE (MGE2), to be held in June 2015 (para. 40a–b).[44] In addition, states recommended that the UN Secretary-General provide further information on the subject and 'encouraged engagement with industry [. . .] to ensure that the parties involved remain fully informed of relevant technical developments' (paras. 27e, 47).[45]

Other provisions. There are few other sources of value added in the ITI section of the BMS5 outcome. At the Second Review Conference, states had undertaken to 'designate, where they have not done so, [. . .] before the next review conference' the national points of contact mandated by the ITI (UNGA, 2012a, annexe II, para. 2f).[46] The BMS5 text reiterates the commitment to designate one or more national points of contact, but without mentioning the deadline of the Third Review Conference, which had been agreed at the Second Review Conference (UNGA, 2014g, paras. 24, 27h). The BMS5 outcome also makes reference to import marking (para. 23), which is important to effective tracing and largely neglected in the BMS4 outcome,[47] but adds nothing to the ITI itself.[48]

One can identify a few new wrinkles in the provisions of the ITI section dealing with international cooperation and assistance, for example:

- the implications of 'developments in small arm and light weapon manufacturing, technology and design [. . .] for international assistance and capacity-building' (para. 27d);
- the possible development of 'a comprehensive international assistance framework' to support ITI implementation (para. 27i); and
- 'adequate technical and financial assistance to strengthen national capacities for ballistics information collection and exchange' (para. 27k).

Yet, as often arises with the topic of international cooperation and assistance, commitments are few, qualifiers many ('consider', 'encourage'). In fact, battle lines were drawn on this very issue during the negotiations on the BMS5 section devoted to international cooperation and assistance.

The BMS5 outcome stresses capacity building, training, and the transfer of technology and equipment.

International cooperation and assistance

The BMS5 outcome document, generally—not only its section on international cooperation and assistance—emphasizes three subjects that were part of the meeting agenda:[49] capacity building,[50] training,[51] and the transfer of technology and equipment.[52] It also puts these topics on the agenda of MGE2 (UNGA, 2014g, para. 40c). In addition, the international cooperation and assistance section, applicable to both the PoA and ITI,[53] reprises some of the themes of past PoA meetings,[54] such as:

- ensuring the 'adequacy, effectiveness and sustainability' of international cooperation and assistance (UNGA, 2014g, paras. 29, 38a, 38(n)(i));[55]
- increasing 'the measurability and effectiveness of international cooperation and assistance' (para. 37);[56]
- improving the 'matching of needs with available resources' (para. 35);
- using national reports on PoA and ITI implementation 'to identify, prioritize and communicate assistance needs' (para. 38f);
- 'preventing and reducing the devastating consequences' of the illicit small arms trade on children (para. 38j);[57]
- strengthening cooperation in addressing the illicit trade in small arms and light weapons across borders, in particular at the sub-regional and regional levels (paras. 33, 38k);[58] and
- facilitating the participation and representation of women in international cooperation and assistance for PoA and ITI implementation (para. 31).[59]

The BMS5 outcome outlines several additional steps for purposes of strengthening international cooperation and assistance for PoA and ITI implementation, including:

- enhancing the exchange and utilization of knowledge, expertise, and lessons learned—including expertise and technical capabilities available in developing countries and at the regional and sub-regional levels (paras. 28, 32, 38h–i);
- avoiding duplication in the provision of, or requests for, assistance, including through coordination with relevant regional and sub-regional organizations (paras. 38g–h);
- cooperating with the UN regional centres for peace and disarmament, the World Customs Organization, INTERPOL, and the UN Office on Drugs and Crime in implementing the PoA and ITI (para. 38l); and
- sustaining collaboration between the UN Secretariat and relevant research and training institutions, including through the provision of information relating to PoA and ITI implementation (para. 38(n)(ii)–(iii)).

Overall, in line with the outcome of the Second Review Conference,[60] the language in the BMS5 text's international cooperation and assistance section is relatively strong. Whereas states typically agree only to 'seriously consider rendering assistance' under the PoA (UNGA, 2001b, para. III.3),[61] they are less equivocal in the BMS5 outcome:

States also reaffirmed that international cooperation and assistance should be rendered upon request, as appropriate, in line with the needs and priorities of recipient States, and that its adequacy, effectiveness and sustainability should be ensured (UNGA, 2014g, para. 29).

Qualifiers remain, however. In the BMS5 outcome, one of the most frequently used is the phrase 'as appropriate', employed in the provision quoted above. Most significantly, text championed by the Non-Aligned Movement, which emphasized that PoA assistance should be unconditional,[62] as reflected in the draft outcome document the chair proposed for BMS5,[63] was dropped from the last versions of the document in the face of opposition from donor countries.

> BMS5 language on international cooperation and assistance is relatively strong.

Follow-up

The follow-up section of the BMS5 outcome document borrows its structure and much of its content from the outcome of the Second Review Conference.[64] Borrowed content includes: a recap of the schedule of meetings agreed for the period from 2012 to 2018;[65] reaffirmation of 'the importance of the early designation of the chair of future [PoA] meetings' (UNGA, 2014g, para. 42);[66] text encouraging 'a maximum of synergies' between national, regional, and global-level meetings and action on small arms (paras. 44–45);[67] two paragraphs encouraging the engagement of civil society, including industry, in the implementation of the PoA and ITI (paras. 46–47);[68] and text promoting the provision of financial support for 'wider and more equitable' PoA meeting participation (para. 50).[69]

While the BMS5 follow-up section also repeats the Review Conference recommendation to 'improve the utility' of national reports on PoA and ITI implementation by synchronizing them with BMSs and review conferences (para. 48),[70] it builds on the Review Conference text by urging the use of national reports 'to identify implementation trends and challenges' (para. 49). Given the UN membership's continuing aversion to the formal monitoring of PoA and ITI implementation, this could help generate an improved picture of overall implementation.[71] The BMS5 text also goes further than the Review Conference outcome by citing 'the important role of regional and subregional organizations [. . .] in building capacity and promoting cooperation and assistance' for PoA and ITI implementation (para. 43).

Most importantly, however, the BMS5 outcome document sketches out the mandate for MGE2. In line with the outcomes of past PoA meetings, in particular the Second Review Conference,[72] the BMS5 text reaffirms that the topic of international cooperation and assistance 'should continue to be an integral element of the agenda of all [PoA] meetings' (para. 41). More specifically, it recommends that MGE2 take up the question of the 'transfer of technology and equipment, as well as capacity-building, in particular training', for PoA and ITI implementation (para. 40c). In addition, it proposes that MGE2 consider 'recent developments in small arm and light weapon manufacturing, technology and design', including '[p]ractical steps to ensure the continued and enhanced effectiveness of national marking, record-keeping and tracing systems in the light of such developments' (paras. 40a–b). In its annual resolution on small arms, the UN General Assembly subsequently confirmed this mandate (UNGA, 2014h, para. 6).

As articulated in the BMS5 outcome, preparatory steps for MGE2 include the presentation, by the UN Secretariat, of options for the enhanced funding of implementation-related activities and for the establishment of PoA- and ITI-related training programmes, as well as a UN study on 'the adequacy, effectiveness and sustainability of financial and technical assistance' since the time of the PoA's adoption in 2001. The BMS5 outcome specifies that the latter study is to be discussed at MGE2 (2015) and considered at BMS6 (2016) (paras. 38m, 38(n)(i)).

While it remains to be seen whether these follow-up measures will yield tangible results over the medium and long term, specifically in terms of strengthened PoA and ITI implementation, they do give the impression of a process striving towards 'coherence, effectiveness and continuity' (UNGA, 2012a, annexe I, sec. III, first preambular para.).[73]

There are several sources of value added in the BMS5 outcome.

Taking stock of BMS5

Although they noted a certain lack of ambition, several observers found much to commend in the BMS5 outcome.[74] In fact, a comparison of this text with the outcomes of the Second Review Conference and the preceding BMSs reveals several sources of value added in the BMS5 outcome:

- the promotion of women's participation and representation in PoA-related policy-making, planning, and implementation processes (UNGA, 2014g, paras. 10, 17d, 31);[75]
- highlighting the potential application of stockpile management to conflict and post-conflict situations, including DDR programmes, UN peacekeeping, and 'other relevant national programmes' (paras. 7–8, 17b);
- the articulation of practical steps for the tracing of small arms in conflict and post-conflict situations, building on general language contained in the outcome of the Second Review Conference (paras. 21, 27f–g);[76]
- some acknowledgement of related Security Council work on small arms (paras. 7, 10, 31);[77]
- relatively strong language on international cooperation and assistance, including the identification of specific follow-up;[78]
- a clear mandate for MGE2 (para. 40);[79] and
- an encouragement to improve the utility of national reports on PoA and ITI implementation by using them to identify implementation trends and challenges (para. 49).

Nevertheless, there were some important omissions from the BMS5 text, such as:

- direct references to ammunition, including the International Ammunition Technical Guidelines;[80]
- greater acknowledgement of UN Security Council work on small arms;[81]
- references to the relationship between the PoA and ATT;[82] and
- mentions of 'security sector reform'[83] and of the International Small Arms Control Standards (ISACS).[84]

At the end of the day, the BMS5 outcome ushers in no normative shifts. For now, the place of ammunition in the UN small arms process remains uncertain, even though the BMS5 text hints that this could change. At the same time, any mention of the connections that exist between the PoA and related Security Council work, or the ATT, remains controversial. More broadly, even though BMS5 mostly managed to build on, rather than repeat, earlier discussions

An officer of the disarmament, demobilization, and reintegration programme of the UN Operation in Côte d'Ivoire (UNOCI) supervises the collection of weapons by UN peacekeepers and the Republican Forces of Côte d'Ivoire (FRCI), Abidjan, February 2012. © Basile Zoma/UN Photo

on stockpile management, the ITI, and international cooperation and assistance, these discussions yielded nothing radically new or different from the PoA and ITI themselves. While that can be seen as a weakness,[85] the action arguably lies elsewhere; the true value of the BMS5 text rests in its enumeration of practical steps that can be taken to advance small arms control in the areas it covered (Marsh, 2014).

This more positive assessment assumes that the measures contained in the BMS5 outcome will be translated into concrete laws, policies, and programmes in the communities, countries, and regions affected by small arms violence. The chapter returns to this question later, in its conclusion, but first focuses on another form of follow-up, namely that which can be conducted in UN meeting halls. As noted above, BMS5 did not consider in any depth the implications of new technologies for ITI implementation, leaving this to the governmental experts who will convene at UN headquarters for MGE2 in June 2015 (UNGA, 2014g, para. 40; 2014h, para. 6). The next section of the chapter, finalized in January 2015, looks ahead to MGE2, examining the subjects with which participants will have to contend at that meeting.

GETTING TO GRIPS WITH NEW TECHNOLOGIES: MGE2

As noted earlier, the topic of 'recent developments in [small arms] manufacturing, technology and design'—in particular their implications for ITI implementation (UNGA, 2014g, para. 40a)—reaches MGE2 via MGE1, the Second

Review Conference, and BMS5. Two general references in the BMS5 outcome aside (paras. 19–20), only MGE1 has looked at the subject in any detail, focusing on two issues: modular weapons design and the use of polymer in the production of firearms, specifically in handgun frames.[86] Between the time of MGE1, in May 2011, and the publication of the UN Secretary-General's report on the new technologies, in May 2014, another issue had drawn widespread attention, namely the production of firearms using additive manufacturing processes—often known as '3D printing'. The UN Secretary-General's report reviews these three issues, along with a fourth, specifically the use, or potential use, of new technologies for improved small arms control (UNGA, 2014a).[87] The following sections review each of the four issues in turn, drawing, above all, on a Small Arms Survey publication that examines them in greater depth (King and McDonald, 2015).

Modular weapons[88]

In some countries, the armed forces are now looking to modular rifles as 'all-in-one' replacements for different rifle types and models. Modular rifles typically feature 'split-receiver architecture'. The primary structural component of these rifles, the 'receiver', is divided into an upper and lower receiver. One of these components serves as a core (fixed) section around which most other major parts and components can be changed. In this way, the user, using relatively basic tools and procedures, can reconfigure the rifle to meet different operational needs—changing the calibre or barrel, for example, in order to optimize rifle use in different environments. Operators can also exchange most parts on a modular rifle with parts from the same or related models. To date, designers have adopted different approaches to modularity. 'Full modularity' allows for the complete reconfiguration of a rifle, including a change of calibre. Under the 'family approach', the same model is produced in different versions, each with its own calibre; while the calibre of a specific rifle cannot be modified, other characteristics can be changed (Persi Paoli, 2015b, pp. 24–34).

Although the concept of modularity has gained traction over the past decade among some national armed forces, consideration of its implications for weapons marking, record-keeping, and tracing has lagged behind. The main problem with modular weapons, simply stated, is that the weapon and its major components cannot be clearly distinguished for tracing purposes. The essential first step in tracing any weapon is to uniquely identify it, based on its physical characteristics (make and model) and identifying marks (in particular, serial number). Yet, if the receiver and one or more additional parts of a modular rifle are marked with identifying information—as the ITI prescribes and recommends, respectively[89]—the rifle will usually bear conflicting identifying information (for example, serial numbers) following a change of parts, hampering attempts to uniquely identify it.

A related problem is that, in addition to certain required identifying marks—manufacturer, country of manufacture, and serial number—the ITI also recommends the marking of additional information, such as weapon calibre (UNGA, 2005, para. 8a). It obviously makes little sense to mark a 'fully modular' rifle with a designation of calibre since this can be changed. In short, record-keeping and tracing become more complicated in a fully—or even partially—modular world. The crucial question is: how can one track a weapon throughout its life cycle, irrespective of changes in its configuration (such as calibre or barrel length)?

Policy options include the identification of a 'control component' for a modular rifle—logically the part around which most other major components can be changed (upper or

A partially-disassembled SCAR-L (Special Forces Combat Assault Rifle).
© weaponsman.com

lower receiver). Decisions also have to be taken as to the identifying information to mark on the control component, whether and how other components of the rifle should be marked, and whether and how records associated with the weapon, presumably linked to the control component, should try to account for the weapon's potential configurations.[90] Useful solutions will need to take account of the inherent complexity of modular weapons, while, at the same time, remaining as simple—and practicable—as possible.

Polymer frames[91]

Gun manufacturers are increasingly using polymers in the production of firearm parts, including the frames of many handguns. The primary reasons for the use of polymers, in place of metal, are the lower weight and cost of polymer parts. Yet, despite these and other advantages, in contrast to metal it is often difficult to mark polymer frames durably, as the ITI prescribes, in order to ensure gun traceability (UNGA, 2005, para. 7).

It is often difficult to mark polymer frames durably, as the ITI prescribes.

The ITI leaves the choice of marking methods to national discretion but indicates that:

States will ensure that, whatever method is used, all marks required under this instrument are on an exposed surface, conspicuous without technical aids or tools, easily recognizable, readable, durable and, as far as technically possible, recoverable (para. 7).

It further specifies that:

A unique marking should be applied to an essential or structural component of the weapon where the component's destruction would render the weapon permanently inoperable and incapable of reactivation, such as the frame and/or receiver, in compliance with paragraph 7 above (para. 10).

Through the use of forensic techniques, markings made on metal can often be recovered following attempts to erase or alter them. This is much more difficult in the case of polymer. Arms traffickers seeking to make a polymer gun untraceable will normally succeed in doing so once they remove the serial number that the manufacturer has applied to the frame. One approach to the problem, used in the United States, is to require manufacturers of polymer frame firearms to embed in the frame a metal tag that is stamped with the weapon's serial number (Persi Paoli, 2015a, p. 13). In practice, however, as some states pointed out at MGE1, criminals intent on preventing the identification of the firearm can often easily remove the tag.[92] An increasing number of manufacturers are, however, embedding the plate in such a way that it can only be pried out by damaging the frame and, as a result, structurally weakening the firearm.

Additional obstacles to the marking of polymer firearms arise after the time of manufacture. Some of the metal tags inserted during production are not large enough to accommodate post-manufacture markings, including import marks. In such cases, the marks have to be made on the polymer frame itself. One advantage of polymer frames is that they can be marked after the time of manufacture without damaging the finish that gun producers often apply to metal firearms. But only a limited number of marking methods can be used to mark polymer, even in a non-durable manner. They include engraving, in particular laser engraving, and, with some limitations, dot-peen (micro-percussion).[93] Laser machines, however, remain relatively expensive, limiting their use in many countries.

As drafted, the ITI takes little account of the specificities of polymer firearms. Guidance is needed on such issues as the use of metal tags, marking methods applicable to polymer firearm parts, and the depth and placement of such markings. International cooperation and assistance, including associated training, will also be important to the broad

diffusion and uptake of technology suitable for the marking of polymer firearms, in particular after the time of manufacture. States could also exchange information on—or collaborate on the development of—new techniques for the
recovery of markings removed or altered from polymer parts.[94] The UN Secretary-General's report, along with international guidelines, such as the International Small Arms Control Standards, also present options for meeting the challenges
posed by polymer frame guns (UNGA, 2014a; UNCASA, 2012).

3D printing[95]

Hobbyists and
others are starting
to print firearms
from polymer.

Falling prices, improved technology, and other factors have led to a boom in additive manufacturing ('3D printing')
in recent years, at both the industrial and consumer (hobbyist) levels. Industry, including aerospace and defence, is
making increasing use of 3D printing due to such advantages as increased speed in the development of designs and
prototypes, reduced material use, easier production of complex products, and inexpensive customization. To date,
firearm manufacturers have mostly used the technology to produce a range of gun components (such as lower
receivers) and accessories (such as sound suppressors). The latter part of 2013, however, saw the printing of the first
complete firearm from metal using a high-end 3D printer. Although several examples of this model—the Solid
Concepts Inc. 1911—have been sold to the public, it is not commercially viable given its price tag of USD 11,900.[96]

Encouraged by the increased availability of relevant materials, software, and hardware—in particular cheaper,
user-friendly printers—hobbyists, craft producers, and small businesses are also starting to print firearms, but from
polymer. In early 2013, Defense Distributed produced the first functioning 3D-printed firearm, the 'Liberator' handgun. Except for a metal firing pin and a metal block designed to ensure compliance with minimum metal (detectable
firearm) laws in the United States, the original Liberator is made entirely of polymer. Initial models were capable of
firing only between 1 and 11 rounds before structural failure occurred, although improved designs were in development
as of late 2014.[97]

The advent of consumer-produced 3D-printed guns has attracted considerable attention from policy-makers and
law enforcement agencies worldwide. In May 2013, two days after Defense Distributed posted the Liberator design
files on its website, the US Department of State directed the firm to remove them, citing a possible violation of US
arms export regulations. In 2013–14, several countries introduced legislation that would ban or otherwise restrict
3D-printed firearms or their components. Some legislators have also called for controls on 3D printers, the materials
used to produce 3D-printed guns, and associated computer files. Such proposals are problematic, however, as the
materials and equipment used to produce 3D-printed firearms are also used to make other 3D-printed products.[98]

In fact, current norms, both national and international, are largely suitable for the control of 3D-printed firearms.
National regulations, or provisions in such instruments as the UN Firearms Protocol (UNGA, 2001a), the PoA (UNGA,
2001b), the ITI (UNGA, 2005), and the Arms Trade Treaty (UNGA, 2013a), relating to small arms manufacture, international transfer, and marking, record-keeping, and tracing, would govern 3D-printed guns in the same way they
govern traditional firearms. Yet it is often more difficult to apply these norms to 3D-printed firearms. Many of the
associated law enforcement challenges stem from the diffusion of increasingly powerful 3D printing technology to
individuals and small groups. Criminals and non-state armed groups may find 3D-printed guns attractive since, when
unmarked, they are untraceable, and because many security screening devices have difficulty detecting firearms made
largely of polymer—although that is not true of the (standard) ammunition they still use. For such reasons, illicit online
markets currently sell Liberator-type pistols.

Additional challenges posed by 3D-printed guns include:

- the control of unlicensed production, or production involving shared resources in so-called 'maker spaces';
- enforcement of restrictions on the flow of weapons-related information over the Internet;
- the limited application of forensics (ballistics) techniques to some 3D-printed firearms;
- the possible routine destruction of low-cost 3D-printed guns by criminals in order to eliminate evidence; and
- the risk of catastrophic weapons failure (consumer safety).[99]

It seems likely that 3D printing, including for firearms production, will pick up more steam. Current predictions are for further declines in the cost of printers and materials and the increased accessibility of related software and weapons design files. Nevertheless, high-end 3D manufacturing technology—capable of producing complete metal firearms or critical structural components in metal or robust metal–polymer hybrids—will remain the preserve of larger, well-resourced companies for the foreseeable future. This will facilitate law enforcement monitoring of sophisticated 3D-printed firearms production. It will also limit the appeal of 3D-printed guns to criminals and non-state armed groups.

On any current measure of relative cost and performance, firearms produced using traditional manufacturing techniques, including craft firearms, easily best their 3D-printed counterparts. For many years to come, individuals and small groups will continue to confront major hurdles to the production of reasonably effective 3D-printed firearms. These include the cost of suitable printers and materials and the required technical skills. That said, as indicated above, 3D-printed guns already present important law enforcement challenges. Governments, moreover, have a clear interest in preparing for the day when fully functional 3D-printed firearms can be easily and economically produced.

> 3D printing, including for firearms production, will likely pick up more steam.

New technologies for improved small arms control[100]

As indicated in the preceding sections, technologies that are new—or at least new to the firearms industry—including modular design, the use of polymer, and 3D printing—pose certain challenges to the implementation of the PoA and ITI. Nevertheless, as indicated in this section, new or underutilized technologies can also improve marking, record-keeping, and tracing, strengthen stockpile security, and prevent unauthorized use—provided critical barriers to their adoption and diffusion can be overcome and the new technologies can be reconciled with existing multilateral control norms.

New marking technologies, such as data matrix codes and microstamping, coupled with improvements to associated scanning technology, could allow users to instantly capture, store, retrieve, and exchange information about a given weapon. Using these technologies, data that uniquely identifies the weapon, in particular its serial number, could be combined with information about its authorized users and ownership or usage history. This presupposes, however, not only the adoption of the new marking and scanning systems, but also the existence or creation of necessary IT infrastructure.[101]

New technology also offers opportunities for improved stockpile management, including access control, increased data accuracy, and the monitoring and protection of weapons in transit from one location to another. Some of these technologies, such as biometric gun safes, are inexpensive and available to individual gun owners, while others, such as the US military's Defense Transportation Tracking System, cost many millions of dollars to set up and run. Radio frequency identification (RFID), in particular, could play an important role in improved weapons management and security. Already used in a wide range of commercial and defence applications, RFID tags and strips, coupled with associated scanners, could be employed, for example, to detect attempts to break a seal on a shipping crate.[102] The transborder application of RFID technology is currently limited, however, due to the use of different RFID frequency bands in different countries (UNGA, 2014a, para. 34).

End-use control is another potential application of new or underutilized technology. Electronically controlled safety mechanisms (ECSMs) may be biometric (such as palm print scanners) or token-based (such as a RFID-tagged wrist watch). They can, for example, prevent a criminal from using a stolen gun—locking it in the absence of the necessary palm print or wrist watch. There is controversy surrounding ECSMs, however, with some observers expressing concerns about their reliability. So far sales of ECSM-equipped firearms have been limited (Schroeder, 2015, p. 83).

There are numerous barriers to the uptake of these new technologies. Foremost among them is cost, including, for many countries, the cost of establishing supporting infrastructure (databases and networked IT). As indicated above, there are also questions about the reliability of some of these technologies, in particular ECSMs, which some fear could prevent the use of a gun by its authorized user when most needed. Additional barriers include the difficulties of sharing information stored in a new format, opposition from political and consumer groups, especially in the United States, the conservative nature of political and military procurement, and the historically slow pace of change in firearms technology.[103] Some technologies, moreover, do not meet the requirements of existing multilateral control instruments.[104]

For all these reasons, 'old' firearms technology is proving surprisingly resistant to the changes that have recently transformed other products and industries. Whatever the future impact of technology on the firearms industry, it is also important to note that the huge number of small arms now circulating in the illicit market, very few of which feature new technology, will define the small arms problem for years to come. Irrespective of the advantages offered by many of the new systems, the same tried and tested methods remain key to small arms control. At the end of the day, the basics of weapons marking, record-keeping, and tracing, stockpile management, and diversion prevention, as defined in the PoA and ITI, are still essential for all countries, whatever their degree of access to new technology.

That said, as described above and as the MGE2 discussions will undoubtedly show, some new technologies, including modular design, polymer frames, and 3D printing, make implementation of the PoA and ITI more difficult. MGE2 will offer participants an important opportunity to share information and lessons learned in each of these areas, but the long-term value of these discussions will be limited unless states go beyond a review of the new challenges to identify specific, cost-effective ways of meeting them.

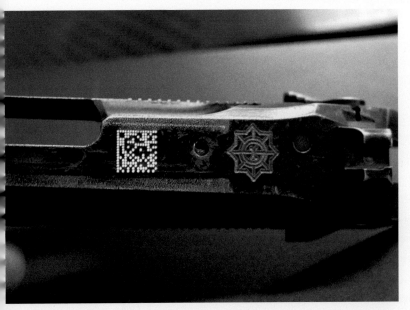

A two-dimensional data matrix code. © Traceability Solutions

CONCLUSION

A meeting was held, but to what end? BMS5, including its preparatory phase, was characterized by intense diplomatic effort, yet the result is not exactly groundbreaking. The BMS5 outcome document is marred by key omissions, such as a mention of obvious linkages between UN General Assembly (PoA) and Security Council work on small arms, and between the PoA and the ATT. The actual contents of the document—covering stockpile management; marking, record-keeping, and tracing; and international cooperation and assistance—only modestly elaborate on issues already solidly anchored in the text of the PoA and ITI. And some discussions, in particular the implications of recent developments in small arms manufacturing, technology, and design, were deferred to a later date.

One can certainly question the amount of diplomatic effort that went into a meeting outcome that, at some level, is self-evident. Yet that outcome, although unexciting, is in fact useful on several levels. First, compared to the outcomes of previous PoA meetings, the BMS5 text clearly builds on preceding discussions concerning subjects such as women's participation in PoA-related processes, conflict tracing, and international cooperation and assistance. Overall, the document defines a series of basic, practical measures for strengthened PoA and ITI implementation. In addition to those just mentioned, these include ensuring the security of small arms stockpiles in conflict and post-conflict settings, exchanging tracing results and other information in order to identify and reduce diversion risks, and putting more emphasis on training as a means of building sustainable capacity for PoA and ITI implementation (STOCKPILE MANAGEMENT).

Second, the BMS5 outcome makes important connections to other PoA meetings—not only past, but future. Although not really advancing consideration of the question, BMS5 has at least put the issue of new technologies squarely on the agenda of MGE2. As described earlier in the chapter, specific challenges to small arms control efforts arise in at least three new areas: modular weapons design (unique identification and tracing), polymer firearm parts (durable marking), and 3D printing (law enforcement). At the same time, certain new technologies offer opportunities for improved control—at least once critical barriers to their adoption are overcome.

For the moment, the basics of stockpile management, marking, record-keeping, and tracing, and international cooperation and assistance, as defined in the PoA, ITI, and many sections of the BMS5 text, remain essential for all countries, whatever their degree of access to new technology. In that light, one could consider BMS5 and its outcome document, focused on practical implementation measures, a clear success. While this is true when one sets the BMS5 outcome alongside other PoA meeting outcomes, real success will depend on the extent to which the measures contained in the BMS5 outcome are translated into concrete laws, policies, and programmes in the communities, countries, and regions affected by small arms violence. This could include, for example: exposing weaknesses in stockpile management through conflict tracing; exchanging information that alerts export licensing officials to specific diversion risks; and building sustainable capacity for PoA and ITI implementation through training.

Clearly, in order to determine the impact BMS5 will have on the small arms problem, one needs to connect the meeting and its outcome document to real-world change. Yet this is difficult for at least two reasons. First, no mechanism currently allows for a systematic assessment of progress made in implementing the PoA and ITI, let alone progress made in achieving their underlying objectives (curbing small arms proliferation and misuse).[105] Second, even if one could measure changes over time, it may be difficult, or impossible, to attribute them to a particular PoA meeting or even to the PoA itself. Individual governments, NGOs, or regional organizations—or some combination of them—may have a better claim to the observed change.

With assistance from soldiers, a MAG (Mines Advisory Group) team take munitions from an open-air stockpile for destruction, near Goma, DRC, September 2012. © Sean Sutton/Panos Pictures

While the real-world impact of BMS5 may thus remain unclear, the time and expense that went into the meeting can still be justified. In contrast to other arms control processes,[106] the UN small arms process continues to move forward—not by leaps and bounds, but in a relatively practical, focused way. All PoA meetings since BMS3, in 2008, have yielded substantive outcomes.[107] What was implicit (and ignored)[108] in the PoA and ITI—for example, weapons tracing in conflict and post-conflict settings—has been made explicit (and actionable).

Whether action is in fact taken is, of course, the critical question, but the PoA was never meant to be a one-stop solution to the small arms problem. It outlines relevant problems and solutions in agreed language, sets priorities, keeps the issue on national and regional agendas, and presumably helps catalyse practical work. Such work can arise, for example, when NGOs push their governments to follow through on commitments they have made in the PoA or ITI. Admittedly, those commitments tend to be quite modest in nature; as demonstrated at BMS5 itself, the UN small arms process suffers from a lowest common denominator effect. But this is a strength as well as a weakness. As politically binding agreements negotiated within the UN framework, the PoA and ITI apply to all UN member states. In theory, everyone is on board.

So far, not bad. But what has worked reasonably well in the past may not be what is needed in the future. One of the strengths of the UN small arms process to date has been its ability to evolve. The MGE, not mentioned in the text of the PoA or ITI, provides states with an expert-led forum to discuss—and potentially strengthen—implementation of the PoA and ITI.[109] MGE1 helped alert states to new developments in small arms manufacturing, technology, and design that made ITI implementation more difficult in several areas. It will be up to MGE2 to engage with these challenges and indicate how to respond.

Another meeting, then. With perhaps only modest gains to show for the time and effort spent. But such is progress. ◾

LIST OF ABBREVIATIONS

ATT	Arms Trade Treaty
BMS	Biennial Meeting of States to Consider the Implementation of the Programme of Action to Prevent, Combat and Eradicate the Illicit Trade in Small Arms and Light Weapons in All Its Aspects
DDR	Disarmament, demobilization, and reintegration
ECSM	Electronically controlled safety mechanism
IANSA	International Action Network on Small Arms
ISACS	International Small Arms Control Standards
ITI	International Instrument to Enable States to Identify and Trace, in a Timely and Reliable Manner, Illicit Small Arms and Light Weapons
MGE	Open-ended Meeting of Governmental Experts
PoA	Programme of Action to Prevent, Combat and Eradicate the Illicit Trade in Small Arms and Light Weapons in All Its Aspects
RFID	Radio frequency identification

ENDNOTES

1   Fifth Biennial Meeting of States to Consider the Implementation of the Programme of Action to Prevent, Combat and Eradicate the Illicit Trade in Small Arms and Light Weapons in All Its Aspects.

2   Programme of Action to Prevent, Combat and Eradicate the Illicit Trade in Small Arms and Light Weapons in All Its Aspects (UNGA, 2001b).

3   International Instrument to Enable States to Identify and Trace, in a Timely and Reliable Manner, Illicit Small Arms and Light Weapons (UNGA, 2005).

4   See UNGA (2001b, para. IV.1.b; 2012a, annexe I, para. III.1; 2012b, para. 5; 2013b, para. 5). For an overview of the UN small arms process up to the time of the PoA's Second Review Conference, see McDonald (2014).

5   See McDonald (2013).

6   See also McDonald (2012).

7   For more on the interplay of politics and substance (research) in the UN small arms process, see McDonald (2014).

8   Simpson took over as ITI moderator in May 2014, replacing Wolfgang Bindseil of Germany, who had begun the work but was unable to continue (Afghanistan, 2014c).

9   The dates for BMS5, 16–20 June 2014, were set by UN General Assembly Resolution 68/48 (UNGA, 2013b, para. 5).

10 In UN terminology, the phrase 'open-ended' means open to all states. This approach differs from that taken by other UN bodies with more restricted participation, such as groups of governmental experts.

11 See UNGA (2005, para. 37; 2012a, annexe I, para. III.3).

12 See Afghanistan (2013; 2014a); UNGA (2014b). Agreement on the agenda during the period of informal consultations was 'provisional', pending the formal adoption of the document at the beginning of BMS5. See Afghanistan (2013).

13 Ambassador Tanin based these draft versions of the BMS5 outcome on national statements made at the informal consultations, 'working papers', other written inputs countries submitted for BMS5, national reports, and past PoA meeting outcome documents. Afghanistan (2014b).

14 On all days of BMS5 except for the last, Ambassador Tanin convened informal consultations in the early morning and evening, and during the day after the completion of formal plenary discussions.

15 See IANSA (2014b, annexe 2); UNODA (n.d.a).

16 The statements are available from IANSA (2014b, annexe 4) and UNODA (n.d.b). See also Goldring (2014).

17 Specifically, Mack (2014).

18 See Lamb and Mack (2014).

19 Among the final sticking points was Egyptian opposition to an 'other issues' section that failed to mention ammunition or 'integrated border control management'—topics it wanted included in the section in order to indicate that, in its view, they were not within the scope of the PoA. See UNGA (2014f, para. 19); Egypt (2014). The 'other issues' section of the outcome document had been used at BMS3 and BMS4 as a dumping ground for subjects states could not agree to integrate into the agreed meeting text, including topics that clearly fell *within* the scope of the PoA but did not figure in the meeting agenda (UNGA, 2008a; 2010a). At BMS5, however, many states expressed reservations about the utility of the 'other issues' section and, as a result, it is much shorter than in the BMS3 and BMS4 outcomes.

20 See Endnote 19, above.

21 See UNGA (2008a, sec. III).

22 Earlier references to 'security sector reform' were dropped in favour of the less specific 'relevant national programmes'. Compare Afghanistan (2014d, paras. 4, 15) with UNGA (2014g, paras. 8, 17b).

23 The PoA has quite a lot to say about the application of stockpile management to DDR, however. See UNGA (2001b, sec. II, paras. 21, 29–30, 34).

24 See Afghanistan (2014d, paras. 1, 3–4); UNSC (2013, paras. 3, 5, 11, 15). Slightly stronger language can also be found in the BMS3 outcome; see UNGA (2008a, para. 27e). Although not mentioned in the BMS5 outcome, stockpile security is important in preventing the diversion of peace-keeper weapons to insurgents or other unauthorized users. See Berman and Racovita (2013).

25 Compare UNGA (2014g, paras. 14, 17g) with UNGA (2008a, paras. 17, 20–23, 27).

26 See Gobinet and Van Beneden (2012).

27 See UNGA (2008a, paras. 27c–d; 2014g, paras. 12, 17f).

28 Examples of qualifiers include 'voluntary application, in accordance with their national legislation' (UNGA, 2014g, para. 12); 'appropriate' (para. 17e); and 'as relevant' (para. 17f).

29 See Bastick and Valasek (2014).

30 Compare UNGA (2014g, paras. 10, 17d, 31) with UNGA (2012a, annexe I, paras. I.14, II.2.i). Value added in the BMS5 outcome includes the terms 'planning and implementation processes', added after 'policymaking', along with references to Security Council Resolution 1325 (UNSC, 2000) and General Assembly Resolution 65/69 (UNGA, 2010b), which supplement the more generic reference to 'relevant resolutions of the Security Council and the General Assembly', found in the Review Conference outcome (UNGA, 2012a, annexe I, para. II.2.i).

31 See UNGA (2008a, sec. III); Bevan, McDonald, and Parker (2009, pp. 136–43).

32 See UNGA (2001b, sec. II, paras. 17–19, 21, 29–30, 34; sec. III, paras. 6, 8, 14).

33 See Bevan, McDonald, and Parker (2009, p. 141).

34 See McDonald (2011, pp. 48–50).

35 See Bevan and McDonald (2012, pp. 4–5); McDonald (2013, p. 173); UNGA (2012a, annexe II, para. 2e).

36 See Bevan (2009, pp. 109–10); Bevan and McDonald (2012, table 1).

37 See UNGA (2012a, annexe II, para. 2e).

38 See UNSC (2013).

39 See UNGA (2012a, annexe II, para. 2d); McDonald (2013, p. 172).

40 See UNGA (2014g, paras. 18, 27a).

41 See UNGA (2014g, paras. 21, 25, 27c, 27g).

42 See UNGA (2014g, paras. 6, 11, 13, 17a, 18, 27a–c).

43 Regarding MGE1, see McDonald (2012, p. 4).

44 The UN General Assembly subsequently endorsed this recommendation (UNGA, 2014h, para. 6).

45 The UN General Assembly subsequently requested that the Secretary-General report further on the subject as part of his annual report on small arms (UNGA, 2014h, para. 22).

46 See UNGA (2005, para. 25).

47 See Bevan (2009, pp. 118–20); McDonald (2011, p. 49).

48 See UNGA (2005, para. 8b).

49 See UNGA (2014b, point 8).

50 In the BMS5 outcome's international cooperation and assistance section, see UNGA (2014g, para. 38b). In other sections of the document, see paragraphs 16, 17i–j, 27d, and 27i–k. With regard to BMS5 follow-up, see paragraphs 40c, 41, and 43.

51 In the BMS5 outcome's international cooperation and assistance section, see UNGA (2014g, paras. 38b–c, 38e, 38m, 38(n)(ii)). In other sections of the document, see paragraphs 16, 17d, 17g, 17j, and 27i–j. With regard to BMS5 follow-up, see paragraph 40c.

52 In the BMS5 outcome's international cooperation and assistance section, see UNGA (2014g, paras. 28, 38a, 38d, 38(n)(i)). In other sections of the document, see paragraphs 15, 17c, 17h, 20, 27d, and 27j. With regard to BMS5 follow-up, see paragraphs 40b–c.

53 This is reflected, for example, in the title of the section (UNGA, 2014g, sec. III).

54 With respect to the Second Review Conference, see McDonald (2013, p. 170).

55 See also paragraph 36 ('reliable and sustained assistance') (UNGA, 2014g).

56 See also UNGA (2014g, para. 38f).

57 The outcome of the Second Review Conference also addresses the problem, specifically from an armed conflict angle. See UNGA (2012a, annexe I, paras. I.14, II.2.j).

58 Note that paragraph 38k reprises, word for word, the provision on border controls agreed at the PoA's Second Review Conference (UNGA, 2012a, annexe I, para. II.3.e).

59 This theme figures, in a more general way, in the outcome of the Second Review Conference. See UNGA (2012a, annexe I, para. I.14, II.2.i).

60 See McDonald (2013, p. 170).

61 See also UNGA (2001b, sec. III, paras. 4, 6, 8, 10).

62 See NAM (2014, paras. 6, 8, 9b).

63 See Afghanistan (2014d, paras. 52, 61, 64).

64 Compare UNGA (2014g, sec. IV) with UNGA (2012a, annexe I, sec. III).

65 In addition to BMS5, the schedule includes MGE2 in 2015, BMS6 in 2016, and the Third Review Conference in 2018 (UNGA, 2012a, annexe I, paras. III.1–2; 2014g, para. 39).

66 See also UNGA (2012a, annexe I, para. III.5).

67 See also UNGA (2012a, annexe I, sec. III, paras. 6–7).

68 See also UNGA (2012a, annexe I, paras. I.15, II.4.e, II.5.a, III.8).

69 See also UNGA (2012a, annexe I, para. III.10).

70 See also UNGA (2012a, annexe I, para. III.9).

71 Concerning the lack of formal implementation monitoring for the PoA and ITI, see McDonald (2013, pp. 161–62, 173–74). Paragraph 49 of the BMS5 outcome also recommends the use of national reports 'to enhance the matching of assistance needs with available resources', a point first made in the BMS3 outcome and echoed, to some extent, in the outcome of the Second Review Conference. See UNGA (2008a, paras. 3, 7d, 7i, 27f; 2012a, annexe I, para. II.5.h, annexe II, para. 3h).

72 See UNGA (2012a, annexe I, para. III.3).

73 See also UNGA (2014g, para. 38e).

74 See IANSA (2014a; 2014b); Marsh (2014). A few articles, written in response to BMS5, were more critical in nature, although the criticism stemmed not from the BMS5 text, but rather from flaws that the authors saw in the PoA itself. See Ficaretta and Reeves (2014); Lamb and Mack (2014).

75 As noted earlier, this language is stronger than its Second Review Conference counterpart. See UNGA (2012a, annexe I, paras. I.14, II.2.i).

76 See UNGA (2012a, annexe II, para. 2e).

77 In addition to these explicit mentions of the Security Council, related Council work is referenced indirectly through, for example, language in the BMS5 outcome on DDR and conflict tracing (UNGA, 2014g, paras. 8, 17b, 21, 27f–g). The outcome of the Second Review Conference contains only one explicit mention of the Security Council (UNGA, 2012a, annexe I, para. II.2.i), those of BMS3 and BMS4 none (UNGA, 2008a; 2010a). Both the PoA and ITI, however, refer explicitly to the Security Council. See UNGA (2001b, paras. I.12, II.15, II.32, II.35; 2005, para. 6b).

78 See the section on international cooperation and assistance, above. Regarding follow-up in this area, see UNGA (2014g, paras. 27i, 38m, 38(n)(i), 40c).

79 The UN General Assembly subsequently confirmed this mandate in its general resolution on small arms (UNGA, 2014h, para. 6).

80 References to 'accidents' and 'accidental explosions at depots' (UNGA, 2014g, paras. 6, 11), as well as to 'ballistics information' (paras. 26, 27k), are indirect references to ammunition. For more on these issues, see Small Arms Survey (2014); INTERPOL (n.d.). The International Ammunition Technical Guidelines were developed by the UN Office for Disarmament Affairs pursuant to a UN General Assembly mandate, but their place in the UN small arms (PoA) process is disputed. See UNODA (2011); McDonald (2014, p. 160).

81 Because of the opposition of some states, references to Security Council embargoes and to its Resolution 2117 (2013) on small arms were expunged from the final BMS5 text. See Afghanistan (2014d, paras. 1, 4, 6, 44, 72–73).

82 The relationship is mentioned only in the 'other issues' section of the BMS5 outcome, which is not part of the agreed outcome (UNGA, 2014g, para. 51d). Some of the states that had taken a sceptical view of the ATT during the negotiations on the instrument, in 2012–13, opposed any mention of the Treaty in the BMS5 text. For more on the ATT's relationship to the PoA and ITI, see Parker (2014, pp. 71–72).

83 See Endnote 22, above.

84 Although several ISACS modules address BMS5 themes, including stockpile management and weapons marking, record-keeping, and tracing, some states opposed any reference to ISACS in the BMS5 outcome. The ISACS were developed by UN agencies participating in the United Nations Coordinating Action on Small Arms mechanism. See UNCASA (n.d.).

85 See Mack (2014).

86 See New Zealand (2011, sec. II); McDonald (2012, p. 4).

87 The report also reviews the implications of the new developments for international assistance, another topic likely to feature at MGE2.

88 This section is based on Persi Paoli (2015b).

89 See UNGA (2005, para. 10).

90   See Persi Paoli (2015b, pp. 36–41).

91   This section is based on Persi Paoli (2015a).

92   See McDonald (2012, p. 4).

93   See Persi Paoli (2010).

94   See Persi Paoli (2015a, pp. 19–20).

95   This section is based on Jenzen-Jones (2015).

96   See Jenzen-Jones (2015, pp. 52–53).

97   See Jenzen-Jones (2015, pp. 50–52).

98   See Jenzen-Jones (2015, pp. 62–65).

99   See Jenzen-Jones (2015, pp. 62–65).

100   This section is based on Schroeder (2015).

101   See Schroeder (2015, pp. 76–79).

102   See Schroeder (2015, pp. 81–82).

103   See Schroeder (2015, pp. 84–88).

104   The ITI, for example, specifies that 'all marks required under this instrument are on an exposed surface, conspicuous without technical aids or tools, easily recognizable, readable, durable and, as far as technically possible, recoverable' (UNGA, 2005, para. 7). Among others discussed in this section, RFID technology would run afoul of several of these requirements.

105   Concerning the lack of formal implementation monitoring for the PoA and ITI, see McDonald (2013, pp. 161–62, 173–74).

106   The most egregious example is the Conference on Disarmament, unable to achieve any substantive progress since 1996. See, for example, RCW (n.d.).

107   Note that the final product of MGE1, while substantive, was not agreed by meeting participants. The MGE1 chair produced a summary that distils key points from the discussions. See New Zealand (2011).

108   With respect to conflict tracing, see Bevan and McDonald (2012).

109   See McDonald (2012).

110   The author served as an adviser to the BMS5 chair, Ambassador Zahir Tanin. The views expressed in this chapter are the author's and should not be attributed to Ambassador Tanin or the Government of Afghanistan.

BIBLIOGRAPHY

Afghanistan. 2013. Letter dated 20 December from Zahir Tanin, Permanent Representative of Afghanistan to the United Nations.
    <http://www.un-arm.org/BMS5/>

—. 2014a. Letter dated 16 January from Zahir Tanin, Permanent Representative of Afghanistan to the United Nations.
    <http://www.un-arm.org/BMS5/>

—. 2014b. Letter dated 5 March from Zahir Tanin, Permanent Representative of Afghanistan to the United Nations.
    <http://www.un-arm.org/BMS5/>

—. 2014c. Letter dated 7 May from Zahir Tanin, Permanent Representative of Afghanistan to the United Nations.
    <http://www.un-arm.org/BMS5/>

—. 2014d. 'BMS5 Outcome.' Draft 4. Annexed to letter dated 11 June from Zahir Tanin, Permanent Representative of Afghanistan to the United Nations.
    <http://www.un-arm.org/BMS5/>

—. 2014e. 'BMS5 Outcome.' Draft 5. 19 June.

Bastick, Megan and Kristin Valasek. 2014. 'Converging Agendas: Women, Peace, Security, and Small Arms.' In Small Arms Survey. *Small Arms Survey 2014: Women and Guns*. Cambridge: Cambridge University Press, pp. 34–63.
    <http://www.smallarmssurvey.org/publications/by-type/yearbook/small-arms-survey-2014.html>

Berman, Eric G. and Mihaela Racovita. 2013. *Diversion of Weapons within Peace Operations: Understanding the Phenomenon*. GCSP Policy Paper 2013/8. Geneva: Geneva Centre for Security Policy. 9 December. <http://www.gcsp.ch/Regional-Development/Publications/GCSP-Publications/Policy-Papers/Diversion-of-Weapons-within-Peace-Operations-Understanding-the-Phenomenon>

Bevan, James. 2009. 'Revealing Provenance: Weapons Tracing During and After Conflict.' In Small Arms Survey. *Small Arms Survey 2009: Shadows of War*. Cambridge: Cambridge University Press, pp. 106–33. <http://www.smallarmssurvey.org/publications/by-type/yearbook/small-arms-survey-2009.html>

— and Glenn McDonald. 2012. *Weapons Tracing and Peace Support Operations: Theory or Practice?* Issue Brief No. 4. Geneva: Small Arms Survey. March. <http://www.smallarmssurvey.org/publications/by-type/issue-briefs.html#c2918>

— , Glenn McDonald, and Sarah Parker. 2009. 'Two Steps Forward: UN Measures Update.' In Small Arms Survey. *Small Arms Survey 2009: Shadows of War*. Cambridge: Cambridge University Press, pp. 134–57.

<http://www.smallarmssurvey.org/publications/by-type/yearbook/small-arms-survey-2009.html>

Čekuolis, Dalius. 2008. 'Tackling the Illicit Small Arms Trade: The Chairman Speaks.' *Arms Control Today*, Vol. 38, No. 8. October, pp. 19–24.

<http://www.armscontrol.org/act/2008_10/Cekuolis>

Egypt. 2014. Note verbale dated 30 June 2014 from the Permanent Mission of Egypt to the United Nations addressed to the Secretariat. A/CONF.192/BMS/2014/3 of 30 June. <http://www.un-arm.org/BMS5/documents/>

Ficaretta, Teresa and Johanna Reeves. 2014. 'The UN Programme of Action and Arms Trade Treaty: Why They Matter to the U.S. Arms Industry.' 20 June. Washington, DC: F.A.I.R. Trade Group. <http://fairtradegroup.org/wp/?p=1>

Gobinet, Pierre and Tom Van Beneden. 2012. *Buy and Burn: Factoring Demilitarization into Ammunition Procurement*. Issue Brief No. 2. Geneva: Small Arms Survey. April. <http://www.smallarmssurvey.org/publications/by-type/issue-briefs.html#c2919>

Goldring, Natalie. 2014. 'On Day 4, the Technical Gives Way to the Personal.' *Small Arms Monitor*, Vol. 6, No. 5. 20 June.

<http://www.reachingcriticalwill.org/disarmament-fora/salw/2014/sam/8969-20-june-2014-vol-6-no-5>

IANSA (International Action Network on Small Arms). 2014a. *Women Win in UN Negotiations on Guns*. 20 June.

<http://www.iansa-women.org/node/851>

—. 2014b. *The Fifth Biennial Meeting of States on Small Arms (BMS5): IANSA Report*. <http://iansa.org/resource/2014/11/iansa-report-on-bms5>

INTERPOL (International Criminal Police Organization). n.d. 'INTERPOL Ballistic Information Network (IBIN).'

<http://www.interpol.int/Crime-areas/Firearms/INTERPOL-Ballistic-Information-Network-IBIN>

Jenzen-Jones, N.R. 2015. 'Small Arms and Additive Manufacturing: An Assessment of 3D-printed Firearms, Components, and Accessories.' In King and McDonald, pp. 43–74.

King, Benjamin and Glenn McDonald, eds. 2015. *Behind the Curve: New Technologies, New Control Challenges*. Occasional Paper No. 32. Geneva: Small Arms Survey. February.

Lamb, Guy and Daniel Mack. 2014. 'Firing Blanks: The Growing Irrelevance of the UN Small Arms Process.' *Global Observatory*. 21 August.

<http://theglobalobservatory.org/analysis/806-firing-blanks-growing-irrelevance-un-small-arms-process.html>

Mack, Daniel. 2014. *An Assessment of the PoA (Or, Why We Are Not in New York)*. Instituto Sou da Paz, Reaching Critical Will, and Women's International League for Peace and Freedom. June.

<http://www.reachingcriticalwill.org/resources/publications-and-research/publications/8909-an-assessment-of-the-poa>

Marsh, Nicholas. 2014. 'What Has BMS5 Done for Us?' *Small Arms Monitor*, Vol. 6, No. 6.

<http://www.reachingcriticalwill.org/disarmament-fora/salw/2014/sam/8979-final-edition-vol-6-no-6>

McDonald, Glenn. 2011. *Fact or Fiction? The UN Small Arms Process*. In Small Arms Survey. *Small Arms Survey 2011: States of Security*. Cambridge: Cambridge University Press, pp. 42–67. <http://www.smallarmssurvey.org/publications/by-type/yearbook/small-arms-survey-2011.html>

—. 2012. *Precedent in the Making: The UN Meeting of Governmental Experts*. Issue Brief No. 5. Geneva: Small Arms Survey. March.

<http://www.smallarmssurvey.org/fileadmin/docs/G-Issue-briefs/SAS-IB5-Precedent-in-the-making.pdf>

—. 2013. 'Second Wind: The PoA's 2012 Review Conference.' In Small Arms Survey. *Small Arms Survey 2013: Everyday Dangers*. Cambridge: Cambridge University Press, pp. 160–177. <http://www.smallarmssurvey.org/publications/by-type/yearbook/small-arms-survey-2013.html>

—. 2014. 'Measures: Informing Diplomacy—The Role of Research in the UN Small Arms Process.' In Peter Batchelor and Kai Kenkel, eds. *Controlling Small Arms: Consolidation, Innovation and Relevance in Research and Policy*. Oxford and New York: Routledge, pp. 150–71.

NAM (Non-Aligned Movement Working Group on Disarmament). 2014. *Full and Effective Implementation of the Programme of Action to Prevent, Combat and Eradicate the Illicit Trade in Small Arms and Light Weapons in All Its Aspects: Enhancing International Cooperation and Assistance— Working Paper submitted by Indonesia on behalf of the Non-Aligned Movement*. 4 March. <http://www.un-arm.org/BMS5/documents/>

New Zealand. 2011. *Summary by the Chair of Discussions at the Open-ended Meeting of Governmental Experts on the Implementation of the Programme of Action to Prevent, Combat and Eradicate the Illicit Trade in Small Arms and Light Weapons in All Its Aspects, 9 to 13 May 2011, New York*. A/66/157 of 19 July (annexe). <http://www.poa-iss.org/mge/Documents/MGE-ChairLetter/A-66-157-MGE-E.pdf>

Parker, Sarah. *2014. A Diplomat's Guide to the UN Small Arms Process: 2014 Update*. June.

<http://www.smallarmssurvey.org/publications/by-type/handbooks/a-diplomats-guide-to-the-un-small-arms-process.html>

Persi Paoli, Giacomo. 2010. *The Method behind the Mark: A Review of Firearm Marking Technologies*. Small Arms Survey Issue Brief No. 1. December. Geneva: Small Arms Survey. <http://www.smallarmssurvey.org/publications/by-type/issue-briefs.html>

—. 2015a. 'Techno-polymers in Firearms Manufacturing: Challenges and Implications for Marking, Record-keeping, and Tracing.' In King and McDonald, pp. 5–22.

—. 2015b. 'From Firearms to Weapon Systems: Challenges and Implications of Modular Design for Marking, Record-keeping, and Tracing.' In King and McDonald, pp. 23–42.

RCW (Reaching Critical Will). n.d. 'Conference on Disarmament.' Accessed 16 January 2015. <http://www.reachingcriticalwill.org/disarmament-fora/cd>

Schroeder, Matt. 2015. 'New Technologies and Small Arms Control: Preventing Unauthorized Acquisition and Use.' In King and McDonald, pp. 75–93.

Small Arms Survey. 2014. 'Unplanned Explosions at Munitions Sites.' Updated 16 June.
<http://www.smallarmssurvey.org/de/weapons-and-markets/stockpiles/unplanned-explosions-at-munitions-sites.html>

UNCASA (United Nations Coordinating Action on Small Arms). 2012. 'International Small Arms Control Standard: Marking and Recordkeeping.' ISACS 05.30. Version 1.0. 27 August. <http://www.smallarmsstandards.org/isacs/>

—. n.d. 'International Small Arms Control Standards.' <http://www.smallarmsstandards.org/>

UNGA (United Nations General Assembly). 2001a. Protocol against the Illicit Manufacturing of and Trafficking in Firearms, Their Parts and Components and Ammunition, Supplementing the United Nations Convention against Transnational Organized Crime ('UN Firearms Protocol'). Adopted 31 May. In force 3 July 2005. A/RES/55/255 of 8 June. <http://www.unodc.org/pdf/crime/a_res_55/255e.pdf>

—. 2001b. Programme of Action to Prevent, Combat and Eradicate the Illicit Trade in Small Arms and Light Weapons in All Its Aspects ('Programme of Action/PoA'). Adopted 21 July. A/CONF.192/15 of 20 July. <http://www.poa-iss.org/PoA/PoA.aspx>

—. 2005. International Instrument to Enable States to Identify and Trace, in a Timely and Reliable Manner, Illicit Small Arms and Light Weapons ('International Tracing Instrument/ITI'). Adopted 8 December. A/60/88 of 27 June (Annexe).
<http://www.poa-iss.org/InternationalTracing/InternationalTracing.aspx>

—. 2008a. Outcome of the Third Biennial Meeting of States to Consider the Implementation of the Programme of Action to Prevent, Combat and Eradicate the Illicit Trade in Small Arms and Light Weapons in All Its Aspects. Adopted 18 July. A/CONF.192/BMS/2008/3 of 20 August (s. IV).
<http://www.poa-iss.org/DocsUpcomingEvents/ENN0846796.pdf>

—. 2008b. Resolution 63/72, adopted 2 December. A/RES/63/72 of 12 January 2009.
<http://www.un.org/ga/search/view_doc.asp?symbol=A/RES/63/72&Lang=E>

—. 2010a. Outcome of the Fourth Biennial Meeting of States to Consider the Implementation of the Programme of Action to Prevent, Combat and Eradicate the Illicit Trade in Small Arms and Light Weapons in All Its Aspects. Adopted 18 June. A/CONF.192/BMS/2010/3 of 30 June (s. V).
<http://www.poa-iss.org/BMS4/Outcome/BMS4-Outcome-E.pdf>

—. 2010b. Resolution 65/69, adopted 8 December. A/RES/65/69 of 13 January 2011.
<http://www.un.org/ga/search/view_doc.asp?symbol=A/RES/65/69>

—. 2012a. *Report of the United Nations Conference to Review Progress Made in the Implementation of the Programme of Action to Prevent, Combat and Eradicate the Illicit Trade in Small Arms and Light Weapons in All Its Aspects.* A/CONF.192/2012/RC/4 of 18 September.
<http://www.poa-iss.org/RevCon2/Documents/RevCon-DOC/Outcome/PoA-RevCon2-Outcome-E.pdf>

—. 2012b. Resolution 67/58, adopted 3 December. A/RES/67/58 of 4 January 2013.
<http://www.un.org/ga/search/view_doc.asp?symbol=A/RES/67/58>

—. 2013a. Arms Trade Treaty. 'Certified True Copy (XXVI-8).' Adopted 2 April. In force 24 December 2014.
<https://treaties.un.org/Pages/ViewDetails.aspx?src=TREATY&mtdsg_no=XXVI-8&chapter=26&lang=en>

—. 2013b. Resolution 68/48, adopted 5 December. A/RES/68/48 of 10 December. <http://www.un.org/ga/search/view_doc.asp?symbol=A/RES/68/48>

—. 2014a. *Recent Developments in Small Arms and Light Weapons Manufacturing, Technology and Design and Implications for the Implementation of the International Instrument to Enable States to Identify and Trace, in a Timely and Reliable Manner, Illicit Small Arms and Light Weapons: Report of the Secretary-General.* A/CONF.192/BMS/2014/1 of 6 May. <http://www.un-arm.org/BMS5/>

—. 2014b. 'Provisional Agenda.' A/CONF.192/BMS/2014/L.1 of 16 May. <http://www.un-arm.org/BMS5/>

—. 2014c. 'Provisional Programme of Work.' A/CONF.192/BMS/2014/L.2 of 2 June. <http://www.un-arm.org/BMS5/>

—. 2014d. *Draft Outcome Document.* A/CONF.192/BMS/2014/WP.1 of 12 June.
<http://papersmart.unmeetings.org/en/secretariat/unoda/poa-iss/bms5/documents/>

—. 2014e. Outcome of the Fifth Biennial Meeting of States to Consider the Implementation of the Programme of Action to Prevent, Combat and Eradicate the Illicit Trade in Small Arms and Light Weapons in All Its Aspects [draft outcome document]. A/CONF.192/BMS/2014/WP.1/Rev.1 of 20 June.

—. 2014f. *Report of the Fifth Biennial Meeting of States to Consider the Implementation of the Programme of Action to Prevent, Combat and Eradicate the Illicit Trade in Small Arms and Light Weapons in All Its Aspects.* Adopted 20 June. A/CONF.192/BMS/2014/2 of 26 June.
<http://www.un-arm.org/BMS5/>

—. 2014g. Outcome of the Fifth Biennial Meeting of States to Consider the Implementation of the Programme of Action to Prevent, Combat and Eradicate the Illicit Trade in Small Arms and Light Weapons in All Its Aspects. Adopted 20 June. A/CONF.192/BMS/2014/2 of 26 June (annexe). <http://www.un-arm.org/BMS5/>

—. 2014h. Resolution 69/51, adopted 2 December. A/RES/69/51 of 11 December. <http://www.un.org/en/ga/search/view_doc.asp?symbol=A/RES/69/51>

UNODA (United Nations Office for Disarmament Affairs). 2011. 'International Ammunition Technical Guidelines.' <http://www.un.org/disarmament/convarms/Ammunition/IATG/>

—. n.d.a. 'Fifth Biennial Meeting of States 2014: Side Events.' <http://www.un-arm.org/BMS5/sideevents/>

—. n.d.b. 'BMS5: Fifth Biennial Meeting of States to Consider the Implementation of the Programme of Action on Small Arms—Statements: 19 June.' <http://papersmart.unmeetings.org/en/secretariat/unoda/poa-iss/bms5/statements/>

UNSC (United Nations Security Council). 2000. Resolution 1325 (2000), adopted 31 October. S/RES/1325 (2000) of 31 October. <http://www.un.org/en/sc/documents/resolutions/2000.shtml>

—. 2013. Resolution 2117 (2013), adopted 26 September. S/RES/2117 (2013) of 26 September. <http://www.un.org/en/sc/documents/resolutions/2013.shtml>

ACKNOWLEDGEMENTS

Principal author

Glenn McDonald[110]

Contributors

N.R. Jenzen-Jones, Giacomo Persi Paoli, Matt Schroeder

An abandoned crate of rocket-propelled grenades lies in the desert near Col. Muammar Qaddafi's hometown of Sirte, Libya, September 2011. © John Cantlie/Getty Images

Trade Update

AFTER THE 'ARAB SPRING'

4

INTRODUCTION

On 19 October 2014, US Air Force C-130 transport aircraft dropped 28 bundles of small arms and ammunition for Kurdish forces defending the Syrian city of Kobani from attack by the non-state armed group Islamic State (IS) (US, 2014a). IS claimed to have picked up at least one of the bundles and showed the seized shipment in a video posted on YouTube two days later (Rogin, 2014). The Pentagon confirmed that IS had intercepted one of the bundles (Simeone, 2014). This is not an isolated example of a state with robust transfer controls authorizing a risky delivery of small arms and ammunition to a non-state armed group in a volatile region of the world. This chapter explores such decisions—and their consequences—in relation to the Middle East and North Africa (MENA), a region with high levels of armed violence and political instability.

The key findings of the chapter include the following:

- In 2012, the top exporters of small arms and light weapons (those with annual exports of at least USD 100 million), according to available customs data from the United Nations Commodity Trade Statistics Database (UN Comtrade), were (in descending order) the United States, Italy, Germany, Brazil, Austria, South Korea, the Russian Federation, China, Belgium, the Czech Republic, Turkey, Norway, and Japan.

- In 2012, the top importers of small arms and light weapons (those with annual imports of at least USD 100 million), according to available customs data, were (in descending order) the United States, Canada, Germany, Australia, France, the United Kingdom, Thailand, and Indonesia.

- The five largest exporters of small arms during 2001–12, according to available customs data, were (in descending order) the United States, Italy, Germany, Brazil, and Austria. The United States was also, according to available customs data, the world's largest importer of small arms during 2001–12. The next four largest small arms importers during this period were Canada, Germany, France, and the UK.

- There is little evidence that the 'Arab Spring' has had a significant impact on the policies of top or major exporters of small arms to the Middle East and North Africa. Considerations that presumably include regional and national security concerns are exerting a strong influence on arms export decision-making, effectively outweighing the risk of misuse or diversion in the eyes of these exporters.

- Small arms exporters have also authorized exports of small arms to non-state armed groups that are inclined to fight extremist groups, again notwithstanding the risk of misuse or diversion in these cases.

- Regional intergovernmental information exchanges on small arms transfers are not contributing to public transparency, yet regional reporting instruments that cover broader categories of conventional arms are releasing annual reports to the public.

The chapter consists of three distinct sections. The first analyses multi-year trends in the authorized small arms trade, focusing on the most significant exporters and importers. The second section examines small arms flows to Egypt, Libya, and Syria, both before and after the 'Arab Spring', with a view to identifying any changes in the export policies of top and major exporters. This section includes a brief overview of small arms supplies pledged or delivered to the Kurdish *peshmerga* (militia) in August–September 2014. The third and final section assesses the contribution made by regional reporting instruments to increased transparency in small arms transfers.

AUTHORIZED SMALL ARMS TRANSFERS

Like previous editions of the *Survey*, this one provides information on authorized small arms transfers. This section presents the top and major exporters and importers of small arms in 2012, according to UN Comtrade,[1] and maps changes in values transferred by top exporters and importers between 2001 and 2012.

Top and major exporters and importers in 2012

In 2012, the top exporters of small arms—having transferred at least USD 100 million that year—were, in descending order, the United States, Italy, Germany, Brazil, Austria, South Korea, the Russian Federation, China, Belgium, the Czech Republic, Turkey, Norway, and Japan (see Table 4.1). There were 13 top exporters in 2012, down from 14 in 2011. The new top exporters in 2012 were Japan (whose exports increased from USD 97 million to USD 106 million) and Norway (USD 81 million to USD 129 million). Israel, Spain, and Switzerland left the group of top exporters in 2012, with exports dropping down to the USD 50–99 million range, while Italy joined the United States in reporting more than USD 500 million worth of exports annually.

The number of top and major exporters—with at least USD 10 million in annual exports—was 38 in 2012, one less than in 2011, but the total value of this group's reported exports increased by USD 340 million

Russian president Vladimir Putin visits a small arms factory in Izhevsk, Russian Federation, September 2013. © Michael Klimentyev/AFP Photo/RIA Novosti

compared to the previous year.[2] The new major exporter in 2012 was Bulgaria (with exports growing from USD 7 million in 2011 to USD 20 million in 2012), while Pakistan and Hong Kong left the rank of major exporters in that year. Overall, the United States remains the largest exporter of small arms, with at least USD 935 million worth exported in 2012, around USD 19 million more than in 2011.

In 2012, the top importers—importing at least USD 100 million of small arms annually—were, in descending order, the United States, Canada, Germany, Australia, France, the United Kingdom, Thailand, and Indonesia (see Table 4.2). While the number of top importers (eight) did not change between 2011 and 2012, Italy left the group as it imported only USD 57 million worth of small arms in 2012 (compared to USD 108 million in 2011) and Indonesia joined the group for the first time since 2001, as it imported USD 111 million in 2012 (up from 32 million in 2011).

As was the case for exporters, the total number of top and major importers decreased, from 64 in 2011 to 56 in 2012, but the total value of their reported imports increased—by USD 341 million.[3] Cambodia, China, Côte d'Ivoire, the Dominican Republic, Honduras, Hungary, Kenya, Luxembourg, Morocco, Sudan, and Venezuela left the rank of top and major importers in 2012. Meanwhile, Egypt (increasing its reported imports from USD 9 million in 2011 to USD 25 million in 2012), Kazakhstan (up from USD 8 million to USD 14 million), and Paraguay (up from USD 8 million to USD 11 million in 2012) joined this group in 2012.

Table 4.1 presents the top and major exporters, by both reported export value and Small Arms Trade Transparency Barometer 2014 score. The latter measure provides some, admittedly imperfect,[4] indication of the likely reliability of estimates of small arms exports for particular countries, since higher Barometer scores reflect a greater availability and specificity of information provided by states on their exports. For example, the estimated value of exports for a tier 2 exporter (with exports of USD 100–499 million in 2012) whose name is highlighted in black (level 1 transparency) is probably more reliable than that of an exporter in the same tier whose name is highlighted in red (level 3 transparency). A general rule of thumb is that if an exporter has a low Barometer score (level 3 or 4), there is a strong possibility that the reported value of its exports is an underestimate.

Table 4.1	**Exporters of small arms based on UN Comtrade, 2012, with transparency indicators**		
Category		**Value (USD)**	**Exporters (listed in descending order of value exported)**
Top exporters by value	Tier 1	≥500 million	2: United States, Italy
	Tier 2	100-499 million	11: Germany, Brazil, Austria, South Korea, Russian Federation, China, Belgium, Czech Republic, Turkey, Norway, Japan
Major exporters by value	Tier 3	50-99 million	10: United Kingdom, Spain, Israel, Croatia, Finland, Canada, Switzerland, Mexico, France, Serbia
	Tier 4	10-49 million	15: Sweden, India, Philippines, Singapore, Portugal, Hungary, Bulgaria, Argentina, Taiwan,[5] Cyprus, Romania, Australia, Ukraine, Denmark, Poland

Transparency indicators (followed by Small Arms Trade Transparency Barometer 2014 scores):

Level 1 (18.75-25.00); Level 2 (12.5-18.5); Level 3 (6.25-12.25); Level 4 (0.00-6.00)

Table 4.2	**Importers of small arms based on UN Comtrade, 2012**		
Category		**Value (USD)**	**Importers (listed in descending order of value imported)**
Top importers by value	Tier 1	≥500 million	1: United States
	Tier 2	100-499 million	7: Canada, Germany, Australia, France, United Kingdom, Thailand, Indonesia
Major importers by value	Tier 3	50-99 million	16: Russian Federation, Mexico, Belgium, Chile, United Arab Emirates, Norway, Philippines, Italy, Saudi Arabia, Estonia, Malaysia, Austria, Israel, Denmark, Turkey, South Korea
	Tier 4	10-49 million	32: Switzerland, Sweden, Spain, Poland, Netherlands, Colombia, Jordan, Lebanon, New Zealand, Singapore, South Africa, Japan, Portugal, Finland, Egypt, Czech Republic, Afghanistan, Slovakia, Pakistan, Iraq, Ukraine, India, Kuwait, Argentina, Kazakhstan, Brazil, Greece, Peru, Oman, Bulgaria, Paraguay, Cyprus

Global trends, 2001–12

The *Small Arms Survey 2014* notes that, according to UN Comtrade, the global value of the small arms trade almost doubled between 2001 and 2011 (Holtom, Pavesi, and Rigual, 2014, p. 113). The value has continued to increase, with the reported global trade reaching its highest value since 2001: USD 5.057 billion worth of small arms were reportedly transferred in 2012. Ammunition still represented the largest category exported from 2001 to 2012, while exports of pistols and revolvers saw the largest value increase from 2011 to 2012 (increasing by USD 169 million) (Holtom, Pavesi, and Rigual, 2014, p. 114; NISAT, n.d; UN Comtrade, n.d.).

Figure 4.1 illustrates changes in the values exported by the eight largest exporters of small arms during the period 2001–12, highlighting the clear domination of the United States in this market. US exports of small arms reached a value of USD 8.464 billion over the period, with a systematic increase since 2010. The next four largest exporters of small arms for the period 2001–12 were Italy (which exported small arms worth USD 5.7 billion), Germany (USD 4.420 billion), Brazil (USD 2.835 billion), and Austria (2.049 billion), according to UN Comtrade (see Table 4.3 on p. 90). The five largest exporters—the United States, Italy, Germany, Brazil, and Austria—accounted for 53 per cent of the reported value of small arms exports between 2001 and 2012. The top and major exporters that have experienced the largest increase in their small arms exports between 2001 and 2012 were, in descending order, China (with an increase of 1,456 per cent), Norway (777 per cent), South Korea (636 per cent), Turkey (467 per cent), and Brazil (295 per cent)

Figure 4.1   **Changes in export values for the eight largest exporters of small arms, based on UN Comtrade (USD million), 2001-12***

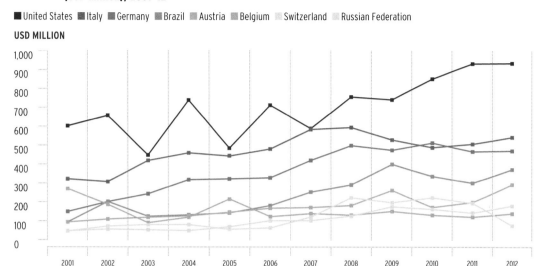

Notes: * All values are expressed in constant 2012 US dollars; all figures have been rounded to the nearest million.

Sources: NISAT (n.d.); UN Comtrade (n.d.)

(see Table 4.3).[6] None of the largest exporters experienced a decrease in their reported exports between 2001 and 2012, except for Belgium (-48 per cent).

Figure 4.2 underlines the United States' unrivalled position as the world's largest importer of small arms as reported to UN Comtrade data.[7] Between 2001 and 2012, the country imported USD 13.884 billion worth of small arms, accounting

Figure 4.2   **Changes in import values for the eight largest importers of small arms, based on UN Comtrade (USD million), 2001-12***

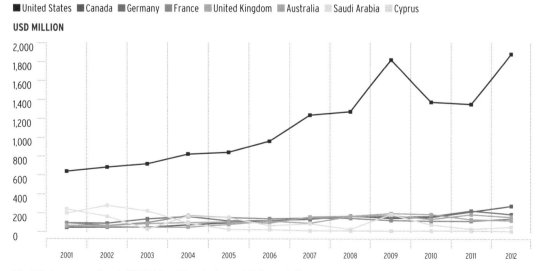

Notes: * All values are expressed in constant 2012 US dollars; all figures have been rounded to the nearest million.

Sources: NISAT (n.d.); UN Comtrade (n.d.)

Table 4.3 Trends in small arms exports per top exporter and for all exporters, as reported to UN Comtrade, 2001-12*

Exporter	Total value exported, 2001-12 (USD million)	2001 value (USD million)	2012 value (USD million)	Absolute change, 2001-12 (USD million)	% change 2001-12
United States	**8,464**	603	935	332	55%
Italy	**5,700**	323	544	221	68%
Germany	**4,420**	150	472	322	214%
Brazil	**2,835**	95	374	280	**295%**
Austria	**2,049**	95	293	198	210%
Belgium	1,822	271	140	-132	-48%
Switzerland	1,440	48	76	28	60%
Russian Federation	1,269	49	181	132	273%
Japan	1,261	77	106	29	38%
South Korea	1,143	37	275	237	**636%**
Spain	1,049	75	89	14	19%
Canada	1,040	64	83	19	29%
Czech Republic	1,025	64	136	72	113%
Turkey	994	23	132	109	**467%**
Israel	961	25	89	64	256%
United Kingdom	949	61	90	29	48%
China	777	10	150	140	**1,456%**
France	731	39	53	14	36%
Norway	716	15	129	114	777%
Sweden	537	23	48	25	112%
All exporters	44,582	2,426	5,057	2,631	108%

Notes: * All values are expressed in constant 2012 US dollars; all figures have been rounded to the nearest million. Each exporter in this table has been ranked as a top exporter (exporting USD 100 million or more annually) for at least one year between 2001 and 2012. Values in bold are the five largest totals and five greatest changes in relevant columns.

Sources: NISAT (n.d.); UN Comtrade (n.d.)

for 30 per cent of reported global small arms imports. After a significant decrease in 2010 and 2011, US imports reached their peak since 2001, with USD 1.907 billion worth of reported small arms imports in 2012.

The next four largest importers during 2001–12 were, in descending order, Canada (with imports totalling USD 1.788 billion), Germany (USD 1.771 billion), France (USD 1.496 billion), and the UK (USD 1.494 billion) (see Table 4.4). The top importers that experienced the largest increase in their small arms imports between 2001 and 2012 were, in descending order, Indonesia (an increase of 8,602 per cent), Pakistan (3,789 per cent), Thailand (558 per cent),

Table 4.4 **Trends in small arms imports per top importer and for all importers, as reported to UN Comtrade, 2001–12***					
Importer	Total value imported, 2001–12 (USD million)	2001 value (USD million)	2012 value (USD million)	Absolute change, 2001–12 (USD million)	% change 2001–12
United States	**13,884**	662	1,907	1,245	188%
Canada	**1,788**	69	296	228	**332%**
Germany	**1,771**	97	188	92	95%
France	**1,496**	64	143	79	125%
United Kingdom	**1,494**	71	121	50	70%
Australia	1,341	62	163	101	162%
Saudi Arabia	1,290	244	54	-190	-78%
Cyprus	928	200	10	-190	-95%
South Korea	894	130	51	-79	-61%
Spain	872	36	44	8	21%
Italy	831	84	57	-26	-31%
Thailand	683	18	116	98	**558%**
Japan	679	38	27	-11	-30%
Egypt	373	7	25	18	**267%**
Indonesia	351	1	111	110	**8,602%**
Pakistan	336	1	21	20	**3,789%**
All importers	45,552	2,624	5,087	2,463	94%

Notes: * All values are expressed in constant 2012 US dollars; all figures have been rounded to the nearest million. Each importer in this table has been ranked as a top importer (importing USD 100 million or more annually) for at least one year between 2001 and 2012. Values in bold are the five largest totals and five greatest changes in each column.

Sources: NISAT (n.d.); UN Comtrade (n.d.)

Canada (332 per cent), and Egypt (267 per cent) (see Table 4.4). For the years 2001–12, nine states were both top exporters and importers: Canada, France, Germany, Italy, Japan, South Korea, Spain, the UK, and the United States.

During 2001–12, the six main importers of US exports were Canada (which imported USD 1.252 billion worth of materiel), South Korea (USD 669 million), Australia (USD 639 million), Japan (USD 444 million), Israel (USD 407 million), and Egypt (USD 311 million). Australia, Canada, Israel, Japan, and South Korea were regularly[8] among the annual top five importers of US small arms during 2001–12; Colombia, Egypt, and Saudi Arabia also figured in the top five on occasion.[9]

In addition to the small arms transfer trends noted in previous editions of the *Survey*—such as the steady global increase in the value of transfers, and the US domination of the trade—emerging trends involve new actors that are increasingly shaping the global market, such as China, whose small arms exports are steadily growing, and Indonesia, a new top importer. As the next section—but also the above figures concerning Egypt—reveal, the recent upheavals in the Arab world do not appear to have disrupted the international flow of small arms to that region.

AUTHORIZED SMALL ARMS TRANSFERS TO THE MIDDLE EAST AND NORTH AFRICA, 2001-14

Parts of the Middle East and North Africa suffer from very high levels of armed violence, armed conflict, and political instability.[10] Between 2007 and 2012, conflict-related deaths were recorded in almost one out of two countries or territories in the region: Algeria, Egypt, Iran, Iraq, Lebanon, Libya, the Palestinian Territories, Syria, and Yemen (Geneva Declaration Secretariat, 2014). These nine countries and territories also rank among the 25 countries and territories with the lowest scores for 'political stability and absence of violence' in 2012, according to the World Bank's worldwide governance indicators (World Bank, n.d.). The risk of small arms diversion to non-state armed groups in these states is also considered high.[11] These factors help to explain why governments in the region seek to import small arms—for example, to bolster weak or recently re-established national security forces that are fighting well-equipped non-state armed groups. The 'Arab Spring' heightened many of the concerns cited above, with parliamentarians and civil society organizations questioning earlier decisions to arm seemingly stable governments that had reputations for serious violations of human rights or that were accused of supporting terrorist organizations.[12]

This section examines the effect of increased armed violence and political instability in Egypt, Libya, and Syria on the policies of significant small arms exporters to the region by comparing the small arms flows of two periods: 2001–10 and 2011–13 (see Boxes 4.1 and 4.2).[13] These three countries have been chosen for two reasons. First, the World Bank's worldwide governance indicators for 'political stability and absence of violence' for Egypt, Libya, and Syria show the largest drops from 2010 to 2011 (the years before and after the Arab uprisings) among all MENA countries. Second, each case offers an opportunity to examine the influence of different multilateral arms restrictions. For example, while agreement was secured in the UN Security Council to impose an arms embargo on Libya in 2011, efforts to impose such an embargo on Syria failed (see Table 4.5). The option has not been discussed with regard to Egypt. As described below, the embargoes on these countries, including several regional and unilateral ones, have not stopped the authorization of small arms transfers that carry a high risk of misuse or diversion to these states.

This section also addresses the supply of small arms to non-state armed groups engaged in conflict with repressive governments or extremist organizations in MENA. On the one hand, there is a risk that non-state armed groups will

Table 4.5 Multilateral arms embargoes targeting government and non-government entities in Egypt, Libya, and Syria, in force during 2001–13

Target country	United Nations	European Union (EU)	League of Arab States
Egypt	None	EU Council Conclusions on Egypt (21 August 2013)*	None
Libya	UN Security Council Resolution 748 (31 March 1992-12 September 2003)	European Political Cooperation Presidency Statement (14 April 1986-11 October 2004)	None
	UN Security Council Resolution 1970 (26 February 2011)	Council Common Position 2011/137/CFSP (28 February 2011)	None
Syria	None	Council Common Position 2011/273/CFSP (9 May 2011)	League of Arab States Statement (3 December 2011)

Notes: * The EU Foreign Affairs Council meeting of 21 August 2013 did not impose an arms embargo on Egypt, but noted that EU member states had agreed (a) 'to suspend licences for export to Egypt of any equipment which might be used for internal repression' and (b) 'to reassess export licences for military equipment and review their security assistance to Egypt' (EU, 2013a, para. 8).

Source: SIPRI (n.d.a)

Box 4.1 Monitoring small arms transfers to MENA: a note on the sources

Monitoring authorized armed transfers is challenging as there is no single, comprehensive source of information and as data is usually provided by states on a voluntary basis. In regions that are experiencing high levels of armed violence, armed conflict, and political instability, small arms procurement can be particularly sensitive. Moreover, the MENA region has generally been relatively opaque with regard to small arms imports, rendering the monitoring of authorized small arms transfers to the region difficult.

Publicly available information on arms transfers, both authorized and delivered, can be found in a variety of sources, including multilateral instruments to which governments provide information–such as the UN Register of Conventional Arms (UN Register) and UN Comtrade–national reports on arms exports, arms company press releases, UN reports, NGO and academic reports, specialist arms trade publications, the media, and social media. This wide range of sources can assist in building a comprehensive picture of authorizations and deliveries of small arms to MENA. Yet these different data sources are rarely comparable and may even provide conflicting information, such as when figures in official reports from exporting and importing states diverge.

The UN Register was established in 1991 to promote transparency in armaments and to build confidence among UN member states (UNODA, n.d.). Since its inception, at least 170 UN member states have voluntarily reported at least once on their annual imports or exports of major conventional arms (UNODA, n.d.). Since 2003, UN member states have been invited to provide background information on international transfers of small arms and light weapons. While 80 states have provided such information at least once (UNGA, 2013a, para. 24), Lebanon is the only MENA country to have done so. In addition, Lebanon, as well as and Qatar, responded to the UN Secretary-General's invitation to provide national 'views' on the inclusion of small arms as a separate category in the UN Register in 2014 (UNGA, 2013b, para. 6(a); 2014, p. 119). At present, the UN Register provides only a partial snapshot of small arms flows to MENA because the major small arms suppliers Belgium, China, Israel, and the Russian Federation do not provide information to the UN Register on their small arms transfers. Some of the most significant small arms transfers to Egypt, Libya, and Syria, as reported to the UN Register by exporters, are presented in Tables 4.6–4.10.

UN Comtrade is not a transparency instrument *per se*, but a repository for national customs data for all commodities. The data provided by countries under 'arms and

ammunition; parts and accessories thereof' (World Customs Organization code 93) can be used to capture some small arms deliveries. Countries voluntarily provide such information and therefore UN Comtrade data is skewed towards transfers involving transparent states. Another limitation to the use of UN Comtrade for small arms trade monitoring is that its categorizations mix small arms with larger-calibre weapons. Moreover, many countries provide little or no data on their transfers of military weapons. For instance, in 2011, nine top exporters did not report to UN Comtrade on their military firearm transfers: Austria, Belgium, Brazil, China, Germany, Italy, the Russian Federation, Spain, and Sweden (Holtom, Pavesi, and Rigual, 2014, annexe 4.1). Yet some MENA countries provide information on certain small arms imports to UN Comtrade rather than to the UN Register.

Tables 4.6–4.10 present two columns for UN Comtrade: one for imports reported by Egypt, Libya, and Syria, and one for exporter reports. The juxtaposition of these two columns highlights many significant, and in some cases very large, discrepancies between the information provided by importers and exporters.

While 39 states have provided information on small arms exports via national or regional arms export reports at least once in 2001–14,[14] none of them is located in the MENA region (SIPRI, n.d.b). National export reports typically provide information on authorizations (licences) and actual deliveries, broken down by destination and 'EU Military List' categorization, which differs from both the UN Register and UN Comtrade weapons categories. Again, these reports are produced by more transparent states. One limitation, however, is that major European exporters tend to provide information only on authorizations for small arms exports, not actual deliveries. Tables 4.6–4.10 contain information on deliveries extracted from national or regional reports.

In an attempt to provide a fuller picture of small arms flows to MENA, this chapter complements official government data with available open-source information. While such information is often considered less reliable than that contained in official government sources, it is useful for monitoring small arms flows to the MENA region. The United Arab Emirates, for instance, did not report to any public transparency instrument on its small arms exports in 2001–14 but has been cited in UN reports as having been involved in small arms transfers to armed groups in Libya and Syria (Small Arms Survey, n.d.; UNSC, 2014a, annexe V). In an effort to map, as comprehensively as possible, small arms flows to Egypt, Libya, and Syria before and after the Arab uprisings, this chapter thus taps into a wide range of complementary sources.

commit human rights abuses or violations of international humanitarian law with transferred weapons, not to mention the risk of them
being diverted to other groups that may be more likely to misuse
them. On the other hand, some non-state armed groups seek to
address the pressing humanitarian needs of civilian populations that
are threatened by armed conflict and repression. The case studies on
Libya and Syria explore various facets of this two-pronged issue, with
Box 4.3 focusing on the arming of the Kurdish militia (the peshmerga)
in Iraq in response to the advance of IS.

Western and Gulf Cooperation Council governments have delivered, or considered the delivery of, small arms to non-state armed
groups that opposed the regimes of Qaddafi in Libya and of al-Assad
in Syria on the following grounds:

- humanitarian intervention: providing non-state armed groups with
  arms to protect civilians at risk of attack from government forces;
- regime change support: assisting non-state armed groups that seek
  to overthrow repressive regimes; and
- counter-terrorism efforts: arming non-state armed groups to help
  them fight 'extremist' non-state armed groups or designated terrorist groups.

All three case studies begin by examining recent levels of internal
armed violence, armed conflict, and political stability; next, they
review authorized small arms transfers for the period 2001–10 and
consider whether conditions in each country since 2011 have had any
impact on small arms export policies and deliveries made in 2011–13.
In short, the question is whether the political instability of 2011–13 in
the three states resulted in any significant changes in decision-making
and small arms flows from significant exporters.

Egypt

Since the establishment of the Republic of Egypt in 1953, the country's
presidents have made use of the Emergency Law (Law No. 162 of
1958) to grant extended powers to state security forces and to restrict
fundamental rights and freedoms (OHCHR, 2011, p. 5). Nevertheless,
Egypt experienced relative political stability until January 2011, when
hundreds of thousands of demonstrators took to the streets, calling
for economic, political, and legal reforms. In several cases, security
forces responded with lethal force involving the use of small arms.

A supporter of ousted Egyptian President Mohammed Morsi displays empty cartridges following clashes with soldiers near the Republican Guard headquarters, Cairo, July 2013. © Mohamed Abd El Ghany/Reuters

Table 4.6 Reported deliveries of small arms to Egypt by known significant exporters, 2001–10*

Exporters	Egyptian reports to UN Comtrade on values imported (year), USD	Exporter reports to UN Comtrade on values exported (year), USD	Exporter national and regional reports on values exported (year), USD	Exporter reports to the UN Register on small arms exported, units
Czech Republic	3,699,452 (2004–05; 2008–10), including at least 2,016 pistols and revolvers, 8 sporting and hunting rifles, shotgun cartridges, and ammunition	6,767,876 (2001–10), including at least 22,455 pistols and revolvers (including parts and accessories), 181 sporting and hunting rifles or shotguns, shotgun cartridges, and ammunition	12,768,703 (2003–09)	–
Germany	577,136 (2001–10), including at least 117 pistols and revolvers (including parts and accessories) and 26 sporting and hunting shotguns	3,421,454 (2001–10), including at least 3,946 pistols and revolvers (including parts and accessories), 1,332 sporting and hunting rifles or shotguns (including parts and accessories), and ammunition	–	2,093 sub-machine guns (2007; 2009)
Italy	4,378,140 (2001–10), including at least 107 pistols and revolvers (including parts and accessories), 17,466 sporting and hunting rifles or shotguns (including parts and accessories), and shotgun cartridges	10,061,335 (2001–10), including at least 7,780 pistols and revolvers (including parts and accessories), 4,144 sporting and hunting rifles or shotguns (including parts and accessories), and shotgun cartridges	–	7,828 pistols and revolvers and 18,823 rifles and carbines (2007–10)
South Korea	–	4,824,809 (2001; 2008–09), including at least military firearms, parts and accessories of pistols or revolvers, shotgun cartridges, and ammunition	–	–
Switzerland	123,369 (2003; 2007; 2009–10), including at least 83 sporting and hunting shotguns, parts and accessories of pistols or revolvers, and shotgun cartridges and barrels	4,430,505 (2001–03; 2005–10), including at least 451 pistols and revolvers (including parts and accessories), 18 sporting and hunting rifles, 1,190 military rifles, 26 grenade launchers, and ammunition	6,619,876 (2001–10)	2 sub-machine guns, 123 assault rifles, and 2 under-barrel grenade launchers (2008)

Table 4.6 **Continued**				
Exporters	Egyptian reports to UN Comtrade on values imported (year), USD	Exporter reports to UN Comtrade on values exported (year), USD	Exporter national and regional reports on values exported (year), USD	Exporter reports to the UN Register on small arms exported, units
Turkey	1,355,116 (2004; 2006; 2009-10), including at least 428 sporting and hunting shotguns or rifles, parts and accessories of pistols or revolvers, shotgun cartridges, and ammunition	5,828,982 (2001-10), including at least 15,720 pistols and revolvers (including parts and accessories), 44,717 sporting and hunting rifles or shotguns (including parts and accessories), military firearms, shotgun cartridges, and ammunition	–	1,312 semi-automatic pistols (2006-08; 2010)
United States	464,887 (2002; 2004; 2008-10), including at least 313 pistols and revolvers (including parts and accessories), 4,677 sporting and hunting rifles or shotguns (including parts and accessories), and ammunition	253,895,514 (2001-10), including at least 1,365 pistols and revolvers (including parts and accessories), 7,771 sporting and hunting rifles or shotguns (including parts and accessories), 60,559 military rifles, 478 military weapons, 148 grenade launchers, shotgun cartridges, and ammunition	95,118,000 (2001-09), including at least 3 carbines, 2,439 machine guns, 992 rifles, and cartridges up through .22 calibre	–

Notes: * Only states that have reported small arms exports to Egypt worth at least USD 1 million using at least one reporting mechanism during the period under review are included in the table. See Box 4.2 for details on the methodology used in developing the table. Official government information on small arms exports to Egypt in 2001-10 is contained in Annexe 4.4.

Sources: EU (n.d.); NISAT (n.d.); SIPRI (n.d.b); UN Comtrade (n.d.); UNODA (n.d.)

The crackdown claimed at least 840 lives and left more than 6,000 people injured (AI, 2011, p. 25); they also prompted President Hosni Mubarak to step down in February 2011, after 30 years in power. The military remained in power under the Supreme Council of the Armed Forces, headed by Field Marshal Mohamed Hussein Tantawi, but promised to hand over power to civilian authorities (Spencer, 2012).

Parliamentary elections took place in November 2011 and presidential elections were held in June 2012. The Muslim Brotherhood and Freedom and Justice Party performed well in both elections, with their candidate, Mohamed Morsi, securing 51.7 per cent of the presidential vote in 2012 (Kirkpatrick, 2012). Morsi took office on 30 June 2012 but was ousted from power by the Egyptian military one year later, on 3 July 2013, following large popular protests against his rule (HRW, 2014, p. 27). Supporters of the Muslim Brotherhood and Egyptian security forces clashed repeatedly and violently in July and August 2013, with several incidents spurring widespread condemnation of the security forces (OHCHR, 2013). Overall, the period 2011–14 has been characterized by acute political instability and the use of force involving small arms by Egyptian security forces against protestors.

Small arms transfers to Egypt, 2001-10

Egypt has its own small arms industry, which has produced licensed copies of Belgian, Italian, Soviet/Russian, and US small arms. It currently produces Helwan 9 mm automatic pistols, Misr assault rifles, semi-automatic rifles, 7.62 × 51 mm general-purpose machine guns, 40 × 35 mm automatic grenade launchers, and 40 × 46 mm under-barrel grenade launchers (MEIC, n.d.).

Egypt reports small arms imports to UN Comtrade but has not provided information on small arms imports to the UN Register as part of so-called 'background' information on small arms transfers.[15] Exporters of small arms and ammunition to Egypt provide information to UN Comtrade that is higher in volume and value than the corresponding information contained in Egypt's own Comtrade reports.[16]

Box 4.2 Methodology and a note on data tables

Tables 4.6-4.10 provide official government information on deliveries of small arms to Egypt, Libya, and Syria during the periods 2001-10 and 2011-13. The three types of sources used for the data contained in the tables are UN Comtrade (importer and exporter reports); national and regional reports on arms exports; and the UN Register of Conventional Arms. Each column in the tables refers to one of these reporting instruments, each of which utilizes different definitions or categories for small arms. For this reason, the values shown in the different columns are not directly comparable. In addition, this chapter applies varying thresholds to determine the minimum value required for the inclusion of an exporter in Tables 4.6-4.10. For example, the threshold for the reported value of small arms exports to Egypt is at least USD 1 million for 2001-10, but USD 500,000 for 2011-13. The threshold for Syria is much lower, at just USD 100,000 for the period 2001-10. The varying thresholds facilitate the monitoring of changes in policies and flows by major suppliers for each country, in view of the fact that the volumes of reported small arms transfers to Egypt, Libya, and Syria vary greatly. A full list of all transactions reported by all countries for Egypt, Libya, and Syria during 2001-13 is available online in Annexe 4.4.

The **first column** in Tables 4.6-4.10 contains the declared value of small arms transfers in US dollars and the number of units transferred to Egypt, Libya, or Syria, as reported to UN Comtrade by the importing countries, for the periods 2001-10 and 2011-13.

The **second column** contains information provided by significant exporters to Egypt, Libya, and Syria. The following UN Comtrade categories are utilized to record small arms transfers: 930100 (military weapons), 930120 (rocket and grenade launchers, etc.), 930190 (military firearms), 930200 (revolvers and pistols), 930320 (sporting and hunting shotguns), 930330 (sporting and hunting rifles), 930510 (parts and accessories of revolvers and pistols), 930521 (shotgun barrels), 930529 (parts and accessories of shotguns and rifles), 930621 (shotgun cartridges), 930630 (small arms ammunition).

The **third column** presents national data drawn from national or regional reports on deliveries of items contained in the European Union Common Military List categories 1, 2, and 3, which cover small arms (and components), light weapons and artillery (and components), and ammunition, respectively (EU, 2014a).[17] It is worth noting that many significant suppliers do not provide delivery information for all small arms transfers. Even if countries provide data on deliveries, the information provided is not always comprehensive. For example, the United States provides data only for small arms and ammunition deliveries conducted as part of government-to-government foreign military sales and does not include items purchased outside government-to-government arrangements. In other cases, states may not disaggregate the data, thereby precluding the identification of the country of import or the end user. For example, Serbian national reports indicate that Libya was one of several potential end users for deliveries of pistols, hunting carbines, sub-machine guns, automatic rifles, hand-held grenade launchers, and ammunition in 2007-09 (Serbia, 2009, pp. 38, 49; 2010, pp. 38, 41, 54, 57; 2011, pp. 49, 62-63). Some reports clearly identify Libya as the end user but include small arms and ammunition with other items, rendering a determination of the actual value of only the small arms and ammunition component of deliveries in a given year impossible. Finally, the third column does not include any of the following categories, which have been omitted as they could also cover items that fall beyond the Survey's definition of small arms and ammunition: missiles, other ammunition and components, rocket launchers and rockets, and weapons spares.

The **fourth column** consists of exporter reports to the UN Register of Conventional Arms for all categories contained in the 'background information' on small arms transfers.

Data for Tables 4.6-4.10 is drawn from EU annual reports (EU, n.d.); the NISAT Database of Small Arms Transfers (NISAT, n.d.); UN Comtrade (n.d.); the UN Register of Conventional Arms (UNODA, n.d); and national reports (SIPRI, n.d.b).

Egypt reported to UN Comtrade the import of USD 25 million worth of small arms from 18 countries during 2001–10, yet 34 countries reported exporting USD 292 million worth of small arms to Egypt over this period. Thirteen countries reported to the UN Register on the export of small arms to Egypt during 2004–10;[18] Table 4.6 lists the largest reported volumes of small arms deliveries to Egypt. Based on reports to UN Comtrade and national report data, the largest exporter of small arms to Egypt during 2001–10 was the United States, followed by Italy, the Czech Republic, Turkey, South Korea, Switzerland, and Germany (see Table 4.6). In the US row of Table 4.6, the third column identifies deliveries of small arms and ammunition under the US foreign military sales programme, which were probably funded as part of US military aid to Egypt.[19]

Small arms exporter policies towards Egypt, 2011–13

Egypt's known significant small arms suppliers differed in their reactions to the events of January–February 2011 and July–August 2013. The response to the former was mixed. Although the US government announced in January 2011 that it was reviewing the provision of military aid to Egypt, arms deliveries continued throughout 2011 on the grounds that maintaining the provision of assistance was in the interests of US national security (US, 2011; Cornwell and Mohammed, 2012; see Table 4.7). In contrast to the United States, several significant European small arms suppliers—the Czech Republic, France, Germany, the Netherlands, and Spain—announced in January and February 2011 that they had frozen or suspended arms export licences and would not approve any new licences (AI, 2011, p. 34). Yet the EU did not impose an arms embargo on Egypt and EU member states authorized and delivered small arms to Egypt in 2011–13 (see Table 4.7).

The EU did not impose an arms embargo on Egypt.

It appears that the United States took a harder line with the Egyptian military following the overthrow of the Morsi government and the use of force by Egyptian security forces in mid-2013. On 3 July 2013, US president Barack Obama urged 'all sides to avoid violence' and initiated a review of US assistance to Egypt, including military aid (US, 2013a). In late August 2013, the White House denied reports that the United States had suspended military aid to Egypt (Klapper, 2013; US, 2013b). Yet in late 2013, the US national security adviser, Susan Rice, stated that in response to the use of force against civilians in July and August, the United States had 'withheld delivery of some major weapons systems pending progress towards democratic reforms and inclusive governance'. She did not comment on whether this also applied to deliveries of small arms and ammunition (Rice, 2013).

The EU reaction to Morsi's ouster and the use of force by Egyptian security forces was muddled. While German chancellor Angela Merkel raised the prospect of imposing an EU arms embargo in response to the Egyptian government's use of force against protestors (Rettman, 2013a), the 28 EU members were divided on this issue (Duquet, 2014, pp. 14–15). These differences were reflected in the conclusions of the Council of the EU's emergency meeting on foreign affairs on 21 August 2013, which failed to reach a consensus on adopting a legally binding arms embargo on Egypt (EU, 2013a). The Council of the EU imposed a politically binding embargo only on the supply to Egypt of 'any equipment which might be used for internal repression', noting that EU member states agreed to 'reassess export licences of equipment covered by Common Position 2008/944/CFSP and review their security assistance with Egypt' (EU, 2013a, para. 8).

The embargo on 'internal repression' equipment leaves considerable room for interpretation in terms of how and for how long it should be applied and the types of equipment to which it applies. To assist with the latter issue, an internal EU guideline was developed for EU member states; it outlined 11 categories of 'internal repression' equipment, including firearms, ammunition, weapons sights, bombs, and grenades (Rettman, 2013b). Similar guidance was provided for sanctions imposed on Belarus in 2011, Côte d'Ivoire in 2010, and Libya in 2011.

Table 4.7   Reported deliveries of small arms to Egypt by known significant exporters, 2011–13*

Exporters	Egyptian reports to UN Comtrade on values imported (year), USD	Exporter reports to UN Comtrade on values exported (year), USD	Exporter national and regional reports on values exported (year), USD	Exporter reports to the UN Register on small arms exported, units
Czech Republic	14,237,459 (2011–13), including at least 15,246 pistols and revolvers (including parts and accessories) and ammunition	27,011,021 (2011–13), including at least 56,076 pistols and revolvers (including parts and accessories), 9 sporting and hunting rifles or shotguns, and ammunition	4,639,125 (2011–12)	53,329 pistols and revolvers and 7,493 assault rifles (2012–13)
Germany	575,437 (2011–13), including at least 13 pistols and revolvers (including parts and accessories), 1,140 sporting and hunting rifles or shotguns, shotgun cartridges, and ammunition	769,776 (2011–13), including at least 1 pistol or revolver (including parts and accessories), 639 sporting and hunting shotguns (including parts and accessories), shotgun cartridges, and ammunition	–	–
Italy	1,634,018 (2011–13), including at least 4 pistols and revolvers (including parts and accessories), 1,360 sporting and hunting shotguns, and shotgun cartridges	1,120,933 (2011–13), including at least 12 pistols and revolvers (including parts and accessories), 193 sporting and hunting rifles or shotguns (including parts and accessories), and shotgun cartridges	–	–
Slovakia	–	1,858,960 (2011–13), mainly small arms ammunition	758 (2011–12)	1 revolver or pistol (2011) and 2 revolvers or pistols (2012)
South Korea	–	1,604,785 (2011–12), including at least shotgun cartridges and ammunition	–	–
Spain	647,518 (2011; 2013), including shotgun cartridges	296,328 (2012–13), including at least 11 sporting and hunting shotguns, shotgun cartridges, and 24 pistols	935,374 (2011–12), including shotguns and shells	–
Turkey	501,786 (2011–12), including at least 3,702 sporting and hunting rifles or shotguns (including parts and accessories) and parts and accessories of revolvers or pistols	2,835,002 (2011–13), including at least 55 pistols and revolvers (including parts and accessories), 11,812 sporting and hunting rifles or shotguns (including parts and accessories), and shotgun cartridges	–	–

Exporters	Egyptian reports to UN Comtrade on values imported (year), USD	Exporter reports to UN Comtrade on values exported (year), USD	Exporter national and regional reports on values exported (year), USD	Exporter reports to the UN Register on small arms exported, units
UK	420 (2012–13), including at least parts and accessories of revolvers or pistols	8,886 (2012), including at least shotgun cartridges	–	94 pistols and revolvers, 150 sporting rifles, 700 rifles and carbines, 200 sniper rifles, 1,900 assault rifles, and 18 heavy machine guns (2012–13)
United States	672,793 (2011–13), including at least 695 pistols and revolvers (including parts and accessories), 1 sporting or hunting rifle, and ammunition	21,522,840 (2011–13), including at least parts and accessories of pistols and revolvers, 4,167 sporting and hunting rifles or shotguns (including parts and accessories), 1,584 military rifles, 5 grenade launchers, and ammunition	1,808,000 (2011), including at least 188 carbines, 47 machine guns, 686 rifles, and cartridges up through .22 calibre	–

Table 4.7 **Continued**

Notes: * Only states that have reported small arms exports to Egypt worth at least USD 500,000 using at least one reporting mechanism during the period under review are included in the table. See Box 4.2 for details on the methodology used in developing the table. Official government information on small arms exports to Egypt in 2011–13 is contained in Annexe 4.4.

Sources: EU (n.d.); NISAT (n.d.); SIPRI (n.d.b); UN Comtrade (n.d.); UNODA (n.d.)

The case of Egyptian orders for Czech small arms provides clear evidence that states apply varying interpretations of the politically binding EU arms embargo. In 2013, the Czech arms producer Česká Zbrojovka won a tender to supply 50,000 CZ P-07 Duty pistols to the Egyptian interior ministry (Radio Praha, 2013). The Czech Republic reported to the UN Register the delivery of 50,000 pistols and 5,000 assault rifles in 2013. Austria, Germany, and Poland all reportedly denied permission for the land and sea transit of the 50,000 pistols (Pavel, 2014). In early 2014 it was announced that Czech companies had signed a contract to export 29,000 CZ 75 P-07 Duty pistols and 10 million 9 mm rounds to Egypt's ministry of interior, with Egypt expressing an interest in an additional 50,000 (Pavel, 2014).

In February 2014, the Russian media reported that 'light weapons and ammunition' were included in a USD 3 billion arms deal that was being discussed between the Russian Federation and Egypt and that was to be paid for by Saudi Arabia and the United Arab Emirates (Nikolskii and Khimshiashvili, 2014). There were indications that this option was being explored in light of delays in the delivery of US arms (Mustafa, 2013). This case shows that a government that is subjected to restrictive practices by some of its established small arms suppliers is likely to seek alternative sources of supply.

Libya

Col. Muammar Qaddafi maintained power and relative stability in Libya for four decades. Yet most of that period was characterized by the country's isolation from the international community, the result of the regime's poor human rights record and support for international terrorist and insurgent groups (Lutterbeck, 2009, p. 511; Mangan and Murtaugh, 2014, p. 7; UNHRC, 2011a, paras. 30–34, 240). Peaceful demonstrations in mid-February 2011, which called for fundamental reforms, were met with the use of lethal force by security forces in several cities. This sparked an armed revolt against Qaddafi's rule, which, by the end of February 2011, had acquired the characteristics of a civil war (UNHRC, 2011a, paras. 37–39, 244).

Anti-Qaddafi forces in Libya, supported by NATO aircraft, defeated the regime after several months of fighting and Qaddafi was executed on 20 October 2011 (Al Jazeera, 2011a). Despite his demise and the relatively peaceful election of a General National Congress in 2012, Libya has since fragmented into rival regional factions (McQuinn, 2012; UNSC, 2014a, p. 5, paras. 18, 39, 41, 94, 98). The factions are well armed following the looting of Libya's extensive arms stockpiles and arms deliveries that took place during the civil war. From 2011 to 2014, Libya experienced high levels of armed violence and political instability; this situation has had a negative impact on the security and stability of the broader Sahel region (UNSC, 2014a, para. 37).

Small arms transfers to Libya, 2001–10

Libya's 2010 national report on the implementation of the UN Programme of Action on small arms stated that 'no weapons are manufactured in the Jamahiriya' (Libya, 2010, p. 2). Yet some reports indicate that the Soviet Union had built, or had almost finished building, a small arms factory in Libya in 1985 (Felgenhauer, 2007; Lenta, 2010). The Russian media reported in February 2010 that a contract had been signed to build a factory and grant a licence to Libya to manufacture Kalashnikov AK-103 assault rifles (Nikolskii, 2010). Nevertheless, Libya relied on imports to meet its small arms procurement needs.

During the cold war, Brazil, France, Italy, and the Soviet Union supplied a significant quantity of small arms and ammunition to Libya.[20] In April 1986 the European Community imposed an arms embargo on Libya in response to the country's support for terrorism, most notably its reported involvement in an attack in Berlin in 1986 (EPCP, 1986; SIPRI, n.d.c). A UN arms embargo was introduced in March 1992, following Libya's lack of cooperation in investigating its connections to terrorist attacks on US and French civilian airliners (UNSC, 1992). Qaddafi's assistance with these investigations in the late 1990s and his cooperation in efforts to combat al-Qaeda following the 11 September 2001 terrorist attacks on the United States, together with his decision to abandon the pursuit of weapons of mass destruction, led to the lifting of the UN arms embargo in 2003 and the EU arms embargo in 2004. This prompted many small arms exporters to explore opportunities to supply Libya with small arms (see Table 4.8 and Annexe 4.4).

During the period 2001–10, Libya reported to UN Comtrade only in 2009 and 2010, noting small arms imported from three countries and valued at USD 83,071 (see Table 4.8a in Annexe 4.4). In contrast, 18 countries reported exporting USD 15 million worth of small arms to Libya during this period. Three countries reported small arms exports to the UN Register in 2009–10. According to UN Comtrade and national reports, the largest exporters of small arms to Libya in 2001–10, by order of importance, were Italy, South Korea, the UK, Austria, and Iran (see Table 4.8 and Annexe 4.4). While Ukraine reported a transfer of 100,000 'assault rifles or sub-machine guns' to Libya in 2006, it did not specify the value of the transfer, as noted in Table 4.8.

Both France and the Russian Federation appear to have delivered small arms to Libya since 2006, although no information was provided to the reporting instruments reviewed for inclusion in Table 4.8. While the Russian Federation has not made public information on small arms deliveries to Libya since 2000, evidence shows that the country exported AK-103-2 assault rifles to Libya between 2007 and 2011 (Jenzen-Jones, 2011a; 2011b). France reportedly delivered 1,000 MILAN-3 anti-tank guided weapons to Libya between 2008 and 2011 (IHS Jane's, 2014, p. 30; SIPRI, n.d.d).

Libya's factions are well armed following the looting of extensive arms stockpiles and arms deliveries.

Table 4.8 **Reported deliveries of small arms to Libya by known significant exporters, 2001–10***				
Exporters	**Libyan reports to UN Comtrade on values imported (year), USD**	**Exporter reports to UN Comtrade on values exported (year), USD**	**Exporter national and regional reports on values exported (year), USD**	**Exporter reports to the UN Register on small arms exported, units**
Austria	–	30,520 (2005–06; 2008–10), including at least 25 sporting and hunting rifles or shotguns (including parts and accessories) and parts and accessories of pistols or revolvers	251,602 (2005–10)	–
Iran	–	255,011 (2004), including at least parts and accessories of pistols and revolvers		
Italy	8,743 (2010), including at least 37 sporting and hunting shotguns	11,647,130 (2009–10), including at least 7,500 pistols and revolvers and 3,770 sporting and hunting rifles and shotguns	–	7,500 pistols and revolvers, and 3,706 rifles and carbines (2009)
Serbia	–	7,182 (2005–06), including at least 4 pistols and revolvers and 23 sporting and hunting rifles or shotguns	–	35,000 light machine guns (2009)
South Korea	–	2,596,616 (2009), including at least grenade launchers and shotgun cartridges	–	–
Turkey	–	81,860 (2006; 2010), including at least ammunition	–	–
UK	–	648,486 (2005; 2008; 2010), including at least 4 sporting and hunting rifles or shotguns, shotgun cartridges, and ammunition	–	4 shotguns (2009) and 1 sniper rifle (2010)
Ukraine	–	–	100,000 units of assault rifles or sub-machine guns (2006), value unknown	–

Notes: * Only states that have reported small arms exports to Libya worth at least USD 50,000 over the period under review using at least one reporting mechanism are included in the table. See Box 4.2 for a detailed explanation of the methodology used in developing the table. Official government information on small arms exports to Libya in 2001–10 is contained in Annexe 4.4.

Sources: EU (n.d.); NISAT (n.d.); SIPRI (n.d.b); UN Comtrade (n.d.); UNODA (n.d.)

Small arms exporter policies towards Libya, 2011–13

Libya is the only state affected by the 'Arab Spring' to be the subject of UN sanctions, including an arms embargo. On 26 February 2011, all 15 members of the UN Security Council voted in favour of Resolution 1970, which imposed an arms embargo on Libya in response to 'the violence and use of force against civilians' and 'the gross and systematic violation of human rights' (UNSC, 2011a; 2011b). The African Union, League of Arab States, and Organization of the Islamic Conference called upon Security Council members to vote in favour of the resolution and its sanctions (UNSC, 2011a, p. 4). Yet there was no consensus on Resolution 1973, which was adopted a month later with abstentions from Brazil, China, Germany, India, and the Russian Federation (UNSC, 2011c). It authorized UN member states to enforce the arms embargo by inspecting suspicious shipments, including on the high seas (UNSC, 2011d, para. 13). It also authorized member states to 'take all necessary measures [. . .] to protect civilians and civilian populated areas under threat of attack', after notifying the Secretary-General (para. 4). Some member states used this language as a justification for delivering small arms and ammunition to non-state armed groups during 2011, but neither the UN Secretary-General nor the UN's Libya Security Council Committee was notified of all such weapons deliveries at that time, as discussed below.

Libya is the only state affected by the 'Arab Spring' to be the subject of UN sanctions.   Indeed, the UN Panel of Experts appointed to monitor the implementation of the sanctions investigated several cases of arms shipments that were delivered to anti-Qaddafi forces during 2011 with the involvement of France and Gulf Cooperation Council states. The Panel did not regard France's delivery of machine guns, rocket-propelled grenades, or anti-tank missiles to non-state actors in the western Nafusa mountains as a violation of the embargo because France had notified the UN Secretary-General of the delivery in accordance with terms of Security Council Resolution 1973 (UNSC, 2012b, paras. 76–78). Russian foreign minister Sergey Lavrov, however, characterized the transaction as a 'flagrant violation of UNSCR resolution 1970' (Russian Federation, 2011a). The Russian Federation and South Africa called for a closed meeting of the UN's Libya sanctions committee to discuss the French delivery; that meeting took place on 7 July 2011 (Lee, 2011; UNSC, 2012a, para. 40). Conversely, the Panel considered re-export of small arms and ammunition to anti-Qaddafi forces from Qatar and the United Arab Emirates, made without the authorization of the original exporting states, to be violations of Resolution 1973 because the deliveries had been carried out without notifying the UN Secretary-General (UNSC, 2012b, paras. 86–102; 2013b, paras. 59–100; 2014a, paras. 56–57).

While noting that officials from the Qaddafi regime also tried to procure arms and ammunition, the Panel of Experts collected 'only limited information relating to potential sanctions violations committed by the Qaddafi government' (UNSC, 2012b, para. 51; 2013b, para. 57). The only specific case discussed in Panel reports refers to meetings that took place in July 2011 between representatives of the Libyan regime and Chinese arms exporters (UNSC, 2012b, paras. 54–56). Yet Chinese government officials have stated that no Chinese companies delivered arms to Libya during the arms embargo (Bromley, Duchâtel, and Holtom, 2013, p. 12).

UN Security Council Resolution 2009 of 16 September 2011, adopted after the insurgents had taken control of most parts of Libya, including Tripoli (SIPRI, n.d.e), changed the terms of the embargo in spite of remaining concerns over the proliferation of arms in the country and permitted transfers of arms 'intended solely for security or disarmament assistance to the Libyan authorities' (UNSC, 2011e, para. 13a). Resolution 2009 requires states to notify the Security Council Committee of their plans to deliver arms or ammunition; the committee then has five days in which to object to the proposed delivery (para. 13a). According to publicly available information, as of February 2014, the Security Council Committee had not objected to any transfer about which it had been notified (UNSC, 2014a, p. 5).[21] For the years 2011–13, UN Comtrade national reports and the UN Register provide information on small arms deliveries to Libya by only four states: Malta, Serbia, Turkey, and the UK (see Table 4.9).

Table 4.9 Reported deliveries of small arms to Libya by known significant exporters, 2011–13*

Exporters	Libyan reports to UN Comtrade on values imported (year), USD	Exporter reports to UN Comtrade on values exported (year), USD	Exporter national and regional reports on values exported (year), USD	Exporter reports to the UN Register on small arms exported, units
Malta	–	129,623 (2011–13), including at least 12 pistols and revolvers, 52 sporting and hunting shotguns (including parts and accessories), and ammunition	5,084 (2012)	–
Serbia	–	–	–	19,000 revolvers and pistols, 1,500 rifles and carbines, 34,000 assault rifles, 11,000 light machine guns, 3,000 heavy machine guns, and 8,600 under-barrel and hand-held grenade launchers (2012–13)
Turkey	–	14,183,192 (2011–13), including at least 9,504 pistols and revolvers (including parts and accessories), 70,428 sporting and hunting rifles or shotguns, shotgun cartridges, and ammunition	–	9,504 semi-automatic pistols (2012–13)
UK	–	28,231 (2013), including at least 38 pistols and revolvers	–	51 pistols and revolvers, 14 rifles and carbines, and 65 assault rifles (2012–13)

Notes: * Official government information on small arms exports to Libya during 2011–13 is contained in Annexe 4.4. See Box 4.2 for details on the methodology used in developing the table.

Sources: EU (n.d.); NISAT (n.d.); SIPRI (n.d.b); UN Comtrade (n.d.); UNODA (n.d.)

The Libyan government has established a military procurement department in its ministry of defence to centralize and coordinate arms procurement in the post-Qaddafi era (UNSC, 2014a, para. 51). In practice, however, other ministries and unauthorized officials within the ministry of defence continue to procure arms (para. 52). Indeed, only one of seven notifications received by the sanctions committee since June 2013 was signed by a representative of the military procurement department—specifically, for material that included 65,000 assault rifles and 42 million rounds of 7.62 × 39 mm ammunition (para. 53). In November 2013, Greek authorities seized a shipment of ammunition that was en route from Ukraine to Libya without an authorization from the sanctions committee (para. 92). Even if a shipment of arms and ammunition to Libya is authorized by the sanctions committee and military procurement department, the risk of post-delivery diversion is considered high (para. 44). First, overall control of the Libyan national stockpile appears tenuous, which means that the risk of leakage, unauthorized sale, and theft is significant (paras. 44, 46). Second, as armed groups are slowly integrated into the formal security sector, there is a risk that officials will share the delivered materiel with them (para. 45).

Syria

The Syrian government has kept the country in a 'state of emergency' since 1963, with state security forces accused of serious human rights violations against political opponents throughout this period (UNHRC, 2011b, paras. 14, 16–17, 26). Limited protests in Syria in February 2011 soon evolved into broader demonstrations and demands for President Bashar al-Assad to undertake wide-ranging economic, legal, and political reforms (paras. 27–28). Government security forces responded with lethal force, followed by countrywide military operations. Beginning in late spring 2011, various non-state armed groups were engaging in all-out war with the Syrian military.

By all accounts, both regime and anti-government forces have committed violations of international humanitarian and human rights law, including crimes against humanity (UNHRC, 2014). Independent observers estimate that the number of fatalities between March 2011 and April 2014 exceeded 190,000 (Price, Gohdes, and Ball, 2014, p. 3); as of mid-2014, almost half of the Syrian population had been displaced.[22] The civil war has undermined regional stability and security as non-state armed groups, in particular IS, have fought not only Syrian government forces and each other, but also government forces in neighbouring states, most notably Iraq. In sum, Syria has experienced high levels of armed violence and political instability during 2011–14, with its civil war destabilizing neighbouring countries and the broader region.

Small arms transfers to Syria, 2001–10

Syria's Industrial Establishment of Defence produces some small arms ammunition (Jenzen-Jones, 2014), but the country relies on imports of small arms and ammunition to meet its needs. There is limited information regarding the

Having been intercepted by Turkey on suspicion of carrying weapons and ammunition to Syria, the Atlantic Cruiser lies at anchor in Iskenderun port, Hatay, Turkey, April 2012.
© Ismihan Ozguven/Anadolu New Agency/AFP Photo

Table 4.10 Reported deliveries of small arms to Syria by known significant exporters, 2001–10*

Exporters	Syrian reports to UN Comtrade on values imported (year), USD	Exporter reports to UN Comtrade on values exported (year), USD	Exporter national and regional reports on values exported (year), USD	Exporter reports to the UN Register on small arms exported, units
Czech Republic	–	120,157 (2001–02), including at least 465 pistols and revolvers	35,412 (2003)	–
Egypt	46,452 (2010), including at least ammunition	2,380,652 (2008–09), including at least 500 military firearms, parts and accessories of military weapons, and ammunition	–	–
Germany	6,444 (2006; 2010), including at least ammunition	116,050 (2002; 2004; 2006; 2008; 2010), including at least 125 pistols and revolvers (including parts and accessories), 77 sporting and hunting rifles (including parts and accessories), and ammunition	–	–
Iran	–	3,013,613 (2004), including at least 964 military firearms, shotgun cartridges and barrels, and parts and accessories of shotguns or rifles	–	–
Turkey	537,833 (2009–10), including at least 1,493 pistols and revolvers	4,547,585 (2003; 2005; 2007–10), including at least 15,116 pistols and revolvers (including parts and accessories) and 51 sporting and hunting rifles	–	10,545 semi-automatic pistols and 2 rifles and carbines (2007–08; 2010)

Notes: * Only states that have reported on small arms exports worth at least USD 100,000 over the period under review using at least one reporting mechanism are included in the table. See Box 4.2 for details on the methodology used in developing the table. Official government information on small arms exports to Syria during 2001–13 is contained in Annexe 4.4.

Sources: EU (n.d.); NISAT (n.d.); SIPRI (n.d.b); UN Comtrade (n.d.); UNODA (n.d.)

volume of small arms exports to Syria in the period preceding the civil war. The United States has maintained an arms embargo on Syria since 1991, in response to reported Syrian support for acts of international terrorism, including the unauthorized re-export of arms to Hezbollah (US, 1991). In the mid- to late 1990s, the Russian Federation supplied Syria with large quantities of AKS-74U and AK-74M assault rifles, 9K111-1 Konkurs and 9K115-2 Metis-M anti-tank guided weapons systems, 9K117 Bastion gun-launched anti-tank guided missiles and guidance equipment, and PG-7VL rounds for RPG-7 and RPG-29 grenade launchers (Aliev, 2007). However, it reportedly denied Syrian requests for the supply of Igla (SA-18 Grouse) man-portable air defence systems in 2005 and 2007 because of fears that these items could be diverted to Hezbollah (Lantratov et al., 2007; RIA Novosti, 2007). Syria's options for small arms imports were thus restricted even before the civil war erupted in 2011.

For the period 2001–10, 14 countries reported to UN Comtrade on small arms exports to Syria valued at USD 10,485,611; however, for that same period, Syria only reported on small arms imports received from seven countries in 2006–10 and valued at USD 776,324. Only Turkey has reported to the UN Register on the export of small arms to Syria in 2004–10. The available official data indicates a limited number of significant suppliers—a list headed by Turkey, Iran, and Egypt—during the period 2001–10 (see Table 4.10 on previous page). Neither China nor the Russian Federation provided information on small arms and ammunition exports to Syria during this period, although they are probably significant small arms exporters to the country.[23]

Small arms exporter policies towards Syria, 2011–13

The emergence of IS has tipped the balance in favour of the supply of arms to non-state armed groups.

Several regional organizations and exporters listed in Table 4.10 introduced arms embargoes in 2011 in response to the Syrian civil war. The EU imposed an arms embargo on Syria on 9 May 2011, Turkey in November 2011, and the League of Arab States in December 2011 (Al Jazeera, 2011b; EU, 2011; League of Arab States, 2011). There have been repeated calls for a UN arms embargo on Syria and a draft UN Security Council resolution to that effect was circulated in mid-2011 (Lauria and Malas, 2011).[24] Yet, to date, the Russian Federation has blocked all efforts to impose a UN arms embargo on Syria, apparently fearing that UN Security Council resolutions on Syria would lead to a Western-led military intervention and regime change, as it deems occurred in Libya (Allison, 2013, pp. 795–96). In November 2011, Russian foreign minister Sergey Lavrov asserted that non-state armed groups that 'maintain contacts with Western and Arab states' are the source of instability and violence in Syria. He indicated, moreover, that Russian opposition to an arms embargo was rooted in 'the Libya experience, and the behavior of some of our partners', citing French and Qatari arms supplies to anti-Qaddafi forces as violations of the Libyan arms embargo (Russian Federation, 2011b).

Western and Arab countries that oppose the Assad regime have given serious consideration to supplying small arms to non-state armed groups. In early 2013, France and the UK called for the terms of the EU arms embargo to be changed to enable the supply of arms to one such group, the Syrian National Coalition. They justified the policy on two grounds. First, it would send a strong signal to Assad and increase pressure for a negotiated peaceful resolution to the conflict. Second, according to former British foreign secretary William Hague and French foreign minister Laurent Fabius, it would represent a 'necessary, proportionate and lawful response to a situation of extreme human suffering' where 'there is no practicable alternative' (Spiegel, 2013). Some EU member states reportedly opposed this proposal as they feared that the arms could be misused by the Syrian National Coalition forces or diverted to radical Islamic groups (Duquet, 2014, pp. 13–14). During a foreign affairs meeting on 27 May 2013, the Council of the EU renewed the arms embargo on Syria for 12 months but included an exemption for EU member states to supply arms to the Syrian National Coalition 'for the protection of civilians' with 'adequate safeguards against misuse' (EU, 2013b). The UK government's support for this option was weakened in July 2013, when the UK's lower house of parliament voted in favour of the motion that 'no lethal support should be provided to anti-government forces in Syria without the explicit prior consent of Parliament' (UKHC, 2013).

Similar divisions have reportedly occurred within the US government (Landler and Gordon, 2013). The emergence of IS has, however, tipped the balance in favour of the supply of arms to non-state armed groups, in particular those willing to fight IS. In 2013 and 2014, several US congressional committees introduced or considered proposals for the provision of non-lethal and lethal military assistance to the Syrian National Coalition (Blanchard, Humud, and Nikitin,

2014, pp. 29–31). In June 2014, the fiscal year 2015 Overseas Contingency Operations funds included a request for USD 500 million for a 'train and equip' programme for 5,000 'appropriately vetted elements of the Syrian opposition and other appropriately vetted Syrian groups or individuals' to defend the Syrian people against attacks from IS and the Syrian regime; protect the United States, its friends, allies, and the people of Syria from threats posed by terrorists in Syria; and promote the conditions for a negotiated settlement to the end of the Syrian conflict (US, 2014b, p. 56).

Media and research reports indicate that Arab countries have facilitated and arranged the supply of arms and ammunition to non-state armed groups in Syria (Chivers and Schmitt, 2013; Holtom, Pavesi, and Rigual, 2014, p. 126; Schroeder, 2014, pp. 9–11), but at the time of writing there was no reliable overview of small arms flows to non-state armed groups in Syria.

Due to the fact that most of Syria's main small arms suppliers are among the least transparent exporters, it is very difficult to chart the impact of the conflict on small arms flows to the Syrian government.[25] Germany and Switzerland provided information to UN Comtrade on limited quantities of small arms exports to Syria in 2011. Turkey reported to Comtrade on the export of 1,016 pistols and revolvers in 2011 and 24,760 sporting and hunting rifles and shotguns in 2013 for a total value of USD 1,918,265 (see Annexe 4.4). Ukraine's national report listed the delivery of 4,000 assault rifles in 2011 (Ukraine, 2012). Open-source information also indicates that Iran, North Korea, and the Russian Federation have sought to supply the Syrian government with small arms (Spencer, Blomfield, and Millward, 2012; UNSC, 2012c; 2014b). Although Russian president Vladimir Putin stated in mid-2012 that 'Russia is not supplying arms that could be used in civil conflicts' (RIA Novosti, 2012), the Russian Federation has maintained Syrian weaponry that has been used in the internal conflict and remains an important supplier of small arms

Box 4.3 Arming the peshmerga in Iraq

In mid-2014, several Western governments decided to provide small arms and ammunition to the Kurdish Regional Government in Iraq, in particular for the Kurdish peshmerga, to respond to the threat posed by IS to regional security and their own nationals working in the region. In early August 2014, the United States had begun to provide the peshmerga with arms and equipment directly and openly, in cooperation with the government of Iraq (Khalilzad, 2014; US, 2014c). The United States also reportedly encouraged European states to supply arms and ammunition to the peshmerga in mid-2014 (Ryan, Hosenball, and Scheer, 2014). On 11 August 2014, French foreign minister Laurent Fabius called for a special meeting of the EU Council of Foreign Ministers to discuss IS and arming the peshmerga (AFP, 2014a). The formal conclusions of the resulting Council meeting, which was held fours days later, encouraged individual EU member states to respond 'positively to the call by the Kurdish regional authorities to provide urgently military material' and noted that the supply of arms 'will be done according to the capabilities and national laws of the Member States, and with the consent of the Iraqi national authorities' (EU, 2014b). Several European states pledged or began to provide small arms and ammunition to the peshmerga in August and September 2014 (see Table 4.11).[26]

Despite the threats posed by IS, the supply of arms to the peshmerga presents clear risks of misuse and diversion. The Kurdistan Security Forces have, for example, been accused of arbitrary arrest and torture (HRW, 2007). As outlined in the opening paragraph of this chapter, diversion risks are also a concern given the challenges of delivering the arms and of ensuring that supplied materiel is not deliberately retransferred to unauthorized end users or lost as a result of poor stockpile management. To mitigate some of these risks, Germany stationed six Bundeswehr officers in Erbil to monitor the German arms provided to the peshmerga, with provisions for the marking and recording of all small arms provided to them (Pöhle, 2014).

Footage released by IS allegedly shows small arms and ammunition dropped by the United States and intercepted by IS, in Kobani, Syria, October 2014. © A3Maq News/YouTube

Table 4.11 **Small arms and ammunition pledged or delivered to peshmerga, August–September 2014**		
Exporter	**Pledged materiel**	**Declared value**
Albania	22 million 7.62 x 39 mm cartridges, 15,000 hand grenades, 15,000 60 mm mortar shells, 12,000 82 mm mortar shells, 20,000 grenades for 40 mm under-barrel grenade launchers	n/a
Bulgaria	1,800 firearms and 6 million rounds of ammunition	USD 3.7 million (BGN 6 million)
Croatia	Undisclosed small arms and ammunition	n/a
Czech Republic	10 million 7.62 x 39 mm cartridges, 8 million 7.62 x 54R mm cartridges, 5,000 RPG-7 rounds, and 5,000 hand grenades	USD 2 million (CZK 41 million)
Estonia	1 million rounds of 7.62 x 39 mm ammunition	n/a
France	Browning M2 heavy machine guns and undisclosed arms and ammunition	n/a
Germany	8,000 G3 rifles and 2 million rounds of 7.62 x 51 mm ammunition, 8,000 G36 assault rifles and 4 million rounds of 5.56 x 45 mm ammunition, 40 MG3 general purpose machine guns and 1 million rounds of 7.61 x 51 mm ammunition, 8,000 P1 pistols and 1 million rounds of 9 x 19 mm ammunition, 30 MILAN anti-tank guided weapons and 500 guided missiles, 200 shoulder-fired Panzerfaust 3 rocket-assisted recoilless guns and 2,500 rockets, 40 Carl Gustaf recoilless guns and 1,000 projectiles, 100 flare guns and 4,000 rounds, and 10,000 hand grenades	USD 91 million (EUR 70 million)
Hungary	7 million cartridges and thousands of mines and armour-piercing shells	n/a
Iran	Undisclosed arms and ammunition	n/a
Italy	100 MG 42/59 general purpose machine guns and 250,000 ammunition rounds, 100 12.7 mm machine guns and 250,000 ammunition rounds, 1,000 RPG-7 grenades, 1,000 RPG-9 grenades, and 400,000 ammunition rounds for 'Soviet-made machine guns'	USD 2.5 million (EUR 1.9 million)
UK	40 Browning M2 heavy machine guns and nearly half a million rounds of ammunition	USD 2.6 million (GBP 1.6 million)
United States	Undisclosed arms and ammunition	n/a

Note: n/a = not available.

Sources: AFP (2014b; 2014c; 2014d); Albania (2014); B92.net (2014); Italy (2014, p. 13); Jones (2014); Kimball (2014); Kominek (2014); Novinite (2014); Payne (2014); UKMoD (2014); author correspondence with a small arms expert, September 2014

to the country (Holtom et al., 2013, pp. 269–70; Human Rights First, 2013). In addition, China and Iran are known to have supplied ammunition to Syrian government forces since 2011 (Jenzen-Jones, 2014).

Several EU member states, Turkey, and the United States have sought to disrupt the flow of arms from Iran, North Korea, and the Russian Federation to the Syrian government via the enforcement of transit controls and controls on the use of their flagged vessels. The United States has applied pressure on Syria's neighbours to interdict shipments heading to Syria from Iran that violate UN sanctions on Iran (Omanovic, 2013, pp. 10–11). Turkey has interdicted aircraft and ships from Iran and North Korea in an effort to prevent the supply of arms to Syria. In March 2011, for example, Turkish authorities intercepted a Yas Air (Iranian cargo airline) flight that was heading from Iran to Syria and seized assault rifles, machine guns, ammunition, and mortar shells (UNSC, 2012c, para. 37). In August 2013, Turkey reportedly found 30,000 rounds of ammunition and 1,400 pistols and rifles on a vessel travelling from North Korea to Syria (Cain, 2013).

For the UK, even the provision of insurance by UK companies to vessels shipping arms to Syria constitutes a breach of the EU arms embargo on Syria. This position caused a UK company to withdraw insurance from the MV *Alaed* as it was transporting munitions from the Russian Federation to Syria (Spencer, Blomfield, and Millward, 2012). The vessel was quickly reflagged with a Russian flag, which was largely seen as a protective measure, and reportedly delivered an arms shipment to Syria (Clover, 2012).

TRANSPARENCY ON SMALL ARMS TRANSFERS: REGIONAL REPORTING INSTRUMENTS

Transparency helps build trust among exporters and importers of small arms. The timely provision of information on small arms transfer authorizations and deliveries also facilitates accountability and oversight of arms transfer decisions. In particular, openness on small arms transfers enables parliamentarians, civil society, and the broader public to check whether a government is complying with its national and international obligations concerning the international arms trade.

Since 2004, the *Small Arms Survey* has featured the Small Arms Trade Transparency Barometer, a tool designed to assess countries' transparency in reporting on their small arms exports. The Barometer examines countries that claim—or are believed—to have exported USD 10 million or more worth of small arms, including their parts, accessories, and ammunition, during at least one calendar year since 2001. The assessment relies on national arms export reports,[27] the UN Register, and UN Comtrade. The Barometer will be presented in the next edition of the *Survey* using new scoring rules that reflect important recent changes to arms trade reporting, including reporting under the Arms Trade Treaty. The revision will also take account of regional reporting instruments, a subject explored in further detail below.

Several regional reporting instruments include information provided by states on their small arms transfers. Reports that are publicly available cover authorizations, and in some cases deliveries, of all conventional arms, while information specific to small arms is currently exchanged only among governments that are part of a regional arrangement.[28] This section first introduces the two publicly available regional reports on arms transfers: the EU Annual Report on arms exports and the regional report on arms exports for South-east Europe. The second part describes two regional instruments that are utilized for exchanging information on small arms transfers: the *Document on Small Arms and Light Weapons* of the Organization for Security and Cooperation in Europe (OSCE) and the Convention on Small Arms and Light Weapons, Their Ammunition and Other Related Materials of the Economic Community of West African States (ECOWAS) (OSCE, 2000; ECOWAS, 2006).

Publicly available regional reports on arms transfers

The **EU Annual Report on arms exports** contains data provided by EU member states on the financial value of their arms export licence approvals and actual arms exports for the preceding calendar year, broken down by destination and the 22 categories of the EU Common Military List. EU member states also provide information on arms export licence denials, although the report aggregates this data by potential recipient and Military List category, with no information provided on states that deny a licence. Categories 1 and 3 of the EU Common Military List cover small arms and ammunition, respectively; light weapons and associated ammunition are included in categories 2 and 4, which also include larger-calibre items, such as artillery pieces (EU, 2014c). The first EU Annual Report on arms exports was produced in 1999. The EU's common position establishing common rules governing the control of exports of military technology and equipment make both the provision of information for the report and its publication legally binding (EU, 2008).

All EU member states provided information on the financial value of their arms export authorizations for 2013.[29] Nineteen of the EU's 28 member states provided disaggregated information on arms deliveries in 2013.[30] However, the three largest arms exporters in the EU—France, Germany, and the United Kingdom—do not provide such information due to difficulties each faces in collecting and submitting data on arms deliveries disaggregated by EU Common Military List categories. In April 2008, EU member states agreed not only to share information on brokering licence authorizations and denials, but also to provide this information in the EU Annual Report on arms exports (EU, 2009). Sixteen EU member states provided such information for 2013, including data on the relevant destination, country of origin, financial value or quantity of items, and EU Common Military List category.[31]

The **South-east Europe Regional Report on Arms Exports** is based on the EU Annual Report, with data on licences authorized or denied and deliveries provided by Albania, Bosnia and Herzegovina, Croatia, the former Yugoslav Republic of Macedonia, Montenegro, and Serbia (SEESAC, n.d.). The production of a regional report was motivated, above all, by the desire to demonstrate the 'ability and willingness by the countries in the region to uphold the commitments associated with the Council Common Position 2008/944/CFSP' (SEESAC, n.d.). The South Eastern and Eastern Europe Clearinghouse for the Control of Small Arms (SEESAC) coordinates the compilation and publication of the reports. The first report was produced in December 2009, covering licences authorized or denied for the calendar year 2007 (Bromley, 2011; SEESAC, 2009). Data on deliveries was included from the second report onwards. At the time of writing, the published reports contained information on arms export authorizations and deliveries undertaken in 2007–11. The information contained in the annual reports is also presented in the form of a searchable database on the SEESAC website (SEESAC, n.d.).

Intergovernmental small arms transfer regional reporting instruments

The **OSCE *Document on Small Arms and Light Weapons*** outlines the rationale, purpose, and procedures of an annual intergovernmental exchange of information on small arms and light weapons transferred between OSCE states (OSCE, 2000). The 57 OSCE participating states provide information only on transfers among themselves, not on exports to or imports from non-OSCE members. A standardized reporting form that is annexed to the *Document* requests information on deliveries of five subcategories of small arms and eight subcategories of light weapons for the preceding calendar year, including the exporting or importing state, the number of items, the state of origin (if not the exporter), any intermediate location,[32] and any additional information that the reporting state wishes to provide (OSCE, 2000). The first information exchange took place in 2002 and data on transfers was submitted as of the following year. While the total number of states that participate in the exchange each year is made publicly available (see Table 4.12), the OSCE does not release details on which states participate or on the information they share.[33]

Table 4.12 OSCE member participation in information exchange on imports and exports of small arms and light weapons

Year	2002	2003	2004	2005	2006	2007	2008	2009	2010	2011	2012	2013
Number of OSCE states exchanging information (out of all participating states)	45 (55)	47 (55)	50 (55)	48 (55)	46 (55)	42 (56)	48 (56)	48 (56)	48 (56)	44 (56)	40 (56)	46 (57)

Source: author correspondence with an OSCE official, 7 January 2015

In June 2014, the OSCE adopted 'Voluntary Guidelines for Compiling National Reports on [small arms and light weapons] exports from/imports to other participating States during the previous calendar year' in order to 'improve the utility and relevance of the information provided' (OSCE, 2014a). In particular, the guidelines are intended to reduce, or at least help clarify, the significant discrepancies arising between information provided by exporters and importers. The guidelines recommend that states share the methodologies used to compile their information on small arms imports and exports and include a 'standardized cover sheet for submissions on [small arms and light weapons] exports and imports' (OSCE, 2014b). The guidelines further urge OSCE participating states to:

- provide descriptions of small arms and light weapons being transferred;
- make wider use of the OSCE small arms and light weapons reporting template;
- provide information on sources used for collecting data;
- provide information on the types of transfers and related end users; and
- carry out bilateral consultations with states from which small arms have been imported or to which they were exported in the preceding year on the contents of the OSCE submissions.

The **ECOWAS Convention on Small Arms and Light Weapons, Their Ammunition and Other Related Materials** was signed by the 15 ECOWAS heads of state and government in Abuja on 14 June 2006 and entered into force on 29 September 2009 (UNREC, 2009). Article 10 of the ECOWAS Convention obliges states parties to provide an annual report on their orders or purchases of small arms to the ECOWAS Executive Secretariat. The Executive Secretary is required to present an annual report on these transactions at the summit of heads of state and government and to develop a subregional database and register of small arms. As of February 2015, ECOWAS had not yet established the database or register, although the ECOWAS Commission reported plans to convene an expert meeting in 2015 to determine how to proceed with their establishment. It indicated that the implementation of the ECOWAS Convention's transparency provisions were 'immediate priorities' for the Commission.[34] It is not yet known whether the resulting information will be made publicly available or remain confidential.

CONCLUSION

This year's trade update chapter reviews significant trends in authorized international small arms transfers since 2001, with a particular focus on the MENA region, before and after the Arab uprisings. In preparation for a revision of the Small Arms Trade Transparency Barometer, to be presented in the 2016 edition of the *Survey*, the chapter also considers the contribution made by regional reporting instruments to overall trade transparency.

With respect to the latter issue, the final section of the chapter highlights that current regional reporting practices are something of a patchwork. The information exchange on small arms transfers undertaken by OSCE participating states remains confidential (restricted to governments) for the time being. In contrast, EU countries and states in South-eastern Europe make publicly available annual reports on export authorizations and on some deliveries of conventional arms. These latter efforts contribute towards greater transparency—as will be reflected in the 2016 edition of the Transparency Barometer.

The first section of the chapter, presenting multi-year trends in the authorized trade, shows that the United States continues to dominate the global small arms market. The country was both the largest exporter and importer of small arms between 2001 and 2012—by a large margin in the case of imports. The top and major exporters that saw the

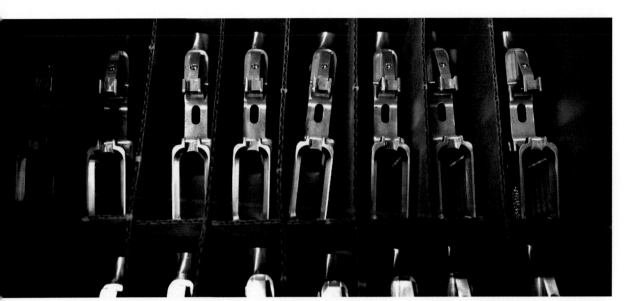

A box of MA-15 rifle lower receivers sits on the production floor at MMC Armory, United States, June 2013. © Daniel Acker/Bloomberg/Getty Images

greatest increases in their small arms exports during the same period were China (with a 1,456 per cent increase), Norway (777 per cent), South Korea (636 per cent), Turkey (467 per cent), and Brazil (295 per cent). The top and major importers that experienced the greatest increase in their small arms imports between 2001 and 2012 were Indonesia (with an 8,602 per cent increase), Pakistan (3,789 per cent), Thailand (558 per cent), Canada (332 per cent), and Egypt (267 per cent), revealing new trade patterns that, in some cases, involved countries that were suffering from high rates of armed violence and political instability.

The bulk of the chapter examines and compares the small arms policies and flows from significant arms exporters to Egypt, Libya, and Syria in 2001–10 and 2011–14, illustrating some of the ways in which these countries responded to increased levels of armed violence, armed conflict, and political instability in MENA during and after the 'Arab Spring'. Somewhat surprisingly, perhaps, with some exceptions, the Arab uprisings do not appear to have led to significant changes in the policies or practices of important small arms exporters to the region. Political instability and increased levels of armed violence in Egypt and Syria did not produce consensus among small arms exporters on the need for a UN arms embargo. While there was such a consensus in the case of Libya, the resulting UN arms embargo was amended after the overthrow of Qaddafi for purposes of re-equipping the new government's security forces with small arms—notwithstanding significant associated risks of diversion and misuse.

A similar dilemma arose with respect to the authorized transfer of small arms to non-state armed groups in MENA. While the issue divided some governments, the emergence of IS tipped the balance in favour of such transfers in the eyes of many important exporters. As described in the chapter, however, arms shipments such as the ones delivered to the Kurdish peshmerga also present heightened risks of diversion and potential misuse. It will be interesting to see whether countries that have exported small arms to non-state armed groups, including the peshmerga, will include this information in their Arms Trade Treaty reports, which do not restrict the information states parties are to provide to transfers between states.[35] In any case, neither the prospect of the adoption and entry into force of the Arms Trade Treaty, nor pre-existing control instruments, nor national legislation or policy appear to have led small arms exporters to exercise much restraint vis-à-vis the turbulence of the Middle East and North Africa. ◾

LIST OF ABBREVIATIONS

ECOWAS	Economic Community of West African States
EU	European Union
IS	Islamic State
MENA	Middle East and North Africa
NISAT	Norwegian Initiative on Small Arms Transfers
OSCE	Organization for Security and Co-operation in Europe
SEESAC	South Eastern and Eastern Europe Clearinghouse for the Control of the Small Arms and Light Weapons
UN Comtrade	United Nations Commodity Trade Statistics Database
UN Register	United Nation Register of Conventional Arms

ANNEXES

Online annexes at <http://www.smallarmssurvey.org/publications/by-type/yearbook/small-arms-survey-2015.html>

Annexe 4.1. Annual authorized small arms and light weapons exports for major exporters (annual exports of at least USD 10 million), 2012

Annexe 4.2. Annual authorized small arms and light weapons imports for major importers (annual imports of at least USD 10 million), 2012

Annexe 4.3 Importers (excluding the United States) and main recipients of shipments from the largest exporters, 2001–12

Annexe 4.4 Authorized transfers of small arms and light weapons to Egypt, Libya, and Syria, 2001–13

ENDNOTES

1   The *Small Arms Survey* relies on the analysis of customs data provided by the Norwegian Initiative on Small Arms Transfers (NISAT) project at the Peace Research Institute Oslo. NISAT considers countries' self-reported exports as well as 'mirror data'—reported imports by destination countries—to generate a single value by transaction; see Marsh (2005). Figures may vary depending on the period of consultation of the UN Comtrade database as countries can revise their submissions to UN Comtrade (see Dreyfus et al., 2009, p. 54, n. 10). Data for this chapter was downloaded between September 2014 and February 2015. For brief definitions of the terms 'authorized transfers' and 'small arms', along with a discussion of the strengths and weaknesses of UN Comtrade as a source of information on the global small arms trade, see Dreyfus et al. (2009, pp. 28–31); Grzybowski, Marsh, and Schroeder (2012, pp. 247–51); Holtom, Pavesi, and Rigual (2014, pp. 110–11). On the challenges of monitoring small arms transfers to MENA, see Box 4.1 in this chapter.

2   See Annexe 4.1 for details on values exported, main partners, and categories reported by top and major exporters for 2012.

3   See Annexe 4.2 for details on values imported, main partners, and categories reported by top and major importers for 2012.

4   Customs (Comtrade) data used by the Barometer to evaluate exporter transparency is derived not only from exporter submissions, but also from 'mirror' data provided by importing states, weakening, at least in some cases, the tie between Barometer score and the amount of information provided by the state receiving that score. It is also important to note that the Barometer assesses the availability, quantity, and level of detail of exporter information, not its veracity. Finally, the Barometer assesses only countries that are known, or believed, to have exported at least USD 10 million worth of small arms in one or more years since 2001, thus omitting a portion of the global small arms trade. See Lazarevic (2010, pp. 11–24).

5   Although not a UN member, Taiwan can issue a national report on its international small arms transfers. The Small Arms Survey estimates Taiwan's small arms exports using UN Comtrade mirror data—reported imports by destination countries—as compiled by NISAT.

6   Note that changes in reported values transferred can be caused by an actual change in small arms transfer flows or by a change in reporting practices (increased or decreased transparency). China's level of transparency has remained within the range of 6.25–12.25 since 2001, but the country has seen the largest increase in reported transfers over the past decade. Given the country's unchanged level of transparency, this reported increase may well reflect an actual surge in exports.

7   A graph presenting the same figures, but excluding the United States, is provided in Annexe 4.3 (see Figure 4.2a).

8   These countries were among the annual top five importers of US small arms at least five times between 2001 and 2012.

9   See Annexe 4.3 for more information on the main recipients of small arms from the five largest exporters in 2001–12. These top exporters are, in descending order, the United States, Italy, Germany, Brazil, and Austria. Figures 4.3 to 4.7 in Annexe 4.3 reveal that Austria, Brazil, Germany, and Italy all had the same main recipient for their small arms exports: the United States.

10 For purposes of this chapter, the Middle East and North Africa region includes Algeria, Bahrain, Egypt, Iran, Iraq, Israel, Jordan, Kuwait, Lebanon, Libya, Morocco, Oman, the Palestinian Territories, Qatar, Saudi Arabia, Syria, Tunisia, the United Arab Emirates, and Yemen.

11 The Small Arms Survey has conducted research into the proliferation of small arms to armed groups in the region. Selected sources that discuss this phenomenon include Holtom, Pavesi, and Rigual (2014, pp. 117–28); Jenzen-Jones (2013; 2014); Kartas (2013); Rigual (2014); Schroeder (2014).

12 AI (2011); Duquet (2014); European Parliament (2012); Vranckx, Slijper, and Isbister (2011).

13 Boxes 4.1 and 4.2 provide details on the sources and methodology for this section. Annexe 4.4 features official data on small arms exports to Egypt, Libya, and Syria for 2001–13.

14 The 39 states are Albania, Austria, Belgium, Bosnia and Herzegovina, Bulgaria, Canada, Croatia, Cyprus, the Czech Republic, Denmark, Estonia, Finland, the former Yugoslav Republic of Macedonia, France, Germany, Greece, Hungary, Ireland, Italy, Latvia, Lithuania, Luxembourg, Malta, Montenegro, the Netherlands, Norway, Poland, Portugal, Romania, Serbia, Slovakia, Slovenia, South Africa, Spain, Sweden, Switzerland, Ukraine, the United Kingdom, and the United States.

15 Egypt provided information on its imports and exports of major conventional weapons to the UN Register in its first year of operation (1993) but stressed that its continuing participation in the instrument would depend on the expansion of the UN Register to include weapons of mass destruction (UNGA, 1993, p. 33). It has provided no information to the Register since 1993.

16 See Table 4.6 and Annexe 4.4. Boxes 4.1 and 4.2 provide further information on sources and methodology.

17 All data from the EU report has been converted into US dollars.

18 Among the 13 countries was the Russian Federation, which reported the export of 98 man-portable air defence systems to Egypt in 2009 under category VII of the UN Register. The Russian Federation has not provided background information on small arms exports to the UN Register.

19 Sections 517 and 644(q) of the US Foreign Assistance Act of 1961 outline the conditions under which the United States designates states non-NATO allies. Egypt was granted the status of major non-NATO ally in 1989, as a result of which it receives US military aid for the purchase or lease of military equipment. Between 1987 and 2014, the United States provided around USD 1.3 billion per year in military aid to Egypt (Sharp, 2014). Small arms and ammunition represent only a very small share of the overall value of US military aid to Egypt.

20 Lutterbeck (2009, p. 510); NISAT (n.d.); SIPRI (n.d.d); UN Comtrade (n.d.).

21 The UN Security Council Committee concerning Libya reported that it received 4 notifications invoking paragraph 13a in 2011 (UNSC, 2012a, para. 25), 53 in 2012 (UNSC, 2013a, para. 29), 20 in 2013 (UNSC, 2013c, para. 31), and 2 in 2014 (UNSC, 2014c, para. 22), none of which received negative decisions. It received two further notifications that did not meet the necessary requirements for a notification in 2013 (UNSC, 2013c, para. 31), and four in 2014 (UNSC, 2014c, para. 22). In these cases, the committee requested further specifications from the notifying member states. It confirmed that the four 2014 incomplete notifications were subsequently completed by the notifying states and that no negative decisions were taken by the committee (UNSC, 2014c, para. 22).

22 Syria had a population of 22 million before the civil war. According to data analysed in April 2014, three million Syrians are refugees in neighbouring states, while a further 6.5 million are internally displaced (Blanchard, Humud, and Nikitin, 2014, p. 3).

23 In relation to China, see Grimmett and Kerr (2012) and Jenzen-Jones (2014).

24 For example, the UN Human Rights Council independent international commission of inquiry on Syria recommended in August 2014 'that the international community impose an arms embargo' on Syria (UNHRC, 2014, para. 146(a)).

25 For example, China scored 7.00 (out of a maximum of 25 points), Iran 0.00, North Korea 0.00, the Russian Federation 10.25, and Ukraine 8.00 in the Small Arms Trade Transparency Barometer 2014 (Holtom, Pavesi, and Rigual, 2014, p. 130).

26 Australia, Canada, France, the UK, and the United States airlifted small arms and ammunition provided by other states to northern Iraq during these months (Payne, 2014).

27 These reports include information EU states have contributed to the EU Annual Report on military exports, produced pursuant to EU Council Common Position 2008/944/CFSP on the control of exports of military technology and equipment by EU states.

28 This section does not include the Inter-American Convention on Transparency in Conventional Weapons Acquisition because it does not currently require states parties to provide information on small arms transfers even though it obliges them to provide an annual report on imports of items falling within the seven categories of the UN Register (OAS, 1999). Nor does this section discuss the confidential reporting mechanism of the Wassenaar Arrangement, a multilateral—rather than regional—export control regime (Wassenaar Arrangement, n.d.).

29   Author correspondence with an EU official, 6 January 2015.

30   Author correspondence with an EU official, 6 January 2015.

31   Author correspondence with an EU official, 6 January 2015.

32   The OSCE does not provide guidance on 'intermediate location'; however, UN guidance explains that states can use the 'intermediate location' column in the UN Register reporting form to identify a state where materiel is integrated into or installed on another item—such as missiles on combat aircraft—before export to the end user (UNODA, 2007, p. 13).

33   Spain unilaterally makes its OSCE submission publicly available by including a copy in its national report on arms exports (Spain, 2014).

34   Author correspondence with the ECOWAS Commission, 11 February 2015.

35   By contrast, according to the 2013 report of the Group of Governmental Experts on the UN Register, the latter does not apply to 'transfers to and holdings of arms by non-State actors' (UNGA, 2013a, para. 62).

BIBLIOGRAPHY

AFP (Agence France-Presse). 2014a. 'France Asks EU to "Mobilise" to Arm Kurds in Iraq.' *Defense News*. 11 August.

    <http://www.defensenews.com/article/20140811/DEFREG04/308110011/France-Asks-EU-Mobilize-Arm-Kurds-Iraq>

—. 2014b. 'Iran Provided Weapons to Iraq's Kurds: Barzani.' 26 August.

    <http://news.yahoo.com/iran-provided-weapons-iraqs-kurds-barzani-135743780.html>

—. 2014c. 'Britain Arming Iraqi Kurds with Machine Guns to Fight IS.' 9 September.

    <http://news.yahoo.com/britain-arming-iraqi-kurds-machine-guns-fight-140021897.html>

—. 2014d. 'Des armes envoyées par la France sont arrivées sur le front irakien.' 14 September.

    <http://www.institutkurde.org/info/depeches/des-armes-envoyees-par-la-france-sont-arrivees-sur-le-front-irakien-5281.html>

AI (Amnesty International). 2011. *Arms Transfers to the Middle East and North Africa: Lessons for an Effective Arms Trade Treaty*. London: AI.

Al Jazeera. 2011a. 'Battle for Libya: Key Moments Timeline of Decisive Battles and Political Developments in Libya's Uprising against Muammar Gaddafi.' 19 November. <http://www.aljazeera.com/indepth/spotlight/libya/2011/10/20111020104244706760.html>

—. 2011b. 'Turkey Imposes Sanctions on Syria.' 30 November.

    <http://www.aljazeera.com/news/middleeast/2011/11/2011113083714894547.html>

Albania. 2014. Cabinet of Ministers Decision No. 542 of 15 August. *Official Bulletin*, No. 132. 19 August, p. 6039.

    <http://www.ufsh.org.al/content/uploads/2014/sep/2/fletorja-zyrtare-132-2014.pdf>

Aliev, Ruslan. 2007. 'Military-Technical Relations between Libya, Syria, Egypt and Russia.' *Moscow Defense Brief*, No. 3.

    <http://mdb.cast.ru/mdb/3-2007/at/article2/?form=print>

Allison, Roy. 2013. 'Russia and Syria: Explaining Alignment with a Regime in Crisis.' *International Affairs*, Vol. 89, Iss. 4, pp. 795–823.

B92.net (Serbia). 2014. 'Croatia Gives Weapons to Kurds in Iraq.' 22 August.

    <http://www.b92.net/eng/news/region.php?yyyy=2014&mm=08&dd=22&nav_id=91376>

Blanchard, Christopher, Carla Humud, and Mary Beth Nikitin. 2014. *Armed Conflict in Syria: Overview and U.S. Response*. Congressional Research Service Report RL33487. Washington, DC: Congressional Research Service. 17 September. <http://fas.org/sgp/crs/mideast/RL33487.pdf>

Bromley, Mark. 2011. *The Development of National and Regional Reports on Arms Exports in the EU and South Eastern Europe*. Belgrade: SEESAC.

—, Mathieu Duchâtel, and Paul Holtom. 2013. *China's Exports of Small Arms and Light Weapons*. Policy Paper 38. Stockholm: Stockholm International Peace Research Institute. October.

Cain, Geoffrey. 2013. 'North Korea Attempts to Sell Gas Masks to Assad.' *Global Post* (United States). 28 August.

    <http://www.globalpost.com/dispatches/globalpost-blogs/today-north-korea/north-korea-attempts-sell-gas-masks-assad>

Chivers, C.J. and Eric Schmitt. 2013. 'Syrian Rebels' Arms Traced to Sudanese; Qatar Buys Weapons and Arranges Shipment via Turkey, Officials Say.' *The New York Times*. 14 August. <https://www.questia.com/newspaper/1P2-36307049/syrian-rebels-arms-traced-to-sudanese-qatar-buys>

Clover, Charles. 2012. 'Confusion Clouds Fate of Syrian Helicopters.' *Financial Times*. 13 July.

    <http://www.ft.com/cms/s/0/590748d4-ccf0-11e1-9960-00144feabdc0.html#axzz3S6OmykI8>

Cornwell, Susan and Arshad Mohammed. 2012. 'Clinton to Let Military Aid to Egypt Continue: State Department Official.' Reuters. 22 March.

    <http://www.reuters.com/article/2012/03/23/us-egypt-usa-aid-idUSBRE82L13D20120323>

Dreyfus, Pablo, et al. 2009. 'Sifting the Sources: Authorized Small Arms Transfers.' In Small Arms Survey. *Small Arms Survey 2009: Shadows of War.* Cambridge: Cambridge University Press, pp. 6–59.

Duquet, Nils. 2014. *Business as Usual? Assessing the Impact of the Arab Spring on European Arms Export Control Policies.* Brussels: Flemish Peace Institute. March.
<http://www.flemishpeaceinstitute.eu/sites/vlaamsvredesinstituut.eu/files/files/reports/report_business_as_usual_web.pdf>

ECOWAS (Economic Community of West African States). 2006. ECOWAS Convention on Small Arms and Light Weapons, Their Ammunition and Other Related Materials.

EPCP (European Political Cooperation Presidency). 1986. 'Statement by Ministers of Foreign Affairs of the Twelve on International Terrorism and the Crisis in the Mediterranean.' The Hague: EPCP. 14 April.
<http://www.sipri.org/databases/embargoes/eu_arms_embargoes/libya/libya-1986/european-political-cooperation-presidency-statement>

EU (European Union). 2008. Council Common Position 2008/944/CFSP of 8 December 2008 Defining Common Rules Governing Control of Exports of Military Technology and Equipment. *Official Journal of the European Union.* L 335/99 of 13 December.

—. 2009. *Eleventh Annual Report according to Article 8(2) of Council Common Position 2008/944/CFSP Defining Common Rules Governing Control of Exports of Military Technology and Equipment.* 2009/C 265/01 of 6 November. Brussels: Council of the EU.

—. 2011. Council Decision 2011/273/CFSP of 9 May 2011 Concerning Restrictive Measures against Syria. *Official Journal of the European Union*, L121. 10 May.

—. 2013a. '3256th Council Meeting: Foreign Affairs.' Press Release 13086/13. Brussels: Council of the EU. 21 August.
<http://www.consilium.europa.eu/uedocs/cms_data/docs/pressdata/EN/foraff/138603.pdf>

—. 2013b. 'Council Declaration on Syria.' Brussels: Council of the EU. 27 May.
<http://www.consilium.europa.eu/uedocs/cms_data/docs/pressdata/EN/foraff/137315.pdf>

—. 2014a. Common Military List of the European Union. Adopted 17 March. *Official Journal of the European Union.* C 107/1. 9 April.

—. 2014b. 'Council Conclusions on Iraq.' Press release. Brussels: Council of the EU. 15 August.
<http://www.consilium.europa.eu/uedocs/cms_data/docs/pressdata/EN/foraff/144311.pdf>

—. 2014c. *Fifteenth Annual Report According to Article 8(2) of Council Common Position 2008/944/CFSP Defining Common Rules Governing Control of Exports of Military Technology and Equipment. Official Journal of the European Union*, C 621. 21 January.

—. n.d. 'Arms Exports Control: Documents—Earlier EU Annual Reports on Arms Exports.'
<http://www.eeas.europa.eu/non-proliferation-and-disarmament/arms-export-control/index_en.htm>

European Parliament. 2012. *EU Action for Human Rights and Democracy in the Middle East and North Africa.* Brussels: Directorate-General for External Policies. December.
<http://www.europarl.europa.eu/RegData/etudes/etudes/join/2012/457141/EXPO-DROI_ET%282012%29457141_EN.pdf>

Felgenhauer, Pavel. 2007. 'Putin Makes Sweetheart Arms Deal to Benefit His Cronies.' *Eurasia Daily Monitor*, Vol. 4, Iss. 91. 9 May.
<http://www.jamestown.org/single/?tx_ttnews%5Btt_news%5D=32730&no_cache=1#.VHm0qzGsXTg>

Geneva Declaration Secretariat. 2014. Global Burden of Armed Violence 2014 Database. Geneva: Geneva Declaration Secretariat.

Grimmett, Richard and Paul Kerr. 2012. *Conventional Arms Transfers to Developing Nations, 2004–2011.* Congressional Research Service Report R42678. Washington, DC: Congressional Research Service. 24 August. <http://www.fas.org/sgp/crs/weapons/R42678.pdf>

Grzybowski, Janis, Nicholas Marsh, and Matt Schroeder. 2012. 'Piece by Piece: Authorized Transfers of Parts and Accessories.' In Small Arms Survey. *Small Arms Survey 2012: Moving Targets.* Cambridge: Cambridge University Press, pp. 240–81.

Holtom, Paul, Irene Pavesi, and Christelle Rigual. 2014. 'Trade Update: Transfers, Retransfers, and the ATT.' In Small Arms Survey. *Small Arms Survey 2014: Women and Guns.* Cambridge: Cambridge University Press, pp. 108–43.

—, et al. 2013. 'International Arms Transfers.' *SIPRI Yearbook 2013: Armament, Disarmament and International Security.* Oxford: Oxford University Press, pp. 241–81.

HRW (Human Rights Watch). 2007. *Caught in the Whirlwind: Torture and Denial of Due Process by the Kurdistan Security Forces.* 3 July.
<http://www.hrw.org/reports/2007/07/02/caught-whirlwind>

—. 2014. *All According to Plan: The Rab'a Massacre and Mass Killings of Protestors in Egypt.* August.
<http://www.hrw.org/sites/default/files/reports/egypt0814web_0.pdf>

Human Rights First. 2013. 'New Document Details Syria's Request for Russian Arms.' 13 May.
<http://www.humanrightsfirst.org/press-release/new-document-details-syria%E2%80%99s-request-russian-arms>

IHS Jane's. 2014. *Navigating the Emerging Markets: Libya.* May.

Italy. 2014. 'Comunicazioni del Governo sullo stato delle missioni in corso e degli interventi di cooperazione allo sviluppo a sostegno dei processi di pace e di stabilizzazione.' Rome: Joint and Combined Commission of Foreign Affairs and Defence. 3 September.
<http://www.difesa.it/Primo_Piano/Documents/2014/04%20settembre/20140903_Audizione.pdf>

Jenzen-Jones, N.R. 2011a. 'Update: AK-103 Exports to Libya.' Rogue Adventurer blog. 16 September.
<http://rogueadventurer.com/2011/09/16/update-ak-103-exports-to-libya/>

—. 2011b. 'Update II: AK-103 Exports to Libya.' Rogue Adventurer blog. 31 October.
<http://rogueadventurer.com/2011/10/31/update-ii-ak-103-exports-to-libya/>

—. 2013. *Small-calibre Ammunition in Libya: An Update*. Security Assessment in North Africa Dispatch No. 2. Geneva: Small Arms Survey.

—. 2014. *Following the Headstamp Trail: An Assessment of Small-calibre Ammunition Documented in Syria*. Working Paper No. 18. Geneva: Small Arms Survey.

Jones, Bruce. 2014. 'Estonia Donates Small-arms Ammo to Iraqi Kurds.' *IHS Jane's 360*. 2 September.
<http://www.janes.com/article/42682/estonia-donates-small-arms-ammo-to-iraqi-kurds>

Kartas, Moncef. 2013. *On the Edge? Trafficking and Insecurity at the Tunisian–Libyan Border*. Working Paper No. 17. Geneva: Small Arms Survey.

Khalilzad, Zalmay. 2014. 'To Fight the Islamic State, Kurdish and Iraqi Forces Need Expedited Aid.' *Washington Post*. 5 August.
<http://www.washingtonpost.com/opinions/zalmay-khalilzad-to-fight-the-islamic-state-kurdish-and-iraqi-forces-need-expedited-aid/2014/08/05/746d8680-1c24-11e4-ae54-0cfe1f974f8a_story.html>

Kimball, Spencer. 2014. 'German Weapons Deliveries to Iraq's Kurdish Region.' *Deutsche Welle*. 1 September.
<http://www.dw.de/german-weapons-deliveries-to-iraqs-kurdish-region/a-17892161>

Kirkpatrick, David. 2012. 'Named Egypt's Winner, Islamist Makes History.' *The New York Times*. 24 June.
<http://www.nytimes.com/2012/06/25/world/middleeast/mohamed-morsi-of-muslim-brotherhood-declared-as-egypts-president.html?pagewanted=all&_r=0>

Klapper, Bradley. 2013. 'Senate Aide: US Military Aid to Egypt Has Stopped.' Associated Press. 20 August.
<http://news.yahoo.com/senate-aide-us-military-aid-egypt-stopped-154230217.html>

Kominek, Jiri. 2014. 'Czechs Donate Ammunition to Iraqi Kurds.' *IHS Jane's 360*. 27 August.
<http://www.janes.com/article/42443/czechs-donate-ammunition-to-iraqi-kurds>

Landler, Mark and Michael Gordon. 2013. 'Obama Could Revisit Arming Syria Rebels as Assad Holds Firm.' *The New York Times*. 18 February.
<http://www.nytimes.com/2013/02/19/world/middleeast/as-assad-holds-firm-obama-could-revisit-arms-policy.html?pagewanted=all&_r=0>

Lantratov, Konstantin, et al. 2007. 'MiGs Will Defend Syria and Iran.' *Kommersant*. 19 June.
<http://www.kommersant.com/p775460/r_527/arms_trade_/1 of>

Lauria, Joe and Nour Malas. 2011. 'Russia Introduces Competing UN Draft on Syria.' *Wall Street Journal*. 26 August.
<http://online.wsj.com/news/articles/SB10001424053111904787404576532921767214848>

Lazarevic, Jasna. 2010. *Transparency Counts: Assessing State Reporting on Small Arms Transfers, 2001–08*. Occasional Paper No. 25. June. Geneva: Small Arms Survey. <http://www.smallarmssurvey.org/fileadmin/docs/B-Occasional-papers/SAS-OP25-Barometer.pdf>

League of Arab States. 2011. Arab Ministerial Council Statement on the Situation in Syria [in Arabic]. 3 December.
<http://www.sipri.org/databases/embargoes/eu_arms_embargoes/syria_LAS/20111203_Arab%20League%20arms%20embargo%20on%20Syria.pdf>

Lee, Matthew Russell. 2011. 'UN Libya Sanctions Consensus Requirement Makes Arms Embargo a Joke.' Inner City Press. 7 July.
<http://www.innercitypress.com/frun6libya070711.html>

Lenta. 2010. 'Russia to Finish Building a Kalashnikov-producing Factory in Libya' [in Russian]. 5 February.
<http://lenta.ru/news/2010/02/05/deal/>

Libya. 2010. *Report of the Libyan Arab Jamahiriya on Implementation of the United Nations Programme of Action to Prevent, Combat and Eradicate the Illicit Trade in Small Arms and Light Weapons in All Its Aspects Submitted Pursuant to General Assembly Resolution 64/50*.
<http://www.poa-iss.org/NationalReport/NationalReports.aspx>

Lutterbeck, Derek. 2009. 'Arming Libya: Transfers of Conventional Weapons Past and Present.' *Contemporary Security Policy*, Vol. 30, No. 3, pp. 505–28.

Mangan, Fiona and Christina Murtaugh. 2014. *Security and Justice in Post-revolution Libya: Where to Turn?* Peacework No. 100. Washington, DC: United States Institute of Peace and Security Assessment in North Africa, Small Arms Survey

Marsh, Nicholas. 2005. 'Accounting Guns: The Methodology Used in Developing Data Tables for the Small Arms Survey.' Background paper. Oslo: Norwegian Initiative on Small Arms Transfers and Peace Research Institute Oslo. 14 November.

McQuinn, Brian. 2012. *After the Fall: Libya's Evolving Armed Groups*. Working Paper No. 12. Geneva: Small Arms Survey.

MEIC (Maadi Engineering Industries Company). n.d. 'Military Products.' <http://fact54.momp.gov.eg/En/MilProduct.aspx>

Mustafa, Awad. 2013. 'Intrigue Deepens Over Egypt–Russia Arms Deals.' *Defense News*. 24 November.
  <http://www.defensenews.com/article/20131124/DEFREG01/311240009/Intrigue-Deepens-Over-Egypt-Russia-Arms-Deals>

Nikolskii, Aleksei. 2010. 'Receiving Tanks and Assault Rifles' [in Russian]. *Vedomosti* (Russia). 5 February.
  <http://www.vedomosti.ru/newspaper/article/2010/02/05/224831>

— and Polina Khimshiashvili. 2014. 'Two Plus Two Equals USD 3 million' [in Russian]. *Vedomosti* (Russia). 14 February.
  <http://www.vedomosti.ru/newspaper/article/623731/dva-plyus-dva-ravno-3-mlrd>

NISAT (Norwegian Initiative on Small Arms Transfers). n.d. 'NISAT Database of Small Arms Transfers: Researcher's Database.' Oslo: NISAT, Peace Research
  Institute Oslo. Accessed November 2014. <http://nisat.prio.org/Trade-Database/Researchers-Database/>

Novinite (Bulgaria). 2014. 'Bulgaria Sends Firearms, Ammo to Iraqi Government.' 30 September.
  <http://www.novinite.com/articles/163717/Bulgaria+Sends+Firearms,+Ammo+to+Iraqi+Government>

OAS (Organization of American States). 1999. Inter-American Convention on Transparency in Conventional Arms Acquisitions. Guatemala City, 7 June.
  <http://www.oas.org/juridico/english/treaties/a-64.html>

OHCHR (Office of the United Nations High Commissioner for Human Rights). 2011. *Report of the OHCR Mission to Egypt, 27 March–4 April 2011*.
  <http://www.ohchr.org/Documents/Countries/EG/OHCHR_MissiontoEgypt27March_4April.pdf>

—. 2013. 'Pillay Calls for Urgent Talks to Save Egypt from Further Disastrous Violence.' 15 August.
  <http://www.ohchr.org/EN/NewsEvents/Pages/DisplayNews.aspx?NewsID=13632&LangID=>

Omanovic, Edin. 2013. 'Effective Embargo Enforcement: Overflight Denial and Control.' Non-Proliferation Papers No. 26. EU Non-Proliferation Consortium.
  February. <http://www.sipri.org/research/disarmament/eu-consortium/publications/nonproliferation-paper-26>

OSCE (Organization for Security and Co-operation in Europe). 2000. Document on Small Arms and Light Weapons. FSC.DOC/1/00/Rev.1, adopted
  24 November 2000, reissued 20 June 2012. Vienna: Forum for Security Co-operation, OSCE. <http://www.osce.org/fsc/20783>

—. 2014a. Decision No. 3/14: Voluntary Guidelines for Compiling National Reports on SALW Exports from/Imports to other Participating States during
  the Previous Calendar Year. FSC.DEC/3/14. 4 June. <http://www.osce.org/fsc/119734?download=true>

—. 2014b. 'Voluntary Guidelines for Compiling National Reports on SALW Exports from/Imports to other Participating States during the Previous Calendar
  Year.' Vienna: OSCE.

Pavel, Otto. 2014. 'Češi dodají egyptské policii desítky tisíc pistolí' [Czechs give tens of thousands of pistols to Egyptian police]. E15.cz. 17 February.
  <http://zpravy.e15.cz/byznys/prumysl-a-energetika/cesi-dodaji-egyptske-policii-desitky-tisic-pistoli-1061249>

Payne, Sebastian. 2014. 'What the 60-plus Members of the Anti-Islamic State Coalition Are Doing.' *Washington Post*. 25 September.
  <http://www.washingtonpost.com/news/checkpoint/wp/2014/09/25/what-the-60-members-of-the-anti-islamic-state-coalition-are-doing/>

Pöhle, Sven. 2014. 'We Can't Track Every Weapon We Deliver.' *Deutsche Welle*. 4 September.
  <http://www.dw.de/we-cant-track-every-weapon-we-deliver/a-17901214>

Price, Megan, Anita Gohdes, and Patrick Ball. 2014. *Updated Statistical Analysis of Documentation of Killings in the Syrian Arab Republic*. Human Rights
  Data Analysis Group. August. <http://www.ohchr.org/Documents/Countries/SY/HRDAGUpdatedReportAug2014.pdf>

Radio Praha. 2013. 'Czech Arms Producer Wins Tender to Supply Pistols to Egypt.' 23 May.
  <http://www.radio.cz/en/section/news/czech-arms-producer-wins-tender-to-supply-pistols-to-egypt>

Rettman, Andrew. 2013a. 'EU Reconsiders Arms Sales, Financial Aid to Egypt.' EUobserver.com. 19 August.
  <http://euobserver.com/foreign/121149>

—. 2013b. 'Loopholes Aplenty in EU "Arms Ban" on Egypt.' EUobserver.com. 2 September. <http://euobserver.com/defence/121277>

RIA Novosti. 2007. 'Russia Denies New Deliveries of Strelets Air Defense System to Syria.' 23 January.
  <http://sputniknews.com/russia/20070123/59565930.html>

—. 2012. 'Russia's Rosoboronexport to Continue Arms Supplies to Syria.' 12 June.

Rice, Susan. 2013. 'Remarks by National Security Advisor Susan E. Rice: "Human Rights: Advancing American Interests and Values."' Presentation at Human
  Rights First Annual Summit, Washington, DC, 4 December.
  <http://www.whitehouse.gov/the-press-office/2013/12/04/remarks-national-security-advisor-susan-e-rice-human-rights-advancing-am>

Rigual, Christelle. 2014. *Armed Groups and Guided Light Weapons: 2014 Update with MENA Focus*. Research Note No. 47. Geneva: Small Arms Survey.

Rogin, Josh. 2014. 'ISIS Video: America's Air Dropped Weapons Now in Our Hands.' *Daily Beast* (New York). 21 October.
  <http://www.thedailybeast.com/articles/2014/10/21/isis-video-america-s-air-dropped-weapons-now-in-our-hands.html>

Russian Federation. 2011a. 'Remarks and Response to Media Questions by Foreign Minister Sergey Lavrov after the Meeting of the State Duma Committee on International Affairs, Moscow, June 30, 2011.' Moscow: Ministry of Foreign Affairs. 30 June.
<http://www.mid.ru/bdomp/brp_4.nsf/e78a48070f128a7b43256999005bcbb3/468f5d0c2073a305c32578c000575f4f!OpenDocument>

—. 2011b. 'Opening Remarks and Answers by Russian Foreign Minister Sergey Lavrov at Press Conference Following Talks with Icelandic Foreign Minister Ossur Skarphedinsson, Moscow, November 29, 2011.' Moscow: Ministry of Foreign Affairs. 29 November.
<http://www.mid.ru/brp_4.nsf/0/910EA870582BC0F344257959001DACE9>

Ryan, Missy, Mark Hosenball, and Steven Scheer. 2014. 'US Seeking European Arms, Ammunition for Kurds: Officials.' Reuters. 14 August.
<http://www.reuters.com/article/2014/08/14/us-iraq-security-usa-arms-idUSKBN0GE18A20140814>

Schroeder, Matt. 2014. *Fire and Forget: The Proliferation of Man-portable Air Defence Systems in Syria.* Issue Brief No. 9. Geneva: Small Arms Survey.

SEESAC (South Eastern and Eastern Europe Clearinghouse for the Control of Small Arms and Light Weapons). 2009. *Regional Report on Arms Exports in 2007.* Belgrade: SEESAC. <http://www.seesac.org/res/files/publication/594.pdf>

—. n.d. 'Regional Reports on Arms Exports.' <http://www.seesac.org/project.php?l1=126&l2=154&l3=185>

Serbia. 2009. *Annual Report on the Transfers of Controlled Goods in 2007.* Belgrade: Ministry of Economy and Regional Development.

—. 2010. *Annual Report on the Transfers of Controlled Goods in 2008.* Belgrade: Ministry of Economy and Regional Development.

—. 2011. *Annual Report on the Transfers of Controlled Goods in 2009.* Belgrade: Ministry of Economy and Regional Development.

Sharp, Jeremy. 2014. *Egypt: Background and U.S. Relations.* RL33003. Washington, DC: Congressional Research Service. 5 June.
<http://fas.org/sgp/crs/mideast/RL33003.pdf>

Simeone, Nick. 2014. 'One Airdrop to Kurds Fighting in Kobani Intercepted.' DoD News. Washington, DC: US Department of Defense. 22 October.
<http://www.defense.gov/news/newsarticle.aspx?id=123464>

SIPRI (Stockholm International Peace Research Institute). n.d.a. 'Arms Embargoes Database.' Accessed February 2015.
<http://www.sipri.org/research/armaments/transfers/databases/embargoes>

—. n.d.b. 'SIPRI National Reports Database.' Accessed February 2015.
<http://www.sipri.org/research/armaments/transfers/transparency/national_reports/sipri-national-reports-database>

—. n.d.c. 'EU Arms Embargo on Libya.' Last updated 23 November 2012.
<http://www.sipri.org/databases/embargoes/eu_arms_embargoes/libya/libya-1986>

—. n.d.d. 'SIPRI Arms Transfers Database.' Accessed 28 September 2014. <http://armstrade.sipri.org/armstrade/page/trade_register.php>

—. n.d.e. 'UN Arms Embargo on Libya.' Last updated 29 August 2014.
<http://www.sipri.org/databases/embargoes/un_arms_embargoes/libya/libya_2011>

Small Arms Survey. n.d. 'The Transparency Barometer.'
<http://www.smallarmssurvey.org/weapons-and-markets/tools/the-transparency-barometer>

Spain. 2014. *Estadísticas Españolas de Exportación de Material de Defensa, de Otro Material y de Productos y Tecnologías de Doble Uso, Año 2013.* Madrid: Ministry of Economy and Finance.

Spencer, Richard. 2012. 'Egypt's Military Council "to Lift 30-year-old State of Emergency".' *Daily Telegraph* (UK). 24 January.
<http://www.telegraph.co.uk/news/worldnews/africaandindianocean/egypt/9036685/Egypts-military-council-to-lift-30-year-old-state-of-emergency.html>

—, Adrian Blomfield, and David Millward. 2012. 'Britain Stops Russian Ship Carrying Attack Helicopters for Syria.' *Daily Telegraph* (UK). 18 June.
<http://www.telegraph.co.uk/news/worldnews/middleeast/syria/9339933/Britain-stops-Russian-ship-carrying-attack-helicopters-for-Syria.html>

Spiegel, Peter. 2013. 'Syria: Fabius–Hague Letter on Lifting Arms Embargo.' *Financial Times* Brussels Blog. 21 April.
<http://blogs.ft.com/brusselsblog/2013/04/21/syria-fabius-hague-letter-on-lifting-arms-embargo/>

UKHC (United Kingdom House of Commons). 2013. 'Arms to Syria.' Hansard, cols. 587–628. 11 July.
<http://www.publications.parliament.uk/pa/cm201314/cmhansrd/cm130711/debtext/130711-0002.htm#13071159000002>

UKMoD (United Kingdom Ministry of Defence). 2014. 'UK Provides Further Support to Kurdish Regional Forces Battling ISIL Insurgents in Northern Iraq.' 9 September. <https://www.gov.uk/government/news/uk-gifts-arms-and-ammunition-to-kurdish-regional-government>

Ukraine. 2012. 'Information on the International Transfer of Certain Categories of Conventional Arms Carried Out by Ukraine in 2011' [in Ukrainian]. Kiev: State Service of Export Control of Ukraine. <http://www.dsecu.gov.ua/control/uk/publish/article?art_id=46460&cat_id=46454>

UN Comtrade (United Nations Commodity Trade Statistics Database). n.d. 'United Nations Commodity Trade Statistics Database.' Accessed November 2014.
<http://comtrade.un.org/db/>

UNGA (United Nations General Assembly). 1993. *General and Complete Disarmament: Transparency in Armaments.* A/48/344 of 11 October.

—. 2013a. *Report of the Secretary-General: Continuing Operation of the United Nations Register of Conventional Arms and Its Further Development.* A/68/140 of 15 July.

—. 2013b. Resolution 68/43: Transparency in Armaments. A/RES/68/43 of 10 December.

—. 2014. *Report of the Secretary-General: Continuing Operation of the United Nations Register of Conventional Arms and Its Further Development.* A/69/124 of 15 July.

UNHRC (United Nations Human Rights Council). 2011a. *Report of the International Commission of Inquiry to Investigate All Alleged Violations of International Human Rights Law in the Libyan Arab Jamahiriya.* A/HRC/17/44 of 1 June.

—. 2011b. *Report of the Independent International Commission of Inquiry on the Syrian Arab Republic.* A/HRC/S-17/2/Add.1 of 23 November.

—. 2014. *Report of the Independent International Commission of Inquiry on the Syrian Arab Republic.* A/HRC/27/60 of 13 August.

UNODA (United Nation Office for Disarmament Affairs). 2007. *United Nations Register of Conventional Arms Information Booklet 2007.*

—. n.d. 'UN Register of Conventional Arms: Annual Consolidated Reports of the Secretary-General.'
<http://www.un.org/disarmament/convarms/Register/>

UNREC (United Nations Regional Centre for Peace and Disarmament in Africa). 2009. 'The Entry into Force of the ECOWAS Convention.' 20 November.
<http://www.unrec.org/index/index.php?option=com_content&view=article&id=152%3Adeclaration-by-the-president-of-the-ecowas-commission&catid=39%3Apolitics&lang=en>

UNSC (United Nations Security Council). 1992. Resolution 748 (1992) of 31 March.
<http://www.un.org/en/ga/search/view_doc.asp?symbol=S/RES/731%281992%29>

—. 2011a. 6491st Meeting Record. S/PV.6491 of 26 February. <http://www.un.org/en/ga/search/view_doc.asp?symbol=S/PV.6491>

—. 2011b. Resolution 1970 (2011). S/RES/1970 (2011) of 26 February.
<http://www.un.org/en/ga/search/view_doc.asp?symbol=S/RES/1970(2011)>

—. 2011c. 6498th Meeting Record. S/PV.6498 of 17 March. <http://www.un.org/en/ga/search/view_doc.asp?symbol=S/PV.6498>

—. 2011d. Resolution 1973 (2011). S/RES/1973 (2011) of 17 March.
<http://www.un.org/ga/search/view_doc.asp?symbol=S/RES/1973%20(2011)>

—. 2011e. Resolution 2009 (2011). S/RES/2009 (2011) of 16 September.
<http://www.un.org/ga/search/view_doc.asp?symbol=S/RES/2009 (2011)>

—. 2012a. *Report of the Security Council Committee Established Pursuant to Resolution 1970 (2011) Concerning Libya.* S/2012/32 of 13 January.
<http://www.un.org/ga/search/view_doc.asp?symbol=S/2012/32>

—. 2012b. *Final Report of the Panel of Experts Established Pursuant to Security Council Resolution 1973 (2011) Concerning Libya.* S/2012/163 of 20 March.
<http://www.un.org/ga/search/view_doc.asp?symbol=S/2012/163>

—. 2012c. *Final Report of the Panel of Experts Established Pursuant to Resolution 1929 (2010).* S/2012/395 of 12 June.
<http://www.un.org/ga/search/view_doc.asp?symbol=S/2012/395>

—. 2013a. *Report of the Security Council Committee Established Pursuant to Resolution 1970 (2011) Concerning Libya.* S/2012/983 of 9 January.
<http://www.un.org/ga/search/view_doc.asp?symbol=S/2012/983>

—. 2013b. *Final Report of the Panel of Experts Established Pursuant to Resolution 1973 (2011) Concerning Libya.* S/2013/99 of 9 March.

—. 2013c. *Report of the Security Council Committee Established Pursuant to Resolution 1970 (2011) Concerning Libya.* S/2013/790 of 31 December.
<http://www.un.org/ga/search/view_doc.asp?symbol=S/2013/790>

—. 2014a. *Final Report of the Panel of Experts Established Pursuant to Resolution 1973 (2011) Concerning Libya.* S/2014/106 of 19 February.
<http://www.un.org/ga/search/view_doc.asp?symbol=S/2014/106>

—. 2014b. *Final Report of the Panel of Experts Established Pursuant to Resolution 1929 (2010).* S/2014/394 of 11 June.
<http://www.un.org/ga/search/view_doc.asp?symbol=S/2014/394>

—. 2014c. *Report of the Security Council Committee Established Pursuant to Resolution 1970 (2011) Concerning Libya.* S/2014/909 of 31 December.
<http://www.un.org/ga/search/view_doc.asp?symbol=S/2014/909>

US (United States). 1991. International Traffic in Arms Regulations Amendments. 22 CFR Part 126. Public Notice 1510. *Federal Register*, Vol. 56, No. 209. 29 October, pp. 55630–31. <http://www.pmddtc.state.gov/FR/1991/56FR55630.pdf>

—. 2011. 'Press Briefing by Press Secretary Robert Gibbs, 1/28/2011.' Washington, DC: Office of the Press Secretary, White House. 28 January.
<http://www.whitehouse.gov/the-press-office/2011/01/28/press-briefing-press-secretary-robert-gibbs-1282011>

—. 2013a. 'Statement by President Barack Obama on Egypt.' Washington, DC: Office of the Press Secretary, White House. 3 July.
<http://www.whitehouse.gov/the-press-office/2013/07/03/statement-president-barack-obama-egypt>

—. 2013b. 'Press Briefing by Principal Deputy Press Secretary Josh Earnest, 8/20/2013.' Washington, DC: Office of the Press Secretary, White House. 20 August.

    <http://www.whitehouse.gov/the-press-office/2013/08/20/press-briefing-principal-deputy-press-secretary-josh-earnest-8202013>

—. 2014a. 'U.S. Military Conducts Aerial Resupply of Kurdish Forces Fighting ISIL.' US Central Command News Release. 19 October.

    <http://www.centcom.mil/en/news/articles/u.s.-military-conducts-aerial-resupply-of-kurdish-forces-fighting-isil>

—. 2014b. 'Estimate #2—FY 2015 Budget Amendments: Overseas Contingency Operations.' 26 June.

    <http://www.whitehouse.gov/sites/default/files/omb/assets/budget_amendments/final_fy_2015_oco_amendment_-_062414.pdf>

—. 2014c. 'Department of Defense Press Briefing by Lt. Gen. Mayville in the Pentagon Briefing Room.' Washington, DC: United States Department of Defense. 11 August. <http://www.defense.gov/Transcripts/Transcript.aspx?TranscriptID=5483>

Vranckx, An, Frank Slijper, and Roy Isbister. 2011. *Lessons from MENA: Appraising EU Transfers of Military and Security Equipment to the Middle East and North Africa—A Contribution to the Review of the EU Common Position.* Gent: Academia Press. November.

Wassenaar Arrangement (Wassenaar Arrangement on Export Controls for Conventional Arms and Dual-Use Goods and Technologies). n.d. Website. <http://www.wassenaar.org/>

World Bank. n.d. 'Worldwide Governance Indicators.' Accessed February 2015.

    <http://info.worldbank.org/governance/wgi/index.aspx#home>

ACKNOWLEDGEMENTS

Principal authors

Paul Holtom and Christelle Rigual

Empty ammunition crates litter the road leading to an ammunition factory at which an unplanned explosion took place, in Gorni Lom, Bulgaria, October 2014.

© Stringer/Keystone

Less 'Bang' for the Buck

STOCKPILE MANAGEMENT IN SOUTH-EAST EUROPE

5

INTRODUCTION

Proper management of conventional ammunition and explosives stockpiles involves safe storage practices that ensure security while reducing the risk of illicit proliferation and enhancing military and police capabilities. Conversely, poor stockpile management can lead to the deterioration of stored ammunition and its accidental explosion.

Around the world, unplanned explosions at munitions sites (UEMS)[1] occur because too many states still view their ammunition stockpiles as assets, rather than as liabilities, regardless of their age and storage conditions. UEMS are widespread and increasingly common. The Small Arms Survey UEMS database shows that, from 1979 to 2014, 520 incidents of this nature were recorded in 103 countries and territories, indicating that UEMS affect more than half of all UN member states and every continent except Antarctica (Small Arms Survey, 2014b).

Most countries in South-east Europe (SEE) face the challenge of managing operational, excess, and ageing weapons and ammunition. In the case of ammunition particularly, tackling the issue comprehensively requires complex and often expensive measures relating to planning, procurement, storage, use, infrastructure, physical security, surveillance, and final disposal. Few SEE governments have the capacity to address each of these issues throughout their national stockpile's life cycle.

The Regional Approach to Stockpile Reduction (RASR) initiative aims at fostering regional solutions to South-east Europe's stockpile management problem. RASR participating states are Albania, Bosnia and Herzegovina (BiH), Bulgaria, Croatia, the former Yugoslav Republic of Macedonia (hereafter Macedonia), Montenegro, Romania, Serbia, and Slovenia.[2] Funded exclusively by the US government, the initiative seeks to address stockpile management challenges by sharing good practices and lessons learned, by building transparency and mutual confidence between RASR participating states, and by pooling transport and destruction capacities.

This chapter focuses on the issue of sustainable weapons and ammunition stockpile management in the nine RASR participating states, while placing a particular emphasis on *training*. The chapter also reviews the surplus stockpile situation in SEE at the end of 2014, more than five years after the launch of RASR in May 2009. The analysis is largely based on data obtained by the Small Arms Survey in its capacity as one of the five RASR Steering Committee members;[3] additional information was obtained in the framework of an ongoing research project on European Union Force (EUFOR) Mobile Training Team (MTT) 2.1.6.1, which was set up in 2011.

The main findings are:

- Poor ammunition stockpile management remains a serious problem in much of South-east Europe.
- While UEMS are a global problem, they have been especially prevalent in South-east Europe, at both state and non-state facilities.

- While most countries reported that surplus stockpile levels were decreasing, some registered little change between 2009 and 2014 as military reform, ageing ammunition, and new acquisitions provided a steady flow of surplus ordnance.

- Sales and donations remain the favoured disposal options. A RASR participating state will only opt to destroy its surplus stockpiles upon determining that its marketability is poor.

- Surplus weapons and ammunition destruction in South-east Europe remains largely donor-driven and donor-funded.

- A number of political, regulatory, and commercial constraints hinder regional cooperation with respect to transport and demilitarization.

- In collaboration with other stakeholders, RASR states are making a concerted effort to build, harmonize, and standardize the stockpile management knowledge base through regional technical training.

- In Bosnia and Herzegovina, a long-term, ongoing initiative that is potentially of wider application seeks to integrate technical training into a broader capacity building effort that promotes host-country ownership, organizational reform, and the integration of international standards into national legislation and policy.

This chapter begins by describing the rationale behind RASR. The second section reviews surplus stockpile, disposal, and storage data declared by RASR participating states between 2008 and 2014. The third section describes the main constraints on regional cooperation with reference to surplus ammunition transport and demilitarization. The final section examines the need, current programmes, and potential opportunities for sustained, comprehensive, and standardized stockpile management capacity building in SEE.

RASR: A PRIMER

Two main developments brought the problem of SEE surplus weapon and ammunition stockpiles to the attention of international policy-makers and fostered the creation of RASR. The first was the downsizing of SEE military structures, coupled with the simultaneous increase in surplus weapons and ammunition stockpiles in the wake of the cold war. The second was a spate of UEMS in the region. The following sections examine each of these issues in turn.

A legacy of surplus

Excess weapons and ammunition in SEE are a legacy of political systems and defence strategies that relied on stockpiling to establish and safeguard national regimes. Prior to 1991, the Socialist Federal Republic of Yugoslavia had one of Europe's best-equipped military forces. The Yugoslav People's Army comprised 195,000 active-duty soldiers, and the country's Territorial Defence Force an estimated 510,000 reservists, with weapons and ammunition depots decentralized throughout the six Yugoslav republics (Bromley, 2007, pp. 3–4). When the wars in Bosnia and Croatia broke out, some weapons and ammunition stockpiles were placed under Army—and thus Serbian—control,[4] while others went to other local governments. Similarly, the communist regime of Enver Hoxha in Albania revolved around a strong and well-equipped military (Arsovska and Kostakos, 2008, p. 362).

After the disintegration of Yugoslavia and the fall of communism in Albania, large stockpiles of weapons and ammunition—some of which were already obsolete—became redundant. For example, after the Montenegrin parliament declared independence from Serbia and Montenegro, on 3 June 2006, the two successor states retained or—in the case of Montenegro, inherited—significant surplus weapons and ammunition stockpiles. Montenegro's ministry of defence (MoD) identified 74,000 different weapons and more than 12,000 tonnes of ammunition in its national stockpiles. It declared more than 9,500 tonnes of the ammunition stores surplus (Montenegro, 2011c, p. 2).[5] Serbia's resulting stockpile figures, thought to be significant, remained largely guesswork due to 'ongoing poor transparency within the MoD' (SEESAC, 2006, p. 91). In April 2007, six months after an accidental explosion at a military depot near Paraćin on 19 October 2006 and after international assistance with the explosive clearance, Serbia declared that its surplus ammunition stockpiles amounted to 23,859 tonnes (GICHD, 2008, p. 10).

Successive military modernization programmes, which mandated force reduction and changes to national military doctrine, also played—and continue to play—a role in the accumulation of surpluses in the region. One process that inevitably added to Serbia's already significant surplus stockpile burden was the trimming of its army from 14 brigades to four under the provisions of the Strategic Defence Review completed in July 2006 (Saferworld, 2007, n. 24). Modernization had a similar effect in Romania, where the military strength of the armed forces declined from 180,000 in the mid-1990s to 71,745 active forces in 2011 (Faltas and Chrobok, 2004, p. 87; IISS, 2011, p. 138). This 60 per cent force reduction generated large surpluses of stockpiled weapons and ammunition. Romania was invited to begin NATO accession negotiations at the Prague Summit in November 2002 and joined the organization on 29 March 2004. The adoption of NATO standards and the subsequent redundancy of some Warsaw Pact weapons led to a further increase in Romania's surplus stockpile (Faltas, 2008, p. 82).

In little time, the surplus weapons and ammunition stockpiles throughout SEE became a financial burden, as well as a safety and security liability. Countries lacked the funds needed to maintain and modernize the high number of ageing military depots and installations, and to invest in associated personnel, training, and equipment requirements. A shortage of appropriate storage facilities meant that ammunition was often stacked in the open air for several years. Derelict explosive storage houses were overloaded with ageing, unstable ammunition for which there were often no technical or historical records. Ultimately, these stockpiles posed two serious threats: accidental explosion during storage or transportation, and diversion to unauthorized end users. UEMS, in particular, brought increasing attention to the SEE surplus problem.

Military modernization programmes play a role in the accumulation of surpluses in the region.

UEMS and stockpile management

While UEMS are a global problem, they have been especially prevalent in SEE, which has witnessed nearly 10 per cent of all incidents worldwide. From 1980 until the end of 2014, 51 UEMS incidents occurred in the region, more than half of them after 2000. With the exception of Macedonia and Romania, every RASR participating state has been affected at least once. Although UEMS can occur for a number of reasons, in RASR participating states some of the main known causes include handling errors and inappropriate working practices, a failure to adjust to external environmental influences, and a lack of surveillance to monitor ammunition deterioration (Carapic and Gobinet, 2014).

Incidents have occurred during storage at both state-owned depots and private manufacturing and demilitarization facilities, suggesting deficiencies in the technical knowledge of staff and lax safety standards (Gobinet, 2013, p. 203). Modern demilitarization facilities—regardless of ownership—need to store large amounts of ammunition before processing it and must meet strict quantity–distance standards.[6] Yet the fact that about one-quarter of all recorded UEMS in SEE occurred at non-state facilities between 2006 and 2013 indicates that the region's private demilitarization industry needs government oversight, which is currently absent in many facilities (Carapic and Gobinet, 2014, p. 1). A case in point is the explosion that killed 15 workers at the Midzhur plant[7] in Bulgaria on 1 October 2014 (Tsolova and Nenov, 2014).

In addition to destroying ordnance and causing extensive damage to public and private infrastructure, UEMS have much broader consequences. The 51 UEMS in SEE resulted in more than 700 casualties (fatalities and injuries). The subsequent clean-up of scattered unexploded ordnance (UXO), provision of health care, and reconstruction efforts involved significant direct and indirect costs to the state and its population, as well as donor countries (Carapic and Gobinet, 2014, p. 1; Lazarevic, 2012). UXO can also have long-term effects on the environment and can pose continuing safety risks to the local population. Albania, for instance, has identified at least 19 'hot spots' that are contaminated by UXO largely as a result of UEMS; between 1997 and 2014, an estimated 149 people lost their lives and 883 were injured by UXOs in the country (Albania, 2014a, slide 12).[8]

Stockpile management, also referred to as physical security and stockpile management (PSSM), aims to ensure safe storage, security, and a reduction in the risk of accidental explosions. The International Ammunition Technical Guidelines (IATG) define stockpile management as the 'procedures and activities regarding safe and secure accounting, storage, transportation and handling of ammunition and explosives'; stockpile safety as 'the result of measures taken to ensure minimal risk of accidents and hazards deriving from explosive ordnance to personnel working with arms and munitions as well as adjacent populations'; and stockpile security as 'the result of measures taken to prevent the theft of explosive ordnance, entry by unauthorized persons into explosive storage areas, and acts of malfeasance, such as sabotage' (UNODA, 2011a).

Developed in 2011 under the UN SaferGuard Programme, the IATG address conventional ammunition stockpile management—from transport to storage to destruction—and are based on the most comprehensive existing standards. Technical specialists generally regard NATO's Allied Ammunition Storage and Transportation Publications 1 and 2 as among the most comprehensive documents covering the principles of safe storage and transportation of ammunition (NATO, 2005; 2010).[9] With respect to best practice at the regional level, experts consult the *Document on Stockpiles of Conventional Ammunition* and the *Best Practice Guide on National Procedures for Stockpile Management and Security*, both published by the Organization for Security and Co-operation in Europe (OSCE) (OSCE, 2003a; 2003b).

> The 51 UEMS incidents in SEE resulted in more than 700 casualties.

RASR

The US government created—and has continued to fund—the RASR initiative in order to address the problems of UEMS and stockpile diversion in SEE. The US Department of State's Office of Weapons Removal and Abatement (WRA) launched the first RASR workshop in Zagreb, Croatia, in May 2009. During this event, PSSM stakeholders identified five areas in which regional cooperation could potentially benefit actors involved in conventional munitions reduction:

- policy;
- infrastructure;
- training and education;
- sharing of information and best practices; and
- standardization (in particular pertaining to ammunition classification and surveillance systems).

Six larger workshops followed: in Budva, Montenegro (2009); Sarajevo, BiH (2010); Ljubljana, Slovenia (2011); Durrës, Albania (2012); Bled, Slovenia (2013); and Sofia, Bulgaria (2014).[10] The events gathered—with varying levels of participation[11]—representatives of MoDs and general staffs of Albania, BiH, Bulgaria, Croatia, Macedonia, Montenegro, Romania, Serbia, and Slovenia; US government officials from the Departments of State and Defense; and representatives of international and regional organizations.[12]

WRA recognized that a core Steering Committee made up of organizations already active in various areas of stockpile management could, with relatively minor funding, coordinate the initiative. The Steering Committee organizes the workshops, which are designed to encourage international, regional, and national PSSM stakeholders to share best practices and lessons learned at the technical or practitioner level. In so doing, the initiative aims to foster transparency and confidence building between RASR participating states in relation to stockpile management.

RASR's website also serves as a clearinghouse for open-source SEE surplus stockpile data. Workshop material can be used to generate a snapshot of SEE's weapons and ammunition surplus stockpiles; it also provides an indication of the current state of stockpile reduction activities in the region.

SURPLUS WEAPONS AND AMMUNITION IN THE NINE RASR COUNTRIES

This section reviews available surplus stockpile, disposal, and storage data for the period 2008–14 in SEE, highlighting relevant data gaps and limitations. The analysis relies on a wide range of open-source data obtained from the following sources:

> The levels of surplus weapons and ammunition in SEE change frequently.

- small arms and light weapons and ammunition assessments performed in the region by international ammunition specialists and explosive ordnance disposal (EOD) specialists;
- presentations given by the representatives of SEE MoDs and international organizations during various regional stockpile management conferences, including those hosted by RASR;
- working group discussions held during annual RASR workshops;
- Small Arms Survey questionnaires answered by eight MoDs during the first quarter of 2011; and
- updates, interviews, and email exchanges with representatives of SEE MoDs and regional organizations carried out in the second half of 2014.

Stockpiles

The levels of surplus weapons and ammunition in SEE change frequently because of the ongoing restructuring of SEE military organizations, the modernization of SEE armed forces, and, as a result, the continuously changing nature of national defence stockpiles, as discussed above.

While most countries reported decreasing surplus stockpile levels, some registered little change between 2009 and 2014 as military reform, ageing ammunition, and new acquisitions provided a steady flow of surplus ordnance (see Table 5.1). Over time, operational, reserve, and training stockpiles are recategorized as excess, obsolete, or unusable (Wilkinson, 2006, p. 231).

Some MoDs have even signalled an *increase* in their surpluses. In 2010, Bulgaria issued its Armed Forces Development Plan, which reviewed the structures, roles, missions, and tasks of its armed forces and implied a 'restructuring of [the] Bulgarian Army's operational stockpile and [increased] surplus stockpiles' (Bulgaria, 2011, p. 2). Despite an 'action plan for future demilitarization of surplus munitions 2012–2015', the Bulgarian MoD projected that its surplus ammunition stockpile would increase to 24,000 tonnes in 2013 and 2014 (Bulgaria, 2012, slide 4/7). Figures provided by Bulgaria in 2014 mention a 6,395-tonne surplus, indicating that the 'new' surplus was not yet accounted for (see Table 5.1). Similarly, Croatia's Strategic Defence Review and Long-Term Development Plan for the period 2011–20

Table 5.1 Surplus conventional ammunition and small arms and light weapons stockpiles declared by RASR participating states, 2008–14

Country		2008	2009	2010	2011	2012	2013	2014
Albania	Ammunition	100,000–120,000	86,421–92,651	67,423–72,170	40,141–69,715	18,902–40,318	8,391–12,845	2,860–4,246
	Small arms and light weapons	n/a	n/a	n/a	258,992	n/a	n/a	100,000–190,000
	Evolution of storage	In 2009, at the start of the demilitarization effort, Albania reported having 34 active ammunition storage sites (ASSs) and weapons storage sites (WSSs). As of 30 September 2014, 24 depots had been closed and certified, eight remained to be closed, and 2 were to be retained for permanent storage.						
Bosnia and Herzegovina	Ammunition	67,000	25,000	22,500	21,389–21,700	18,378	n/a	16,305–16,546
	Small arms and light weapons	n/a	100,000	65,878–99,882	53,000	n/a	n/a	28,231–40,052
	Evolution of storage	In 2011, Bosnia and Herzegovina reported having 20 ASSs, including 5 or 6 'prospective' ASSs, and 30 WSSs, including 2 prospective WSSs. In September 2014, the ASS number had dropped to 17–of which 6 are prospective,[13] 1 is temporary, 6 are non-prospective, and 4 are non-prospective pending closure–and the WSS number remained unchanged.						
Bulgaria	Ammunition	153,000	n/a	n/a	15,000	11,000	7,075	6,395
	Small arms and light weapons	46,577	n/a	n/a	n/a	n/a	10,380	11,590
	Evolution of storage	n/a						
Croatia	Ammunition	35,000	21,000	n/a	20,000	18,000	18,000	17,000–20,000
	Small arms and light weapons	190,000	n/a	n/a	0	2,028 (pistols)	2,028 (pistols)	2,028 (pistols)
	Evolution of storage	In 1995, Croatia reported 68 ASSs. By 2013 that number had dropped to 16 and in 2014 it stood at 10.						
Macedonia	Ammunition	n/a	n/a	n/a	No tonnage provided, but more than 360,000 items	915	n/a	n/a
	Small arms and light weapons	n/a	n/a	n/a	n/a	n/a	n/a	n/a
	Evolution of storage	n/a						

Table 5.1 Continued

Country		2008	2009	2010	2011	2012	2013	2014
Montenegro	Ammunition	9,751–12,000	7,241	4,692–5,611	4,500–5,155	4,045–4,384	3,674	3,188–3,852
	Small arms and light weapons	59,538–76,000	17,212	13,685–16,969	13,000–16,203	16,203	16,134	16,094
	Evolution of storage	In 2010, Montenegro reported having 10 ASSs; in 2011, there were 9 ASSs and 2 WSSs in Kapino Polje and Lepetani; by 2014, the ASS number had dropped to 8. The MoD's stated goal is to downsize to three ASSs.						
Serbia	Ammunition	24,000	19,000	14,000	8,712–9,000	n/a	n/a	6,000–7,000
	Small arms and light weapons	n/a	n/a	n/a	>90,000	n/a	n/a	n/a
	Evolution of storage	n/a						

Notes: n/a = not available. Ammunition volumes are listed in metric tonnes all-up weight (AUW), unless stated otherwise; ranges reflect the lowest to the highest documented tonnage. One tonne AUW is equivalent to 1 cubic metre, or one unit of space for storage and transportation planning (for approximately 50,000 rounds of small arms ammunition, such as 7.62 x 39 mm cartridges). For small arms and light weapons, the table lists the number of documented weapons. At the time of writing, no open-source surplus stockpile data was available for Romania or Slovenia.

Source: Small Arms Survey (2014a)

earmarked increased levels of surplus ammunition for open burning and open detonation (OB/OD) and industrial demilitarization (Croatia, 2013, slide 14).

Although useful for external observers, the surplus stockpile estimates provided by the MoDs are often limited on several counts:

- They do not take ministry of interior (MoI) stockpiles into account. In all RASR countries, MoIs also hold small arms, light weapons, and ammunition.[14]
- They provide much more information on surplus ammunition than on surplus small arms and light weapons. The risks and consequences of UEMS, coupled with increased donor pressure to address the unsafe management of large conventional ammunition, have prompted RASR countries to generate surplus ammunition data as a priority.
- They do not indicate the physical condition of the depots in which the ammunition is stored. Significant quantities of ordnance are sometimes stored in the open.[15] Rain, dampness, high temperatures, and humidity speed up the degradation of ammunition and can cause it to become dangerous when stored, handled, and used.
- They make no qualitative assessment of the stability of surplus ammunition, nor do they indicate whether trained personnel have ever carried out periodic technical inspection or chemical analysis of stocks of particularly sensitive items, such as pyrotechnics and propellants,[16] to ensure safety and stability. As a result, there is little analysis of the public safety risks particular ammunition storage sites might pose.
- They offer no indication of the physical security measures[17] applied around the depots, nor whether surplus stockpiles benefit from the same security measures as operational stockpiles.

There is also significant variation in the level of detail of the data that MoDs provide, which complicates cross-country comparison. Countries rarely provide information on item type, location, net explosive weight, or number—details that are frequently considered classified. Generally, countries that host extensive donor-funded PSSM and demilitarization assistance programmes, sometimes involving intrusive stockpile assessments by international experts, furnish the most detailed surplus weapons and ammunition figures.

Most countries do not specify whether their figures reflect (US) tons, metric tonnes, or gross weight (also known as all-up weight, or AUW) when declaring their surplus. Logistics planning for storage and demilitarization, for example, traditionally uses gross weight as a reference, covering both ammunition and its packaging. In addition, there are differences between US and UK tons.[18] Few—if any—SEE countries reveal the actual number of items of surplus ammunition by specific type. Unless otherwise stated, this chapter provides ammunition figures for RASR countries in metric tonnes AUW. For small arms and light weapons, the numbers of weapons, rather than the total weight, is recorded.

Some countries simply do not know the precise quantities of ammunition (whether surplus or operational) in their stockpiles, often because of poor stockpile accounting practices. In such cases, government bureaucracy or the reorganization of state agencies in charge of military logistics leads to poor accounting, inaccurate reporting, and stockpile opacity. In order to remedy such problems, the Armed Forces of Bosnia and Herzegovina (AF BiH) are carrying out an inventory of all of their stockpiles with five mobile inspection teams in the framework of a project called Explosive Ordnance and Remnants of War Destruction, or EXPLODE (OSCE, 2014, slide 32); they are also testing software for inventory record-keeping with European Union (EU) and OSCE support.[19]

Surplus disposal in SEE is largely donor-driven and donor-funded.

Disposal and storage

Donor funding

Surplus weapons and ammunition disposal in SEE is largely donor-driven and donor-funded. Table 5.2 lists a selection of large, ongoing donor-funded projects implemented by international or regional organizations in RASR countries as of November 2014. The projects usually apply a mix of surplus destruction, infrastructure refurbishment, and capacity building measures. Recent and ongoing examples include the third Partnership for Peace Trust Fund project of the NATO Support Agency (NSPA) in Albania, a joint demilitarization programme of the OSCE and the UN Development Programme (UNDP) in Montenegro, a joint OSCE–UNDP capacity development programme for conventional ammunition stockpile management (CASM) in Serbia, and ITF Enhancing Human Security (ITF) projects in BiH, Croatia, and Montenegro.

Donor-funding shortages often mean that disposal programmes are put on hold. For instance, the first phase of the Montenegro demilitarization (MONDEM) project destroyed 430 tonnes of ammunition out of a 1,300-tonne stockpile initially earmarked for destruction in two phases in 2010 (Montenegro, 2011d, slides 12–13). Yet the second MONDEM phase—during which the remaining 870 tonnes of ammunition were to be destroyed (Montenegro, 2011b)—was put on hold due to funding shortfalls that persisted throughout 2010 and 2011.[20]

National weapons and ammunition disposal figures are usually associated with donor-funded destruction campaigns. Yet the information is often incomplete and disposal timeframes frequently overlap, making comparison challenging. Figures seldom disaggregate the types of ammunition and the net explosive quantities that were destroyed. The following examples nevertheless provide a sense of magnitude. Albania disposed of more than 90,000 tonnes of ammunition in six years, from 2009 to 2014 (Albania, 2014a, slide 3; 2014b, slide 10; NSPA, 2014, slide 18). Croatia disposed of approximately 5,000 tonnes of ammunition in 2013 (Croatia, 2014, slide 6). Montenegro reportedly disposed of more than 7,000 tonnes of ammunition between 2006 and 2014 (Montenegro, 2014a, slide 11).

Donor-funded stockpile management and demilitarization projects often involve some in-kind or financial con-tribution from the host government. In some cases, host-country participation has been significant. Albania is a good example. Following the Gërdec explosion on 15 March 2008,[21] Albania's Plan of Action for the Elimination of the Excess Ammunition in the Armed Forces foresaw the identification and disposal of all old surplus ammunition and explo-sives from the Albanian Armed Forces (AAF) inventory by the end of 2013 (Albania, n.d., p. 4). In September 2009 the AAF declared more than 85,000 tonnes of ammunition surplus. The government subsequently allocated some EUR 3–4 million (USD 3.8–5 million) annually to cover the costs of destruction, *in addition to* the funds and demil-itarization equipment received from various international donors, including Denmark and Germany (both via the OSCE) and the US State Department (via NSPA) (Albania, 2014b). Albania reportedly covered 83 per cent of the EUR 23 million required to dispose of more than 90,000 tonnes of surplus ammunition between 2009 and September 2013, while the NSPA covered the remaining 17 per cent with US funding (Albania, 2014b).

Another best practice example is Montenegro, where the MoD reinvested more than EUR 1.2 million (USD 1.8 million) obtained mostly from the sale of scrap metal—generated by the destruction and recycling of heavy weapons systems—into ammunition demilitarization (OSCE, 2014). Croatia[22] and Slovenia, among other SEE states, have also covered all or part of the costs of conventional ammunition destruction, infrastructure refurbishment, or depot construction.

Members of an explosive ordnance disposal team prepare a batch of high-explosive projectiles prior to open detonation at the Krivolak range near Mushanci, Macedonia, 2011. © Macedonian EOD team

Table 5.2 Selected ongoing small arms and ammunition destruction and infrastructure refurbishment projects implemented by international or regional organizations in RASR countries, as of November 2014

Country	Project	Period	Lead implementing agency	Cost
Albania	Third NATO Partnership for Peace project	October 2010–late 2014	NSPA	EUR 6,037,000 (USD 8,174,000) overall budget (including transportation, administrative costs, NSPA management team)
BiH	EXPLODE	2012–15	UNDP-BiH	EUR 4,604,830 (USD 5.2 million) over a period of 36 months
	SECUP	2013–16	OSCE	EUR 1,052,460 (USD 1.2 million)
Montenegro	MONDEM	2007–ongoing	UNDP-Montenegro	OSCE: EUR 870,706.13 (USD 1.1 million) + Government of Montenegro: EUR 1.2 million (USD 1.5 million) + UNDP: EUR 3.2 million (USD 4 million) = EUR 5.27 million (USD 6.6 million) total as of October 2014 The total includes USD 1.8 million for the reconstruction of Taraš and an estimated investment of USD 2.5 million for the reconstruction of Brezovik.
Serbia	CASM	February 2012 until 31 December 2015	UNDP-Serbia and SEESAC	USD 1,246,431, since the start of the project
	Serbia IV Trust Fund	Feasibility study, December 2012–June 2013 NATO Political and Partnerships Committee 15 July 2013 (Due to start mid-2015) Delay due to resolution of legal agreements	NSPA	EUR 3.7 million (USD 4.2 million)

Sources: OSCE (2014); author correspondence with David Towndrow, NSPA, 10 December 2014; with Jasmin Porobic, UNDP-BiH, 30 December 2014; and with Tamara Svircev, SEESAC, 25 February 2015

Table 5.2 **Continued**

Activities

- Destruction of 12,069 tonnes of surplus ammunition;
- destruction of 70,000 small arms and light weapons; and
- development of an industrial demilitarization factory at ULP Mjekës, including: 120 mm mortar and large-calibre lines; 14.5 mm and anti-tank mine lines; and improvements to the explosive waste incinerator.

- Disposal of more than 11,000 tonnes of ammunition and 140,000 pieces of small arms and light weapons since 2006;
- successful implementation of the High Hazardous Munitions Destruction project, which includes the destruction of all reported quantities of cluster bombs, rockets, and other cluster munitions;
- infrastructure improvements of 50 storage facilities in four prospective storage sites: Krupa, Kula, Rabić, and Teufik Buza;
- new technologies for ammunition disposal installed, doubling technological capacities for ammunition disposal; and
- building capacities of senior officers and officials of the BiH MoD on ammunition stockpile management.

Security Upgrade programme in 4 prospective storage sites–Krupa, Kula, Rabić, and Teufik Buza–including:
- partial replacement of fencing;
- installation of vehicle beam barriers;
- replacement of gates and installation of standardized signs at all four storage sites;
- additional fencing around high-security buildings (small arms and light weapons);
- technical documentation for intruder detection system packages, which include closed-circuit TV, touch sensors, alert lighting, and back-up power systems; and
- the installation of intruder detection system packages.

- Disposal of 120 tonnes of toxic hazardous substances (mélange oxidizer, rocket fuel, and napalm thickener);
- destruction and recycling of heavy weapons systems (some 3,300 tonnes, including 60 battle tanks, some 900 different field artillery pieces, and rocket launchers);
- conventional ammunition demilitarization, with 430 tonnes of surplus ammunition destroyed in 2010; 715 tonnes destroyed in 2011 and 2012; and 1,350 tonnes earmarked for destruction before the end of 2015; and
- the completed reconstruction of Taraš, an MoD ammunition storage site in Danilovgrad, which reopened in May 2011, and ongoing reconstruction of a larger ammunition storage site at Brezovik.

Component 1
- Demilitarizing and destruction of 1,133.86 tonnes of surplus stocks of white phosphorus (WP), CS-filled, and napalm powder-based ammunition. This includes the disposal of: 162 tonnes of napalm powder-filled ammunition (completed in 2013); 550 tonnes of WP-filled ammunition shells (ongoing); and special CS ammunition (planning/preparatory activities ongoing).
- Infrastructure improvement to the existing demilitarization facilities at TRZ Kragujevac (the Serbian MoD's centre for demilitarization); including the provision of closed-circuit TV system (ongoing); sprinkler systems (ongoing); and the installation of antistatic floors (completed).

Component 2
- Storage reconstruction in Mrsać and Mirnićka Reka.

Making sense of 'disposal' figures

The term 'disposal' refers to the removal of ammunition and explosives from a stockpile through a variety of methods that do not necessarily involve destruction. Four traditional methods of disposal are used by armed forces around the world: increased use during training; sales; donations; and destruction via industrial demilitarization or OB/OD. The distinction between 'destruction' and 'disposal' is often lost in translation and in SEE the MoDs will often use the term 'demilitarization' erroneously, thus complicating data collection and comparability.

Destruction

Most governments cannot afford to fund their demilitarization facilities continuously.

Small arms destruction is technically straightforward and largely donor-driven. Serbia destroyed 49,500 small arms between 2010 and 2013 (Serbia, 2014a, slide 8). The figure includes the EU-funded destruction, via SEESAC, of 28,285 items in 2010 and 17,000 items in 2012, undertaken with the support of the Serbian MoI. SEESAC and the EU also led destruction initiatives in Croatia, where 33,091 items were destroyed during 2011 and 2012 (SEESAC, n.d.). In Albania, 70,000 items were destroyed under a US-funded NSPA managed project at the Gramsh weapons factory from April to September 2014. The United States allocated funding for another 30,000 items, but the Albanian authorities blocked the plan, allegedly arguing that these weapons had significant commercial value. The funds were then reallocated (Cubic and USDTTA, 2014).[23]

OB/OD has been used to destroy conventional ammunition throughout most of SEE. OB/OD capacities vary across countries. Albania destroyed 31 per cent of its 90,000-tonne ammunition surplus using OB/OD between 2009 and 2014 (Albania, 2014a, slide 4; 2014b, slide 16; NSPA, 2014, slide 16). Croatia destroyed about 6,800 tonnes of various types of ammunition using OB/OD between 2001 and 2012 (Croatia, 2014, slide 4). OB/OD has, however, fallen out of favour with many demilitarization practitioners who consider it a source of uncontrolled soil, groundwater, and air pollution. Wherever environmental considerations are the decisive factor, OB/OD is controversial (Gobinet, 2013, p. 206). For the moment, however, OB/OD remains economically viable for countries with smaller (yet potentially unstable) stockpiles and suitably remote areas in which to carry it out. According to some practitioners and subcontractors, the advantages of OB/OD outweigh its drawbacks, making it a much easier—and thus preferred—solution whenever government or donor funds are scarce (King and Diaz, 2011, p. 40).

The industrial demilitarization of surplus ammunition is a more complex activity, as it uses assembly lines that apply industrial processes to disassemble the ammunition and separate the energetic from the inert materials through a combination of melting, cutting, and crushing, or by directly burning out the energetic materials (Gobinet, 2013, pp. 196–97). A well-functioning industrial demilitarization process can destroy large quantities of ammunition and recover commercially valuable materials for use in commercial applications. All US demilitarization facilities, for instance, can reportedly process up to 110,000 tonnes annually (NSPA, 2014, slide 18).

By mapping the SEE network of indigenous demilitarization facilities—many of which were previously unknown to the donor community—the Small Arms Survey showed that industrial demilitarization capacities vary across states in the region (Gobinet, 2012). Most governments cannot afford to fund their demilitarization facilities continuously. Destruction is thus carried out intermittently, in batches, whenever (donor) funding permits. In order to remain commercially viable in a competitive market, government-owned facilities and private contractors must combine their demilitarization operations with more lucrative activities, such as industrial explosive or ammunition production.

Generally, RASR countries that held large quantities of similar types of surplus items that needed to be destroyed were the ones that developed or upgraded industrial demilitarization processes, thereby making economies of scale possible. In 2009, for instance, the AAF categorized its 90,000-tonne ammunition surplus into several generic types of ammunition, allowing for the development of targeted industrial processes with long production runs (Gobinet, 2011, pp. 32–35). Between 2009 and 2014, more than half of this surplus was destroyed using industrial demilitarization (Albania, 2014b, slide 16); some sources cite as many as 57,000 tonnes of ammunition demilitarized industrially at Gramsh, Mjekës, and Poliçan during this period (Albania, 2014a, slide 5).[24]

Large government-owned facilities tend to declare their capacity figures and approximate demilitarization costs. As these are context-specific, care must be taken when making comparisons between nations. Albania's main plant—ULP Mjekës—has a total capacity of more than 5,000 tonnes per year across a broad spectrum of ammunition types, at approximately EUR 500/tonne (USD 565/tonne) (NSPA, 2014, slide 23). The Serbian MoD's TRZ plant in Kragujevac reportedly dismantled approximately 4,000 tonnes of ammunition per year between 2006 and 2010 (Serbia, 2011a, slide 4; 2011b, slide 5). Serbia has repeatedly stated that the plant is underutilized and that it could increase its capacity to anywhere between 6,000 to 10,000 tonnes per year by opening additional demilitarization lines (Serbia, 2011b, slide 13; 2011d, p. 3). In 2011, the plant reported an average demilitarization cost of EUR 780 (USD 1,080) per tonne, but calculated that economies of scale linked to the potential capacity increases could bring the cost down to

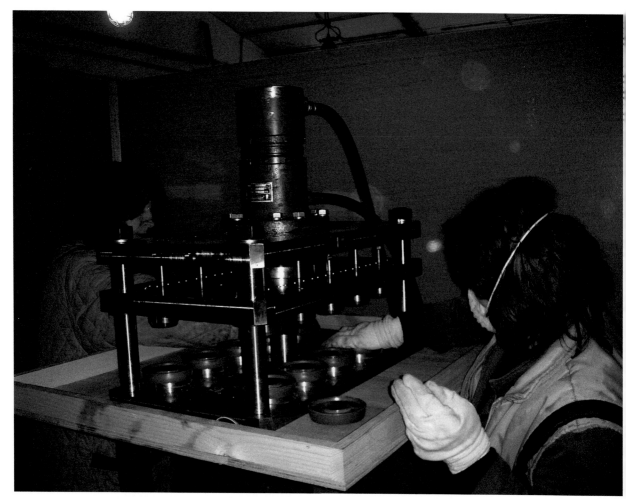

Trained staff dismantle anti-personnel mines at TRZ technical overhauling facilities in Kragujevac, Serbia, April 2007. © TRZ Kragujevac

approximately EUR 500 (USD 640) per tonne (Serbia, 2011a, slide 13). The CASM programme, initiated in 2012, involves incremental infrastructure upgrades to improve the plant's safety and capacity (Serbia, 2014a, slide 5).

In other RASR countries, national (that is, government-owned) industrial demilitarization capacity is either structurally limited or underused. Demilitarization relies heavily on donor funding as well as private, civilian contractors. The annual destruction capacity of the AF BiH's main facility, the GOF-18/TROM Doboj plant, is estimated at approximately 1,200–1,300 tonnes (EWG, 2010a, slides 7, 9; NATO, 2011, slide 21).[25] In reality, however, the plant processes far less, despite facility upgrades carried out under the EXPLODE project (OSCE, 2014, slide 31). Since 2006, BiH has processed decreasing amounts of ammunition using OB/OD and industrial demilitarization; at the time of writing, the country was destroying less than 1,000 tonnes per year (AF BiH AWE, 2014). Croatia reportedly destroyed only around 600 tonnes of conventional ammunition using industrial demilitarization between 2011 and 2013, even though the civilian company contracted for this work, ISL Spreewerk, in Gospić, has a demilitarization capacity of approximately 3,000 tonnes per year, depending on the type of ammunition being processed (Croatia, 2014, slide 5).

Sales and donations

Most countries test the marketability of their surplus stocks before deciding whether to destroy them. Likewise, RASR countries dispose of surplus weapons and ammunition through sales[26] and donations,[27] provided the items are in sufficiently good condition.

National export reports do not disaggregate sales of surplus from sales of new ordnance, yet RASR countries have provided some information. Bulgaria noted that it sold more than 5,000 tonnes of excessive ammunition in 2011, more than 8,775 tonnes in 2012, and 2,208 tonnes in 2013, with the latter figure representing about 31 per cent of its estimated 7,075 tonnes of surplus in 2013 (Bulgaria, 2012, slide 4; 2013, slide 5). The Croatian MoD reported sales

During Operation Impact, a Royal Canadian Air Force aircraft–photographed in the Czech Republic–transports pallets of military supplies donated by Albania and the Czech Republic to security forces in Iraq, September 2014. © Marc-Andre Gaudreault/Canadian Forces Combat Camera

of 6,035 tonnes of various types of ammunition, worth approximately EUR 15 million (USD 16.9 million), between 2001 and 2012 through its government-owned export company Agencije Alan, based in Zagreb (Croatia, 2013, slide 7). In 2014, Serbia earmarked 1,570 tonnes of mostly small arms ammunition for sale out of its 6,000-tonne ammunition surplus (Serbia, 2014b, slide 3).

Some national laws prioritize the sale of surplus state-owned property, including arms and ammunition, over destruction (Montenegro, 2009, arts. 21–22). MoDs usually earmark more ammunition for sale than they are able to sell. International demand for surplus weapons and ammunition is quite volatile, and signed contracts do not necessarily translate into actual sales. MoDs then face the costs of storing and ultimately destroying the items.

Albania recently earmarked 14 per cent of the abovementioned 90,000-tonne surplus, representing 12,603 tonnes of ammunition, for export or donation (Albania, 2014a, slide 16; 2014b, slide 9). Of the 12,600 tonnes earmarked for sale, 7,088 tonnes of artillery, mortar, and small arms ammunition were effectively sold and exported via the Military Export–Import State Company (MEICO) between 2009 and 2013 (Albania, 2014a, slide 6).

Montenegro encountered a similar situation. In May 2011, the MoD declared that it had sold—but not delivered—1,400 tonnes of surplus ammunition. The Montenegrin MoD stated that it was likely to offer another 1,300 tonnes for sale during 2011 (Montenegro, 2011c, p. 3). Phase three of the MONDEM programme, which started in June 2013, aims to destroy a similar tonnage (that is, some 1,350 tonnes total) of unstable and obsolete ammunition before the end of 2015 (OSCE, 2014); this information suggests that a large portion of the 1,300 tonnes earmarked for sale by the Montenegrin MoD in 2011 has not been sold.

> MoDs usually earmark more ammunition for sale than they are able to sell.

Donations to countries whose security forces use former Warsaw Pact firearms and ammunition are also frequent, although states do not report on them regularly. Albania, for instance, donated 10,000 AK-47 assault rifles to the Afghan National Police in 2010, and another 10,000 assault rifles in 2014 (Cubic and USDTTA, 2014; IBNA, 2014). In addition, in September 2014, the Albanian MoD announced that it was donating 785 tonnes of ammunition[28] and 10,000 Kalashnikov-pattern rifles to support Iraqi Kurds (Cubic and USDTTA, 2014). As the Canadian Armed Forces report, in August–September 2014 Albanian and Czech military supplies—including small arms and ammunition—were delivered to security forces working in Baghdad and Erbil, in the framework of a multinational coalition against the non-state armed group Islamic State (ND and CAF, n.d.).

Depot reduction, refurbishment, and construction

Among RASR participating states, the overall tendency is to reduce the number of ammunition storage sites (ASSs) and weapons storage sites (WSSs) in order to lower storage and staffing costs. The ones that are to be retained as permanent storage sites after all surpluses are disposed of are dubbed 'prospective' sites and benefit from donor-funded refurbishment programmes to bring them up to international standards.

Technical ammunition depot assessments in SEE usually highlight one or more of the following security and safety risks:

- The buildings where ammunition is stored suffer from significant structural damage.
- Ammunition is not stored in accordance with principles relating to hazard division and compatibility group.
- The sites are overstocked far in excess of capacity.
- Large quantities of ammunition are left unpackaged, stored in the open, or in temporary facilities.
- Leaking containers of unidentified chemicals are stored alongside other explosives.
- Firefighting equipment is inadequate or out of date.

- Ammunition surveillance systems do not exist or, if they do exist, there are no records of inspections.
- Perimeter security at storage sites is cursory, with inadequate personnel, inactive intruder detection systems, and insufficient internal and external lighting (Gobinet, 2011, pp. 27–29).

Storage facility and infrastructure upgrades are meant to improve physical security through the renovation of disused buildings, the repair of existing equipment, and the installation of appropriate security systems. Examples include the SECUP programme in four BiH storage sites[29] (OSCE, 2014, slides 15–28); the infrastructure upgrade of Montenegro's Taraš and Brezovik ammunition depots under the MONDEM programme (Montenegro, 2014b, slide 24); and reconstruction and infrastructure upgrades of Serbia's Mrsać and Mirnićka Reka storage sites under the CASM programme (SEESAC, 2014, slides 7–10). Storage facility and infrastructure upgrades are also meant to improve the management of stockpiles, including the safe storage of ammunition, for instance through ammunition accounting and management systems.

Reducing the number of storage sites creates new challenges. Reducing the number of storage sites creates new challenges. In most countries ammunition disposal rates cannot keep up with the reduction of storage capacity so that ammunition has to be transported and then crammed into 'prospective' depots that are often already full. Transporting ammunition always carries some risk, but without proper equipment and appropriately trained personnel, the risk is significantly higher. Non-existent or deteriorating packaging associated with poor ammunition management increases the likelihood of an incident considerably.

STOCKPILE REDUCTION IN SEE: PRACTICAL CONSTRAINTS

It is difficult to quantify the impact of RASR—an expert discussion forum without dedicated staff or a permanent building—on SEE surplus stockpile levels. While the RASR Steering Committee has sought to increase regional ownership over stockpile management and reduction, to date the initiative has received very little attention from the region's high-level cooperative processes and frameworks. Among others, the South-Eastern Europe Defense Ministerial[30] and the Regional Cooperation Council,[31] which could provide much-needed political leverage, have yet to engage with RASR.

Individual participant interviews and testimonies have stressed the value of RASR workshops as informal forums through which donors and host countries can coordinate the implementation of PSSM and demilitarization projects in SEE. For instance, NSPA used the RASR forum to circulate and bench-test the idea of a joint pilot project, which eventually led to the destruction of 17 tonnes of Montenegrin 20 mm anti-aircraft cannon ammunition at ULP Mjekës in Albania between 25 November and 4 December 2014 (see Box 5.1).

RASR has also prompted most participating states to provide information on their levels of surplus, and to share their stockpile management challenges publicly and regularly. Yet despite the added transparency and networking opportunities provided by the forum, a number of practical constraints continue to hinder the more complete development of a regional approach to stockpile destruction.

Challenges and impediments
Transport and ammunition categorization
A regional approach to stockpile reduction necessitates the cross-border transport of surplus munitions, usually by road or rail, from one country's depot to another country's demilitarization facility. Both modes of transport are

governed by comprehensive directives and regulations such as (1) the UN Recommendations on the Transport of Dangerous Goods: Model Regulations, also known as 'The Orange Book' (UN, 2013); (2) the European Agreement concerning the International Carriage of Dangerous Goods by Road (UNECE, 2009); and, in certain circumstances, (3) the Basel Convention on the Control of Transboundary Movements of Hazardous Wastes and Their Disposal (UNEP, 1989).[32]

Yet arranging for import and export permits and associated documentation, developing emergency plans, and securing insurance for the transported items represent significant administrative and logistical hurdles that most SEE MoDs are reluctant to tackle. Surplus ammunition in SEE stockpiles is rarely marked with the hazard labels—such as a UN serial number, hazard division, and compatibility group[33]—that are required for transportation under international norms. A large quantity of surplus ammunition has been repackaged into non-original boxes. Moreover, box contents and quantities do not always match markings and labelling. Consequently, the ammunition cannot be moved easily. In addition to international transport regulations, national laws prevent the cross-border transportation of weapons and ammunition. Some national legislation, such as Bulgaria's, prohibits the export of weapons and ammunition for demilitarization purposes, allowing only revenue-generating exports and imports (Bulgaria, 2011, p. 6).

This situation can only be remedied if existing ammunition management processes are brought in line with the principles contained in the IATG or in NATO's Allied Ammunition Storage and Transportation Publications 1 and 2 (NATO, 2005; 2010). Among other things, this means classifying ammunition according to the UN Globally Harmonized System of Classification and Labelling of Chemicals and the UN Recommendations on the Transport of Dangerous Goods: Model Regulations.

The difficulty of establishing a regional demilitarization hub

Although technically possible, the establishment of a regional demilitarization centre is difficult in practical terms and, moreover, does not have the support of all regional demilitarization practitioners (Gobinet, 2012).

Relatively well-developed capacity in some countries would suggest that bilateral cooperation could yield benefits through the disposal of surpluses, perhaps coordinated at the regional level. The Mjekës factory in Albania and Kragujevac's TRZ plant in Serbia benefited from significant donor-funded upgrades that increased their ammunition processing capacities. In fact, both countries have offered to support the demilitarization efforts of other SEE states in relation to a broad spectrum of ammunition types (NSPA, 2014, slide 3; Serbia, 2014b, slide 14).

Yet despite ad hoc offers of help, closer cooperation is not yet a reality in much of the SEE region. First, the issue of surplus ammunition destruction is sensitive within and among RASR nations. In each state, it can be highly politicized, which means that most—if not all—decisions and directives that address surplus destruction are taken by high-level government officials, including from the ministries of economy and finance. In BiH, for instance, the lack of progress in disposing of surplus weapons and ammunition largely stems from a lack of political consensus among the entities regarding the application of the 2008 Doboj Agreement and the BiH Defence Law (BiH, 2005;[34] 2008; 2009). Consequently, the BiH MoD is not authorized to carry out surplus destruction without obtaining authorization from the BiH presidency.

Such stumbling blocks largely limit collaboration at the regional level with countries bearing certain historical and cultural affinities. For instance, the Montenegrin authorities collaborate with the Serbian facility in Kragujevac to test propellant stability. But the traditionally low levels of trust among many of the region's governments do not facilitate burden sharing for the potential funding of a regional plant or the transfer of surplus ammunition across borders, even for demilitarization.

Surplus ammunition destruction—within and among RASR nations—can be highly politicized.

High-explosive projectiles are processed for demilitarization using an industrial bandsaw (top), and the resulting opened shells are transported away on forklifts, for the removal of energetics (bottom), ULP Mjekës, Albania, 2011. © NATO Support Agency (NSPA)

Secondly, it is unclear to what extent MoD-owned plants such as Mjekës and TRZ Kragujevac can become commercially viable and competitive in the open market. Such facilities often function as military units, featuring older technology and lower production volumes than their private, civilian competitors. In particular, they are not able to adapt to the constraints of regional or international demilitarization markets, where commercial considerations play an increasingly important role. The NSPA completed US-funded destruction activities at the ULP Mjekës and Gramsh plants at the end of December 2014. At the time of writing it was unclear how they would pursue their demilitarization activities without donor assistance.

Finally, while most countries claim to support the concept of a regional demilitarization facility, they actually have competing interests. Nations often have an economic interest in developing national demilitarization capability, rather than paying for such services in another nation. If states that have invested in national demilitarization infrastructure ship their ordnance to a neighbouring state, they lose a potential source of employment and income in the process. Practitioners who favour the regional destruction option face a tough sell at a time when work is scarce and unemployment is high.

One consequence of the factors cited above is that regional implementation organizations that compete for donor funds, and that face short project timescales and stringent delivery requirements, tend to opt for national disposal and storage refurbishment programmes, instead of using existing demilitarization facilities in neighbouring states. Another consequence is that some of these facilities—despite significant donor investment—may eventually become idle. The NSPA's recent facilitation of a pilot project, involving a surplus munitions transfer from Montenegro to Albania, has, however, demonstrated the feasibility of transferring ammunition across state lines for demilitarization (see Box 5.1).

Disparate knowledge bases

Another impediment to implementing a regional approach to stockpile management in SEE are the disparate levels of ammunition expertise in the region, which are partly the consequence of varying attention to training.

Generally, much of the donor-funded capacity building in the region has prioritized EOD skills. Specifically, donors provided support and training following UEMS in many of the countries. Such was the case in Albania in 2009, when the MoD reorganized and strengthened its military EOD capability in order to carry out OB/OD activities following the Gërdec explosion. The United States largely funded the training of AAF EOD personnel (Albania, 2011, p. 8). BiH,[35] Bulgaria, and Macedonia[36] benefited from similar EOD training programmes (Bulgaria, 2012, slide 4/6; SEESAC, 2009, slide 4). Yet EOD training does not address the full scope of challenges associated with the planning, management, and implementation of conventional ammunition storage.

> **Box 5.1 The complexities of cross-border demilitarization: the example of Albania and Montenegro**
>
> The Mjekës factory in Albania benefited from significant donor-funded upgrades that increased its ammunition processing capacities. During the fifth RASR workshop, held in Durrës, Albania, from 23 to 25 April 2012, NSPA officials and the Albanian authorities discussed the possibility of capitalizing on these investments by dedicating a portion of the plant's excess capacity to the demilitarization of surplus ammunition from neighbouring countries.
>
> In September 2012, the NSPA officially submitted the idea to the Albanian MoD. The goal was to demonstrate that procedures were in place that would allow the transfer of surplus munitions across borders to SEE demilitarization facilities with available capacity. Once the option was seen as viable, it would be up to SEE nations to pursue it further. The concept grew into a pilot project involving the movement of a relatively small (trial) quantity of surplus Montenegrin ammunition from an MoD storage site in Montenegro to ULP Mjekës (Albania), where it was to be destroyed in an incinerator under NSPA oversight. The Montenegrin MoD offered to cover the cost of transportation of the munitions. The NSPA (accessing WRA funds) offered to pay for the disposal at ULP (at a cost of less than EUR 20,000, or USD 22,600).
>
> In August 2014, the Albanian and Montenegrin MoDs resolved the final details and signed a technical agreement for the pilot demilitarization of approximately 17 tonnes of Montenegrin anti-aircraft cannon ammunition (50,380 rounds of 20 mm API PZ ammunition) at ULP Mjekës. Although arrangements relating to transportation, import and export licences, and end-user certification took some time to complete, the greatest delay was Albanian political endorsement as a new government struggled to reconcile the importation of 'waste' with the opportunity to provide demilitarization services to neighbouring countries.
>
> The cross-border transport and delivery at ULP Mjekës took place on 25 November 2014, with the Albanian agency MEICO arranging for the escort of the convoy from the Montenegrin border to the ULP Mjekës factory. Destruction of the rounds started on 1 December 2014 and finished on 4 December. The whole operation was overseen by the NSPA, which countersigned the certificate of disposal that ULP Mjekës provided to the Montenegrin government.

Some RASR countries have an indigenous stockpile management training programme in place for personnel in field units and at headquarters. For instance, Croatia's Logistics Training and Doctrine Centre, headquartered in Požega, trains logistics personnel—officers and non-commissioned officers—among them ammunition specialists (Croatia, 2014). In Serbia, the Military Academy in Belgrade provides technical training programmes for demilitarization and stockpile security personnel of the Serbian Armed Forces and the TRZ Kragujevac Technical Repair Facility (Serbia, 2014b).

Some countries report having an indigenous stockpile management training curriculum in place within their respective training and doctrine command structures while relying heavily on donor-funded courses to train their personnel.

Macedonia's training command and the military academy have reportedly developed a specific training programme for ammunition and armament storage and destruction (Macedonia, 2011, p. 3). Yet research indicates a reliance on short, ad hoc technical seminars provided on a one-off basis to mid-level logistics officers by the US Defense Department (DTRA, 2011). Slovenia has no military school or civilian universities involved in stockpile management; ammunition handlers get 'on-the-job' training.[37]

Other countries rely *exclusively* on donor-funded training initiatives. In Montenegro, training is undertaken in the MONDEM framework, with additional training provided by NATO (Montenegro, 2011a, slide 19; 2011c, p. 8). Yet the Montenegrin MoD reported that its logistics staff was not sufficiently trained, particularly in NATO storage and maintenance standards (Montenegro, 2011a, slide 27). BiH had no indigenous stockpile management training capacity and largely relied on EUFOR training programmes until the Mobile Training Team 2.1.6.1 began to hand over courses to training and doctrine command in Travnik in mid-2014, as discussed below. The BiH MoD, in concert with international partners, has highlighted the recurring need to train personnel to take on different roles, including ammunition technicians and handlers (BiH, 2011, slides 34, 41, 45; EWG, 2010b, slide 13). At the time of writing, EUFOR was providing training at all technical levels, and the process was expected to take several years to complete.

MoDs of SEE countries have highlighted the shortage of qualified technical staff. The majority of SEE MoDs have repeatedly drawn attention to a shortage of qualified technical staff, including ammunition technical officers and handlers with experience in applying best international ammunition management and demilitarization practices, and who are familiar with sophisticated ammunition such as shaped charges, missiles, and other special ordnance.[38] MoDs also report problems with personnel retention and replacement. Technical knowledge and experience are often lost when the restructuring of national armed forces leads trained demilitarization, stockpile maintenance, and security personnel to find employment in the private sector.

A REGIONAL APPROACH TO STOCKPILE MANAGEMENT CAPACITY BUILDING

As discussed above, it has proven difficult to operationalize a regional approach to ammunition demilitarization; however, SEE governments have expressed interest in—and have proven receptive to—a regional approach to stockpile management training. This section begins with a presentation of selected donor-funded training initiatives in SEE. It then focuses on a particular case to illustrate some of the difficulties, as well as important opportunities, associated with the building of sustainable capacity for stockpile management.

Training

Several RASR Steering Committee members organize specialized—and regionally standardized—technical training sessions aimed at participants of SEE armed forces. The courses cover a wide array of issues, including the IATG, ammunition surveillance, handling, transport, and management, as well as demilitarization techniques and technologies.[39]

In 2012, for instance, ITF organized a course on the 'Physical Security and Stockpile Management of Arms, Ammunitions and Explosives' at TRZ Kragujevac, in Serbia. The two-week course, conducted in collaboration with Serbia's MoD, was primarily geared towards Serbian government representatives, but was also open to participants from BiH, Croatia, and Montenegro. In 2013 ITF organized a course entitled 'Ammunition Safety, Ammunition Stockpile Management and Ammunition Demilitarization Technology'. Also held at TRZ Kragujevac and open to representatives from the MoDs of BiH, Croatia, Macedonia, Serbia,[40] and Slovenia, the course focused on ammunition design, the safe storage and maintenance of ammunition, as well as dangers arising from inadequate stockpile management.

SEESAC supports and organizes a 'Regional Training Course on Stockpile Management', the last of which consisted of three five-day modules held in 2011 at the Faculty of Mechanical Engineering of the University of Sarajevo. The event gathered 58 members of the ministries of defence and interior from BiH, Croatia, Macedonia, Montenegro, and Serbia. Perhaps the most long-standing regional PSSM training course offered to representatives from RASR countries is the 'Physical Security and Stockpile Management Course' organized by RACVIAC. Since its launch in 2010, the course has been offered on an annual basis to about 125 representatives of RACVIAC member states, including employees of governmental organizations and agencies involved in the management of national stockpiles of small arms and conventional ammunition (RASR, n.d.b).

Donor-funded industrial demilitarization programmes also provide training. Project documents of the third NATO Partnership for Peace project in Albania, for instance, emphasize that NATO Maintenance and Supply Agency equipment supply contracts were to include the provision of training to Albanian equipment operators, including courses in business, logistics, technical supervision, management processes, and safety (NAMSA, 2009, p. 12; 2012).

> It can take years for trainees to become proficient in ammunition management and handling.

Yet this form of training is limited in time and scope. In particular, such efforts address only specific aspects of stockpile management and surplus destruction. Personnel also tend to receive dedicated training on certain types of ammunition, leaving other (often more sophisticated) types of ammunition beyond their expertise.

Beyond training

The impact of donor-funded stockpile management courses on the capacities and competencies of SEE armed forces is difficult to evaluate. After the courses, staff are often transferred or relocated to posts where their new skills are of little use. The courses, moreover, tend to be ad hoc, in the sense that they are held irregularly and infrequently. Ensuring that the most relevant people receive the training is a problem in some cases. Linguistic hurdles must also be overcome. Using full-time interpreters is expensive, yet knowledgeable staff often lack the necessary language skills. On the flip side, some individuals attend technical courses solely because of their language skills, rather than because their job requires the skills being taught.

Funding tends to limit the duration of the courses to a few weeks at most. Yet, as Priestley (2011, pp. 53–58) explains, it can take several months, and often years, for trainees to acquire a basic level of proficiency in many aspects of ammunition management and handling. Those who are familiar with or accustomed to handling munitions but acquired much of their professional knowledge 'in-house' may need to unlearn old practices before learning new ones that are consistent with regional and international standards.

There is also a tendency for donor-funded training to benefit mainly staff officers and high-level civilian ammunition experts and to overlook the basic training needs of personnel involved in depot management and physical security. Yet securing and transporting ammunition has considerable manpower requirements. Albania reported in 2011 that a total of 1,472 people, representing approximately 12.5 per cent of all AAF personnel, had been assigned to guarding depots (Albania, 2011, p. 4). The BiH MoD assigns approximately 200 soldiers to guard its ASS and WSS (EWG, 2010a; NATO, 2011). In 2011, Macedonia reported that a total of 115 army personnel were assigned to provide security to army warehouses (Macedonia, 2011).

For most RASR countries, stockpile reduction means disposing of surplus ammunition through sales, donations, and destruction, coupled with the sustained implementation of ammunition management processes, including:

- carrying out ammunition surveillance[41] and maintaining an inventory;
- transitioning to UN (and, where applicable, NATO) classification systems for ammunition and explosives;

- conducting consequence risk analysis and managing risk;[42]
- upgrading and refurbishing prospective storage depots; and, ultimately,
- replacing old and obsolete ammunition with new types of ammunition for new combat systems.

Each of these processes requires specific expertise. Stockpile management specialists increasingly understand that improving stockpile management competencies requires more than training (UNODA, 2015). Regional training seminars—although important—are too limited in their scope and duration to alter a host country's stockpile management practices in a sustainable way. During the seventh RASR workshop,[43] there was broad agreement that training is most effective not when offered as a standalone solution, but when integrated into comprehensive capacity building measures that aim at long-term ownership, organizational reform, and the integration of international standards into existing national legislation, policy, and practices (Berman, 2014).

The following section describes an ongoing initiative in BiH that offers a possible template for building sustainable stockpile management capacity in the region.

The EUFOR Mobile Training Team 2.1.6.1

Long-term capacity building requires long-term commitment. Yet few donor countries are willing to invest the human, material, and financial resources needed over several years to build comprehensive stockpile management capacity in any SEE country, let alone the region.

A participant is trained in firefighting skills during the Ammunition Transportation Safety Course held at Rajlovac, Sarajevo, Bosnia and Herzegovina, mid-2014.
© Swiss Armed Forces

One exception is the Mobile Training Team 2.1.6.1, set up in 2011, led by Switzerland, and implemented in coordination with Austria and Sweden. The EU-led Operation EUFOR ALTHEA established MTTs to rebuild lost capacities of AF BiH personnel in various domains. MTT 2.1.6.1. coordinates training for, and oversees the equipment and infrastructure aspects of, the life-cycle management of weapons and ammunition. The MTT faces a series of challenges in BiH, including a high number of overloaded ammunition depots, transportation constraints, and the risks of explosion. Achieving project objectives is expected to take at least seven years.

The Small Arms Survey has requested access to interim reports and documents as part of an ongoing study of the project's rationale, inception, and activities, along with the obstacles it encountered and the solutions it found.

The MTT 2.1.6.1 rationale revolves around six key pillars of sustainable stockpile management capacity building:

1. **MTT courses address the needs of AF BiH** personnel working on different aspects of weapons and ammunition life-cycle management. Participants—officers as well as non-commissioned officers—include ammunition technical appointees for advanced ammunition handling and surveillance; facility protection and validation specialists (risk assessment); specialists in the transportation of dangerous goods; and data management specialists. All modules follow relevant international standards and can be adapted by the AF BiH to meet its future needs.

   > Coherence between training supplied and available equipment is essential.

2. **MTT courses are progressively transferred** to the training and doctrine command of the AF BiH. The MTT's moderating, mentoring, and monitoring train-the-trainers approach means that every module it provides is taught at least three times with increasing responsibility and autonomy conferred on pre-selected AF BiH trainers. For the first course, the staff is composed of experts from the MTT's troop-contributing nations, namely Austria, Switzerland, and Sweden. Staff for the second course include MTT-mentored trainers from the AF BiH. The third course is fully organized and staffed by the AF BiH, which is asked to (i) integrate the modules in training and doctrine command's routine training curriculum, (ii) conduct the courses, and (iii) establish related regulations. Although the MTT does not certify participants, it grants a certificate of attendance; meanwhile, the AF BiH awards a national certification to participants once it is in charge of the course. At the end of the process, the AF BiH assumes full responsibility for the certification of its personnel.

3. **Coherence is ensured between training and equipment.** Since MTT trains the AF BiH to manage its stockpiles in accordance with international standards, associated material and equipment also need to meet such standards. The troop-contributing nations provide the AF BiH with necessary equipment, such as forklifts to move ammunition boxes around the depot. Perhaps the best example of the confluence of training and equipment is the refurbishment of the ASS in Krupa, where the MTT provides on-site training. In collaboration with the AF BiH, the site is being transformed into a model site[44]—that is, weapons and ammunition storage practices, depot infrastructure, and perimeter security are all being brought in line with international standards.

4. **Simultaneous reforms at strategic levels** address high-level aspects of ammunition life-cycle management. The building of stockpile management capacity presupposes wider institutional, structural, and organizational reforms of the AF BiH for long-term sustainability. Such reforms might involve, for instance, higher salaries to entice course participants to become instructors. In Bosnia, this reform process is coordinated by a strategic board, chaired by the BiH minister of defence, and a coordination body, led by the deputy chief of staff for resources. At the time of writing, the coordination body oversaw three working groups (including one on ASS Krupa) to address interrelated issues, including normative standardization, surveillance, record-keeping, training and certification, personnel allocation, and infrastructure.

5. **Coordination with international PSSM partners** is necessary to support reforms to each host country's normative and institutional framework. Hence the strategy must be endorsed by the main international stakeholders, including the OSCE Mission in BiH, NATO headquarters in Sarajevo, the EU special representative, the US Embassy, and UNDP–BiH.

6. **The host nation must take ownership** of the project at an early stage. Among other things, this entails identifying and allocating key personnel to the courses; assessing the normative framework and identifying changes needed to bring it in line with international standards; anticipating human resource needs and allocating tasks; and clarifying the chain of command for stockpile management.

The MTT model seeks to combine a bottom–up approach (delivery of technical courses) with top–down reform initiatives (involving changes to force structure, a country's normative framework, and personnel allocation). While the project is still under way and final results are not yet in, the model appears to address many of the abovementioned gaps. To date, several courses have been handed over to training and doctrine command in Travnik. Challenges remain, but ultimately it is conceivable that AF BiH trainers could contribute to PSSM courses elsewhere in the region, with the MTT serving as a model that could assist other countries in need of stockpile management capacity building.

CONCLUSION

The RASR initiative gathers representatives of ministries of defence and general staffs of Albania, Bosnia and Herzegovina, Bulgaria, Croatia, Macedonia, Montenegro, Romania, Serbia, and Slovenia to explore options for cooperation in the field of stockpile management, and particularly the management of surpluses. This chapter compiles surplus stockpile data provided, for the most part, by these states, and documents the evolution of surplus weapons and ammunition stockpiles in South-east Europe since 2008. More specifically, it seeks to identify the most promising means of building on the stockpile management and destruction efforts already undertaken in the nine RASR countries.

RASR has prompted more and more participating states to declare their levels of surplus ordnance, and especially large conventional ammunition. While most countries report decreasing surplus stockpile levels, the ongoing restructuring of SEE military organizations and the upgrading of small arms and light weapons in use by SEE armed forces are processes that add to national stockpiles, creating new surpluses. The creation of weapons and ammunition surpluses is normal for any country, yet in SEE it presents a continuing problem because the disposal process is politically sensitive. Despite examples of catastrophic accidents associated with surplus, and sometimes unsafe, ammunition, governments generally regard surplus stockpiles as having a high commercial value (if sold) and are reluctant to allocate the budgets required for demilitarization. For this and other reasons, surplus destruction tends to be slow.

The record of UEMS in the region—including during storage at private demilitarization plants—underlines the potential dangers of neglected surpluses. Donor-funded destruction and infrastructure refurbishment programmes are thus instrumental, and, in fact, currently the main driving force behind stockpile reduction. At the national level, such projects have helped to destroy surpluses, revamp infrastructure, and build capacity; however, synergies have proven difficult to create at the regional level, particularly in efforts to pool resources to optimize cross-border transport to facilitate destruction. A number of political, regulatory, and logistical hurdles still hinder regional cooperation in the field of ammunition demilitarization.

RASR workshop discussions have revealed disparities and shortfalls in expertise across SEE, specifically in the areas of stockpile safety and security. Technical knowledge and experience are often lost with the restructuring of armed forces and the consequent reassignment or loss of personnel, which thwarts sustainable capacity building. Critically, many soldiers assigned to guard duty at ammunition and weapons storage sites lack the basic training necessary for ensuring the adequate physical security of these sites.

Regional organizations acknowledge that this loss of know-how jeopardizes the sustainability of previous donor and host-country demilitarization and infrastructure investments; they are addressing the problem by funding and organizing regional technical training courses for national personnel. This new phase adopts a bottom–up approach, placing emphasis on personnel rather than on infrastructure. It also uses detailed and comprehensive curricula that integrate international standards and best practices into national legislative frameworks.

As practitioners acknowledge, however, technical training alone does not guarantee sustainability. Building stockpile management capacity over the long term presupposes wider institutional, structural, and organizational reforms. The ideal—but resource-intensive—solution may lie in combining technical courses with concurrent, top–down reforms that address national normative frameworks, force structures, and personnel allocation. BiH will prove an interesting test case in this regard. ◼

ABBREVIATIONS AND ACRONYMS

AAF	Albanian Armed Forces
AF BiH	Armed Forces of Bosnia and Herzegovina
ASS	Ammunition storage site
AUW	All-up weight
BiH	Bosnia and Herzegovina
CASM	Conventional ammunition stockpile management
EOD	Explosive ordnance disposal
EU	European Union
EUFOR	European Union Force
EXPLODE	Explosive Ordnance and Remnants of War Destruction
IATG	International Ammunition Technical Guidelines
MEICO	Military Export–Import State Company
MoD	Ministry of defence
MoI	Ministry of interior
MONDEM	Montenegro demilitarization
MTT	Mobile Training Team
NATO	North Atlantic Treaty Organization
NSPA	North Atlantic Treaty Organization Support Agency
OB/OD	Open burning/open detonation
OSCE	Organization for Security and Co-operation in Europe
PSSM	Physical security and stockpile management
RACVIAC	Regional Arms Control Verification and Implementation Assistance Centre
RASR	Regional Approach to Stockpile Reduction
SEE	South-east Europe
SEESAC	South Eastern and Eastern Europe Clearinghouse for the Control of Small Arms and Light Weapons

UEMS	Unplanned explosions at munitions sites
UNDP	United Nations Development Programme
UXO	Unexploded ordnance
WP	White phosphorus
WRA	Office of Weapons Removal and Abatement
WSS	Weapons storage site

ENDNOTES

1 The Small Arms Survey defines UEMS as 'accidents that result in an explosion of abandoned, damaged, improperly stored, or properly stored stockpiles of munitions at a munitions site' (Berman and Reina, 2014, p. 3).

2 Kosovo attended the workshops as an observer. The designation of Kosovo is without prejudice to positions on status and is in line with UN Security Council Resolution 1244 and the relevant opinion of the International Court of Justice (UNSC, 1999; ICJ, 2010).

3 The four other members are the Regional Arms Control Verification and Implementation Assistance Centre (RACVIAC–Centre for Security Cooperation), ITF Enhancing Human Security, the NATO Support Agency (NSPA), and the South Eastern and Eastern Europe Clearinghouse for the Control of Small Arms and Light Weapons (SEESAC).

4 By 1991, the Serbian government had inherited an estimated 3.5 million Yugoslav small arms and light weapons (Griffiths, 2010, p. 184).

5 Small Arms Survey interview with Lt.-Col. Vukadin Tomašević, MoD, Podgorica, Montenegro, 6 July 2010.

6 These standards include those found in the *Manual of NATO Safety Principles for the Storage of Military Ammunition and Explosives*, International Ammunition Technical Guideline 02.20, and US Army's Ammunition and Explosives Safety Standards (NATO, 2010; UNODA, 2011b; USDA, 2011).

7 Owned by the company Vitex JSC, the plant is located in Gorni Lom, north-western Bulgaria.

8 This number excludes land mine-related deaths and injuries that have occurred on the Albania–Kosovo border.

9 The following RASR countries are NATO members: Albania (since 2009), Bulgaria (2004), Croatia (2009), Romania (2004), and Slovenia (2004).

10 See RASR (n.d.a).

11 Romania, for instance, only attended the seventh workshop. Kosovo attended some of the workshops as an observer.

12 Among these organizations were ITF Enhancing Human Security, the NSPA, the OSCE, RACVIAC, SEESAC, and the UN Development Programme.

13 In contrast, EUFOR advocated three prospective ASSs (EUFOR, 2014).

14 Confiscated, seized, and collected small arms, for instance, are distinct from 'surplus' and often fall within the responsibility of MoIs. See Lazarevic (2010) for a review of the disparate disposal policies in SEE for this category, which often include the absorption of these weapons into state arsenals and their reuse by state forces.

15 In 2006 Serbia was reportedly storing around 12,600 tonnes of ammunition in open-air facilities (statement by Serbian representative, third RASR workshop, Sarajevo, BiH, 3 November 2010). In mid-2011, the MoD declared that it had completed the removal of all ammunition from open-air storage areas (Serbia, 2011c, slides 7–8).

16 For propellants, the primary risk is autocatalytic decomposition, which has the potential to result in spontaneous ignition, leading to mass explosions in ammunition storage areas.

17 Physical security measures include controlled access and perimeter measures, such as fencing and external lighting, security guards, cameras, perimeter intruder detection systems, and any other measure designed to minimize the risk of illegal entry, which might result in the loss or diversion of weapons and ammunition.

18 The following conversions apply: 1 US ton=0.907 metric tonnes; 1 UK ton=1.016 metric tonnes.

19 Author correspondence with Alexander Savelyev and Gerhard Faustmann, OSCE, 6 November and 4 December 2014.

20 Statement by Montenegrin representative, third RASR workshop, Sarajevo, BiH, 3 November 2010.

21 The explosion took place during surplus ammunition disposal operations conducted by a private contractor hired by the Albanian MoD. See Carapic and Gobinet (2014, p. 3) and Lazarevic (2012).

22 Author correspondence with Ivanela Krizanovic, Ministry of Defence, Croatia, 24 December 2014.

23 Author correspondence with David Towndrow, NSPA, 4 December 2014.

24 By comparison, BiH destroyed only 6,300 tonnes of surplus ammunition, mines, and explosives by combining OB/OD and industrial demilitarization over the same period (AF BiH AWE, 2014, slide 12).

25   Author briefing by BiH Ammunition, Weapons and Explosives (AWE) Task Force, Sarajevo, BiH, 16 September 2014.

26   For more on surplus sales, see Gobinet (2011) and Gobinet and Gramizzi (2011).

27   Ammunition that is donated is transferred free of charge or for a nominal fee, with someone paying the transport.

28   According to the media, the donated ammunition included 22 million 7.62 x 39 mm cartridges, 15,000 hand grenades, and 32,000 artillery shells of various calibres (IBNA, 2014).

29   Kula near Mrkonjić Grad, Krupa near Pazarić, Rabić near Derventa, and Teufik Buza near Visoko.

30   A joint ministerial statement issued in October 2010 endorses a regional approach to stockpile management but does not specifically mention RASR (SEDM, n.d.).

31   The Council is the successor to the Stability Pact for South Eastern Europe.

32   Government-owned ammunition is almost always controlled, accounted for, and secured during transport under instruments (1) and (2). Surplus munitions are subject to the Basel Convention in addition to instruments (1) and (2) only when they are categorized as 'waste'. However, most nations do not regard surplus munitions, even when destined for demilitarization, as waste. Some have specific explosive legislation dealing with final transport for disposal (Gobinet, 2013, p. 200; author correspondence with David Towndrow, NSPA, November 2014).

33   For the purposes of classification for transport, the UN hazard class and compatibility system assigns explosives to one of six hazard divisions depending on the type of hazard they present, and to one of 13 compatibility groups, which identify the kinds of explosives substances and articles that are deemed to be compatible for storage.

34   See Articles 70(1), 79(2), and 70(3) of the Defence Law (BiH, 2005).

35   Author briefing by Michael Aramanda, Sarajevo, BiH, September 2014.

36   Small Arms Survey correspondence with Macedonian EOD team leader, 17 September 2011.

37   A stockpile management training programme is reportedly being developed (Slovenia, 2014).

38   Such special ordnance includes the Grad, Šturm, Igla SA-18, OFAB-100, OFAB-250, S-8, cluster bombs, and ammunition containing white phosphorous (Macedonia, 2011, p. 3; EWG, 2010b, slide 12).

39   For the full array of courses as of November 2014, see RASR (n.d.b).

40   Representatives from the Serbian MoI attended the course as well (author correspondence with Blaz Mihelic, ITF, November 2014).

41   Ammunition surveillance is defined as a 'systematic method of evaluating the properties, characteristics and performance capabilities of ammunition throughout its life cycle in order to assess the reliability, safety and operational effectiveness of stocks and to provide data in support of life reassessment' (UNODA, 2011a).

42   See IATG risk reduction process levels (UNODA, 2012).

43   The workshop, held in Sofia from 12 to 15 May 2014, focused on RASR countries' training curricula in the field of stockpile management.

44   International organizations—and particularly the OSCE and SEESAC—are implementing infrastructure upgrades, including fencing and intruder detection systems. See Table 5.2.

BIBLIOGRAPHY

AF BiH AWE (Armed Forces of Bosnia and Herzegovina Ammunition, Weapons and Explosives Task Force). 2014. 'General Briefing.' Presentation given to Small Arms Survey staff, Sarajevo, BiH, 16 September.

Albania. 2011. 'Small Arms Survey Questionnaire for Albanian MoD Authorities and Experts on Demilitarization of Surplus Ammunition.' Unpublished translation of completed questionnaire.

—. 2012. 'Information Sheet about RASR and Albania.' Presented at the 5th RASR Workshop, Durrës, Albania, 23–25 April.
<http://www.rasrinitiative.org/pdfs/workshop-5/RASR-Workshop-5-Albania-RASR-Information-Handout.pdf>

—. 2014a. 'Ongoing Demilitarization and PSSM Training Capacities.' Presented at the 7th RASR Workshop, Sofia, Bulgaria, 12–15 May.
<http://www.rasrinitiative.org/pdfs/workshop-7/RASR-Workshop-7-PPT-Albania-Demil-PSSM-training.pdf>

—. 2014b. *The Process of Demilitarization of Stockpile Ammunition and Armaments in Albanian Armed Forces.* Presented at the RACVIAC Physical Security and Stockpile Management Workshop, Rakitje, Croatia, 18–20 February.

—. n.d. Plan of Action for the Elimination of Excess Ammunition in the Armed Forces of the Republic of Albania 2009–13. Tirana: Ministry of Defence.

Arsovska, Jana and Panos Kostakos. 2008. 'Illicit Arms Trafficking and the Limits of Rational Choice Theory: The Case of the Balkans.' *Trends in Organized Crime,* Vol. 11, No. 4, pp. 352–78.

Berman, Eric G. 2014. 'Wrap-up Slide for the 7th RASR Workshop.'
    <http://www.rasrinitiative.org/pdfs/workshop-7/RASR-Workshop-7-PPT-PSSM-training-Wrap-up.pdf>

— and Pilar Reina. 2014. *Unplanned Explosions at Munition Sites (UEMS): Excess Stockpiles as Liabilities rather than Assets*. Geneva: Small Arms Survey.
    <http://www.smallarmssurvey.org/?uems-handbook>

BiH (Bosnia and Herzegovina). 2005. Defence Law (Zakon o odbrani Bosne i Herzegovine). Sarajevo: Government of BiH.
    <http://www.mod.gov.ba/files/file/zakoni/Zakon-o-odbrani-bs.pdf>

—. 2008. Agreement on Final Disposal of All Rights and Obligations over Movable Property that Will Continue to Serve Defence Purposes (also known
    as the Doboj Agreement). Sarajevo: Presidency of Bosnia and Herzegovina. January.

—. 2009. Decision for Dealing with Surplus Weapons and Ammunition of the Armed Forces of Bosnia and Herzegovina. 8 October.
    <http://www.predsjednistvobih.ba/zaklj/sjed/default.aspx?id=36656&langTag=bs-BA>

—. 2011. 'Surplus Weapons and Munitions Disposal.' Presented at the conference 'Towards a Sustainable Solution for Excess Weapons and Ammunition,'
    Pula, Croatia, 30 May–1 June 2011.

Bromley, Mark. 2007. 'UN Arms Embargoes: Their Impact on Arms Flows and Target Behaviour—Case Study: Former Yugoslavia, 1991–96.' Stockholm:
    Stockholm International Peace Research Institute. <http://books.sipri.org/files/misc/UNAE/SIPRI07UNAEYug.pdf>

Bulgaria. 2011. 'Small Arms Survey Questionnaire for Bulgarian Ministry of Defense Authorities and Experts on Demilitarization of Surplus Ammunition.'
    Unpublished questionnaire.

—. 2012. 'Bulgarian Demilitarization Activities: A Step Forward.' Presented at the 5th RASR Workshop, Durrës, Albania, 23–25 April.
    <http://www.rasrinitiative.org/pdfs/workshop-5/RASR-Workshop-5-Bulg-MOD-PPT-Demilitarization.pdf>

—. 2013. 'Demilitarization of Surplus Ammunition.' Presented at the 6th RASR Workshop, Bled, Slovenia, 3–5 April.
    <http://www.rasrinitiative.org/pdfs/workshop-6/RASR-Workshop-6-PPT-Bulgaria-MoD.pdf>

Carapic, Jovana and Pierre Gobinet. 2014. 'Taking Stock of Excess Stockpiles: UEMS in South-east Europe.' Research Note No. 41. Geneva: Small Arms Survey.
    <http://www.smallarmssurvey.org/fileadmin/docs/H-Research_Notes/SAS-Research-Note-41.pdf>

Croatia. 2013. 'Ammunition and Weapons Surplus Treatment in the Croatian Armed Forces.' Presented at the 6th RASR Workshop, Bled, Slovenia, 3–5 April.
    <http://www.rasrinitiative.org/pdfs/workshop-6/RASR-Workshop-6-PPT-Croatia-MoD.pdf>

—. 2014. 'Ammunition Management and Education in the Croatian Armed Forces.' Presented at the 7th RASR Workshop, Sofia, Bulgaria, 12–15 May 2014.
    <http://www.rasrinitiative.org/pdfs/workshop-7/RASR-Workshop-7-PPT-Croatia-ammo-mgmt-training.pdf>

Cubic and USDTTA (United States Defense Transformation Team Albania). 2014. 'Surplus SALW and Ammunition Statistics.' Unpublished document.

DTRA (Defense Threat Reduction Agency). 2011. 'Physical Security and Stockpile Management of Arms, Ammunition and Explosives.' Presented at the
    4th RASR Workshop, Ljubljana, Slovenia, 23–25 May.
    <http://www.rasrinitiative.org/pdfs/workshop-4/RASR-Workshop4-DTRA-PSSM-May11.pdf>

EUFOR (European Union Force). 2014. 'BiH/IC Master Plan on Ammunition.' Unpublished presentation given to Small Arms Survey researchers by
    Colonel Martin F. Trachsler, EUFOR Mobile Training Team 2.1.6.1. September.

EWG (Expert Working Group). 2010a. 'Disposal Surplus of Weapons and Ammunition in AF BiH: Management of Storage Sites.' Presented at the Ministry
    of Defence Conference, Zenica, Bosnia and Herzegovina, 3 March.

—. 2010b. 'Disposal of Surplus of Weapons and Ammunition in AF BiH: Management of Storage Sites.' Presented at the 3rd RASR Workshop, Sarajevo,
    Bosnia and Herzegovina, 3 November.
    <http://www.rasrinitiative.org/pdfs/workshop-3/RASR-workshop-EWG-Surplus-in-AF-BiH-3Nov10.pdf>

Faltas, Sami. 2008. 'Bulgaria and Romania: Quick Start, Ambiguous Progress.' In Aaron Karp, pp. 82–105.

— and Vera Chrobok, eds. 2004. *Disposal of Surplus Small Arms: A Survey of Policies and Practices in OSCE Countries*. Bonn: Bonn International Center
    for Conversion. <http://www.smallarmssurvey.org/fileadmin/docs/E-Co-Publications/SAS-BICC-2004-OSCE-surplus-small-arms.pdf>

GICHD (Geneva International Centre for Humanitarian Demining). 2008. *A Guide to Ammunition Storage*. Geneva: GICHD. November.
    <https://www.gichd.org/fileadmin/pdf/publications/Ammunition-Storage-2008.pdf>

Gobinet, Pierre. 2011. *Significant Surpluses: Weapons and Ammunition Stockpiles in South-east Europe*. Special Report No. 13. Geneva: Small Arms Survey.
    <http://www.smallarmssurvey.org/fileadmin/docs/C-Special-reports/SAS-SR13-Significant-Surpluses.pdf>

—. 2012. *Capabilities and Capacities: A Survey of South-east Europe's Demilitarization Infrastructure*. Special Report No. 15. Geneva: Small Arms Survey.
    April. <http://www.smallarmssurvey.org/fileadmin/docs/C-Special-reports/SAS-SR15-South-East-Europe-Demilitarization.pdf>

—. 2013. 'Burning the Bullet: Industrial Demilitarization of Ammunition.' In Small Arms Survey. *Small Arms Survey 2013: Everyday Dangers*. Cambridge:
    Cambridge University Press, pp. 189–217.

— and Claudio Gramizzi. 2011. *Scraping the Barrel: The Trade in Surplus Ammunition*. Issue Brief No. 2. Geneva: Small Arms Survey. April.
<http://www.smallarmssurvey.org/fileadmin/docs/G-Issue-briefs/SAS-IB2-Scraping-the-barrel.pdf>

Griffiths, Hugh. 2010. 'Serbia: Choosing Between Profit and Security.' In Aaron Karp, pp. 179–205.

IBNA (Independent Balkan News Agency). 2014. 'Albania Donates Iraq 22 Million Cartridges, Shells and Grenades, 10 Thousand Kalashnikovs to Afghanistan.' 30 September.
<http://www.balkaneu.com/albania-donates-iraq-22-million-cartridges-shells-grenades-10-thousand-kalashnikovs-afghanistan/>

ICJ (International Court of Justice). 2010. *Opinion on the Kosovo Declaration of Independence*. 22 July.
<http://www.unmikonline.org/Documents/ICJ%20decision%20on%20Kosovo%2022%20July%202010.pdf>

IISS (International Institute for Security Studies). 2011. *The Military Balance 2011*. London: Routledge.

Karp, Aaron, ed. 2008. *The Politics of Destroying Surplus Small Arms*. New York: Routledge.

King, Benjamin and F. David Diaz. 2011. 'Preparing PSSM Programmes: Avoiding the Inevitable Problems?' In Benjamin King, ed. *Safer Stockpiles: Practitioners' Experiences with Physical Security and Stockpile Management (PSSM) Assistance Programmes*. Geneva: Small Arms Survey, pp. 8–47.

Lazarevic, Jasna. 2010. *South-east European Surplus Arms: State Policies and Practices*. Issue Brief No. 1. Geneva: Small Arms Survey. November.
<http://www.smallarmssurvey.org/fileadmin/docs/G-Issue-briefs/SAS-RASR-IB1_SE-European-Surplus-Arms.pdf>

—. 2012. *Costs and Consequences: Unplanned Explosions and Demilitarization in South-east Europe*. Special Report. Geneva: Small Arms Survey.
<http://www.smallarmssurvey.org/fileadmin/docs/C-Special-reports/SAS-SR18-costs-and-consequences.pdf>

Macedonia. 2011. 'Small Arms Survey Questionnaire for Macedonian MoD authorities and Demilitarization Experts.' Unpublished questionnaire.

Montenegro. 2009. Zakon o drzavnoj imovini (Law on State-owned Property). Unofficial translation.

—. 2011a. 'Logistics and Regional Cooperation.' Presented at the conference 'Towards a Sustainable Solution for Excess Weapons and Ammunition,' Pula, Croatia, 30 May.

—. 2011b. 'Update on NATO Trust Fund Project for Munitions Disposal in Albania.' Presented at the 4th RASR Workshop, Ljubljana, Slovenia, 24 May.

—. 2011c. 'Small Arms Survey Questionnaire for Montenegrin Ministry of Defense Authorities and Demilitarization Experts.' Unpublished questionnaire.

—. 2011d. 'Surplus Weapon and Ammunition Destruction in Montenegro.' Presented at the 4th RASR Workshop, Ljubljana, Slovenia, 30 May.
<http://www.rasrinitiative.org/pdfs/workshop-4/RASR-Workshop4-Montenegro-SurplusAmmunition-24May11.pdf>

—. 2014a. *Safe Storage of Ordnance in Army of Montenegro*. Presented at the 7th RASR Workshop, Sofia, Bulgaria, 12–14 May.

—. 2014b. *Ammunition Maintenance and Disposal in the Armed Forces of Montenegro*. Presented at the RACVIAC Physical Security and Stockpile Management Workshop in Rakitje, Croatia, 18–20 February.

NAMSA (North Atlantic Treaty Organization Maintenance and Supply Agency). 2009. 'Proposal to Albania and United States Department of State Bureau of Political–Military Affairs Office of Weapons Removal and Abatement for the Destruction of Surplus Ammunition Stocks in Albania.' Capellen, Luxembourg: NAMSA. December.

—. 2012. 'Update on NATO Trust Fund Project for Munitions Disposal in Albania.' Presented at the 5th RASR Workshop, Durrës, Albania, 23–25 April.
<http://www.rasrinitiative.org/pdfs/workshop-5/RASR-Workshop-5-NAMSA-Alb-Trust-Fund-Project-Update.pdf>

NATO (North Atlantic Treaty Organization). 2005. *Manual of NATO Safety Principles for the Transport of Military Ammunition and Explosives*. AASTP-2, first edn. September. Brussels: NATO. <http://www.unog.ch/80256EDD006B8954/%28httpAssets%29/A80AD5A6BEBCAC05C12579FE00489A2A/$file/ManualofNATOSafetyPrinciplesfortheTransportofMilitaryAmmunitionandExplosives.pdf>

—. 2010. *Manual of NATO Safety Principles for the Storage of Military Ammunition and Explosives*. AASTP-1, first edn., change 3. May. Brussels: NATO.
<http://www.rasrinitiative.org/pdfs/AASTP-1-Ed1-Chge-3-Public-Release-110810.pdf>

—. 2011. 'NATO Support to the Reduction of BiH Small Arms, Light Weapons, Ammunition and Ammunition Storage Sites.' Presented at the conference 'Towards a Sustainable Solution for Excess Weapons and Ammunition,' Pula, Croatia, 30 May.

ND and CAF (National Defence and the Canadian Armed Forces). n.d. 'Operation IMPACT.' Updated 3 February 2015.
<http://www.forces.gc.ca/en/operations-abroad-current/op-impact.page>

NSPA (North Atlantic Treaty Organization Support Agency). 2014. 'NATO/NSPA Demilitarisation Trust Fund Projects in the Balkans.' Presented at the 7th RASR Workshop, Sofia, Bulgaria, 12–15 May. <http://www.rasrinitiative.org/pdfs/workshop-7/RASR-Workshop-7-PPT-NSPA.pdf>

OSCE (Organization for Security and Co-operation in Europe). 2003a. *OSCE Document on Stockpiles of Conventional Ammunition*. 19 November.
<http://www.osce.org/fsc/15792>

—. 2003b. *Best Practice Guide on National Procedures for Stockpile Management and Security*. 1 December. <http://www.osce.org/fsc/13637>

—. 2014. 'Montenegro Demilitarization Programme—MONDEM: Synopsis.' October.

Priestley, Steve. 2011. 'Implementing PSSM Programmes in Least-developed Nations: The Bottom-up.' In Benjamin King, ed. *Safer Stockpiles: Practitioners' Experiences with Physical Security and Stockpile Management (PSSM) Assistance Programmes*. Geneva: Small Arms Survey, pp. 48–73.

RASR (Regional Approach to Stockpile Reduction). n.d.a. '7th RASR Workshop.' <http://www.rasrinitiative.org/workshop-7th.php>

—. n.d.b. 'Courses.' <http://www.rasrinitiative.org/events-courses.php>

Saferworld. 2007. *Measuring up? Arms Transfer Controls in Serbia*. London: Saferworld. October.
    <http://www.saferworld.org.uk/downloads/pubdocs/SEE%20Serbia-English.pdf>

SEDM (South-Eastern Europe Defense Ministerial). n.d. 'Priority Goals: MPFSEE-SEDM.'
    <http://www.mapn.ro/sedm/concept/MPFSEE-SEDM/index.php>

SEESAC (South Eastern and Eastern Europe Clearinghouse for the Control of Small Arms and Light Weapons). 2006. *South Eastern Europe SALW Monitor 2006: Serbia (including the UN administered Entity of Kosovo)*. Belgrade: SEESAC.
    <http://www.seesac.org/res/files/publication/400.pdf>

—. 2009. 'Regional Focus.' Presented at the 1st RASR Workshop, Zagreb, Croatia, 5–7 May.
    <http://www.rasrinitiative.org/pdfs/workshop-1/RASR-8-IOs-Dimov-SEESAC.pdf>

—. 2014. 'Training, Education, and Building Capacity: Presentation of SEESAC Activities.' Presented at the 7th RASR Workshop, Sofia, Bulgaria, 12–15 May.
    <http://www.rasrinitiative.org/pdfs/workshop-5/RASR-Workshop-5-SEESAC-PPT.pdf>

—. n.d. *SALW Destruction Activities Strengthening Safety and Security through Regional Cooperation in South East Europe*.
    <http://www.seesac.org/project.php?&l1=126&l2=156&l3=181>

Serbia. 2011a. 'Surplus Ammunition in the Serbian Armed Forces' (translation). Presented at the 4th RASR Workshop, Ljubljana, Slovenia, 23–25 May.

—. 2011b. 'Surplus Ammunition.' Presented at the 11th South Eastern and Eastern Europe Clearinghouse for the Control of Small Arms and Light Weapons, Belgrade, 25–27 May.

—. 2011c. 'Towards a Sustainable Solution for Excess Weapons and Ammunition.' Presented at the conference 'Towards a Sustainable Solution for Excess Weapons and Ammunition,' Pula, Croatia, 30 May.

—. 2011d. 'Small Arms Survey Questionnaire for Serbian MoD Authorities and Demilitarization Experts.' Unpublished translation of completed questionnaire.

—. 2014a. 'Physical Security and Stockpile Management Workshop.' Presented at the RACVIAC Physical Security and Stockpile Management Workshop in Rakitje, Croatia, 18–20 February.

—. 2014b. 'Training Curriculum in the Field of Physical Security and Stockpile Management.' Presented at the 7th RASR Workshop, Sofia, Bulgaria, 12–15 May.
    <http://www.rasrinitiative.org/pdfs/workshop-7/RASR-Workshop-7-PPT-Serbia-PSSM-training.pdf >

Slovenia. 2014. 'Slovenian MoD AF PSSM Training Capacities and Curriculum.' Presented at the 7th RASR Workshop, Sofia, Bulgaria, 12–15 May.
    <http://www.rasrinitiative.org/pdfs/workshop-7/RASR-Workshop-7-PPT-Slovenia.pdf>

Small Arms Survey. 2014a. 'Ammunition and Small Arms and Light Weapons Surplus Database by RASR participating state 2009–14.' Unpublished database.

—. 2014b. Unplanned Explosions at Munitions Sites Database. Geneva: Small Arms Survey. <http://www.smallarmssurvey.org/?uems>

Tsolova, Tsvetelia and Stoyan Nenov. 2014. 'Blasts Kill 15 People at Bulgaria Explosives Plant.' Reuters. 2 October.
    <http://www.reuters.com/article/2014/10/02/us-bulgaria-blast-idUSKCN0HR12Q20141002>

UN (United Nations). 2013. UN Recommendations on the Transport of Dangerous Goods: Model Regulations. Vol. 1, 18th edn. New York and Geneva: UN.
    <http://www.unece.org/trans/danger/publi/unrec/rev18/18files_e.html>

UNECE (United Nations Economic Commission for Europe). 2009. European Agreement concerning the International Carriage of Dangerous Goods by Road. As applicable from 1 January 2011. ECE/TRANS/215, Vols. I–II. Geneva: UNECE.
    <http://www.unece.org/trans/danger/publi/adr/adr2011/11contentse.html>

UNEP (United Nations Environment Programme). 1989. Basel Convention on the Control of Transboundary Movements of Hazardous Wastes and Their Disposal. Châtelaine, Switzerland: UN. 22 March.
    <http://www.basel.int/Portals/4/Basel%20Convention/docs/text/BaselConventionText-e.pdf>

UNODA (United Nations Office for Disarmament Affairs). 2011a. *International Ammunition Technical Guidelines (IATG) 01.40: Glossary of Terms, Definitions and Abbreviations*. 10 January.
    <http://www.un.org/disarmament/convarms/Ammunition/IATG/docs/IATG01.40-Glossary_and_Definitions%28V.1%29.pdf>

—. 2011b. *International Ammunition Technical Guidelines (IATG): Quantity and Separation Distances*. IATG 02.20, 1st edn.
    <http://www.un.org/disarmament/convarms/Ammunition/IATG/docs/IATG02.20-Quantity_and_Separation_Distances(V.1).pdf>

—. 2012. *International Ammunition Technical Guidelines (IATG) 02.10: Introduction to Risk Management Principles and Processes*, 1st edn.
    <http://www.un.org/disarmament/convarms/Ammunition/IATG/docs/IATG02.10.pdf>

—. 2015. *International Ammunition Technical Guidelines (IATG) 01.90: Ammunition Management Personnel Competences.*

UNSC (United Nations Security Council). 1999. Resolution 12444 (1999). S/RES/1244 of 10 June 1999.

<http://daccess-dds-ny.un.org/doc/UNDOC/GEN/N99/172/89/PDF/N9917289.pdf?OpenElement>

USDA (United States Department of the Army). 2011. 'Ammunition and Explosives Safety Standards.' Washington, DC: USDA.

Wilkinson, Adrian. 2006. 'Stockpile Management of Ammunition.' In Stéphanie Pézard and Holger Anders, eds. *Targeting Ammunition: A Primer.* Geneva: Small Arms Survey, pp. 229–59.

<http://www.smallarmssurvey.org/fileadmin/docs/D-Book-series/book-03-targeting-ammunition/SAS-Targeting-Ammunition-13-Chapter-8.pdf>

ACKNOWLEDGEMENTS

Principal authors

Pierre Gobinet and Jovana Carapic

لا إله إلا الله

Militiamen belonging to the jihadist group Ansar Dine, Kidal, June 2012.
© Adama Diarra/Reuters

Expanding Arsenals

INSURGENT ARMS IN NORTHERN MALI

6

INTRODUCTION

Armed violence persisted in northern Mali throughout 2014 although the government and secessionist rebel groups had signed a preliminary peace agreement in June 2013. While rebels clashed with the army and community self-defence groups, violent jihadists attacked armed forces and international peacekeepers. Fighting between armed groups over smuggling routes and competition among tribal and ethnic groups further heightened insecurity. Amid these complex dynamics, armed actors have stepped up and diversified their means of sourcing weapons.

This chapter focuses on arms and ammunition used by rebel groups struggling for independence or greater auton-omy, jihadists fighting for the implementation of Islamic law, and militias and self-defence groups that formed in opposition to rebels and jihadists. The analysis is based on original field investigations conducted in 2012–14, includ-ing the documentation of 1,500 small arms and light weapons cartridges identified at some 20 sites of armed clashes[1] and 300 weapons the Malian army recovered from armed groups in 2012–14.[2] The chapter also draws on previously published reports on arms and ammunition whose possession by armed groups was documented in 2012–13, compar-ing new findings with research conducted in northern Mali by the Small Arms Survey in 2005.

The chapter's main findings are as follows:

- Armed groups are better armed than they were a decade ago, including with larger-calibre weapons. Of particu-lar concern is jihadist possession of man-portable air defence systems (MANPADS), although many of these may be inoperable.

- Insurgents use materiel that consists largely of cold war-era Soviet and Chinese arms and ammunition, but they also use more recently produced materiel from Bulgaria and China, among other states.

- Armed groups appear to have obtained much of their materiel through diversion from Malian army stockpiles; however, Libyan stockpiles have also been an important source of materiel, including of more recently acquired larger-calibre weapons.

- There is no evidence that foreign states have directly supplied rebels with arms and ammunition or violated the UN arms embargo by supplying jihadists with arms and ammunition, despite accusations to the contrary.

- Armed groups use trans-Saharan smuggling routes to obtain resupply from illicit markets in Libya and elsewhere in the region.

- Violent jihadists are likely to pose an ongoing threat in northern Mali. Relevant stakeholders, including the UN peacekeeping mission, may have to consider ways to best adapt to this long-term challenge.

This chapter begins by offering background information on the armed insurgency that broke out in 2012 and by providing an overview of current security challenges in northern Mali. It then examines arms and ammunition used by armed groups in northern Mali as well as their countries and years of manufacture. The findings are contrasted against

Map 6.1 **Map of northern Mali**

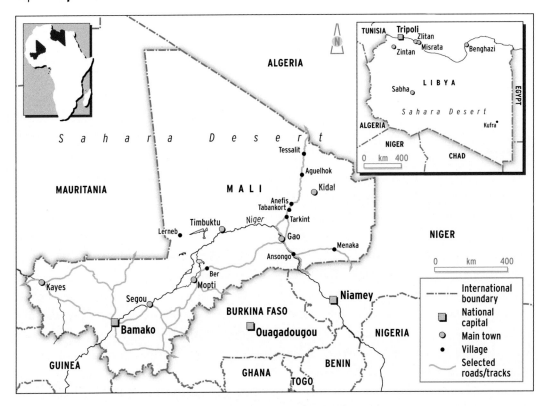

what is known about the holdings of armed groups in previous rebellions in the area. The chapter then identifies the major sources of the materiel and discusses the allegations that foreign states have supplied armed groups with arms and ammunition. The chapter's conclusion considers the findings in relation to the threat of enduring insecurity and continuing jihadist attacks on national and international forces in northern Mali.

THE 2012 INSURGENCY AND ITS AFTERMATH

In January 2012, rebels under the banner of the Mouvement National pour la Libération de l'Azawad (MNLA) and allied jihadist groups launched a sweeping campaign against the national army in northern Mali. Their week-long attack on the army base in Aguelhok began on 18 January 2012 and culminated in the killing of 82 Malian soldiers, including through summary executions (RFI, 2012). The rebel and jihadist groups, hereafter referred to as insurgents, included local Tuareg and subsequently also Arab groups as well as Tuareg fighters who had left Libya in the wake of Col. Muammar Qaddafi's downfall the previous year (UNSC, 2013a, para. 144). For rebels, the declared aim was independence for northern Mali until, in light of developments in 2013, some of them narrowed their demands to greater autonomy. Jihadists also included radical Tuareg and Arab fighters who followed an al-Qaeda-inspired agenda with the goal of establishing Islamic law in northern Mali (Keenan, 2012). The advance of the insurgent groups triggered the formation of additional armed groups that aligned themselves with the Malian government or emerged for self-defence purposes, to protect their local interests, and to counter the perceived threat of domination by secessionist Tuaregs.

By April 2012, insurgents were occupying the major population centres and provincial capitals of Gao, Kidal, and Timbuktu. On 6 April, the MNLA unilaterally declared what they call 'Azawad' (northern Mali) independent (Al Jazeera, 2012). Yet their decision was not universally supported among insurgents or the local population. Among the dissenters were sedentary farmers and pastoralists of the Songhai and Fulani groups who feared Tuareg domination and wished the region to remain firmly within the Republic of Mali. There were also disagreements between groups that supported secular structures and those in favour of Islamic structures, including jihadist groups that were not fighting for the independence of Azawad but for the introduction of Islamic law in Mali. In 2012, when Gao, Timbuktu, and other areas were under their control, the jihadist groups implemented a radical interpretation of sharia law that included the prohibition of alcohol, music, and cigarettes as well as public beatings of individuals accused of adultery and the amputation of limbs of individuals accused of theft or buying or selling stolen goods (Bennoune, 2013).

Jihadist groups eventually turned on the rebels they had previously supported and consolidated their dominance in northern Mali. Responding to the crisis, the UN Security Council mandated the African-led International Support Mission in Mali (AFISMA) in December 2012 and, in April 2013, the UN Multidimensional Integrated Stabilization Mission in Mali (MINUSMA), to which AFISMA transferred its authority in July of the same year (MINUSMA, n.d.). As jihadists pushed farther south in January 2013, raising fears that they could take over Mali's capital, Bamako, the Malian

A woman walks down a street reduced to ruins following an attack by armed groups, Gao, February 2013. © Joel Saget/AFP Photo

government requested urgent assistance. That same month, French troops arrived in Mali and launched, together with AFISMA troops and the Malian army, a counter-insurgency campaign that drove jihadists out of the major population centres (MINUSMA, n.d.). Nevertheless, jihadists have continued their attacks and remain committed to fighting the Malian army as well as French and UN forces in northern Mali.

In contrast, rebel groups that had fought the Malian army in 2012 signed a preliminary agreement with the Malian government for inclusive peace talks in Ouagadougou, Burkino Faso, in June 2013. The Ouagadougou agreement officially restored the territorial integrity of Mali and paved the way for a tentative restoration of state authority in northern Mali. Yet the Malian government and rebel groups were slow in the implementation of key provisions of the agreement, including the cantonment and disarmament of rebel groups (SCR, 2014). Moreover, the national army and insurgents clashed violently in May 2014, when the then Malian prime minister, Moussa Mara, visited the town of Kidal in the heartland of the Tuareg rebellion, which had remained under the de facto control of secessionist rebels. The clashes resulted in the routing of the national army from Kidal; the national defence and security forces subsequently withdrew from various locations in northern Mali to focus on Gao and Timbuktu (Bozonnet, 2014; Diarra, 2014; Offner, 2014). Armed groups then repositioned themselves in various areas of northern Mali, ostensibly to provide protection to the civilian population, but also, according to one observer, to gain political leverage in view of upcoming peace negotiations.[3]

The Malian government and rebel groups met again in Algiers, Algeria, in July 2014 to prepare for the peace talks (Ramzi and Oumar, 2014). Further meetings took place between September and November 2014, gathering representatives of the Malian government, rebel groups, and armed groups that had formed to defend their communities and interests. At the time of writing, discussions remained hamstrung due to ongoing disagreements between the participants, especially with respect to the future status of northern Mali. Rebel groups that had initially called for independence

Table 6.1 Prominent armed groups in northern Mali, 2014

Group		Principal membership
Coordination Group (separatist, federalist)	Haut Conseil pour l'Unité de l'Azawad (High Council for the Unity of Azawad)	Tuareg
	Mouvement Arabe de l'Azawad (Arab Movement of the Azawad)-Sidati	Arab
	Mouvement National pour la Libération de l'Azawad (National Movement for the Liberation of Azawad)	Tuareg
Platform Group (pro-Malian unity, decentralist)	Coordination des Mouvements et Forces Patriotiques de Résistance (Coordination of Patriotic Movements and Forces of the Resistance)	Songhai and Fulani
	Coalition pour le Peuple de l'Azawad (Coalition of the People for Azawad)	Tuareg and Arab
	Mouvement Arabe de l'Azawad (Arab Movement of the Azawad)-Sidi Mohamed	Arab
Jihadist groups	Al-Mourabitoune	Arab and other
	Al-Qaeda au Maghreb Islamique (al-Qaeda in the Islamic Maghreb)	Arab
	Ansar Dine	Tuareg

and formed the 'Coordination Group' were insisting on greater autonomy for northern Mali, to be provided through a new federal structure. Other armed groups that had formed to defend their communities and interests established the 'Platform Group', which defended Malian unity, generally aligned itself with the positions of the Malian government, and promoted decentralization as opposed to federalism. Table 6.1 lists prominent members of the Coordination and Platform groups in the Algiers peace talks. The table also lists prominent jihadist groups, although these have not participated in the peace talks.

Moreover, northern Mali's security situation remained precarious towards the end of 2014. Following the withdrawal of the national army from large parts of northern Mali, members of the Coordination and Platform groups clashed with one another, possibly also over the control of trade and trafficking routes, as discussed below.

Meanwhile, jihadist groups were continuing their attacks against what they perceived to be 'the enemies of Islam' and seeking to undermine a possible peace agreement between rebels and the Malian government. In 2014 they assaulted French and UN forces in northern Mali by carrying out suicide attacks, setting roadside bombs, and shelling camps with mortar projectiles and rockets. Suicide bombers drove vehicles laden with explosives into UN camps in Aguelhok in June 2014 and in Ber in August 2014, killing six peacekeepers and wounding another 17 (AFP, 2014a; UN News Centre, 2014). On 3 October 2014, jihadists attacked a convoy of UN peacekeepers on the road between Ansongo and Menaka in Gao region, killing nine blue helmets from Niger (Diarra and Lewis, 2014).

> Northern Mali's security situation remained precarious towards the end of 2014.

SECURITY CHALLENGES: AN OVERVIEW

The sources of enduring insecurity in northern Mali are multi-layered and often interconnected. They include armed rebellion for greater autonomy and independence, religiously motivated violence, inter-communal clashes, and trafficking of drugs and other illicit goods. Complex ethnic, tribal, and clan-based structures as well as competition for scarce resources, which takes place in an environment of shifting alliances between and within different groups, further complicate the situation. The following sections discuss relevant factors in their historical context with a view to identifying changes in northern Mali's security situation. 'New' challenges are discussed in addition to long-standing issues.

Armed rebellions and jihadist groups

An important factor in northern Mali's insecurity is the enduring rejection, especially by some sections of Tuareg society, of Malian state rule. Armed rebellion broke out in 1963 and was brutally suppressed by the Malian army. In the following decades, grievances grew among the northern population, much of which perceived themselves as marginalized and neglected by the state despite environmental hardship (Keita, 1998, pp. 11–13). Further rebellions, also aimed at greater autonomy in the Tuareg heartlands north of the river Niger, broke out in 1991 and 2006. While the rebellion that began in 2012 came on the heels of these uprisings, it aimed for independence rather than for greater autonomy within Mali.

The current rebellion is also notable for the capacities of armed groups. The past decades have seen numerous Tuaregs leave northern Mali in search of employment and better living conditions. Some of them fought in Libyan armed groups under Qaddafi before returning to Mali in late 2011. They brought with them military training and combat experience. Previously, the rebels had had limited numbers of arms and had faced a scarcity of ammunition (Florquin and Pézard, 2005, p. 48). By 2013 these constraints had apparently been lifted: Malian army commanders argued that insurgent-held materiel was 'pretty much the same' as that held by the Malian army and that it had the destructive power 'indicative of an army, or groups that have the capacity of an army' (AFP, 2013).

A major new factor in 2012 was the presence of jihadist fighters seeking to establish Islamic law in northern Mali. Jihadist combatants have been present in northern Mali for at least a decade, but in 2012 observers saw them emerge as a dominant group of fighters. Their presence is closely related to the spread of violent jihadist ideology in Mali and elsewhere in Africa (see Box 6.1). One such group is al-Qaeda in the Islamic Maghreb (AQIM), which has reportedly profited from some USD 90 million in ransoms paid for kidnapped Westerners since 2003 and has generated further revenue by taxing trafficking convoys for safe passage through its areas of control (Kustusch, 2012). Another prominent group, Ansar Dine, is composed largely of radicalized Tuaregs from northern Mali.

Box 6.1 Violent Salafism in Mali

Islamic roots in Mali reach back to the ninth century. The majority of Malians follow tolerant Islamic traditions that reflect mystical beliefs and ancestor worship. It was only in the past decades that Salafist thought established itself among sections of Malian society. Salafist organizations that run religious schools and that receive financial support from Kuwait, Qatar, and Saudi Arabia have been a key element in the spread of Salafism in Mali.[4]

Salafism, a puritanical movement that does not necessarily advocate violence, sees Islam as having strayed from its origins. It holds that only the return to the teachings of Mohammed and his early disciples will allow the Muslim community to be free from enemy oppression and to re-establish the perceived former glory of Islam (Livesey, 2005). Salafists reject mystical beliefs and therewith the established traditions that underpin Malian Islamic culture.

Violent Salafism was popularized by al-Qaeda, which complemented the Salafist worldview with radical Islamic arguments. It contended that Islam was under attack by infidel 'crusaders' and their allies and that it was a divine obligation for each 'true' Muslim to engage in violent jihad, or holy war, in the defence of Islam against its enemies (FAS, 1998). In Africa, violent Salafism and jihadist groups exist mainly in Arab countries, although some operate in Nigeria, Somalia, and elsewhere on the continent.

In northern Mali violent Salafism is present mainly among radicalized Arab and Tuareg communities. Their sworn enemies include what jihadists perceive as a deeply corrupted and Westernized Malian state and army, as well as French 'crusaders' and their 'mercenaries' (international peacekeeping troops). The presence of violent Salafism in northern Mali is illustrated by a statement by Iyad Ag Ghaly, founder of Ansar Dine, that was published on a website linked to AQIM in early August 2014:

Since the beginning of the Crusader aggression against us [. . .] we [. . .] fulfil the duty of defending our religion [. . .]. The war between us and them is still ongoing, as you see with the martyrdom-seeking operations carried out against the enemy successively, and the rockets launched from time to time, and the mines that were placed for them everywhere (SITE Intelligence Group, 2014, p. 1, translation by SITE).

A soldier of the Malian army stands guard before a sign promoting sharia law after the liberation of Gao by national and international forces in January, Gao, February 2013. © Joel Saget/AFP Photo

An internal AQIM document dated June 2012 and recovered by journalists in Timbuktu in 2013 reflects on the jihadist rule in northern Mali in early 2012. In the document, AQIM leader Abdel Malek Droukdel admonishes fellow jihadists for their harsh implementation of sharia law in northern Mali, stressing that their approach could turn the local population against them. He urges the jihadist community to focus instead on educating the population on 'true' Islam as a step to win their support (RFI, 2013). This strategy appears to have been implemented by 2014, as 'preaching convoys' of jihadists arrived in villages to 'teach' locals about 'true' Islam. At the same time, jihadists were threatening to kill anyone who informed their enemies about their presence.[5]

Box 6.2 Environmental hardship and armed conflict

Northern Mali has experienced repeated droughts, including in the 1970s and 1980s. The droughts contribute to the continuing encroachment of the Saharan desert into the Sahel and the resulting loss of land suitable to human populations and livestock herding. These environmental pressures increase competition between populations over remaining natural resources. The droughts also caused significant loss of livestock, aggravating the impoverishment of pastoralist communities and increasing the number of internally displaced people in the northern part of the country (Benjaminsen, 2008; Brooks, 2012; Holthuijzen and Maximillian, 2011).

There is no evidence that environmental hardship is a root cause of armed conflict in northern Mali, although it arguably contributes to conditions that, together with other elements, facilitate armed conflict. One factor in this regard is that some people who are affected by environmental hardship consider themselves neglected and marginalized by the Malian state. Rebel groups and jihadists exploit these perceptions by claiming that greater autonomy or independence and the imposition of Islamic law will improve living conditions in northern Mali.[6] In so doing, they promote insurgent recruitment and garner support among sections of the local population.

Likewise, economic hardship in the harsh environment of northern Mali may facilitate recruitment by rebels and jihadists, especially given insurgent payments to fighters and supporters. Some jihadist groups reportedly offer recruits USD 300 or more per month, depending on their function.[7] These payments represent a substantial income in northern Mali and are particularly attractive in the absence of comparable income-generating opportunities, other than engagement in smuggling and banditry.

Inter-communal violence

The current armed violence in northern Mali takes place against the background of complex competition between and within ethnic groups, tribes, and clans as well as groups with cross-cutting membership and interests. Traditional hierarchies characterize both Tuareg and Arab tribal structures, whereby 'subaltern' tribes do not necessarily share the aims and views of 'noble' tribes. Indeed, the aim of greater autonomy for northern Mali is by no means common to all Tuareg and Arab tribes in northern Mali, as 'subaltern' tribes often side with the Malian government.[8] Fractured social relations are also reflected in the multitude of armed groups and splinter groups in northern Mali.

Competition between communities has occasionally turned violent. In July and August 2014 members of the Coordination and Platform groups repeatedly clashed with each other in the area of Tabankort, Gao region, and Lerneb, Timbuktu region. The clashes claimed the lives of fighters and triggered flows of civilians seeking refuge (Diakité, 2014; Diop, 2014a–b; Koba, 2014).[9] The armed groups reportedly fought over control of important trade and smuggling routes, with a view to imposing taxes on merchants and drug trafficking convoys.[10]

In parallel, inter-ethnic competition over scarce resources has long been established in northern Mali, including over grazing and land rights, as well as access to water. These rivalries can involve conflicts between nomadic livestock herders and farmers. Competition is arguably intensified by enduring environmental hardship and the absence of mechanisms to mitigate environmental pressures, such as drought and desertification. Poverty and a perceived absence of development opportunities exacerbate these dynamics (see Box 6.2).

Drug trafficking and other smuggling

Entrenched cross-border smuggling networks have long provided the backdrop to armed violence in northern Mali. In the recent past, cocaine has been smuggled through the north Malian desert on its way from Latin America towards northern Africa and Europe. In the widely publicized 'Air Cocaine' incident of 2009, a burnt-out Boeing 727 was discovered in the desert near Tarkint in northern Mali. Investigations revealed that the plane had originated in Venezuela and had carried several tonnes of cocaine. After loading the narcotics onto 4×4 vehicles, the traffickers may have torched the plane, which was already in poor condition (Hawley, 2010).

As one observer notes, traffickers and the networks they operate in northern Mali are key players at the local level, as they make temporary alliances with armed groups to protect and further their economic interests. In addition, trafficking networks allegedly enjoy close ties to political circles both in northern Mali and in Bamako, where money may be laundered in construction projects.[11] The thin line between traffickers and insurgents is well illustrated by the case of Mokhtar Belmokhtar, founder of the jihadist group Al-Mourabitoune, which operates in northern Mali. Belmokhtar was known as 'Mr. Marlboro' for his sophisticated cigarette smuggling racket across the Sahara before he branched out into kidnappings of Westerners and violent jihad (Beaumont, 2013).

A prominent means of trafficking is the use of convoys of 4×4 vehicles to cross the Sahara and Sahel, a modern version of the caravan trade. Numerous convoys carrying arms and ammunition for insurgents in northern Mali have been documented (Al Jazeera, 2014; UNSC, 2012a, paras. 120–22, 130–33; 2013a, paras. 126f, 144). In some cases, convoys leave from northern Mali to Libya to return with materiel required by insurgents. The materiel is sometimes ordered beforehand.[12] Convoy organizers include rebels and jihadists, as well as criminal networks that traffic in people, drugs, and other contraband. This illustrates again the close inter-linkages that can exist between the armed insurgency and transnational crime in northern Mali.

ARMS AND AMMUNITION IN NORTHERN MALI

As in many other African conflicts, armed violence in northern Mali is carried out predominantly with small arms and light weapons, although insurgents have also accessed some larger-calibre weapons. Armed groups also use 'technicals'—4×4 pick-up trucks with mounted machine guns—which play an important role in their mobility and firepower. In addition, rebels and jihadists hold a variety of large conventional weapons systems, including recoilless guns and autocannons, as well as launch systems other than MANPADS for rockets and missiles (CAR and Small Arms Survey, 2013).

A further feature of the current violence in northern Mali is the jihadist use of improvised explosive devices (IEDs). These include pressure-operated mines, which can function as main charges of IEDs, and homemade explosives that are planted at roadsides and

Jihadist combatants use a 4x4 vehicle mounted with a light weapon near Timbuktu, June 2012.
© Romaric Ollo Hien/AFP Photo

Malian soldiers stand next to arms and ammunition seized from jihadist fighters, Gao, February 2013.
© Joel Saget/AFP Photo

airstrips and, like IED suicide attacks, target armed forces in northern Mali. Jihadists also use mortar projectiles against military camps and airstrips. On 7 October 2014, they hit the MINUSMA camp in Kidal with mortar projectiles, killing one Senegalese peacekeeper (RFI, 2014). Likewise, jihadists use improvised rocket launches in attacks. While often lacking precision, such launches can be easy and quick to set up. Altogether, the IED events and attacks contribute to a climate of fear and insecurity that restricts the presence of humanitarian actors and the assistance they can provide.

The following sections detail prominent types of arms and ammunition that armed groups use in northern Mali, with a focus on where and when the materiel was produced. The documented ammunition also includes samples that the Malian army uses. Reference to ownership of ammunition by specific groups, such as rebels or jihadists, is only made if the ownership could be confirmed, which was not always the case. There were no significant differences in terms of origin and age of ammunition documented at the various sites in northern Mali.

Arms and ammunition that were produced in the former Soviet Union, Eastern Bloc countries, and China are considered first, followed by NATO-standard materiel. In assessing the materiel and its distribution, this section then highlights quantitative and qualitative changes in the holdings of armed groups in today's rebellion as compared to previous uprisings in northern Mali.

Eastern Bloc- and Chinese-standard material

The most prevalent arms in northern Mali are Eastern Bloc- and Chinese-standard assault and sniper rifles, light- and general-purpose machine guns, and rocket-assisted recoilless weapons. Also frequently found are heavy machine guns on technicals, which serve as mobile platforms for various weapons. At a minimum, jihadists reportedly possess 81 mm mortars and MANPADS.[13] Research conducted for this study in northern Mali in 2014 documented about 300 small arms and light weapons that were produced in Bulgaria, China, Romania, the Russian Federation (while still part of the Soviet Union), and Serbia (including when Serbia was still part of Yugoslavia). The years of production typically fell within the cold war period, but materiel also included, for example, Chinese light machine guns that were exported in 2007 and Bulgarian assault rifles that were produced in 2011 (CAR and Small Arms Survey, 2013; UNSC, 2012a; 2013a; 2014).

Less common, larger-calibre weapons in insurgent possession include recoilless guns, multiple-launch rocket systems (MLRS), auto-cannon, and launch systems for 122 mm rockets. These weapons were largely produced in the Soviet Union and China during the cold war. Table 6.2 provides an overview of the main types of Eastern Bloc- and Chinese-standard materiel, relevant patterns, and calibres. In some cases, exact models could not be identified because physical access to the materiel could not be secured. Some larger-calibre weapons, for instance, could only be identified on the basis of long-distance photos taken by journalists in northern Mali in 2012 and 2013.

Of the 1,500 small arms and light weapons cartridge cases that were physically documented with armed groups for this study in northern Mali in 2014, some 1,200 were for use in small arms such as the rifles and light and general-purpose machine guns listed in Table 6.2. The remaining 300 cartridge cases were mostly for use in light weapons, such as the heavy machine guns listed in Table 6.2. The distribution of small arms and light weapons ammunition cartridges appears to reflect the relative proportions of small arms and light weapons observed in the hands of armed actors in northern Mali.

The vast majority of the cartridges had case markings, or 'headstamps', indicating that they had been produced in China or the Soviet Union. Other countries of production identified by marks on the cases include Algeria, Bulgaria,

Table 6.2 Eastern Bloc- and Chinese-standard materiel documented with armed groups in northern Mali, 2012-14*

Type	Pattern	Calibre (mm)
Assault rifle	AK-type	7.62 x 39
Light machine gun	RPD	7.62 x 39
Sniper rifle	SVD	7.62 x 54R
General-purpose machine gun	PK	7.62 x 54R
Heavy machine gun	DShKM	12.7 x 108
	KPV/KPVT	14.5 x 114
Rocket-assisted recoilless weapon	RPG-7	40
Rocket pod (aerial)	UB-32-57	57
Recoilless gun	SPG-9	73
MLRS	Type 63 and BM21	107 and 122
Auto-cannon	2A14	23 x 152B
	ZU-23-2	23 x 152B
MANPADS	9K32 (SA-7a) and 9K32M (SA-7b)	72

Note: * The table includes materiel documented by researchers and journalists.

Sources: CAR and Small Arms Survey (2013); UNSC (2012a; 2013a; 2014); author interviews and fieldwork, 2014.

Figure 6.1 **Distribution of ammunition documented with armed groups in northern Mali in 2014, by producer country**

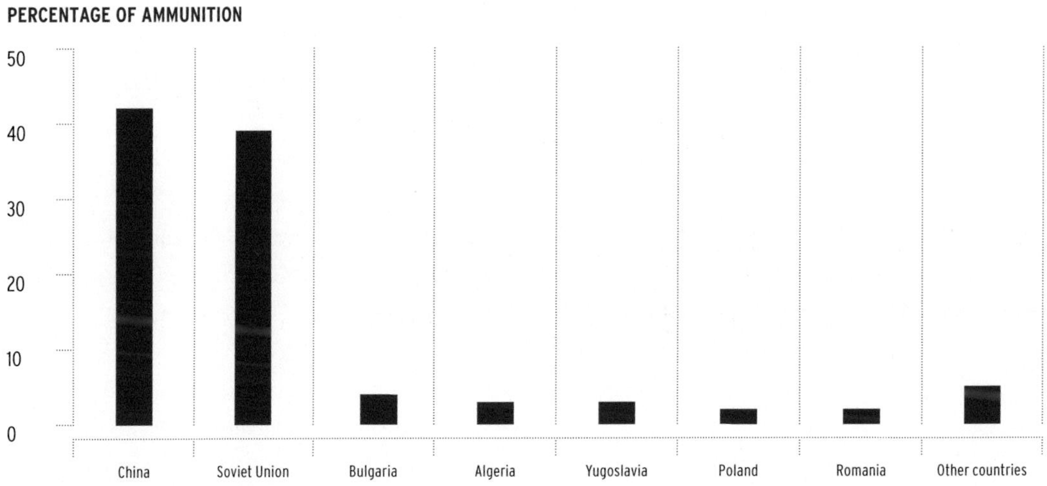

PERCENTAGE OF AMMUNITION

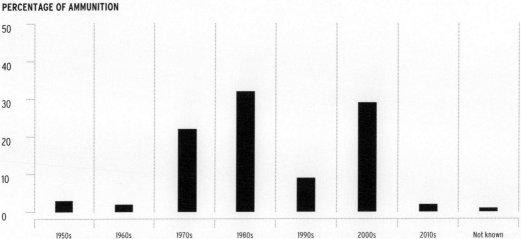

Poland, Romania, and Yugoslavia. Further producer countries, each of which accounts for at most 1 per cent of the 1,500 documented cartridge cases, include Czechoslovakia, Egypt, the German Democratic Republic, North Korea, the Russian Federation, and Sudan. Figure 6.1 illustrates the distribution of documented ammunition cartridges per producer country.

The production years of the physically documented ammunition range from the 1950s to the current decade. About 54 per cent of the ammunition was produced in the 1970s and 1980s; a further 29 per cent was produced in the first decade of the 21st century (see Figure 6.2). The most recent ammunition, produced in or since 2010 and representing 2 per cent, comprises Chinese ammunition produced in 2010, Bulgarian ammunition from 2011, and one Sudanese cartridge from 2012. About 1 per cent of the cartridge cases did not bear year-of-production marks. Photos 6.1–6.3 show Bulgarian ammunition from 2011 and Chinese ammunition from 2010.

Figure 6.2 **Production dates of ammunition documented with armed groups in northern Mali in 2014, by decade**

PERCENTAGE OF AMMUNITION

Photos 6.1-6.3

Photo 6.1: Bulgarian 7.62 x 39 mm cartridge from 2011 (10_11).
Photo 6.2: Bulgarian 7.62 x 54R mm cartridge from 2011 (10_11).
Photo 6.3: Chinese 7.62 x 54R mm cartridge from 2010 (945_10).

Also of note is the distribution of unique combinations of calibres and headstamps. For this quantitative analysis, cartridges that are identical in calibre and have the same headstamp (usually consisting of a producer code and a year-of-production code) are considered the same variety. This approach shows that one-third of the 1,500 documented cartridge cases consisted of only six different varieties. The most prominent ammunition variety in this context was 7.62 × 54R mm calibre with the Chinese producer mark 945 and year-of-production mark for 2005. Other prominent varieties, also of 7.62 × 54R mm calibre, had the identifications marks 17_88 and 188_88, which indicate production in the Soviet Union (now Russia). In contrast, the remaining ammunition varieties consisted of ammunition with more than 120 different combinations of calibre, producer marks, and year-of-production marks. Table 6.3 and Photos 6.4–6.9 present the six most prominent ammunition varieties and the number of cartridge cases documented for each of these varieties.

Table 6.3	**Prominent ammunition varieties documented with armed groups in northern Mali, 2014**				
Country	**Factory**	**Calibre (mm)**	**Year of production**	**Marking**	**Quantity**
China	Unknown state factory (code 31)	7.62 x 39	1994	31_94	73
	Unknown state factory (code 71)	7.62 x 54R	1990	71_90	36
	Unknown state factory (code 945)	7.62 x 54R	2005	945_05	188
Soviet Union (now Russia)	Barnaul Machine Tool Plant JSC	7.62 x 54R	1988	17_88	88
	Novosibirsk LVE Plant JSC	7.62 x 54R	1988	188_88	84
	Ulyanovsk Machinery Plant SPA	14.5 x 114	1987	3_*_87_*	40

Notes: * Denotes five-pointed star. The current names of the formerly Soviet plants are, in order of appearance in Table 6.3: Barnaul Cartridge Plant CJSC, LVE Novosibirsk Cartridge Plant JSC, and OJSC Ulyanovsk Cartridge Works.

Photos 6.4–6.9

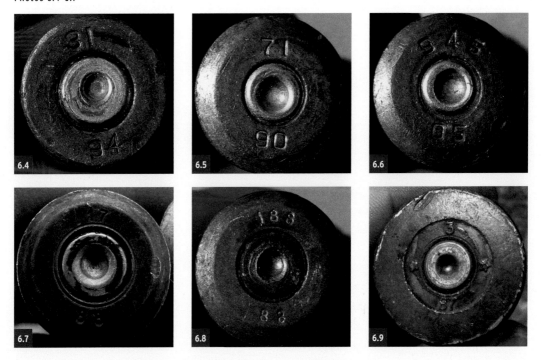

Photo 6.4: Chinese 7.62 x 39 mm cartridge from 1994 (31_94).

Photos 6.5–6.6: Chinese 7.62 x 54R mm cartridges from 1990 (71_90) and 2005 (945_05).

Photos 6.7–6.8: Soviet 7.62 x 54R mm cartridges from 1988 (17_88 and 188_88).

Photo 6.9: Soviet 14.5 x 114 mm cartridge from 1988 (3_*_87_*). The Soviet ammunition was produced in what is now the Russian Federation.

NATO-standard materiel

In comparison to Eastern Bloc- and Chinese-standard materiel, far fewer Western-made small arms and light weapons have been documented among armed groups. Materiel recorded in 2014 included Belgian- and Portuguese-produced assault rifles from the 1950s and 1970s as well as Belgian-produced sub-machine and general-purpose machine guns (years of production unknown). Relevant light weapons documented in northern Mali in 2013 and 2014 included US heavy machine guns from the 1970s and recoilless guns (origin and years of production unknown) (CAR and Small Arms Survey, 2013; UNSC, 2012a; 2013a; 2014). The NATO-standard arms and weapons listed here represent around 2 per cent of the materiel that was physically analysed for this study in 2014.

Corresponding ammunition documented in northern Mali for this study in 2014 includes 7.62 × 51 mm cartridges, produced in Belgium in the 1970s and 1980s, as well as in Pakistan in the 1980s. The relevant cartridge cases accounted for about 0.5 per cent of the documented ammunition. In 2013, Belgian mortar projectiles (60 mm) and recoilless gun projectiles (106 mm) were observed in northern Mali, as were anti-tank mines used in IED events. Also reported but not observed are French 81 mm mortar projectiles.[14]

Tables 6.4 and 6.5 provide an overview of documented NATO-standard arms and weapons, as well as of their related ammunition. Quantities for documented arms and weapons are only given for materiel that was physically observed for this study in 2014.

Table 6.4 NATO-standard materiel documented in northern Mali, 2012–14*

Type	Pattern	Calibre (mm)	Quantity
Sub-machine gun	P90	5.7 x 28	1
Assault rifle	FAL and G3	7.62 x 51	3
General-purpose machine gun	MAG	7.62 x 51	1
Heavy machine gun	M2	12.7 x 99	2
Recoilless gun	M40	106 x 607R	*
Mortar projectiles	Not known	60, 81, and 82	*
Recoilless gun cartridges	NR160	106 x 607R	*
Anti-tank mines	M3 and M3A1	n/a	*

Notes: * Includes materiel documented by researchers and journalists.

Table 6.5 Country of origin of NATO-standard ammunition documented in northern Mali, 2014

Country	Factory	Calibre (mm)	Year of production	Marking	Quantity
Belgium	Fabrique Nationale d'Herstal	7.62 x 51	1977	*_77_FN	4
			1980	*_7.62_80_FNB	2
Pakistan	Pakistan Ordnance Factories	7.62 x 51	1981	POF_81_L2A2	1

Note: * Denotes NATO design mark.

Assessment

The types, origins, and age of documented materiel broadly reflect Mali's recent history. Following independence, the country turned to the Soviet Union and Warsaw Pact members for its military procurement needs (Library of Congress, 2005, p. 18). Likewise, Sino–Malian military relations date back to the 1960s (Chinese Foreign Ministry, 2006). These interactions are mirrored in the study findings, which show that the bulk of materiel in northern Mali consists of cold war-era production from the former Eastern Bloc and China. As noted, procurement from former Eastern Bloc countries and China continued after the cold war. Bulgaria, for example, exported small arms, light weapons, and related ammunition worth some EUR 15 million (USD 18 million) to Mali between 2010 and 2012 (CEU, 2011; 2012; 2014).

These findings also corroborate the claim that armed groups have significant capacities in terms of available materiel. Rebels and jihadists use weapons such as cannon and rocket launchers, which were traditionally associated exclusively with military forces and had not been seen with armed groups in northern Mali in 2005 (Florquin and Pézard, 2005, p. 52). Of particular note is the jihadist possession of MANPADS, which, if operational, could be used against helicopters and planes, threatening lines of supply and movement of French and international forces in northern Mali (see Box 6.3).[15]

Some observers have suggested that insurgents also possess considerably more vehicle-mounted heavy machine guns and related ammunition than a decade ago.[16] These changes have allowed insurgents to conduct larger, more

A French soldier holds the launch tube of a surface-to-air missile before it is destroyed along with other seized weapons, Timbuktu, March 2013.
© Olivier Debes/ECPAD/AP Photo

Box 6.3 **MANPADS in northern Mali**

In June 2013, journalists with the Associated Press inspected a house in Timbuktu that had previously served as quarters for al-Qaeda-linked fighters. Among the documents was a 26-page MANPADS training manual in Arabic (Callimachi, 2013). The discovery fuelled fears that jihadists intended to use such missile launch systems in northern Mali. Three months before, observers had already identified a jihadist fighter with a shouldered MANPADS in a YouTube video (Jenzen-Jones, 2013a). In addition, French forces recovered 13 MANPADS–Soviet type 9K32M (SA-7B)–from jihadists in northern Mali in 2013 (UNSC, 2014, para. 119).

Jihadists in northern Mali typically store MANPADS in substandard conditions, potentially rendering them inoperable. In particular, the batteries that are required to launch the missiles may undergo depletion over time. But a French technical analysis of two of the recovered MANPADS, built in 1978 and 1979, concluded that they were fully operational some 35 years after their production, 'despite rustic storage conditions and handling without caution'.[17] Moreover, jihadists may be able to acquire additional functioning MANPADS in the region. Instructions on how to build home-made batteries for MANPADS are available on the Internet. Syrian jihadists have reportedly used such improvised batteries with success (Smallwood, 2014). The presence of operational MANPADS in jihadist possession in northern Mali is, therefore, a continuing security risk.

Of note in this context is why jihadists appear to refrain from using operational MANPADS. As of December 2014, there had been no successful MANPADS attacks against French or UN air assets in northern Mali. Two observers noted in this regard that jihadists might reserve operational MANPADS to defend 'high-level' targets, such as leaders of jihadist groups.[18] Yet jihadists could arguably employ MANPADS in offensive roles should they obtain greater numbers of operational systems.

intense campaigns than in previous insurgencies (DefenceWeb, 2013). Moreover, insurgents use materiel that is not known to be in use by the Malian army, suggesting that they secured it via illicit trafficking into northern Mali from abroad rather than through battlefield capture or the looting of army stockpiles.

SOURCES OF MATERIEL OF ARMED GROUPS

Non-state actors secure a considerable portion of their holdings by capturing army stockpiles.

Armed groups in northern Mali sourced the bulk of their arms and ammunition through capture from Malian army stockpiles. But there are other sources in the region. Insurgents sourced large conventional weapons from Libyan stockpiles in particular. They also possess materiel that was sourced from, among other countries, Algeria, Burkina Faso, and Côte d'Ivoire (see below). There are allegations that individual countries supplied arms and ammunition to al-Qaeda-linked groups in northern Mali that are under a UN arms embargo.[19] There is, however, no concrete evidence that any state in the region or elsewhere has directly transferred military materiel to rebels or jihadists in northern Mali.

Malian stockpiles

There do not seem to be significant differences in types, models, and years of production of arms and weapons held by the Malian army and armed groups. Likewise, the ammunition varieties most commonly used by armed groups in northern Mali are all found in the possession of both state and non-state actors. These findings support the assessment that much of the groups' materiel was sourced from Malian army stockpiles.

Non-state actors secure a considerable portion of their holdings by capturing army stockpiles. Examples are the capture of army bases in Aguelhok, Gao, and Timbuktu in early 2012. A more recent incident involved the raiding of army materiel in the Kidal events of May 2014. According to their statements, rebels captured 50 new 4×4 vehicles—which the EU had provided to the Malian army as part of its support for military training—as well as 'several tonnes of arms and ammunition' (AFP, 2014b; Observateur Paalga, 2014). This probably included 7.62 × 39 mm ammunition that Bulgaria produced in 2011 and that Mali imported in 2012 (BBC, 2012). Some 7.62 × 39 mm ammunition with marks indicating Bulgarian production in 2011 was subsequently documented with non-state actors.

Research published in 2005 already identified Malian army stockpiles as a primary source of arms and ammunition for armed groups. According to that report, which analysed the arsenals of rebels fighting between 1990 and 2004, rebel holdings 'largely comprised weapons seized and captured from Malian army stockpiles' (Florquin and Pézard, 2005, p. 51). Non-state actors also acquired materiel from new recruits who had deserted the army with their weapons, and through misappropriation by state officials, as when individual soldiers sold their weapons to rebels (Florquin and Pézard, 2005; Republic of Mali, 2008, p. 2). In addition, the Malian government provided arms to self-defence units and pro-government militias (Keita, 1998, p. 20). This further increased the amount of arms in non-state actor possession in northern Mali. According to some observers, such means continue to play a role in the domestic availability of arms and ammunition in the area.[20]

Libyan stockpiles

Libyan stockpiles represent another important source of materiel for rebels and jihadists in northern Mali. Tuareg fighters who left Libya for Mali following the collapse of the Qaddafi regime in 2011 did so with their arms and weapons (UNSC, 2013a, para. 144). Widespread, poorly controlled arms held by Libyan revolutionary brigades and other groups continue to be a central source of materiel for armed groups in northern Mali.[21] The flow of trafficking convoys

Box 6.4 The Libyan arsenal and trafficking dynamics

Dispersal of the Qaddafi arsenal

A full assessment of the Qaddafi-era arsenal is difficult to provide, but Libyan imports increased significantly following the lifting of the EU embargo in 2004 and US sanctions in 2004. EU member states granted Libya arms export licences worth some EUR 1.13 billion (USD 1.39 billion) over the period from 2005 to 2010 (Hansen and Marsh, 2014, p. 13). Force estimates and standard arms-to-soldier multipliers would suggest that on the eve of the 2011 conflict, the regime held between 250,000 and 700,000 firearms, 70–80 per cent of which would have been assault rifles; the number of trafficked firearms was probably in the low tens of thousands (UNODC, 2013, pp. 36–37). Qaddafi's particular brand of 'coup-proofing' relied on massive arms caches—more than 100 depots and warehouses around the country—that could be accessed quickly and distributed to allies in emergencies (UNSMIL, 2013).[22]

By the end of 2011, revolutionary brigades in Benghazi, Misrata, and Zintan controlled much of Qaddafi's 'vast arsenal of conventional weapons' (McQuinn, 2012, p. 43). The rebels' victory in Zliten in August 2011, in particular, led to their acquisition of hundreds of Soviet-era T-55 tanks, Grad rocket launchers, and enormous quantities of small arms and light weapons ammunition. In mid-2011, the Misrata brigades alone had some 30,000 small arms that they had either captured in battle or looted from arms depots. Anti-Qaddafi forces soon had large quantities of light weapons, as well, including 12.7 mm machine guns, 14.5 mm anti-aircraft guns, rocket-propelled grenades, and 20 mm, 23 mm, and 33 mm anti-aircraft machine guns—perhaps as many as 4,000 of the latter (McQuinn, 2012, pp. 46–47). According to British intelligence sources, more than one million tonnes of weapons were looted from arms dumps *after* Qaddafi was toppled (Drury, 2013). Of major concern was the possible proliferation of chemical agents and MANPADS.

Revolutionary armed groups' control over weapons stockpiles has been uneven at best, and generally poor. Even in the midst of the conflict, arms were reportedly being trafficked out of Libya, including some ultimately destined for groups in Mali. Research suggests that Malian stockpiles were the primary source of weapons to insurgents in the region for years (Florquin and Berman, 2005; Lebovich, 2013; Republic of Mali, 2008); since 2011, however, Libyan-sourced weapons have been noted in or en route to northern Mali.

UN investigators have documented some of the trafficking routes and intermediaries from Libya to Mali. In June 2011, the armed forces of Niger intercepted a Mali-bound vehicle loaded with 640 kg of Semtex explosives and 335 detonators originating in Libya. The car accompanying the shipment had been contracted in Benghazi in 2010. According to the presumed trafficker, Abta Hamedi, the weapons were destined for AQIM cells in Mali (UNSC, 2012a). Tuareg leaders arrested for smuggling weapons and explosives were subsequently released by Nigerien authorities, leading to speculation about an appeasement strategy (Lacher, 2013, p. 71).

In October 2014, French troops intercepted and destroyed an AQIM convoy in northern Niger. The convoy consisted of six 4x4 vehicles that had started in Libya and were destined for AQIM fighters in northern Mali. The convoy carried several tonnes of materiel, including missiles for use in MANPADS, 23 mm anti-air cannon, ammunition of 7.62 to 23 mm and larger calibres, machine guns, and about 100 anti-tank rockets (Al Jazeera, 2014; Le Mamouth, 2014).

The UN Panel of Experts on Libya has also documented Libyan stockpiles of small arms and heavy weapons in Mali—including ammunition that had been bought by the United Arab Emirates and that was presumably transferred to Libyan revolutionaries in 2011 (UNSC, 2014). AK-pattern rifles, rocket-propelled grenades, and vehicles seized during the second half of 2011 in Libya helped Tuareg rebels launch their offensives in northern Mali in 2012. Professional smugglers from southern Libya joined later (Diffalah, 2013).

Shifting trafficking dynamics

Qualitative research has helped clarify some of the changing dynamics involved in the trafficking of weapons and other contraband from the Libyan Fezzan (southern region), where state border control is weak and specific tribes have long claimed rights to trade routes. Given that Mali lies on the other side of some 1,800 km of burning Nigerien and Algerian sands, cross-national tribal relationships are crucial to moving goods.

In the Fezzan, access to the border during the Qaddafi era was a privilege granted to tribes that enjoyed prominent positions in the regime's elite units and intelligence services (Lacher, 2014). Big men who financed the contraband and controlled the markets headed the trafficking networks. Around Sabha, towards Niger and Chad, the cartels of the Awlad Suleiman, Qadhadhfa, and Warfalla dominated. In contrast, the Tubu remained on the margins of profitable enterprise, mainly serving as drivers and smugglers.[23]

The political upheavals that have swept across North Africa upset the established smuggling and trafficking networks and cartels. In the south of Libya violent armed struggles over the borders and urban markets between Tubu armed groups and the Awlad Suleiman in Sabha and the Zwayya in Kufra resulted in reconfigurations. In both regions the Tubu gained control of the borders and started to feed surplus weapons into contraband routes through Kufra and Dongola (Sudan), towards northern Egypt, the Sinai Peninsula, or Yemen. The old routes following the traditional patterns of Tubu tribal alliances re-emerged. Conflicts erupting in the Sahel and the Middle East altered the new routes, accelerating their growth and diversification.

▶

By the end of the Libyan armed conflict in 2011, fleeing officers from the former 32nd Brigade had hidden most of their highly sophisticated weaponry in the desert. In early 2014, the Tubu allegedly gained access to the weapons after initiating a series of conciliatory steps with the Qadhadhfa and other tribes close to the former regime. The Tubu armed groups rehabilitated several military cadres of the Jamahiriya from Sabha. By forging new tribal alliances, the Tubu consolidated their sway over contraband and arms trafficking in the Fezzan, gaining control of the vast border region that gives them access to Chad, Egypt, Niger, and Sudan. The Tuareg, in contrast, have seen their control of the routes gradually erode (Shaw and Mangan, 2014); such has been the case since a Zintani-led brigade was mandated to patrol the border with Algeria and Tubu gained control of Sabha and the roads to the north.

Other dynamics quite apart from the collapse of the Libyan regime have also altered trafficking dynamics in the region. These include the gradual rise in the share of illicit products (including drugs, alcohol, and counterfeit goods) in the informal trade over the last 20 years; the influence of criminal activities in the Sahel on desert trade; and inter-tribal clashes for the control of routes, water, and land. Jihadist groups from Algeria moved southward, finding in the southern Sahara not only safe haven for planning their fight for the 'Grand Sahara emirate', but also vital supply lines deeply intertwined with smuggling and informal trade.

As late as October 2014, French action against alleged AQIM convoys carrying weapons from the Fezzan across Niger have shown that southern Libya remains a 'Tesco for terrorists' (Strazzari and Tholens, 2014). The combination of quickly rising demand for weapons in Libya, a net of tribal alliances expanding over large areas of the Sahel–Sahara, and access to a broad sample of weaponry have catalysed the transformation of the Fezzan into a dynamic hub for arms trafficking.[24]

Authors: Francesco Strazzari, Rafaâ Tabib, and Moncef Kartas

from Libya to northern Mali also confirms that at least jihadists in northern Mali exhibit a continued demand for arms and related ammunition (see Box 6.4).

The presence of Libyan-sourced materiel appears linked to qualitative changes in insurgent stockpiles. For example, a scarcity of heavy machine guns and related ammunition was reportedly overcome through Libyan-sourced materiel in previous insurgencies in northern Mali (Florquin and Pézard, 2005, p. 51; UNSC, 2012a, para. 129). Further, Libya is a prominent source of the larger-calibre weapons that were observed in insurgent hands in 2012, including vehicle-mounted ZU-23-2-pattern anti-aircraft auto-cannon, employed primarily to engage ground targets (CAR and Small Arms Survey, 2013). Likewise, Libya served as a source of MANPADS and their missiles that are now in the possession of jihadists in northern Mali (UNSC, 2014, para. 119).

Insurgents in northern Mali also use other materiel that was probably sourced in Libya, including Belgian and Yugoslavian 60 mm mortar projectiles; French 81 mm mortar projectiles; Belgian 106 × 607R mm projectiles; Chinese-produced 107 mm and 130 mm artillery rockets; and Soviet-produced 122 mm artillery rockets (UNSC, 2014, paras. 122–25; Spleeters, 2014).[25] In its February 2014 report, the UN Panel of Experts on Libya observes that some armed groups in northern Mali 'possess heavy ammunition without launchers [. . .] which may be diverted for use in improvised explosive devices. A lot of such old heavy ammunition can be found in Libyan stockpiles' (UNSC, 2014, para. 126). Belgian-produced anti-tank mines have been observed in roadside bombs and French-produced mortar projectiles in jihadist arms caches in northern Mali. Belgian-produced anti-tank mines and French-produced mortar projectiles with matching identification codes (lot numbers) are known to exist in Libya.[26]

Among the documented small arms that armed groups in northern Mali sourced in Libya, two were Russian-produced AK 103-2 rifles that the Russian Federation identified, on the basis of their markings, as having been delivered to Libya between 2005 and 2008 (UNSC, 2014, para. 118). A further possible case concerns a Belgian P90 sub-machine gun, manufactured by FN Herstal, that UN personnel observed in rebel possession in northern Mali in June 2014.[27] As confirmed in interviews with Malian army personnel, P90 sub-machine guns are not found in their stockpiles. Belgium has, however, sold

Photos 6.10-6.14

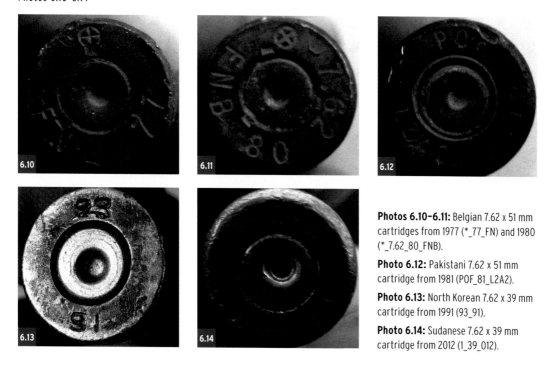

Photos 6.10–6.11: Belgian 7.62 x 51 mm cartridges from 1977 (*_77_FN) and 1980 (*_7.62_80_FNB).

Photo 6.12: Pakistani 7.62 x 51 mm cartridge from 1981 (POF_81_L2A2).

Photo 6.13: North Korean 7.62 x 39 mm cartridge from 1991 (93_91).

Photo 6.14: Sudanese 7.62 x 39 mm cartridge from 2012 (1_39_012).

P90s to other states in the region, including to Libya—which imported 367 of them, along with other materiel, in 2009—as well as to Mauritania and Nigeria (Spleeters, 2012).[28]

Armed groups in northern Mali also possess small arms ammunition that is known to exist in Libya but not in Malian state stockpiles. An example is Belgian-produced 7.62 × 51 mm ammunition with production dates of 1977 and 1980 (see Photos 6.10–6.11).[29] Another example is ammunition in the same calibre that was produced in Pakistan in 1981 (see Photo 6.12). The Small Arms Survey and the UN Panel of Experts on Libya documented identical ammunition in Libya (Jenzen-Jones, 2013b, pp. 22–23; UNSC, 2013a, paras. 67–70). The Panel reported that the ammunition found in Libya probably originated from a retransfer from Qatar, which had initially acquired the ammunition from Pakistan in the 1980s (UNSC, 2013a, paras. 67–70). Of further note is a 7.62 × 39 mm cartridge with production marks from North Korea in 1991 (see Photo 6.13); it was found at the site of an attack on UN peacekeepers in Gao region on 3 October 2014. Not known to exist in army stockpiles in Mali or in neighbouring countries, 7.62 × 39 mm ammunition with identical markings was also documented in Libya in 2012.[30] This raises the possibility that the cartridge case found in northern Mali came from Libya. Similarly, the abovementioned Sudanese ammunition produced in 2012 may have come from Libya, where other recently produced Sudanese ammunition is known to exist (see Photo 6.14).[31]

Other regional stockpiles

Besides Libyan-sourced materiel, research has identified Algerian small arms ammunition—specifically, 7.62 × 39 mm and 7.62 × 54 R mm cartridges produced at the Entreprise des Réalisations Industrielles de Seriana in 1999, 2007, and 2009 (see Photos 6.15–6.17)—that is in use by both the national army and armed groups in northern Mali. Research also identified small arms ammunition that may have been diverted from army stockpiles in Burkina Faso. The

Photos 6.15-6.19

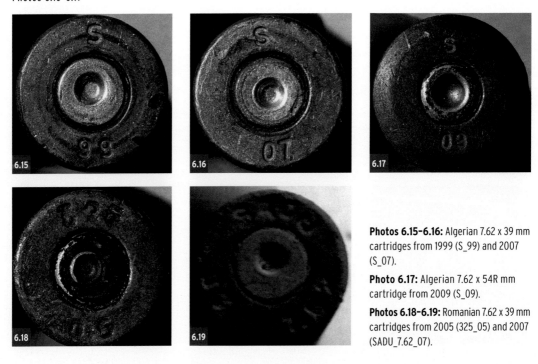

Photos 6.15–6.16: Algerian 7.62 x 39 mm cartridges from 1999 (S_99) and 2007 (S_07).

Photo 6.17: Algerian 7.62 x 54R mm cartridge from 2009 (S_09).

Photos 6.18–6.19: Romanian 7.62 x 39 mm cartridges from 2005 (325_05) and 2007 (SADU_7.62_07).

ammunition in question is from Romania, 7.62 × 39 mm in calibre, and produced in 2005 and 2007 (see Photos 6.18–6.19). Rebels in Côte d'Ivoire have used ammunition of the same calibre with identical markings. The UN Group of Experts concerning Côte d'Ivoire established that Romania had exported the relevant ammunition encountered in western Africa exclusively to Burkina Faso (UNSC, 2012b, paras. 24–26). It is possible, therefore, that rebels in Côte d'Ivoire obtained the ammunition after its diversion from army stockpiles in Burkina Faso. It is also possible that some of the ammunition diverted from these stockpiles found its way into northern Mali. Further regional sources, particularly of small arms and related ammunition, include Côte d'Ivoire itself as well as Guinea, Liberia, Mauritania, Niger, and Sierra Leone (Berghezan, 2013, p. 32; Florquin and Pézard, 2005, p. 61).

Comparing small arms ammunition varieties documented in northern Mali and Côte d'Ivoire is informative. Fewer than 1 per cent of the varieties found in northern Mali were also found in Côte d'Ivoire (Anders, 2014). Moreover, the relevant ammunition varieties were documented in only very small quantities in northern Mali. If armed groups did source the ammunition from Ivorian stockpiles and circulation, the overall quantities seem conspicuously low. The findings support the view of some observers that materiel from sources other than Malian and Libyan stockpiles is typically limited in quantity and obtained by individuals and small criminal networks.[32]

Of further interest is a Polish assault rifle that the author documented in northern Mali in June 2014. The rifle is of the AK type and bears production marks for 1976. Its distinguishing feature is the use of Arabic in the markings of the rifle's rear sight. The Arabic script suggests that the rifle was previously held by armed forces in an Arabic-speaking country, possibly in North Africa. Research has identified a second such rifle in northern Mali; its serial number was removed, presumably in an effort to prevent the identification of the source. The same model of Polish rifle, also from the 1970s and with Arabic sights, was found in rebel possession in Côte d'Ivoire. The rifles documented in Côte d'Ivoire all had their serial numbers removed, suggesting that they had been trafficked into Côte d'Ivoire (UNSC, 2013b, para. 62). It is possible that the two assault rifles in northern Mali and those documented in Côte d'Ivoire were diverted from the same, still unidentified, state stockpile in North Africa.

Foreign state support to armed groups

While the majority of materiel among armed groups in northern Mali came into their possession through diversion, the question of whether foreign states directly supplied armed groups with materiel remains a particular concern in light of the UN sanctions regime relating to al-Qaeda-linked entities and individuals. The regime includes the prohibition of arms transfers to jihadist groups in northern Mali (UNSC, n.d.). In 2012, there was repeated speculation as to whether Qatar and other Arab Gulf countries had supported such groups with arms that were delivered under the guise of humanitarian assistance (Muratet, 2012). Other speculation concerned the possible role of Burkina Faso in arms deliveries to insurgents in northern Mali.

A soldier of the Malian army crouches behind a wall sprayed with the term 'Azawad', Gao, February 2013. © Joel Saget/AFP Photo

One specific allegation of an embargo violation involved a Qatari Red Crescent flight to northern Mali on 6 April 2012, which may have carried not only humanitarian goods, but also arms and money for the jihadist Ansar Dine (Berghezan, 2013, pp. 33–34). The allegation, which remains unproven, gained credibility in view of the apparent delivery of arms and ammunition to Libyan insurgents by Qatar (UNSC, 2013a, paras. 67–70). Similarly, the government of Burkina Faso was accused of delivering arms to insurgents in northern Mali or, at a minimum, of failing to prevent such transfers from its territory. For example, Burkina Faso was accused of allowing truck deliveries of arms destined for the jihadist fighters to leave from its territory in September 2012, although these charges remain unsubstantiated (Berghezan, 2013, p. 34).

There is no concrete evidence for state-sponsored embargo violations in northern Mali. Nor does any particular materiel support allegations of such violations, as was the case in Cote d'Ivoire. There, embargoed actors possessed tens of thousands of small-calibre ammunition cartridges produced in Sudan in 2010. The cartridges could be found throughout the country beginning in early 2011. The quantity and age of the particular ammunition variety suggested that it was trafficked in one or more high-volume transfers from Sudanese government stockpiles (UNSC, 2013b, paras. 45–46). No comparable materiel whose quantity, age, or origin might suggest possible embargo violations by foreign states was identified in northern Mali so far.

CONCLUSION

Rebels and jihadists in northern Mali are better armed and possess larger conventional weapons than they did in 2005. Evidence presented here indicates that Malian army stockpiles represent the primary source of weapons for these groups. While a negotiated peace agreement between rebels and the government seems necessary to reduce violence over the long term, improvements to the army's physical security and stockpile management appear to be urgent.

Preventing weapons from reaching northern Mali from other parts of the region is another pressing need. The dispersal of the Libyan arsenal into the hands of revolutionary brigades has upended trafficking dynamics in the Sahara–Sahel and facilitated more direct linkages between Libyan suppliers and jihadists, especially in northern Mali. Countering these developments will probably require regional initiatives beyond the UN embargo on jihadists—which has been largely ineffective to date. With many of the border areas controlled by non-state or semi-autonomous groups, this is likely to be a long-term challenge.

Since falling out with secessionist rebels, violent jihadists have emerged as perhaps the most pressing security concern in northern Mali. Countering these groups will require dynamic responses from the international community, and the record so far has not been promising. In August 2014, French forces reduced their numbers in northern Mali in favour of a new Sahel-wide anti-jihadist initiative. Since MINUSMA does not have the capacity to engage in offensive counter-jihadist action, a French presence, even with reduced numbers, seems essential to limit violent jihadist activity in northern Mali.

In short, a peace agreement between the Malian government and rebels seems crucial to addressing insecurity in northern Mali, but it is probably only one element of a broader set of required actions. While the jihadist campaign presents different challenges, it shares with the secessionist rebellion a reliance on ongoing, and apparently expanding, access to small arms and light weapons. Identifying ways of preventing the tools of armed violence from reaching these groups should be among the prioritized efforts designed to bring security to northern Mali. ◾

LIST OF ABBREVIATIONS

AFISMA	African-led International Support Mission in Mali
AQIM	Al-Qaeda in the Islamic Maghreb
IED	Improvised explosive device
MANPADS	Man-portable air defence system
MINUSMA	United Nations Multidimensional Integrated Stabilization Mission in Mali
MLRS	Multiple-launch rocket system
MNLA	Mouvement National pour la Libération de l'Azawad

ENDNOTES

1   The sites are located mainly in and near Aguelhok, Anefis, Gao, Kidal, Tabankort, and Timbuktu.

2   In addition to the field investigations, the chapter relies on a range of interviews with mainly Malian officials as well as representatives of the French armed forces and the United Nations, mostly conducted in Bamako in June–October 2014. Many of the interviewees requested anonymity and are therefore not identified by name.

3   Author interview with a UN political affairs officer, Bamako, July 2014.

4   Author interview with a UN political affairs officer, Bamako, July 2014.

5   Author interview with a UN terrorism analyst, Bamako, August 2014.

6   Author interview with a UN political affairs officer, Bamako, July 2014.

7   Author interviews with a UN terrorism analyst and security analysts of the French armed forces, Bamako, August–September 2014.

8   Author interview with a UN political affairs officer, Bamako, July 2014.

9   Author interview with a UN information analyst, Bamako, August 2014.

10   Author interview with a UN information analyst, Bamako, August 2014.

11   Confidential author interviews, Bamako, July–August 2014.

12   Author interview with fighters of an Imghad Tuareg militia, Tabankort, August 2014.

13   Author interview with security analysts of the French armed forces, Bamako, September 2014.

14   Author interview with security analysts of the French armed forces, Bamako, September 2014.

15   At the time of writing, no Malian air assets were active in northern Mali.

16   Author interviews with representatives of the Malian armed forces and a UN terrorism analyst, Bamako, July–August 2014.

17   Author interview with security analysts of the French armed forces, Bamako, September 2014.

18   Author interview with a UN terrorism analyst, Bamako, August 2014.

19   The main jihadist groups in northern Mali (Al-Mourabitoune, Ansar Dine, and AQIM) fall under the UN sanctions regime on al-Qaeda and al-Qaeda-linked actors that the UN Security Council established with resolutions 1267 (1999) and 1989 (2011). The Security Council extended the embargo to the relevant groups in northern Mali on separate occasion since 2011, including Al-Mourabitoune, for example, in the sanctions list of June 2014. See UNSC (1999; 2011) and Al-Qaida Sanctions Committee (2014).

20   Confidential author interviews, Bamako, July–August 2014.

21   Author interviews with a representative of the Malian armed forces, a UN terrorism analyst, and security analysts of the French armed forces, Bamako, July–September 2014.

22   Confidential author interview with an officer of the UN Support Mission in Libya, Geneva, 2014.

23   Confidential author interviews conducted in southern Libya, September–October 2013.

24   This conclusion reflects the findings of the authors' field-based research in southern Libya and several interviewers with heads of armed groups and traders in Awbari, Murzug, and Sebha, October 2013.

25   Author interviews with security analysts in the French armed forces, Bamako, September 2014.

26   Author interviews with security analysts in the French armed forces, Bamako, September 2014.

27   Author interview with a UN terrorism analyst, Bamako, August 2014.

28   Author correspondence with a conflict armament researcher, August 2014.

29   The Small Arms Survey documented ammunition cartridges that were identical in calibre and markings in Libya (Jenzen-Jones, 2013b).

30   Author correspondence with an arms trafficking investigator in Libya, October 2014.

31   Author correspondence with an arms trafficking investigator in Libya, October 2014.

32   Author interviews with a representative of the Malian armed forces and a UN terrorism analyst, Bamako, July–August 2014.

BIBLIOGRAPHY

AFP (Agence France-Presse). 2013. 'Malian Rebels Have "Destructive Power" of an Army: Colonel.' 24 February.
    <http://www.dawn.com/news/788431/malian-rebels-have-destructive-power-of-an-army-colonel>

—. 2014a. 'Suicide Bomber Kills Four Chadian UN Peacekeepers in Mali.' Reliefweb. 11 June.
    <http://reliefweb.int/report/mali/suicide-bomber-kills-four-chadian-un-peacekeepers-mali>

—. 2014b. 'Mali: une quarantaine de militaires maliens tués, 50 blessés et 70 faits prisonniers (MNLA).' 22 May.
    <http://www.maliweb.net/armee/mali-quarantaine-militaires-maliens-tues-50-blesses-70-faits-prisonniers-mnla-318722.html>

Al Jazeera. 2012. 'Tuaregs Claim "Independence" from Mali.' 6 April. <http://www.aljazeera.com/news/africa/2012/04/20124644412359539.html>

—. 2014. 'France Destroys al-Qaeda Convoy in Niger.' 10 October.
    <http://www.aljazeera.com/news/middleeast/2014/10/france-destroys-al-qaeda-convoy-niger-201410101520138060828.html>

Al-Qaida Sanctions Committee (United Nations Security Council Committee Pursuant to Resolutions 1267 (1999) and 1989 (2011) Concerning Al-Qaida
    and Associated Individuals and Entities). 2014. 'The List Established and Maintained by the Al-Qaida Sanctions Committee with Respect to
    Individuals, Groups, Undertakings and other Entities Associated with Al-Qaida.' Last updated 12 December 2014.
    <http://www.un.org/sc/committees/1267/pdf/AQList.pdf>

Anders, Holger. 2014. *Identifying Sources: Small-calibre Ammunition in Côte d'Ivoire.* Special Report. Geneva: Small Arms Survey. June.
    <http://www.smallarmssurvey.org/fileadmin/docs/C-Special-reports/SAS-SR21-CotedIvoire.pdf>

BBC (British Broadcasting Corporation). 2012. 'Guinea Frees Blocked Mali Arms Shipments.' 18 October.
    <http://www.bbc.com/news/world-africa-19990480>

Beaumont, Peter. 2013. 'Mr Marlboro: The Jihadist Back from the "Dead" to Launch Algerian Gas Field Raid.' *Guardian.* 17 January.
    <http://www.theguardian.com/world/2013/jan/17/mokhtar-belmokhtar-algeria-hostage-crisis>

Benjaminsen, Tor. 2008. 'Does Supply-Induced Scarcity Drive Violent Conflicts in the African Sahel? The Case of the Tuareg Rebellion in Northern Mali.'
    Journal of Peace Research, Vol. 45, No. 6, pp. 819–36. <http://jpr.sagepub.com/content/45/6/819>

Bennoune, Karima. 2013. 'The Taliban of Timbuktu.' *The New York Times.* 23 January.
    <http://www.nytimes.com/2013/01/24/opinion/the-taliban-of-timbuktu.html?_r=0>

Berghezan, Georges. 2013. *Côte d'Ivoire et Mali, au Coeur des trafics d'armes en Afrique de l'Ouest.* Brussels: Groupe de Recherche et d'Information
    sur la Paix et la Sécurité. <http://www.grip.org/sites/grip.org/files/RAPPORTS/2013/Rapport%202013-1.pdf>

Bozonnet, Charlotte. 2014. 'A Kidal l'armée malienne mise en déroute par les rebelles touareg.' *Le Monde.* 22 May.
    <http://www.connectionivoirienne.net/99587/kidal-larmee-malienne-mise-en-deroute-les-rebelles-touareg>

Brooks, Nick. 2012. 'Climate, Development and Conflict in the Sahel: A Review.' Background paper for International Alert and the University of East
    Anglia. <http://nickbrooksconsultancy.files.wordpress.com/2012/03/cc_conflict_sahel_brooks_revised2012.pdf>

Callimachi, Rukmini. 2013. 'Mali Manual Suggests al-Qaida Has Feared Weapon.' Associated Press. 11 June.
    <http://www.ap.org/Content/AP-In-The-News/2013/Mali-manual-suggests-al-Qaida-has-feared-weapon>

CAR (Conflict Armament Research) and Small Arms Survey. 2013. *Rebel Forces in Northern Mali: Documented Weapons, Ammunition and Related
    Materiel.* London and Geneva: CAR and Small Arms Survey.
    <http://www.smallarmssurvey.org/fileadmin/docs/E-Co-Publications/SAS-SANA-Conflict-Armament-Research-Rebel-Forces-in-Northern-Mali.pdf>

CEU (Council of the European Union). 2011. *Thirteenth Annual Report According to Article 8(2) of Council Common Position 2008/944/CFSP Defining
    Common Rules Governing Control of Exports of Military Technology and Equipment.* 2011/C 382/01. 30 December.
    <http://eur-lex.europa.eu/LexUriServ/LexUriServ.do?uri=OJ:C:2011:382:0001:0470:EN:PDF>

—. 2012. *Fourteenth Annual Report According to Article 8(2) of Council Common Position 2008/944/CFSP Defining Common Rules Governing Control
    of Exports of Military Technology and Equipment.* 2012/C 386/01. 14 December.
    <http://eur-lex.europa.eu/LexUriServ/LexUriServ.do?uri=OJ:C:2012:386:0001:0431:EN:PDF>

—. 2014. *Fifteenth Annual Report According to Article 8(2) of Council Common Position 2008/944/CFSP Defining Common Rules Governing Control
    of Exports of Military Technology and Equipment.* 2014/C 621/01. 21 January.
    <http://eeas.europa.eu/non-proliferation-and-disarmament/arms-export-control/docs/15_annual_report_en.pdf>

Chinese Foreign Ministry. 2006. 'Mali.' 10 October. <http://www.china.org.cn/english/features/focac/183436.htm>

DefenceWeb. 2013. 'Mali Rebels Used Libyan Weapons—Report.' 19 April. <http://www.defenceweb.co.za/index.php?option=com_content&view=
article&id=30210:mali-rebels-used-libyan-weapons-report&catid=49:National%20Security&Itemid=115>

Diakité, Abdoulaye. 2014. 'Nord-Mali: affrontements sanglants entre MNLA et MAA à Anefis, Tabankort.' MaliJet.com. 11 July.
<http://malijet.com/actualte_dans_les_regions_du_mali/rebellion_au_nord_du_mali/106731-nord-mali-affrontements-sanglants-entre-mnla-
et-maa-à-anefis,-ta.html>

Diarra, Abdoulaye. 2014. 'Après plus de sept heures de combat féroce: Kidal tombe sous le contrôle du MNLA et de ses alliés terroristes d'AQMI et du
MUJAO.' 22 May. <http://www.maliweb.net/la-situation-politique-et-securitaire-au-nord/apres-sept-heures-combat-feroce-kidal-tombe-controle-
du-mnla-ses-allies-terroristes-daqmi-du-mujao-317902.html>

Diarra, Adama and David Lewis. 2014. 'Nine U.N. Troops Killed in Worst Attack Yet on Mali Force.' Reuters. 3 October.
<http://uk.reuters.com/article/2014/10/03/us-mali-un-peacekeepers-idUSKCN0HS0ZH20141003>

Diffalah, Sarah. 2013. 'Mali: L'Arsenal des Islamistes en Question.' *Le Nouvel Observateur.* 14 January.
<http://tempsreel.nouvelobs.com/guerre-au-mali/20130114.OBS5313/mali-l-arsenal-des-islamistes-en-question.html>

Diop, Massiré. 2014a. 'Le MNLA ouvre le feu sur un campement arabe hier près de Tabankort: Un mort et 3 blessés civils.' MaliActu.net. 22 July.
<http://maliactu.net/le-mnla-ouvre-le-feu-sur-un-campement-arabe-hier-pres-de-tabankort-un-mort-et-3-blesses-civils/#sthash.cZNlM1l4.dpuf>

—. 2014b. 'Querelle de leadership entre groupes armés dans la région de Gao: Les affrontements entre deux factions du MAA à Tabancort font 7 morts
et 15 blessés.' Maliweb.com. 28 May. <http://www.maliweb.net/la-situation-politique-et-securitaire-au-nord/querelle-leadership-groupes-armes-
region-gao-les-affrontements-factions-du-maa-tabancort-font-7-morts-15-blesses-330532.html>

Drury, Ian. 2013. 'Don't Turn Syria into a "Tesco for Terrorists" like Libya, Generals Tell Cameron.' *Daily Mail.* 17 June.
<http://www.dailymail.co.uk/news/article-2342917/Dont-turn-Syria-Tesco-terrorists-like-Libya-generals-tell-Cameron.html>

FAS (Federation of American Scientists). 1998. 'Jihad against Jews and Crusaders.' World Islamic Front Statement. 23 February.
<http://fas.org/irp/world/para/docs/980223-fatwa.htm>

Florquin, Nicolas and Eric Berman, eds. 2005. *Armed and Aimless: Armed Groups, Guns, and Human Security in the ECOWAS Region.* Geneva:
Small Arms Survey.
<http://www.smallarmssurvey.org/fileadmin/docs/D-Book-series/book-01-Armed-and-Aimless/SAS-Armed-Aimless-1-Full-manuscript.pdf>

— and Stéphanie Pézard. 2005. 'Insurgency, Disarmament, and Insecurity in Northern Mali, 1990–2004.' In Florquin and Berman, pp. 46–77.
<http://www.smallarmssurvey.org/fileadmin/docs/D-Book-series/book-01-Armed-and-Aimless/SAS-Armed-Aimless-Part-1-Chapter-02.pdf>

Hansen, Susanne Therese and Nicholas Marsh. 2014. 'Normative Power and Organized Hypocrisy: European Union Member States' Arms Export to Libya.'
European Security. 23 October. <http://www.tandfonline.com/doi/pdf/10.1080/09662839.2014.967763>

Hawley, Chris. 2010. 'South American Gangs Flying Vast Quantities of Cocaine to Europe.' *Guardian.* 15 November.
<http://www.theguardian.com/world/2010/nov/15/south-american-gangs-flying-cocaine-to-europe>

Holthuijzen, Wieteke and Jacqueline Maximillian. 2011. 'Dry, Hot, and Brutal: Climate Change and Desertification in the Sahel of Mali.' *Journal of
Sustainable Development in Africa*, Vol. 13, No. 7, pp. 245–68.
<http://www.jsd-africa.com/Jsda/Vol13No7-Winter2011A/PDF/Dry%20Hot%20and%20Brutal.Wieteke%20Holthuijzen.pdf>

Jenzen-Jones, N.R. 2013a. 'MUJAO Fighters with 9K32 or 9K32M MANPADS in Mali.' Rogue Adventurer Blog. 22 March.
<http://rogueadventurer.com/2013/03/22/mujao-fighters-with-9k32-or-9k32m-manpads-in-mali/>

—. 2013b. *The Headstamp Trail: An Assessment of Small-calibre Ammunition Found in Libya.* Small Arms Survey Working Paper No. 16. Geneva:
Small Arms Survey. <http://www.smallarmssurvey.org/fileadmin/docs/F-Working-papers/SAS-WP16-Headstamp-Trail-Ammunition-Libya.pdf>

Keenan, Jeremy. 2012. 'Mali's Tuareg Rebellion: What Next?' Al Jazeera. 20 March.
<http://www.aljazeera.com/indepth/opinion/2012/03/20123208133276463.html>

Keita, Kalifa. 1998. *Conflict and Conflict Resolution in the Sahel: The Tuareg Insurgency in Mali.* Carlisle, PA: Strategic Studies Institute, US Army War
College. <http://www.strategicstudiesinstitute.army.mil/pdffiles/pub200.pdf>

Koba, S. Badou. 2014. 'Affrontements dans la région de Tombouctou: Le MNLA continue ses massacres.' MaliJet.com. 15 August. <http://malijet.com/
actualte_dans_les_regions_du_mali/rebellion_au_nord_du_mali/109437-affrontements-dans-la-region-de-tombouctou-le-mnla-continue-ses-.html>

Kustusch, Timothy. 2012. 'AQMI's Funding Sources: Kidnapping, Ransom, and Drug Running by Gangster Jihadists.' 361Security. 28 November.
<http://www.361security.com/analysis/AQMIs-funding-sources-kidnapping-ransom-and-drug-running-by-gangster-jihadists>

Lacher, Wolfram. 2013. 'Organized Crime and Conflict in the Sahel–Sahara Region.' In Frederic Wehrey and Anouar Boukhars, eds. *Perilous Desert:
Insecurity in the Sahara.* Washington, DC: Carnegie Endowment for International Peace, pp. 61–82.

—. 2014. *Libya's Fractious South and Regional Instability.* Security Assessment in North Africa Dispatch No. 3. Geneva: Small Arms Survey. February.
<http://www.smallarmssurvey.org/fileadmin/docs/R-SANA/SANA-Dispatch3-Libyas-Fractuous-South.pdf>

Lebovich, Andrew. 2013. 'The Sahel Is Awash with Weapons—but Whose?' Dakar: Open Society Initiative for West Africa. 28 March.
<http://www.osiwa.org/Sahel-Notes-Blog-on-recent-events.html?lang=en>

Le Mamouth. 2014. 'Niger: le point focal de Barkhane.' Blog post. 16 October.
<http://lemamouth.blogspot.com/2014/10/niger-le-point-focal-de-barkhane.html>

Library of Congress. 2005. 'Country Profile: Mali.' Washington, DC: Federal Research Division, Library of Congress. January.
<http://lcweb2.loc.gov/frd/cs/profiles/Mali.pdf>

Livesey, Bruce. 2005. 'The Salafist Movement.' *Frontline*. 25 January.
<http://www.pbs.org/wgbh/pages/frontline/shows/front/special/sala.html>

McQuinn, Brian. 2012. *After the Fall: Libya's Evolving Armed Forces*. Working Paper No. 12. Geneva: Small Arms Survey.
<http://www.smallarmssurvey.org/fileadmin/docs/F-Working-papers/SAS-WP12-After-the-Fall-Libya.pdf>

MINUSMA (United Nations Multidimensional Integrated Stabilization Mission in Mali). n.d. 'MINUSMA: United Nations Stabilization Mission in Mali.'
<http://www.un.org/en/peacekeeping/missions/minusma/background.shtml>

Muratet, Christine. 2012. 'La présence du Qatar au nord du Mali: les doutes persistent.' Radio France Internationale. 2 November. <http://www.rfi.fr/
afrique/20121102-presence-qatar-nord-mali-doutes-persistent-mujao-mnla-dioncounda-traore-niger-aide-humanitaire-cooperation/>

Observateur Paalga. 2014. 'Le bilan des affrontements de Kidal selon le MNLA (lors d'une conférence de presse à Ouagadougou).' 23 May.
<http://malijet.com/actualte_dans_les_regions_du_mali/rebellion_au_nord_du_mali/102558-le-bilan-des-affrontements-de-kidal-selon-le-
mnla-lors-d-une-con.html>

Offner, Fabien. 2014. 'Les autorités maliennes déclarent être "en guerre".' Radio France Internationale. 18 May.
<http://www.rfi.fr/afrique/20140518-mali-affrontements-kidal-guerre-mnla-maa-morts-moussa-mara/>

Ramzi, Walid and Jemal Oumar. 2014. 'Algeria Hosts Mali Peace Talks.' Magharebia.com. 17 July.
<http://magharebia.com/en_GB/articles/awi/features/2014/07/17/feature-02>

Republic of Mali. 2008. *Report to the Biennial Meeting of States of the National Commission to Combat the Proliferation of Small Arms*. Bamako: Office
of the President of the Republic. 0057/PR/CNLPAL. 8 April. <http://www.poa-iss.org/NationalReport/NationalReports.aspx>

RFI (Radio France Internationale). 2012. 'Tuareg Rebels behind January Killings, Confirms Mali Army.' 13 February.
<http://www.english.rfi.fr/africa/20120213-tuareg-rebels-behind-january-killings-confirms-mali-army>

—. 2013. 'Aqim Leader Condemns Destruction of Mali Mausoleums in Secret Papers Found by RFI Journalist.' 8 March.
<http://www.english.rfi.fr/africa/20130225-aqim-leader-condemns-destruction-mali-mausoleums-secret-papers-found-rfi-journalist>

—. 2014. 'Mali: nouvelle attaque meurtrière visant un camp de la Minusma à Kidal.' 8 October.
<http://www.rfi.fr/afrique/20141008-mali-nouvelle-attaque-meurtriere-camp-minusma-kidal-casque-bleu-senegalais/>

SCR (Security Council Report). 2014. 'January 2014 Monthly Forecast, Mali.' January.
<http://www.securitycouncilreport.org/monthly-forecast/2014-01/mali_11.php?print=true>

Shaw, Mark and Fiona Mangan. 2014. *Illicit Trafficking and Libya's Transition: Profits and Losses*. Washington, DC: United States Institute of Peace.
24 February. <http://www.usip.org/publications/illicit-trafficking-and-libya-s-transition-profits-and-losses>

SITE Intelligence Group. 2014. 'AQIM Releases Visual Speech by Ansar Dine Leader on Situation in Mali.' 6 August.
<https://news.siteintelgroup.com/Jihadist-News/aqim-releases-visual-speech-by-ansar-dine-leader-on-situation-in-mali.html>

Smallwood, Michael. 2014. 'Improvised MANPADS Batteries Used in Syria.' Armament Research Services. 22 July.
<http://www.armamentresearch.com/improvised-manpads-batteries-employed-in-syria/>

Spleeters, Damien. 2012. 'FN P90 Sold by Belgium to Libya.' Blog post. February.
<http://damspleet.com/post/25249165697/one-of-the-367-fn-p90-sold-by-belgium-to-libya-in>

—. 2014. 'UN Report Confirms Diversion of Belgian Weapons to and from Libya.' Blog post. March.
<http://damspleet.com/post/79383031282/un-report-confirms-diversion-of-belgian-weapons-to-and>

Strazzari, Francesco and Simone Tholens. 2014. 'Tesco for Terrorists Reconsidered: Arms and Conflict Dynamics in Libya and in the Sahara–Sahel Region.'
European Journal on Criminal Policy and Research, Vol. 20, No. 3, pp. 343–60.

UN (United Nations) News Centre. 2014. 'Mali: Security Council Condemns Recent Deadly Suicide Attack on UN Base.' 18 August.
<http://www.un.org/apps/news/story.asp?NewsID=48514#.VAHUMtxur1o>

UNODC (United Nations Office on Drugs and Crime). 2013. *Transnational Organized Crime in West Africa: A Threat Assessment*. February.
<http://www.unodc.org/documents/data-and-analysis/tocta/West_Africa_TOCTA_2013_EN.pdf>

UNSC (United Nations Security Council). 1999. Resolution 1267. S/RES/1267 (1999) of 15 October.
<http://www.un.org/ga/search/view_doc.asp?symbol=S/RES/1267(1999)>

—. 2011. Resolution 1989. S/RES/1989 (2011) of 17 June. <http://www.un.org/ga/search/view_doc.asp?symbol=S/RES/1989(2011)>

—. 2012a. *Letter Dated 17 February 2012 from the Panel of Experts on Libya Established Pursuant to Resolution 1973 (2011) Addressed to the President of the Security Council.* S/2012/163 of 20 March. <http://www.un.org/ga/search/view_doc.asp?symbol=S/2012/163>

—. 2012b. *Letter Dated 15 October 2012 from the Chair of the Security Council Committee Established Pursuant to Resolution 1572 (2004) Concerning Côte d'Ivoire Addressed to the President of the Security Council.* S/2012/766 of 15 October. <http://www.un.org/ga/search/view_doc.asp?symbol=S/2012/766>

—. 2013a. *Letter Dated 15 February 2013 from the Panel of Experts on Libya Established Pursuant to Resolution 1973 (2011) Addressed to the President of the Security Council.* S/2013/99 of 9 March. <http://www.un.org/ga/search/view_doc.asp?symbol=S/2013/99>

—. 2013b. *Letter Dated 12 April 2013 from the Chair of the Security Council Committee Established Pursuant to Resolution 1572 (2004) Concerning Côte d'Ivoire Addressed to the President of the Security Council.* S/2013/228 of 17 April. <http://www.un.org/ga/search/view_doc.asp?symbol=S/2013/228>

—. 2014. *Letter Dated 15 February 2014 from the Panel of Experts on Libya Established Pursuant to Resolution 1973 (2011) Addressed to the President of the Security Council.* S/2014/106 of 19 February. <http://www.un.org/ga/search/view_doc.asp?symbol=S/2014/106>

—. n.d. 'Security Council Committee Pursuant to Resolutions 1267 (1999) and 1989 (2011) Concerning Al-Qaida and Associated Individuals and Entities.' <http://www.un.org/sc/committees/1267/>

UNSMIL (United Nations Support Mission in Libya). 2013. 'UN Experts Assist in Aftermath of Brak Al-Chati Ammunition Explosion.' 5 December. <http://unsmil.unmissions.org/Default.aspx?ctl=Details&tabid=3543&mid=6187&ItemID=1773377>

ACKNOWLEDGEMENTS

Principal author

Holger Anders

Contributors

Francesco Strazzari, Rafaâ Tabib, and Moncef Kartas

Former FDLR executive secretary Callixte Mbarushimana attends the opening hearing of the confirmation of charges against him, conducted at the International Criminal Court in The Hague, the Netherlands, September 2011. © Jerry Lampen/Reuters

Waning Cohesion
THE RISE AND FALL OF THE FDLR-FOCA

INTRODUCTION

In a declaration issued on 30 December 2013, leaders of the Forces Démocratiques de Libération du Rwanda (Democratic Forces for the Liberation of Rwanda, FDLR) in the Democratic Republic of the Congo (DRC) 'committed themselves to put down their weapons and rather undertake a political struggle' (UNSC, 2014b, annexe 12). By mid-2014, some 200 combatants of the estimated 1,400-strong force had surrendered and turned in weapons, raising hopes that the claim was being followed by concrete action (Radio Okapi, 2014; UNSC, 2014b, para. 42; Vogel, 2014a). While the FDLR has not demobilized in its entirety—and was the target of new attacks by the Forces Armées de la République Démocratique du Congo (Armed Forces of the DRC, FARDC) in early 2015—these figures illustrate the dramatic decline in the group's strength, down from an estimated 11,500 men in 2002.

This chapter analyses armed groups' internal cohesion and control mechanisms, including procedures for the acquisition, management, and use of weapons and ammunition. Specifically, it examines the FDLR and its armed wing, the Forces Combattantes Abacunzi (Abacunzi Fighting Forces, FOCA), arguably one the most enduring and destabilizing of the many armed groups operating in the eastern DRC (Rodríguez, 2011, p. 176; Vogel, 2013). By studying the weakening of the group, the chapter attempts to document and provide a better understanding of some of the internal workings of armed groups, including from a demobilization and weapons recovery standpoint. More precisely, it seeks to answer the following questions:

- What were the key internal mechanisms put in place by the FDLR–FOCA to ensure cohesion and control over the areas it held?
- What mechanisms specifically address controls over weapons acquisition, management, and use?
- What factors, internal and external, have contributed to the recent weakening of the FDLR–FOCA?

The chapter's main findings include:

- The FDLR–FOCA put in place state-like institutions and procedures to control territory and refugee camps in the DRC, while the structure of its armed wing resembled that of a regular army. Such unusually strong organizational control mechanisms were critical to the group's ability to generate income, recruit new combatants, and carry out military operations.
- The FDLR–FOCA sourced its weapons primarily from other armed actors in the region—either through battlefield capture or support received from allies. Standing orders issued by the group's military command placed great importance on the need for combat units to acquire new weapons and to use ammunition sparingly.
- The group's small arms holdings are diverse but ageing. Little is known about the current size and state of its light weapons stockpiles, however.

Map 7.1 Approximate areas of influence of selected armed groups in the eastern DRC, October 2014

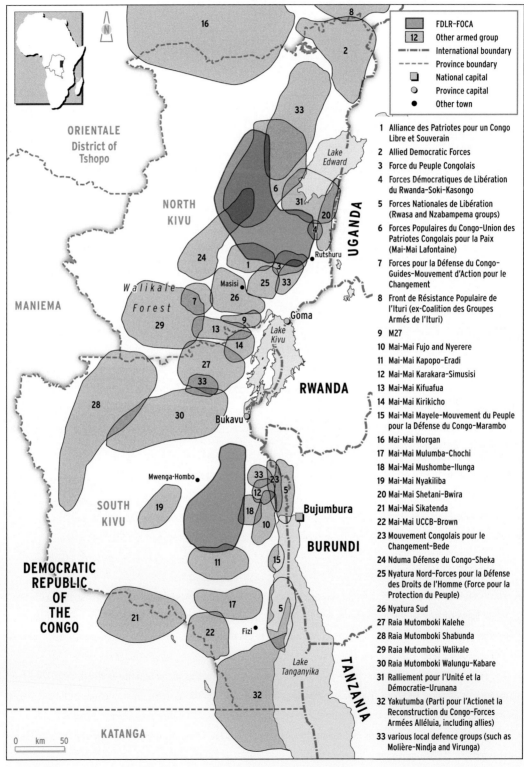

Legend

FDLR-FOCA
12 Other armed group
—·—·— International boundary
— — — Province boundary
☐ National capital
◦ Province capital
• Other town

1   Alliance des Patriotes pour un Congo Libre et Souverain
2   Allied Democratic Forces
3   Force du Peuple Congolais
4   Forces Démocratiques de Libération du Rwanda-Soki-Kasongo
5   Forces Nationales de Libération (Rwasa and Nzabampema groups)
6   Forces Populaires du Congo-Union des Patriotes Congolais pour la Paix (Mai-Mai Lafontaine)
7   Forces pour la Défense du Congo-Guides-Mouvement d'Action pour le Changement
8   Front de Résistance Populaire de l'Ituri (ex-Coalition des Groupes Armés de l'Ituri)
9   M27
10 Mai-Mai Fujo and Nyerere
11 Mai-Mai Kapopo-Eradi
12 Mai-Mai Karakara-Simusisi
13 Mai-Mai Kifuafua
14 Mai-Mai Kirikicho
15 Mai-Mai Mayele-Mouvement du Peuple pour la Défense du Congo-Marambo
16 Mai-Mai Morgan
17 Mai-Mai Mulumba-Chochi
18 Mai-Mai Mushombe-Ilunga
19 Mai-Mai Nyakiliba
20 Mai-Mai Shetani-Bwira
21 Mai-Mai Sikatenda
22 Mai-Mai UCCB-Brown
23 Mouvement Congolais pour le Changement-Bede
24 Nduma Défense du Congo-Sheka
25 Nyatura Nord-Forces pour la Défense des Droits de l'Homme (Force pour la Protection du Peuple)
26 Nyatura Sud
27 Raia Mutomboki Kalehe
28 Raia Mutomboki Shabunda
29 Raia Mutomboki Walikale
30 Raia Mutomboki Walungu-Kabare
31 Ralliement pour l'Unité et la Démocratie-Urunana
32 Yakutumba (Parti pour l'Actionet la Reconstruction du Congo-Forces Armées Alléluia, including allies)
33 various local defence groups (such as Molière-Nindja and Virunga)

Source: Vogel (2014b)

- External interventions, including the military operations that targeted the FDLR–FOCA in 2009–11, and the UN's demobilization programme, dealt severe blows to the group's internal cohesion and accelerated its decline.

- While the current weakened state of the FDLR–FOCA represents an opportunity for regional peace efforts, the remaining force has gone into hiding by mingling with the civilian population, putting the latter at risk in the event of further military attacks.

The chapter is divided into four sections. The first explains the relevance of analysing armed groups—beyond a focus on their sources of armaments—for the small arms control community. The second provides a general profile of the FDLR–FOCA. The third focuses on the group's weapons holdings and the control mechanisms it placed over them. Finally, the last section examines internal and external factors that appear to have contributed to the movement's decline.

The chapter relies primarily on an extensive study of the FDLR authored by Raymond Debelle, who served as a member of the UN Group of Experts on the DRC between 2009 and 2011 (Debelle, 2014). It also draws from research carried out by Debelle for the Small Arms Survey in 2013, including travel to Rwanda in May of that year. Overall, he conducted more than 250 interviews with former and active members of the FDLR–FOCA. In addition, the chapter includes information on weapons and ammunition that the group surrendered in 2014, based on photographs and identification of materiel provided by Conflict Armament Research (CAR, 2014).

ARMED GROUP COHESION AND WEAPONS MANAGEMENT

Small arms analysts have long considered armed groups through the framework of diplomatic efforts to try to regulate international small arms transfers. As a result, armed groups have been seen mainly as controversial, if not illicit, recipients of such transfers. From the late 1990s and into the next decade, UN Panels of Experts monitoring compliance with Security Council sanctions such as arms embargoes led much of this work, including with respect to groups operating in Angola, Liberia, and Sierra Leone (Vines, 2003, p. 248). Today, efforts to trace armed groups' weapons back to their sources continue to mobilize the resources of UN panels, the diplomatic community, and non-governmental actors such as the Small Arms Survey.

Identifying the sources of armed groups' armaments can reveal important information on their military capabilities, sources of support, and strategic alliances. Yet their arsenals represent policy challenges that go beyond controls of international small arms transfers, warranting scrutiny both during and after conflict.

Whether directly or indirectly, armed groups' weapons holdings pose 'real and diverse threats to civilians living in situations of armed conflict', including the deliberate targeting of civilians, safety risks associated with the groups' arsenals, and the further diversion of weapons to other entities that may misuse them (Florquin, 2010, p. 325). Improving the assessments of the size and nature of armed groups' stockpiles, as well as command and control structures, can contribute to efforts to disarm, demobilize, and reintegrate irregular fighters by establishing more reliable baselines for designing programmes and measuring their success (Richards, 2013, pp. 2–3). After the end of hostilities, armed groups may still possess large stockpiles of arms and ammunition, as was the case in Libya in 2012; given that such arsenals raise the risks of unplanned explosions and further arms diversion, they deserve targeted attention (McQuinn, 2012, p. 13; Schroeder, 2013, pp. 1–2).

A key element in understanding the threats posed by armed groups' small arms during and after conflict relates to these actors' levels of cohesion. Organizational cohesion can be understood as:

1) the extent to which a central leadership of an organization exists that is able to reach decisions without internal violence or defection, and 2) the extent to which members of an organization (including commanders) comply with this central leadership in pursuit of shared political-military goals, engage in high-risk combat activities over long periods of time when ordered to do so, and do not defect with resources and manpower previously pledged to the organization (Staniland, 2010, p. 34).

Closely linked is a group's capacity to remain united in times of stress:

Splits, feuds, and defiance on the ground are all characteristics of a lack of cohesion, suggesting a disconnect between individual or factional perceptions of interest and those of the broader organization (Staniland, 2010, p. 35).

The FDLR initially adopted 'state-like' structures and regulations.

A growing body of work is examining the cohesion of insurgent organizations as a factor that affects conflict dynamics in general and that influences their military effectiveness, patterns of violence against civilians (including gender-based violence), and the ability to negotiate and demobilize.[1] This approach inherently suggests that cohesion affects the way armed groups manage, control, and use their small arms in times of conflict, while also influencing the way they engage in post-conflict disarmament initiatives. Highly fragmented armed groups will find it challenging to ensure that fighters follow military tactics or a commitment to respect international humanitarian law while handling or using their weapons. In theory, a strongly united group will not undergo disarmament unless its leadership makes a political decision to that effect; in contrast, disorderly groups are only likely to disarm in response to complex strategies and incentives that target multiple levels in their loose chains of command.

Analysing armed groups' mechanisms for cohesion is challenging, yet a number of indicators provide important clues. Like regular armies, numerous groups have generated extensive written rules and regulations, including codes of conduct, standing orders, operation orders, and penal codes that provide important insight into their inner workings and capacity to remain united. While the more general regulations, such as oaths and codes, are usually short and too broad to address weapons issues directly, small arms-specific language is typically included into standing and operation orders (Bangerter, 2012, p. 3). Assessing whether these procedures are effectively enforced requires field observation and research, in particular through interviews with active or former combatants, and other first-hand witnesses. Reports by independent observers and human rights monitors can also provide important information.

As discussed below, the FDLR–FOCA was initially a strongly cohesive organization that adopted a number of 'state-like' structures and regulations, yet it suffered a remarkable decline over time. In particular, this case study highlights the impact of cohesion on weapons management and use, and the factors that may lead united groups to erode over time.

PROFILING THE FDLR–FOCA

This section presents a broad profile of the FDLR–FOCA, including its historical origins, leadership and structure, objectives and ideology, sources of financing and support, territorial control, and record of abuses.

Origins

From 1990, the Hutu-led Rwandan government and Forces Armées du Rwanda (Rwandan Armed Forces, FAR) fought a civil war with the insurgency of the Tutsi-led Front Patriotique Rwandais (Rwandan Patriotic Front, FPR) (Omaar, 2008, pp. 35–36; UNDPKO, 1994, p. 2). The assassination on 6 April 1994 of President Juvénal Habyarimana sparked a genocidal wave, during which the Hutu-led Interahamwe militias and members of the FAR killed an estimated 800,000 Tutsis and moderate Hutus in a period of only three months (UNSC, 1999, pp. 3, 15). The FPR gained control of the capital Kigali and of most of the Rwandan territory by July–August 1994. By that time, an estimated 1.7 million Rwandan Hutus had fled to Zaire (which became the Democratic Republic of the Congo in 1997), Tanzania, and other neighbouring countries (UNSG, 1998, para. 11). An estimated 34,000–37,000 members of the ex-FAR, presidential guard, gendarmerie, and Interahamwe, along with hundreds of thousands of Rwandan refugees, formed part of the exodus. Most of them gathered in two provinces in Zaire: 20,000 fighters and 850,000 refugees in Goma, North Kivu, and 5,000–7,000 fighters and 332,000 refugees in Bukavu, South Kivu (Prunier, 2009, p. 53; UNDPKO, 1994, pp. 2–3).

The ex-FAR and former Rwandan civil servants transferred a large part of the former Rwandan state security apparatus into exile in Zaire, where they built a quasi-state run by their 'government in exile'. In April 1995, the Rassemblement pour le Retour des Réfugiés et la Démocratie au Rwanda (Rally for the Return of Refugees and Democracy in Rwanda) replaced the latter as the main political formation (Omaar, 2008, p. 36). The Hutu rebels exploited Rwandan refugees and local resources, taking advantage of the weakness of local authorities to consolidate their strength in these remote regions. For the rebel leaders, these refugees would become human shields, a pool for recruitment, and a source of income and political legitimacy (Omaar, 2008, pp. 37–38; Survie, 1996, p. 1).

Reports suggest that only about half of the ex-FAR and associated groups entering Zaire were disarmed (UNDPKO, 1994, p. 2). Although weakened by their defeat in Rwanda, the fleeing armed factions were able to keep a large part of their military capacity as they regrouped in the Zairian refugee camps. While they were based in 'these areas, between mid-1994 and late 1996, tens of thousands of the [ex-FAR] and Interahamwe trained, rearmed and plotted to retake control of their country' (UNSG, 1998, para. 11). These groups staged increasingly well-coordinated cross-border raids into Rwandan territory to attack the new authorities (para. 85).

> **The rebels exploited Rwandan refugees and local resources.**

In late 1996, the Rwandan government, working with its allies Burundi and Uganda, responded to the cross-border attacks by supporting the Alliance des Forces Démocratiques de Libération (Alliance of Democratic Forces for the Liberation, AFDL), an alliance of Congolese rebel groups led by Laurent-Désiré Kabila that toppled President Mobutu Sese Seko of Zaire in May 1997 (Omaar, 2008, p. 39; Pole Institute, 2010, p. 20; UNSG, 1998, paras. 8–86). The Rwandan-led coalition attacked the refugee camps in North and South Kivu; these operations led to the dismantling of the refugee camps in October–November 2006 and the dispersion of Rwandan Hutu combatants and civilians (Omaar, 2008, p. 39).

While the 1996–97 war in Zaire caused the ex-FAR and Interahamwe to flee, their combatants were eventually able to regroup due to persistent fighting in the DRC and changing alliances. As President Kabila sought to free himself from Rwandan influence, a new Congolese rebellion formed under the Rassemblement Congolais pour la Démocratie (Congolese Rally for Democracy, RCD), leading to the Second Congolese War of 1998–2003 (Pole Institute, 2010, p. 20). In a dramatic shift, Kabila, supported by Angola, Chad, Namibia, and Zimbabwe, allied himself with his former ex-FAR and Interahamwe enemies to fight the RCD rebels and their alleged sponsors, Rwanda and Uganda (UNSG, 1998, para. 87).

In 1997, an estimated 5,000 ex-FAR and Interahamwe rebels who had dispersed in North Kivu regrouped to create the Armée de Libération du Rwanda (Rwanda Liberation Army, ALIR) and its political branch, the Peuple en Action pour la Libération du Rwanda (People in Action for the Liberation of Rwanda, PALIR) (Omaar, 2008, pp. 40–41). Meanwhile, Rwandan Hutus who had fled to the western DRC, but also to Angola, the Central African Republic, the Republic of the Congo, and Sudan, formed ALIR-2. Its political branch—the FDLR—was created in 2000 out of the Kinshasa-based Comité de Coordination de la Résistance (Coordination Committee for Resistance). Contacts between ALIR/PALIR and ALIR-2/FDLR were initiated in 1999, with the support of Kinshasa (Debelle, 2014, pp. 100–11; ICG, 2003, p. 6; Pole Institute, 2010, p. 21).

ALIR recognized the FDLR's political leadership in 2000, but ALIR and ALIR-2 combatants only joined their military forces in 2003 in South Kivu, thereby creating the FDLR's armed wing, the FOCA, a force comprising more than 10,000 men at that time (Debelle, 2014, p. 116; see Figure 7.1).

Organization and structure

The FDLR's political leaders also held key military positions.

While the organization's political (FDLR) and military (FOCA) wings have their own distinct names and acronyms, they are actually closely intertwined and part of a single organization. Political leaders who held key military positions were integrated into the organization's decision-making bodies alongside the military leaders (Debelle, 2014, p. 128).

Leadership

Until 2009–10, the FDLR's senior political leadership was based abroad, also exercising key military functions. Among them were the FDLR president and supreme commander of the armed forces, Ignace Murwanashyaka (based in Germany), the FDLR vice president and president of the military high command, Straton Musoni (also in Germany), and the FDLR executive secretary and vice president of the high military command, Callixte Mbarushimana (based in France) (UNSC, 2009, para. 91).

Murwanashyaka and Musoni were arrested on 17 November 2009 in Germany,[2] while Mbarushimana was arrested in France on 3 October 2010.[3] Mbarushimana replaced Murwanashyaka as president after the latter's 2009 arrest. The DRC-based FDLR second vice president, Brig. Gen. Gaston Iyamuremye (also known as Victor Byiringiro, alias Rumuli), became interim president after October 2010 and still holds that position. Ignace Nkaka, alias Laforge Fils Bazeye, is the group's current spokesperson. The FOCA commander, Maj. Gen. Sylvestre Mudacumura, took over from Musoni as first vice president, while Laurent Ndagijimana (also known as Wilson Irategeka or Rumbago) became executive secretary (Omaar, 2012, p. 15).

As a result of these developments, the political leadership, formerly led by civilians who were based in Europe, was quickly transferred to the military leaders in North Kivu. Other leaders based in France and Germany went quiet as judiciary persecutions in Europe continued (*Jeune Afrique*, 2013; Karuhanga, 2014; Omaar, 2012, p. 15).

Political structure

Although the FDLR statute identifies a number of internal decision-making organs, in practice the FDLR's 32-member *comité directeur* (steering committee) meets once or twice a year and takes the most important decisions on war, peace, attack, and defence (FDLR, 2005, arts. 39–43; Schlindwein and Johnson, 2014). This committee includes the 15 highest-ranking FOCA commanders, the FDLR president and his two vice presidents, an executive secretary, as well as about ten executive commissioners responsible for defence, social affairs and reconciliation, status of women and promotion of the family, political affairs, mobilization and propaganda, legal affairs and human rights, information, finance and inheritance, external relations, and documentation and security. In case of an emergency, the statutes authorize the president to make decisions after consulting his two vice presidents and the FOCA commander (FDLR, 2005, arts. 36, 41).

Military structure

The military force, FOCA, was formed through the union of ALIR and ALIR-2 forces in South Kivu in 2003. In 2006, it was reorganized into two operational sectors: former ALIR combatants formed the core of the FDLR–FOCA's Secteur Opérationnel Nord Kivu (SONOKI) while ALIR-2 was the basis for Secteur Opérationnel Sud Kivu (SOSUKI). Like a regular army, and until mid-2012, each sector comprised a general staff, a headquarters battalion, and four combat battalions (Debelle, 2014, p. 128).

The FOCA structure between 2006 and 2012 also included a reserve brigade, composed of a general staff, a head-quarters battalion, and three combat battalions (Debelle, 2014, p. 128). Led to this day by Col. André Kalume (whose real name is Lucien Nzabamwita), the reserve brigade was responsible for protecting FOCA headquarters—it only deployed to the front for special operations (Schlindwein and Johnson, 2014). In 2006–12 this brigade was deployed in the territory situated between the two operational sectors. Only one battalion from this brigade was based in South Kivu (Debelle, 2014, p. 128). The reserve brigade fell under the direct orders of the FOCA commander, Maj. Gen. Mudacumura, without coordinating systematically with the political leadership (Schlindwein and Johnson, 2014). The preferential treatment it received is believed to have been a source of tension between Mudacumura and some of his commanders. In addition to the above units, the FOCA also comprised a military police battalion, a *groupement des écoles* (training camp), a close protection unit for the FOCA commander, and a number of support units (Debelle, 2014, pp. 128–29).

This structure was drastically changed after mid-2012, following the military operations led by the FARDC from 2009 to 2011, which weakened the FOCA militarily, as discussed below. SONOKI was renamed 'Secteur 1' (or 'Secteur Nord', also called 'Apollo'), while SOSUKI became 'Secteur 2' (or 'Secteur Sud', also called 'Columbia'), although the names SOSUKI and SONOKI were still commonly used as of late 2014. Each sector now comprises only two subsectors— Sinayi and Kanani in North Kivu, and Jupiter and Venus in South Kivu—all formed from the remains of the original battalions. The reserve brigade has been reorganized into a subsector called 'Comète' (Debelle, 2014, pp. 366–72);[4] it has also been fully redeployed to North Kivu.[5]

Leaders have tried to position the group as a political player in Rwanda.

Objectives and ideology

The FDLR officially strives for peace and reconciliation in Rwanda and the Great Lakes region. It envisions that reaching that goal requires the establishment of inclusive dialogue in Rwanda—with the FDLR at the table—and the revelation of the truth about the Rwandan 'tragedy' (Romkema, 2007, p. 39). More recently, in the context of the FDLR's dwindling military fortunes, its leaders have positioned the group as a political player whose main demand resides in its participation in the Rwandan political system. At a 26 June 2014 meeting hosted by the Sant'Egidio community in Rome, FDLR representatives met with UN special representatives Martin Kobler and Mary Robinson, the special envoys of Belgium, the United States, and the European Union, as well as government delegates from the DRC. The FDLR's key demand at the meeting was the opening of 'dialogue with the Rwanda government and reform of the Rwandan security forces permitting FDLR representation at a leadership level' (Schlindwein and Johnson, 2014). On 12 January 2014, shortly after its December 2013 commitment to lay down weapons, the FDLR announced the beginning of the activities of its new Front Commun pour la Libération du Rwanda (Common Front for the Liberation of Rwanda)– Ubumwe alliance with the Rwandan opposition Parti Social (Social Party)–Imberakuri (Schlindwein and Johnson, 2014).

Behind the official narrative, argues Romkema, the group also has semi-official and hidden objectives (Romkema, 2007, p. 39). He maintains that in their communication with combatants and refugees, FDLR leaders have stated more clearly their intention to overthrow the Rwandan government, to pardon the actors of the genocide, and to create a Hutu-majority government. He reports that FDLR–FOCA combatants in North Kivu told Rwandan refugees that they were still Interahamwe and that the genocide was not over. He concludes that continuing the armed struggle is a necessity for leaders and members suspected of participation in the Rwandan genocide or subject to international sanctions: the FDLR protects them from prosecution while providing them with a source of income (Romkema, 2007, p. 40).

As the group is partially composed of former FAR and Interahamwe members, its narrative and ideology are centred around the ethnic and historical clichés that prevailed in Rwanda between independence and the FPR's access to power in 1994. The following extracts of the FDLR's website, which was active from 2000 to 2009, highlight discourse used to present Hutus as victims, Tutsis as the 'evil' perpetrators, and violent action against the Rwandan government as the legitimate solution:

- 'The Hutu people are persecuted, despised, and excluded. The FPR–Inkotanyi[6] restored pre-1959 ethnic discrimination and erected a social system similar to South Africa's apartheid.'
- 'The Rwandan tragedy finds its profound origins in the political philosophy of Tutsi monarchs whose most striking characteristics are their bloodthirsty spirit, genocidal practices, hegemonic tendencies, and expansionism.'
- 'Rwandans rise up as a single man and fight the forces of evil incarnated by deceit, trickery, contempt, hatred, revenge, violence, and murder, which continue to be seen through the macabre crimes perpetrated in Rwanda and the Great Lakes region by the FPR–Inkotanyi and its accomplices' (FDLR, 2009; as cited in Debelle, 2014, pp. 21–22, authors' translation).[7]

Several FDLR leaders are suspected of involvement in the 1994 genocide. The group's stated position on the genocide is marked by inconsistencies. Officially, as declared in the 2005 Rome Communiqué signed by President Ignace Murwanashyaka, the FDLR 'condemns the genocide committed in Rwanda and its perpetrators [and] commits itself to fight against all ideologies of hatred and emphasizes once again its willingness to cooperate with international justice' (Pole Institute, 2010, p. 24). Yet a 2003 International Crisis Group report notes that the FDLR questioned whether the 1994 genocide was planned, arguing that it was a spontaneous reaction of a population confused by the assassination of its president, and panicked by the FPR's military attacks (ICG, 2003, p. 10). Several members of the FDLR's top leadership are suspected of involvement in the 1994 genocide, including Callixte Mbarushimana, the former executive secretary; Gen. Apollinaire Hakizimana, alias Amikwe Lepic, defence commissioner; and Martin Gatabazi, alias Enock Dusabe (Omaar, 2008, pp. 65–66, 236–312).

Sources of financing and support

Kinshasa and the FARDC

Although Laurent-Désiré Kabila's support to ALIR and the FDLR was key to the latter group's formation, this relationship proved neither sustainable nor reliable, as regional alliances shifted once again. President Kabila was assassinated in January 2001; having replaced him, his son, Joseph Kabila, sought to improve relations with Rwanda. A meeting with President Paul Kagame in 2001 paved the way for political dialogue and for a UN-led peace process that contributed to end the Second Congolese War. A series of agreements followed, including the Pretoria Peace Agreement between Rwanda and the DRC, signed on 30 July 2002. The terms of the agreement included the withdrawal of the Rwandan army from the DRC, while the DRC committed to dismantling ex-FAR and Interahamwe forces on its territory (DRC and Rwanda, 2002).

The formation of the Government of Transition on 30 June 2003, led by President Joseph Kabila, marked the formal end of the conflict and Kinshasa's support to the FDLR officially ended around the same time. Yet collaboration between the FDLR and the Congolese army—the FARDC—continued in the field. Specifically, the FDLR was found to collaborate with FARDC units in operations against the Congrès National pour la Défense du Peuple (National Congress for People's Defence, CNDP) in 2007 and 2008 (UNSC, 2008, paras. 102–13).

A new Congolese–Rwandan agreement sealed in December 2008 called for joint military action against the Rwandan Hutu rebels. The joint FARDC and the Rwanda Defence Force (RDF) operation—known as 'Umoja Wetu' (Our Unity)—unfolded from 20 January to 25 February 2009 with the objective of dismantling the FDLR–FOCA in North Kivu (UNSC, 2009, paras. 13–15). From March to September 2009 'Kimia II', an operation led by the FARDC and supported by the UN, also targeted FDLR–FOCA (UNSC, 2009, paras. 16–20).

Although official support from Kinshasa to the FDLR–FOCA had ceased, some reports point to continued assistance from and collaboration with some members of the FARDC, including the supply of arms and ammunition, during the 2009 operations and as late as April–May 2014 (UNSC, 2009, paras. 22–43; 2014a, paras. 97–98; 2014b, paras. 54–55).

The diaspora

The FDLR could initially count on the external support of hundreds of Rwandans who had emigrated after 1994. The UN Group of Experts documented regular communications between the FDLR commanders' satellite telephones in the field and 25 countries in Africa, Europe, and North America between September 2008 and August 2009 (UNSC, 2009, para. 99). The diaspora supported the FDLR through fundraising, money laundering, and outreach activities (UNSC, 2009, para. 90).

The significance of this source of income was limited, however. A large portion of the funds collected by the diaspora was spent on communication (satellite phones), travel, and the organization of meetings (Debelle, 2014, pp. 325–26). In fact, the Group of Experts' 2009 report suggests that money also flowed in the opposite direction—from eastern DRC to Europe—to help finance the FDLR political leadership's activities (UNSC, 2009, para. 95).

As described above, the FDLR's top political leaders were based in Europe until 2009. In addition, the group relied on a network of eight *comités de résistance régionaux* (regional resistance committees) that were based abroad and acted as the movement's official antennae around the world. At least until 2009–10, such *comités* were present in the following regions: Central Africa, West Africa, Southern Africa, Western Europe, Scandinavia, Eastern Europe, Canada, and the United States (Debelle, 2014, pp. 309–12). It is unclear how many of them remain operational today, as foreign-based FDLR members became more prudent following the 2009–10 arrests of their European-based senior leaders.

Exploitation of natural resources

As support from Kinshasa and the diaspora proved limited, the FDLR–FOCA essentially relied on income-generating activities within the DRC to meet its units' daily needs for subsistence, fund its combat operations, and support the costs of the entire organization (Debelle, 2014, pp. 184–90; Romkema, 2007, pp. 47–50). These activities often involved identifying and seizing entire economic sectors in the geographical areas where members of the group were deployed, as well as exploiting refugees and the local population. Estimates suggest the FDLR–FOCA controlled as much as 20 per cent of the territory of North and South Kivu in 2007, while directing as much as half of the region's trade in minerals (Romkema, 2007, pp. 49, 51). Each FOCA unit devoted more than 20 per cent of its human resources to generating income (Debelle, 2014, p. 185).

Table 7.1 **Redistribution of income generated through the FDLR-FOCA's 'unconventional logistics'**				
Unit	War loot	Mining taxes	Market taxes	Other income
Company	20 per cent	Nothing	Self-managed	Self-managed
Battalion	40 per cent	60 per cent	Self-managed	Self-managed
Sector	20 per cent	20 per cent	Self-managed	Self-managed
FOCA command	10 per cent	10 per cent	Self-managed	Self-managed
Executive committee	10 per cent	10 per cent	Self-managed	Self-managed

Source: internal FDLR-FOCA documentation for the period 26 December 2008-4 April 2009, cited in Debelle (2014, pp. 189-90)

The resource-generating system emerged in the early days of the organization and was referred to internally as *logistique non-conventionelle* ('unconventional logistics'). The FOCA command issued specific guidelines instructing all units in the field to generate income. Table 7.1 illustrates how the funds from various sources were to be redistributed within the different layers of the FDLR–FOCA structure in 2008–09. Logistics officers had to submit detailed quarterly, biannual, and annual reports on the financial gains their units had generated. These profits served not only to improve the officers' and fighters' daily conditions, but also to buy arms and ammunition, mostly within the DRC (Debelle, 2014, pp. 184–90).

As a result, commanders who controlled areas with natural resources—especially gold and cassiterite (tin ore)—tended to become the wealthiest (VIOLENCE AND RESOURCE EXTRACTION). The 2009 report of the UN Group of Experts estimates that the FDLR–FOCA may have generated several million US dollars from gold mining every year, and up to a few million US dollars from cassiterite (UNSC, 2009, paras. 124, 164).

In addition to their quasi-monopoly on mining activities in areas under their control, the FOCA also became involved in trading coal, wood, food, and other goods of first necessity; agriculture and cattle raising; fishing and poaching; trafficking of cannabis; taxing markets and main roads; and looting and kidnapping for ransom (Debelle, 2014, pp. 185–87; Pole Institute, 2010, p. 11; POACHING IN AFRICA). Before the joint FARDC–RDF operation 'Umoja Wetu' was launched, FDLR–FOCA units had become the primary production and control mechanism of the local economy in their areas of operation. Depending on their geographical location, each unit would generate USD 3,000–10,000 and sometimes up to USD 15,000 per month (Debelle, 2014, p. 190). As discussed below, this system was severely destabilized after the group lost influence over territory in 2009–11.

Miners handle cassiterite extracted at one of the many mines once run profitably by the FDLR, in Nampego, South Kivu, DRC, August 2009.
© Dominic Nahr/Magnum Photos

Control over territory and refugee camps

As it settled in eastern Zaire's refugee camps in 1994, the Rwandan 'government-in-exile' established an administrative structure similar to the one in place in the Rwandan state. The camps, made of tents, were divided into prefectures, communes, and sectors (Debelle, 2014, p. 316).

The FDLR created similar structures to administer the territory they controlled in the eastern DRC (Vogel, 2014a). The FDLR's second vice president, Gaston Iyamuremye (who also served as FDLR interim president) supervised the administration of territory and camps in the DRC, together with the group's commissioners for mobilization and propaganda, and for social affairs. Four regional committees were set up in the DRC: two in North Kivu (Rutshuru and Masisi) and two in South Kivu (Mwenga-Hombo and Fizi). Within the regional committees, administrative boundaries were inspired by the system used by the Congolese authorities. Each committee was divided into *groupements* (groups), which themselves contained *localités* (localities), and *notabilités*. The smallest unit was the *nyumba kumi*, corresponding to ten households (Debelle, 2014, p. 316).

In 2006, an estimated 20,000–25,000 Rwandan civilians were living in South Kivu, and at least as many in North Kivu. The majority had settled on territory controlled by the FDLR and were considered members of the movement (Romkema, 2007, p. 42). Groups of 50–100 refugees were supervised by the relevant head of *notabilité*, who reported to the above structure. A military structure called the *poste d'intervention populaire* (post of popular intervention) provided security to, but also monitored, the refugee population. Moreover, it provided military training to civilians, including children, in an effort to build a recruitment pool among the refugee population (Debelle, 2014, p. 317).

> An estimated 5.4 million people have died due to conflict in the DRC.

The *groupement* chief acted as the local administration official, recording births, marriages, and deaths every quarter. He also collected the monthly USD 1 dues to the FDLR from the refugees, or an equivalent in-kind 'contribution'. These resources were then redistributed to the corresponding *notabilité* (5 per cent), *localité* (5 per cent), and *groupement* (5 per cent), with the remaining portion divided between the regional committee and the executive committee. The *notabilités*, *localités*, and *groupements* used these resources mainly to purchase school supplies (Debelle, 2014, p. 321).

Rwandan refugees, along with Congolese civilians who lived in FDLR–FOCA-controlled areas, were thus kept under close watch. They played a part in generating income for the organization, while representing an important pool for voluntary and forced recruitment. According to data from the UN-led Disarmament, Demobilization, Repatriation, Reintegration, and Resettlement (DDR-RR) programme, 20 per cent of the 1,997 FOCA combatants who joined the programme in 2009 were Congolese. This figure increased to 30 per cent in 2010, illustrating the extent of recruitment from the Congolese population (Debelle, 2014, p. 297).

Abuses

Conflict in the DRC has had a particularly devastating human toll. Based on a series of surveys, the International Rescue Committee estimates that a total of 5.4 million people died as a direct or indirect result of the conflict between 1998 and 2007 (Coghlan et al., 2007, p. 2), although this figure has been challenged.[8] The UN reports that the FARDC and various armed groups active in the eastern DRC perpetrated a large range of abuses against civilians, including summary executions; sexual and gender-based violence; torture and other cruel, inhuman, or degrading treatment or punishment; arbitrary arrest and detention; enforced disappearances; forced labour and extortion; child recruitment; forced recruitment; and pillage.[9]

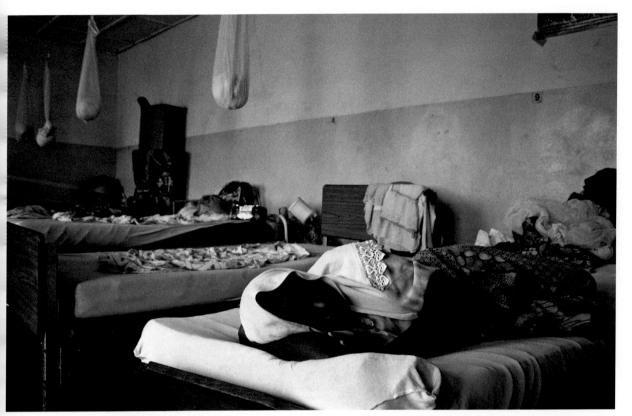

A teenager who was kept as a sex slave, allegedly by the FDLR, awaits her fistula repair surgery, in a hospital in Goma, DRC, February 2009.
© Alissa Everett/Reuters

The FDLR is no exception and is often singled out as a particularly ruthless actor in the region, with combatants involved in rape and sexual violence, the killing of people of all ages, and the burning of schools, churches, and health centres (HRW, 2009; Rodríguez, 2011, p. 177; UNSC, 2009, paras. 317–20, 345–56). The group is on the UN's 2014 list of entities that recruit and use children, commit rape and other forms of sexual violence against children, and engage in attacks on schools and hospitals (UNGA, 2014, annexe 1).[10]

The 2009 'Umoja Wetu' and 'Kimia II' military operations led to particularly gruesome reprisal attacks planned and organized by the FDLR–FOCA against the local population, which it accused of aiding the enemy (Schlindwein and Johnson, 2014; UNSC, 2009, paras. 347–56). The International Criminal Court issued an arrest warrant against FOCA Maj. Gen. Sylvestre Mudacumura on 13 July 2012 for allegedly committing:

> nine counts of war crimes, from 20 January 2009 to the end of September 2010 [. . .] including: attacking civilians, murder, mutilation, cruel treatment, rape, torture, destruction of property, pillaging and outrages against personal dignity (ICC, 2012).

The UN Group of Experts documented 1,199 human rights violations committed by the FDLR between February and October 2009, including 384 killings, 135 cases of sexual violence, 521 abductions, 38 cases of torture, and 5 cases of mutilation (UNSC, 2009, paras. 345, 347). Human Rights Watch quotes victims who reported that, at the time, FDLR combatants had stressed that they would not leave Congo 'without first exterminating the Congolese people' (HRW, 2009).

WEAPONS HOLDINGS AND CONTROL

This section reviews the FDLR–FOCA's military equipment, as well as the group's rules and regulations regarding the management and use of weapons.

Sources

Over the years, the FDLR–FOCA acquired weapons through a variety of sources. The primary patterns of supply include:

- weapons brought by the ex-FAR from Rwanda in 1994;
- weapons provided by President Mobutu of Zaire and his allies in 1996;
- equipment provided by President Laurent-Désiré Kabila of the DRC and his allies between 1998 and 2001;
- purchases and transfers from the FARDC and, starting in 2002, other Congolese armed groups;
- weapons captured from enemy forces such as the Armée Patriotique Rwandaise (Rwandan Patriotic Army, APR), the CNDP, and the FARDC; and
- to a limited extent, supplies and transfers from allied foreign armed groups also operating in the Kivu provinces, such as the Burundian Forces Nationales de Libération (National Liberation Forces) and Forces de Défense de la Démocratie (Forces for the Defence of Democracy) (Debelle, 2014, pp. 274–75; Romkema, 2007, pp. 46–47).

In recent years, the FDLR–FOCA appears to have procured weapons and ammunition primarily from sympathetic segments within the FARDC. In its 2009 report, the UN Group of Experts cites 'evidence and testimony demonstrating that certain FARDC officers, particularly senior officials in control of the tenth military region (South Kivu), [were]

United Nations peacekeepers record the details of weapons recovered from FDLR members, surrendered in Kateko, DRC, May 2014.
© Kenny Katombe/Reuters

implicated in the deliberate diversion' of arms and ammunition to FDLR–FOCA and other armed groups (UNSC, 2009, para. 23). Ammunition supplies from the FARDC to the FDLR–FOCA gained further momentum in 2012, as the former were eager to count on the latter's support to contain the new rebellion initiated by the Mouvement du 23 Mars (23 March Movement, M23) (SSRC, 2014, p. 5; UNSC, 2013, paras. 106–09). While this collaboration petered out in late 2013, after the defeat of M23, reports suggest individual FARDC soldiers continued to barter or sell their weapons, ammunition, and uniforms to the FDLR–FOCA as late as April–May 2014 (UNSC, 2014a, paras. 97–98; 2014b, para. 54).

Weapons holdings

The FDLR procured ammunition mainly through small-scale purchases and battlefield capture.

Table 7.2 summarizes the models and types of weapons and ammunition known to be held by the FDLR–FOCA. It lists equipment held by FDLR–FOCA in 2009–11 as documented in Debelle (2014, pp. 275–84), based on interviews with former and active combatants and other confidential sources. It also shows the types and quantities of weapons and ammunition surrendered by combatants who demobilized in 2014, as reported in CAR (2014). On 30 May 2014, in the presence of the FDLR interim president, Gaston Iyamuremye, and other senior group leaders in Kateko, North Kivu, more than 100 FDLR–FOCA combatants from the SONOKI sector surrendered 102 weapons and limited quantities of ammunition (CAR, 2014; Schlindwein and Johnson, 2014; Vogel, 2014a). Shortly thereafter, on 9 June in Kigogo, more than 80 combatants from the SOSUKI sector surrendered 83 weapons and some ammunition (CAR, 2014; Schlindwein and Johnson, 2014).

As the FDLR–FOCA sourced its weapons mainly from diverted regional stockpiles, its diverse holdings contain a significant proportion of ageing and relatively unreliable weapons. These weapons suffered from years of exposure to unfavourable climatic and inappropriate storage conditions. Unsurprisingly, most weapons surrendered in 2014 were small arms in poor condition, including ageing AK-pattern rifles and several M-16 A1 rifles as well as other NATO-calibre weapons (see Table 7.2). The scarcity of NATO ammunition in the region helps to explain why FDLR–FOCA combatants abandoned a variety of NATO-calibre weapons in 2014, including the M-16, SAR-80, R4, and UZI (Debelle, 2014, p. 275; see Table 7.2).

Although the entire FOCA stockpile is ageing, it is clear that the weapons surrendered in 2014 were particularly old, and that the most functional weapons remain in the control of the group.[11] Only one rocket-propelled grenade launcher and two mortars were turned in during the 2014 ceremonies, suggesting the disarmament ceremonies did little to diminish the FDLR–FOCA's holdings of light weapons. Since the FDLR–FOCA probably holds few heavy weapons, its ability to carry out large-scale operations, or to defend territory against a well-equipped opponent, may be limited (Debelle, 2014, p. 275).

Ammunition stockpiles are in particularly short supply. Until 2011, the FDLR–FOCA's main strategic ammunition stockpile was located in the Nyamaboko refugee camp, near the group headquarters; it was guarded by the group's military police. In addition to ammunition of the calibres described in Table 7.2, the holdings included 107 mm rockets. In April 2011, however, the FARDC attacked the refugee camp, leading FDLR–FOCA combatants to disperse with the ammunition they could carry. Reflecting the group's difficulties in securing systematic procurements, combatants sourced ammunition primarily through small-scale purchases from the FARDC and Congolese armed groups, as well as battlefield capture (Debelle, 2014, p. 275).

With limited heavy equipment and ammunition stockpiles, the FDLR–FOCA's ability to defend territory has always been weak. Yet the equipment under the group's custody is adequate for guerrilla warfare and the conduct of targeted operations to capture materiel from its enemies.

Table 7.2 Materiel held and surrendered by the FDLR-FOCA

Calibre	Holdings in 2009-11		Weapons surrendered in May–June 2014	Ammunition surrendered in May–June 2014
	Weapon type and production	Sources and details		
9 x 19 mm	Belgian-manufactured Browning HP pistols	Multiple sources, including ex-FAR and FARDC; held primarily by officers or given as a reward for brave conduct	None	None
	UZI sub-machine guns of Belgian or Israeli manufacture	Sourced from ex-FAR, FARDC, and Forces Armées du Congo (Congolese Armed Forces, FAC)	1 machine gun dated 1971 (unidentified country of production) surrendered by SOSUKI	
7.62 x 39 mm	AK-pattern rifles manufactured in Bulgaria, China (Type 56), Romania, the Soviet Union, and Yugoslavia (M70 B1/B2)	Multiple sources, including FARDC; M70 sources also include APR, CNDP, and RDF; some of the CNDP and RDF M70 models feature grenade-launching adapters for firing anti-personnel and anti-tank grenades	12 Type 56-2 Chinese-manufactured rifles and 5 other AK-pattern rifles by SONOKI; 1 AKM- and 5 AK-pattern rifles by SOSUKI (including Chinese- and Russian- manufactured)	This calibre accounted for most rounds in the small piles of surrendered ammunition, with various headstamps indicating Albanian manufacture in the 1980s; Bulgarian manufacture in 1990-2001; Chinese manufacture in the 1970s and 1996-2007; East German manufacture in the 1970s; Iranian manufacture in 2003 and 2007; Sudanese manufacture in 2001 and 2007; Egyptian manufacture (no date); North Korean manufacture in the 1980s; Soviet/Russian manufacture in the 1950s, 1960s, and 1980s; Ukrainian manufacture (no date); Yugoslav manufacture in the 1970s and 1980s; and Zimbabwean manufacture in the 1990s
	Chinese- and Russian-made SKS rifles	Various sources	1 Russian-made rifle surrendered by SONOKI	
	Chinese- and Russian-made RPD machine guns	Undetermined source	surrendered by SOSUKI (unidentified country of production)	
	n/a		1 Czech-manufactured Vz. 58 rifle surrendered by SOSUKI; 1 Czech-produced Vz. 52/57 rifle surrendered by SONOKI	
5.56 x 45 mm	South African-produced R4 rifles	Originated from ex-FAR stockpiles	4 rifles surrendered by SONOKI, 2 by SOSUKI	Only 6 cartridges surrendered by SONOKI, with headstamps indicating French, Israeli, and Portuguese manufacture in the 1980s
	US-manufactured M16 A1 rifles	Originated from the special presidential division of ex-Forces Armées Zaïroises (Armed Forces of Zaire, FAZ) stockpiles	8 US-manufactured and US government-stamped rifles surrendered by SONOKI, 2 US-manufactured rifles surrendered by SOSUKI	
	Singapore-manufactured SAR 80 rifles	Originated from ex-FAZ stockpiles	2 rifles surrendered by SONOKI, 3 by SOSUKI	

Calibre	Holdings in 2009–11		Weapons surrendered in May–June 2014	Ammunition surrendered in May–June 2014
	Weapon type and production	Sources and details		
7.62 x 51 mm	South African-produced SS-77 machine guns	Captured from RDF	None	4 varieties of Sudanese-produced cartridges manufactured in 1997, 1999, and 2001, surrendered by SONOKI
	Belgian-produced FN FAL M2/M3 and FALO rifles	Originated from ex-FAR and ex-FAZ stockpiles	1 FN FAL rifle surrendered by SOSUKI	
	G3 rifles, country of production unclear	Sourced from ex-FAZ or the Uganda People's Defence Force, with fixed or telescopic stock	4 rifles surrendered by SONOKI, 3 by SOSUKI	
	Belgian-produced FN MAG machine guns	Originated from ex-FAR, ex-FAZ, and FARDC stockpiles	1 surrendered by SONOKI, 1 by SOSUKI	
7.62 x 54R mm	Russian-produced PKM machine guns	Multiple sources, including FARDC; sometimes nick-named 'PIKA' by combatants	None	6 varieties of Egyptian, Chinese (produced in 1971 and 2001), Czech (pro-duced in 1967), Iranian, and unidentified cartridges surrendered by SONOKI
	Vz. 59 machine gun manu-factured in Czechoslovakia	Originated from FARDC stockpiles	None	
	Russian-produced SGM machine guns	Originated from FARDC stockpiles; sometimes nicknamed 'MILOU' (from mitrailleuse lourde) by combatants	None	
12.7 x 108 mm	Soviet- and Chinese-produced DShK machine guns	Originated from FARDC stockpiles; often referred to as 'MIAA' (from mitrailleuse anti-aérienne) by combatants	None	None
12.7 x 99 mm	Belgian- or US-produced Browning .50 machine guns	Originated from FARDC stockpiles	None	None
Other weapons	Russian-made 40 mm BG-15 grenade launcher for AK-pattern rifles	Originated from FARDC stockpiles	None	None
	US-produced Browning .30 machine guns	Originated from ex-FAZ stockpiles	None	None
	40 mm South African- or Croatian-produced multiple grenade launchers	Originated from APR, ex-FAR, and RDF; several were held by SOSUKI	None	None
	Rocket-propelled grenade (RPG) launchers produced by the Russian Federation (RPG-2) or China (Type 56 RPG).	Undetermined source	None	None
	RPGs produced by the Russian Federation (RPG-7) and China (Type 69)	Multiple sources, including FARDC	2 Chinese-produced Type 69 variants surren-dered by SONOKI;	None

Calibre	Holdings in 2009–11		Weapons surrendered in May–June 2014	Ammunition surrendered in May–June 2014
	Weapon type and production	Sources and details		
Other weapons			1 Chinese-produced Type 69 variant, 2 RPG-7Vs (1 Russian- and 1 Bulgarian-produced) surrendered by SOSUKI	
	Russian-produced RPG-18 launchers	Possibly donated in 1998 by the Chadian Army; only a few units are still in the possession of FOCA combatants	None	None
	60 mm mortars of various manufacturers, including South Africa and the United States	Originated from FARDC stockpiles	2 mortars of unidentified origin surrendered by SOSUKI	None
	Various 81 mm (NATO) and 82 mm (Soviet or Chinese) mortars	Originated from FARDC stockpiles	None	None
	Chinese-produced 107 mm multiple rocket launchers, with modifications made in Likasi, DRC, to single and dual tube launchers	Originated from FAC stockpiles during the 1998-2002 war	None	None
	Russian-produced SA-7 Strela man-portable air defence systems	Two such systems were captured by ALIR combatants in September 1998 during an attack on APR positions near Mount Ngoma, south of Goma; the possession of these weapons was kept secret and associated rules of engagement were under the strict authority of the FOCA commander; they were allegedly kept under custody at FOCA headquarters	None	None
	93 mm Soviet-produced RPO-A 'Shmel' launchers	Allegedly given to FOCA by Zimbabwean soldiers during fighting with APR; one rocket of this type was seized by the UN Organization Mission in the DRC (MONUC) in October 2009, in the Goma area; only the FOCA units based in North Kivu possessed this armament	None	None

Calibre	Holdings in 2009–11		Weapons surrendered in May–June 2014	Ammunition surrendered in May–June 2014
	Weapon type and production	Sources and details		
Other weapons	Z1 anti-personnel mines	Allegedly originated from the stocks of the Zimbabwean army, deployed in the DRC until 2002 to repel Rwandan troops; this type of munition is usually centralized at the level of the general staff and used with parsimony; nicknamed 'chaponer' (phonetic spelling), apparently in reference to 'shrapnel'	n/a	None
	VS 50 anti-personnel mines	Undetermined source; nicknamed 'shoebox'	n/a	None
	Anti-vehicle mines, unknown models	Testimonies suggest possession of anti-tank mines at the unit level; they may have been supplied by foreign forces involved in the Second Congolese War	n/a	None

Notes: Information on holdings relies on interviews conducted by Raymond Debelle in 2009–11 with more than two dozen active and former FDLR-FOCA cadres and combatants, notably ex-FAR soldiers with specialized knowledge of the group's armaments; details were cross-checked through field observation, the analysis of equipment recovered by MONUC and the DDR-RR section of the UN Organization Stabilization Mission in the DRC (MONUSCO), and a review of information collected by observers who had been in contact with the FDLR-FOCA, including journalists.

Sources: holdings: Debelle (2014, pp. 275–84); materiel surrendered: CAR (2014)

Weapons control

The FDLR–FOCA can count on a number of internal regulations to guide the behaviour of its members, including a statute and manifest, a code of discipline, a penal code, internal order regulations, as well as guidelines for electoral processes. Not all of these regulations are relevant to weapons management or their use by the combatants; previous analysis suggests that standing orders and operation orders provide the most insight into the controls over the management and use of arms by fighters (Bangerter, 2012, p. 3). Standing orders 'specify which type of behaviour is expected of all group members in a given situation, though not necessarily at all times' (p. 17). Operation orders are guidelines issued for a specific military operation; it is worth noting that 'most armed groups are reluctant to write orders down, generally due to security concerns' (p. 19).

In the case of the FDLR–FOCA, the military command approves orders, which are then transferred to the two operational sectors and subsequently to the relevant battalions. Many of these orders focus on improving the efficiency of military operations against the enemy while limiting the risk of human and material loss. These guidelines tend to prioritize operations that could result in the capture of weapons and ammunition, communications equipment, and medicine. Fighters are expected to use ammunition sparingly, and units are ordered to submit detailed accounts of their arms holdings every three months. If units have a surplus of arms or ammunition, they hide it in caches, the location of which is known only by a restricted number of individuals (Debelle, 2014, pp. 206–11). Overall, the group's standing orders reflect the FDLR–FOCA command's concerns regarding the scarcity of weapons and ammunition.

In theory, orders emanating from the FOCA command are systematically transmitted to the units in the field. In practice, however, SONOKI and SOSUKI sector commanders are occasionally asked to adapt the orders to reflect local realities. These modified instructions are then submitted back to the FOCA command for approval. Units must also inform their superiors of the level of implementation of the orders (Debelle, 2014, pp. 211–12).

The military operations that targeted the FDLR–FOCA as of 2009 damaged this chain of command, in part by rendering the transmission of orders and guidelines from the FOCA command to the operational units more difficult. As a result, unit commanders have become more self-reliant and no longer execute the central command's orders as systematically as they used to. Until the 2009 operations, the management and maintenance of the arsenal was the responsibility of a former low-ranking FAR officer in charge of the movement's weapons maintenance service at FOCA headquarters; he had received armoury training from the Belgian army prior to 1994. The officer was also responsible for the two SA-7 launchers held by the group (Debelle, 2014, p. 275). The reliance on centralized structures and qualified human resources is unlikely to remain intact in the current context.

THE DECLINE OF THE FDLR-FOCA

Over the past 15 years, the FDLR survived a number of military operations by the Rwandan army and other armed actors—including its former allies. Yet it has been severely weakened in recent years, its strength decreasing from about 11,500 troops in 2002 to fewer than 1,200 in late 2014 (see Figure 7.1). While the FDLR has declined continuously since its formation in 2000, it lost considerable strength from 2009 to 2012, a period during which the estimated number of FDLR combatants was cut to less than one-third of its 2008 strength. This section reviews some of the main external and internal factors that contributed to this trend and puts this numerical decline into broader perspective.

Figure 7.1 **Estimated number of FDLR combatants, 2002-14**

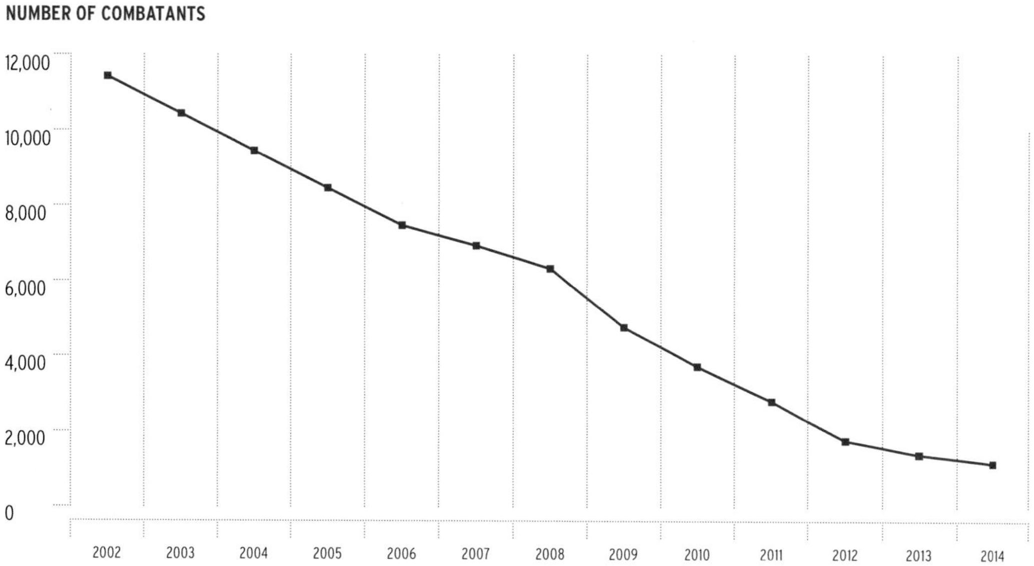

NUMBER OF COMBATANTS

Source: MONUSCO DDR-RR data, provided in correspondence with Ines Rahmi Soued, DDR-RR officer, 21 January 2015

External factors

Targeted military interventions

Improvements in Rwandan–Congolese relations in late 2008 resulted in the joint 2009 FARDC–RDF 'Umoja Wetu' and the Congolese-led 'Kimia II' operations against the FDLR–FOCA, both of which severely weakened the group militarily (Debelle, 2014, pp. 291–93; Omaar, 2012, pp. 10–13). While the rank and file was not prepared to resist such large-scale operations, the high command's response was chaotic and irrational. In late 2009, a member of the group's executive committee reported that during the operations FDLR President Ignace Murwanashyaka had called on civilians and combatants to pray and fast, arguing that god was their only hope (Debelle, 2014, pp. 291–93). FARDC operations continued from 2010 to 2012 under the name 'Amani Leo' (Peace Today), sustaining the pressure on the group (SSRC, 2014, p. 10).

In 2012, FDLR–FOCA also came under attack by a number of Congolese militias—some of which, such as the Raia Mutomboki, formed self-defence groups to protect communities (SSRC, 2014, p. 11). One analyst observed that, 'prior to 2009, no Congolese militia group would have contemplated an assault on the FDLR in its heartland', highlighting the FDLR–FOCA's new state of military weakness in 2012 (Omaar, 2012, p. 9). Other groups that targeted the FDLR–FOCA include the Forces pour la Défense du Congo (Congolese Defence Forces)–Guides, which was reportedly involved in a Rwandan-supported operation that led to the killing of the FDLR–FOCA chief of staff, Brig. Leodomir Mugaragu, in January 2012 (Stearns, 2012). Almost a dozen FOCA commanders were killed in commando operations in 2012 alone (Schlindwein and Johnson, 2014).

Villagers, telling of the atrocities their community endured at the hands of the FDLR, include a youth who claims to have subsequently become a Mai-Mai recruit, in Walikale District, DRC, February 2009. © Susan Schulman/Getty Images

These operations took a significant toll on the FDLR. 'Umoja Wetu' reportedly claimed the lives of 153 FDLR–FOCA combatants, while 13 were wounded, 37 captured, and 103 deserted (ICG, 2009, p. 9). Casualties affected primarily elite units such as the reserve brigade, which was in charge of protecting the FOCA headquarters. Other units apparently abandoned their positions and dispersed with little resistance. While these operations did not result in the neutralization of the FDLR–FOCA, they strongly destabilized the group and triggered significant waves of desertions (Schlindwein and Johnson, 2014). The operations also led the remaining FOCA military force to break up into units of six to eight men and go into hiding (SSRC, 2014, p. 10). Commanders abandoned the previously safe headquarters in the Walikale forests in 2012, as a diminished reserve brigade and headquarters battalion could no longer guarantee their protection. From mid-2012, sources reported significant restructuring of the FOCA. As noted above, the SONOKI and SOSUKI sectors were renamed and their battalions dissolved, with each sector keeping only two sub-sectors, while the reserve brigade was also downgraded to sub-sector level (Debelle, 2014, pp. 366–72).[12]

Loss of territorial control

FDLR units now have to secure resources for their own survival.

The attacks left the FDLR–FOCA incapable of maintaining control over territory where it could generate income. The group lost much of its access to natural resources, while the civilians who had run their exploitation schemes fled the fighting. In practice, the operations helped to disrupt the group's 'unconventional logistics', keeping the FOCA away from areas that used to be key for the group's economic sustainability (Debelle, 2014, p. 292; Omaar, 2012, pp. 23–24).

The FDLR–FOCA has since become increasingly reliant on revenue-generating activities such as looting and cattle raiding, taxing markets and roads, and exploiting mining areas. In 2010, these activities only brought the group an estimated USD 5,000 per month in North Kivu and USD 4,000 in South Kivu—negligible amounts compared with the fortunes previously generated through the extensive unconventional logistics. Each layer of the group now has to secure resources for its own survival rather than for the overall organization (Debelle, 2014, p. 190).

Furthermore, the loss of territorial control meant that FDLR units in North and South Kivu became separated by a gap of several hundred kilometres, which created logistical challenges and isolated southern commanders who could no longer physically participate in high command meetings (Schlindwein and Johnson, 2014; see Map 7.1). The FDLR's military schools have been relocated several times since 2009, hindering efforts to inculcate young Hutu recruits, who belong to a generation of exiles who know little about their country of origin (Schlindwein and Johnson, 2014). The group also reportedly began recruiting combatants of diverse ethnic backgrounds and from other armed groups, further altering the FDLR's composition (SSRC, 2014, p. 10).

DDR-RR

The DDR-RR programme of the UN Organization Stabilization Mission in the DRC (MONUSCO) further contributed to weakening the FDLR. Some 12,000 Rwandan fighters, the majority from the FDLR–FOCA, participated in the programme and were repatriated to Rwanda between 2002 and 2013 (APDHUD, 2014, p. 13). Large numbers of combatants appear to have been attracted to the programme in the context of the 2009–12 operations (see Figure 7.1). In 2009 alone, 1,564 FOCA combatants were repatriated to Rwanda.[13]

Part of the programme's success can be attributed to steady improvements in its outreach activities, which specifically targeted FOCA field commanders and cadres. By promoting the desertion of senior officers, the programme also affected the morale of FDLR troops, who were 'bound to ask themselves why they should believe there is a cause if their leaders do not' (Omaar, 2012, pp. 13–14). Furthermore, from 2009, the UN moved its DDR-RR transit centres closer to the FDLR–FOCA headquarters and increased its use of mobile teams, thereby reducing the distance combatants needed to travel to find a MONUSCO post (Omaar, 2012, p. 13). Many of the combatants who took advantage of the DDR-RR programme used to play a role in the FDLR–FOCA's 'unconventional logistics'. Faced with the prospect of losing access to natural resources in the DRC, they were more easily enticed to defect and take their profits with them. Other combatants fled to be reunited with their families, many of which had been forced to return to Rwanda by the latest military operations (Debelle, 2014, p. 292).

The Rwandan Demobilization and Reintegration Commission's record in supporting combatants repatriated in Rwanda with training and reintegration packages also helped establish trust among FDLR–FOCA fighters. Although around a dozen individuals in the group's top leadership are genocide suspects, the vast majority of fighters are too young to have participated or were involved as children—meaning that they cannot be prosecuted upon return in Rwanda (Schlindwein and Johnson, 2014; Waldorf, 2009, pp. 8, 26). Indeed, interviews conducted with ex-fighters repatriated in Rwanda suggest that they generally did not fear prosecution and trusted the Rwandan authorities to treat them fairly (Waldorf, 2009, p. 26). Although the Rwandan programme had some shortcomings,[14] the fact that it treated returning fighters fairly helped debunk the FDLR leadership's warnings that returnees were systematically arrested and tortured in Rwanda. It also encouraged FDLR elements, many of whom were already demoralized by hard living conditions in the DRC and a lack of employment prospects, to withdraw from the movement. Since many defectors who joined the demobilization programme maintained regular telephone communication with their former brothers-in-arms still deployed in the DRC, their testimonies served to erode the FDLR leadership's credibility among the rank and file.[15]

As part of their demobilization and reintegration process, former FDLR members set to return to civilian life in Rwanda attend classes on politics and history, including the 1994 genocide, held in Mutobo, Rwanda, April 2014. © Chip Somodevilla/Getty Images

Internal factors

Leadership issues

As the group's prospects for military success worsened, the morale among FDLR–FOCA combatants deteriorated, leading to desertion and participation in the DDR-RR programme. The situation of the FDLR's leadership in exile did not improve matters (Omaar, 2012, pp. 14–16). As of November 2005, FDLR leaders who were subject to sanctions imposed by the UN Security Council (a travel ban and asset freeze) included FDLR President Murwanashyaka and the FOCA commander, Maj. Gen. Mudacumura (UNSC, 2005). The number of FDLR leaders subject to UN sanctions has since grown to ten, and the FDLR as an entity was added to the list in December 2012 (UNSC, 2014c). As discussed above, key leadership members in Germany and France were arrested in 2009 and 2010 on charges of war crimes.

The splintering of the FDLR illustrates the group's diminishing cohesion.

Back in the field, the 'unconventional logistics' backfired. Commanders took advantage of the system for their personal gain, by keeping some of the generated income for themselves, or by creating their own companies using their units' assets and, in some cases, loans from the FDLR–FOCA's central command (Debelle, 2014, p. 190). While the unconventional income-generating system had been created to help the organization grow, it ultimately distracted the different layers of the FDLR–FOCA's hierarchy from their military mission, creating internal tensions and irrevocably weakening the organization's cohesion.

Splintering

The splintering of the FDLR–FOCA into a number of new armed factions further illustrates the group's diminishing cohesion. Some splinter groups formed after several senior FDLR leaders became disenchanted with the decisions of the top political leadership, including Murwanashyaka's commitment to aim for demobilization, which he made at the 2005 talks hosted by the Sant'Egidio community in Rome (Schlindwein and Johnson, 2014). The main split occurred when senior leaders, including Vice President Jean-Marie Vianney Higiro and Secretary General Félicien Kanyamibwa, formed the Ralliement des FDLR (Rally of the FDLR), which would later become the Ralliement pour l'Unité et la Démocratie (Rally for Unity and Democracy, RUD)–Urunana. Its armed wing, the Armée Nationale (National Army)–Imboneza, could count on more than 400 fighters in 2006 (APDHUD, 2014, p. 12; Debelle, 2014, p. 242). Other splinter groups include the 100-strong Soki (formed by a dissident RUD-Urunana member), the 50-strong Rastas (composed of deserted FARDC, FDLR, and Mai-Mai fighters), the 50-strong Mandevu (led by Gaston Mugasa 'Mandevu'), and the Commandement Militaire pour le Changement (Military Command for Change, formed in 2005 by dissident officers).[16] While seemingly limited in their military capabilities, several of the new groups reportedly became actively involved in illegal profit-making activities.

The external and internal factors discussed in this section point to an erosion of the FDLR–FOCA's pre-2009 'state-like' structure and cohesion. The nature of the threat posed by the group's remaining force remains poorly understood, however. Although diminished, the group's estimated strength has decreased only slightly since 2012, suggesting that a core of fighters, although in hiding, may still be able to regroup and reorganize.[17] In response to the FDLR's failure to meet a series of deadlines for demobilization, the UN Security Council and regional African governments threatened to carry out joint FARDC–MONUSCO military operations in January 2015 (ICG, 2014, pp. 11–14; RFI, 2014; UNSC, 2014d). After reportedly rejecting the UN's backing, the FARDC launched attacks against FDLR–FOCA positions in South Kivu in late February 2015. It remained unclear at the time of writing to what extent the operations would succeed in eradicating the FDLR in its current configuration. A key challenge will involve protecting civilians while seeking out FOCA units that are hiding among—and blending in with—the local population, having co-existed with them for two decades (Schlindwein and Johnson, 2014; Vogel, 2015).

CONCLUSION

Long considered one of the principal obstacles to peace in the region, the FDLR–FOCA appears severely weakened and no longer able to threaten the government in Kigali. The loss of Kinshasa as a key supporter, especially in the 2009–12 period, and international pressure on its leadership, followed by joint Congolese-Rwandan attacks on its positions, seem to have eroded the FDLR–FOCA's cohesion and, consequently, its overall strength. The killing and arrests of many of the group's leaders and commanders, along with the formation of splinter factions, constitute serious strains on the group's decision-making processes. In response to its military retreat, the FDLR–FOCA has also lost control over much of the territory and resources it once held, poisoning morale and accelerating the desertion and repatriation of combatants to Rwanda. From a 'state within a state' with a unifying objective—reclaiming power in Rwanda—the organization has transformed into a loose grouping of armed factions in hiding that are essentially preoccupied with their daily survival.

Yet the current weakened state of the FDLR–FOCA should not be taken as the group's epitaph. The structures it previously established could easily be revived should the region's strategic alliances shift once more and become more favourable to the movement—as they have in the past. The international community and regional leaders will therefore need to maintain their efforts to neutralize the FDLR–FOCA through complementary military and diplomatic means. They would also do well to understand the factors that underpinned the group's formerly high levels of cohesion, so as to be able to counter them again, should the FDLR–FOCA revive in the future. As this chapter describes, the aggressive international and military pressure on the FDLR leadership, combined with the implementation of credible demobilization and repatriation programmes that targeted commanders and facilitated the desertion of the rank and file, are policies that accelerated the group's decline.

A disorganized FDLR–FOCA also presents new challenges. The group's weapons holdings, perhaps ageing but largely unknown, have now dispersed with the combatants in hiding. This complicates prospects for a comprehensive demobilization and disarmament programme, as agreements with the group's leadership may not translate into participation of the various small units that currently constitute the group. The FDLR–FOCA's waning cohesion may also be bad news for civilians, who have already suffered greatly from the group's reprisal attacks and criminal activities. With group commanders and combatants hiding in communities, civilians are at risk of being caught in the crossfire should attacks occur. Keeping military pressure on the FDLR–FOCA under these new conditions is a major challenge for the international community and the Congolese government. Maintaining the option for exiled Rwandan Hutus to return to Rwanda under good conditions will be crucial. ◼

ABBREVIATIONS

AFDL	Alliance des Forces Démocratiques de Libération
ALIR	Armée de Libération du Rwanda
APR	Armée Patriotique Rwandaise
CNDP	Congrès National pour la Défense du Peuple
DDR-RR	Disarmament, Demobilization, Repatriation, Reintegration, and Resettlement
DRC	Democratic Republic of the Congo
FAC	Forces Armées du Congo
FAR	Forces Armées du Rwanda

FARDC   Forces Armées de la République Démocratique du Congo

FAZ   Forces Armées Zaïroises

FDLR   Forces Démocratiques de Libération du Rwanda

FOCA   Forces Combattantes Abacunzi

FPR   Front Patriotique Rwandais

M23   Mouvement du 23 Mars

MONUC   Mission des Nations Unies en République démocratique du Congo

               (United Nations Organization Mission in the Democratic Republic of the Congo)

MONUSCO   Mission de l'Organisation des Nations Unies pour la Stabilisation de la République démocratique du Congo

               (United Nations Organization Stabilization Mission in the Democratic Republic of the Congo)

NATO   North Atlantic Treaty Organization

PALIR   Peuple en Action pour la Libération du Rwanda

RCD   Rassemblement Congolais pour la Démocratie

RDF   Rwanda Defence Force

RPG   Rocket-propelled grenade

RUD   Ralliement pour l'Unité et la Démocratie

SONOKI   Secteur Opérationnel Nord Kivu

SOSUKI   Secteur Opérationnel Sud Kivu

ENDNOTES

1   See, for instance, Bakke et al. (2012), Cohen (2013), Cunningham (2013), Staniland (2010), and Wood (2012).

2   In June 2002, Germany introduced a law to deal with genocide and other crimes against humanity, enabling prosecutors to try a civilian for command responsibility over atrocities committed outside Germany. German prosecutors acknowledged that Murwanashyaka and Musoni led the FDLR in a conflict in which hundreds were killed, women were raped, and children were enlisted; the trial was still ongoing as of December 2014 (Karuhanga, 2014).

3   Mbarushimana was arrested under an International Criminal Court warrant and transferred to The Hague in January 2011 (UNSC, 2014c).

4   Interviews by Raymond Debelle with former FOCA officers and combatants, Rwanda, May 2013.

5   Author correspondence with Christoph Vogel, DRC analyst, 20 November 2014.

6   *Inkotanyi*, which means 'invincible warrior' in Kinyarwanda, was a nickname given to the FPR's armed branch, the Armée Patriotique Rwandaise (Rwandan Patriotic Army).

7   In addition to its online presence, the FDLR communicated through a number of other means, including its own internal training, a magazine (*Umucunzi* or 'Liberator', published in 2000–02), flyers, and a Twitter account.

8   While experts disagree on the reliability of this total figure, there is no doubt that the conflict in the region was among the deadliest of the decade. See Geneva Declaration Secretariat (2011, p. 71).

9   See, for example, UNGA (2010, paras. 18, 22–24) and UNSC (2009, paras. 317–20).

10 In addition to the FDLR, nine other DRC-based non-state groups and the FARDC also made the list by engaging in one or more types of violations of the rights of children in armed conflict (UNGA, 2014, annexe 1).

11 Author correspondence with an international source in the DRC, November 2014.

12 Interviews by Raymond Debelle with former FOCA officers and combatants, Rwanda, May 2013.

13 MONUSCO DDR-RR data, provided in correspondence with Ines Rahmi Soued, DDR-RR officer, 21 January 2015.

14 Some flaws were related to technical and management issues, including inadequate sensitization and a 'poorly implemented microcredit scheme' (World Bank, 2009, p. 6). There are also reports that the Congolese M23 rebel group recruited former FDLR fighters in Rwanda in 2013 (UNSC, 2013, para. 40).

15 Author correspondence with Claudio Gramizzi, senior field investigator, Conflict Armament Research, and former member of the UN Group of Experts on the DRC, 16 November 2014.

16 See APDHUD (2014, p. 12); Debelle (2014, pp. 266–74); Schlindwein and Johnson (2014).

17 See, for instance, Enough Project (2014).

BIBLIOGRAPHY

APDHUD (Action pour la Protection des Droits Humains et de Développment Communautaire). 2014. *Rapport sur la Récurrence et Activisme des Groupes Armés à l'Est de la République Démocratique du Congo 2010–2014*. Bunyakiri, Democratic Republic of the Congo: APDHUD. 22 October.

Bakke, Kristin, et al. 2012. 'A Plague of Initials: Fragmentation, Cohesion, and Infighting in Civil Wars.' *Perspectives on Politics,* Vol. 10, No. 2. June.

Bangerter, Olivier. 2012. *Internal Control: Codes of Conduct within Insurgent Armed Groups*. Occasional Paper 31. Geneva: Small Arms Survey. November.

CAR (Conflict Armament Research). 2014. *Weapons and Ammunition Surrendered by FDLR–FOCA in 2014*. Unpublished background paper. August.

Coghlan, Benjamin, et al. 2007. *Mortality in the Democratic Republic of Congo: An Ongoing Crisis*. New York: International Rescue Committee.

Cohen, Dara. 2013. 'Explaining Rape during Civil War: Cross-National Evidence (1980–2009).' *American Political Science Review,* Vol. 107, No. 3. August.

Cunningham, Kathleen. 2013. 'Actor Fragmentation and Civil War Bargaining: How Internal Divisions Generate Civil Conflict.' *American Journal of Political Science,* Vol. 57, No. 3, pp. 659–72. July.

Debelle, Raymond. 2014. *Leadership et idéologie des FDLR-FOCA: Dossier pour appréhender les enjeux cachés*. Unpublished manuscript.

DRC (Democratic Republic of the Congo) and Rwanda. 2002. Peace Agreement between the Governments of the Republic of Rwanda and the Democratic Republic of the Congo on the Withdrawal of the Rwandan Troops from the Territory of the Democratic Republic of the Congo and the Dismantling of the Ex-FAR and Interahamwe Forces in the Democratic Republic of the Congo (DRC). 30 July. <http://www.usip.org/sites/default/files/file/resources/collections/peace_agreements/drc_rwanda_pa07302002.pdf>

Enough Project. 2014. 'How to Dismantle a Deadly Militia: Seven Non-military Tactics to Help End the FDLR Threat in Congo.' November. <http://www.enoughproject.org/files/FDLRReport-HowToDismantleADeadlyMilitia-EnoughProject-Nov2014.pdf>

FDLR (Forces Démocratiques de Libération du Rwanda). 2005. 'Manifeste–Programme et Statuts des Forces Démocratiques de Libération du Rwanda—F.D.L.R.' 24 May. <http://umudendezo-news.blogspot.ch/2013/08/manifeste-programme-et-statuts-des.html>

—. 2009. Official website. Online until 2009. <http://www.fdlr.org>

Florquin, Nicolas. 2010. 'Options for Engagement: Armed Groups and Humanitarian Norms.' In Small Arms Survey. *Small Arms Survey 2010: Gangs, Groups, and Guns*. Cambridge: Cambridge University Press, pp. 305–33.

Geneva Declaration Secretariat. 2011. *Global Burden of Armed Violence 2011: Lethal Encounters*. Cambridge: Cambridge University Press.

HRW (Human Rights Watch). 2009. 'DR Congo: Rwandan Rebels Slaughter over 100 Civilians.' 13 February. <http://www.hrw.org/news/2009/02/13/dr-congo-rwandan-rebels-slaughter-over-100-civilians>

ICC (International Criminal Court). 2012. 'The Prosecutor *vs*. Sylvestre Mudacumura.' ICC-01/04-01/12. <http://www.icc-cpi.int/iccdocs/PIDS/publications/MudacumuraEng.pdf>

ICG (International Crisis Group). 2003. *Rwandan Hutu Rebels in the Congo: A New Approach to Disarmament and Reintegration*. Africa Report No. 63. Nairobi and Brussels: International Crisis Group. 23 May. <http://www.crisisgroup.org/~/media/Files/africa/central-africa/rwanda/Rwandan%20 Hutu%20Rebels%20in%20the%20Congo%20a%20New%20Approach%20to%20Disarmament%20and%20Reintegration.pdf>

—. 2009. *Congo: Une stratégie globale pour désarmer les FDLR*. Rapport Afrique No. 151. Nairobi and Brussels: ICG. 9 July. <http://www.crisisgroup.org/~/media/Files/africa/central-africa/dr-congo/151%20Congo%20-%20A%20Comprehensive%20Strategy%20to%20 Disarm%20the%20FDLR%20-%20ENGLISH.pdf>

—. 2014. *Congo: Ending the Status Quo*. Africa Briefing No. 107. 17 December.

Jeune Afrique. 2013. 'Rwanda: trois membres présumés des FDLR jugés en Allemagne.' 11 June. <http://www.jeuneafrique.com/Article/ARTJAWEB20130611172211/>

Karuhanga, James. 2014. 'Rwanda: German Court Convicts Three over FDLR Links.' AllAfrica. 6 December. <http://allafrica.com/stories/201412080197.html>

McQuinn, Brian. 2012. *After the Fall: Libya's Evolving Armed Groups*. Working Paper 16. Geneva: Small Arms Survey. October.

Omaar, Rakiya. 2008. *The Leadership of Rwandan Armed Groups abroad with a Focus on the FDLR and RUD/Urunana*. Report commissioned by the Rwanda Demobilization and Reintegration Commission. December. <http://musabyimana.be/uploads/media/Report_for_the_RDRC_on_the_Leadership_of_Rwandese_ArmedGroups_in_the_DRC_1_.pdf>

—. 2012. *Updates on the Leadership of Rwandan Armed Groups Operating in the DRC: The FDLR and RUD-Urunana*. Report commissioned by the Rwanda Demobilization and Reintegration Commission. 27 March. <http://demobrwanda.org.rw/fileadmin/templates/publication/Updates_on_Leadership_of_Rwandan_Armed_Groups_1_.pdf>

Pole Institute. 2010. *Guerillas in the Mist: The Congolese Experience of the FDLR War in Eastern Congo and the Role of the International Community*. Goma: Pole Institute.

Prunier, Gérard. 2009. *Africa's World Wars: Congo, the Rwandan Genocide, and the Making of a Continental Catastrophe*. Oxford: Oxford University Press.

Radio Okapi. 2014. 'RDC: les FDLR refusent de rejoindre le camp de transit de Kisangani.' 13 August.
    <http://radiookapi.net/actualite/2014/08/13/rdc-les-fdlr-refusent-de-rejoindre-le-camp-de-transit-de-kisangani/>

RFI (Radio France Internationale). 2014. 'RDC: les FDLR promettent de poursuivre le processus de désarmement.' 23 November.
    <http://www.rfi.fr/afrique/20141123-rdc-fdlr-promettent-poursuivre-le-processus-desarmement/>

Richards, Joanne. 2013. *Demobilization in the DRC: Armed Groups and the Role of Organizational Control*. Armed Actors Issue Brief 1. Geneva: Small Arms Survey. April.

Rodríguez, María Paz Ortega. 2011. 'The FDLR as an Obstacle to Peace in the DRC.' *Peace Review: A Journal of Social Justice*. Vol. 23, Iss. 2, pp. 176–82.

Romkema, Hans. 2007. *Opportunités et contraintes relatives au désarmement et au rapatriement des groupes armés étrangers en RD Congo: Cas des FDLR, FNL et ADF/NALU*. Washington, DC: World Bank. June. <http://www.mdrp.org/PDFs/MDRP_DRC_COFS_Study_fn.pdf>

Schroeder, Matt. 2013. *Ad Hoc Arsenals: PSSM Practices of Selected Non-state Actors*. Armed Actors Issue Brief 2. Geneva: Small Arms Survey. May.

Schlindwein, Simone and Dominic Johnson. 2014. 'Endgame or Bluff? The UN's Dilemma with the FDLR Militia in DRC.' Briefing Paper. 15 August.
    <http://blogs.taz.de/kongo-echo/files/2014/08/2014-Endgame-or-bluff-UNs-dilemma-with-the-FDLR-in-DRC_Schlindwein-Johnson.pdf>

SSRC (Social Science Research Council). 2014. *FDLR: Past, Present, and Policies*. Report prepared on behalf of the DRC Affinity Group. March.
    <https://s3.amazonaws.com/ssrc-cdn1/crmuploads/new_publication_3/%7BCD664AA5-24B4-E311-93FD-005056AB3675%7D.pdf>

Staniland, Paul Stephen. 2010. *Explaining Cohesion, Fragmentation, and Control in Insurgent Groups*. Ph.D. thesis, Massachusetts Institute of Technology. September.

Stearns, Jason. 2012. 'The FDLR Suffer Another Blow and Launch Reprisals.' Congo Siasa Blog. 14 January.
    <http://congosiasa.blogspot.ch/2012/01/fdlr-suffer-another-blow-and-launch.html>

Survie. 1996. *Zaïre–Rwanda: les parties en conflit*. Billet d'Afrique No. 40. Paris: Survie. November.
    <http://survie.org/IMG/pdf/BDAF040_Novembre1996.pdf>

UNDPKO (United Nations Department of Peacekeeping Operations). 1994. *Background Paper for U.S. Mission, United Nations: Former Rwandan Army (Ex-FAR) Capabilities and Intentions*. UNRES-4125/J2m-2 of 1 September.
    <http://www.francerwandagenocide.org/documents/DpkoSpecialReportRwanda1septembre1994.pdf>

UNGA (United Nations General Assembly). 2010. *Second Joint Report of Seven United Nations Experts on the Situation in the Democratic Republic of the Congo*. A/HRC/13/63 of 8 March.

—. 2014. *Children and Armed Conflict: Report of the Secretary-General*. A/68/878 of 15 May.

UNSC (United Nations Security Council). 1999. *Report of the Independent Inquiry into the Actions of the United Nations during the 1994 Genocide in Rwanda*. S/1999/1257 of 16 December. <http://daccess-dds-ny.un.org/doc/UNDOC/GEN/N99/395/47/IMG/N9939547.pdf?OpenElement>

—. 2005. 'Security Council Committee Issues List of Individuals and Entities Subject to Measures Imposed by Resolution 1596 (2005).' Press Release SC/8546. 1 November. <http://www.un.org/press/en/2005/sc8546.doc.htm>

—. 2008. *Final Report of the Group of Experts on the Democratic Republic of the Congo*. S/2008/773 of 12 December.
    <http://www.un.org/ga/search/view_doc.asp?symbol=S/2008/773>

—. 2009. *Final Report of the Group of Experts on the Democratic Republic of the Congo*. S/2009/603 of 23 November.
    <http://www.un.org/sc/committees/1533/egroup.shtml>

—. 2013. *Midterm Report of the Group of Experts on the Democratic Republic of the Congo*. S/2013/433 of 19 July.
    <http://www.un.org/sc/committees/1533/egroup.shtml>

—. 2014a. *Final Report of the Group of Experts on the Democratic Republic of the Congo*. S/2014/42 of 23 January.
    <http://www.un.org/sc/committees/1533/egroup.shtml>

—. 2014b. *Midterm Report of the Group of Experts Submitted in Accordance with Paragraph 5 of Security Council Resolution 2136 (2014)*. S/2014/428 of 25 June. <http://www.un.org/sc/committees/1533/egroup.shtml>

—. 2014c. 'The List Established and Maintained by the 1533 (2004) Committee.' Updated on 30 June.
    <http://www.un.org/sc/committees/1533/pdf/1533.pdf>

—. 2014d. Resolution 2147. S/RES/2147 of 28 March.

UNSG (United Nations Secretary-General). 1998. *Final Report of the International Commission of Inquiry (Rwanda)*. S/1998/1096 of 18 November.
    <http://www.un.org/en/sc/documents/letters/1998.shtml>

Vines, Alex. 2003. 'Monitoring UN Sanctions in Africa: The Role of Panels of Experts.' In Trevor Findlay and Kenneth Boutin, eds. *Verification Yearbook 2003*. London: Vertic.

Vogel, Christoph. 2013. 'The FDLR: A Never Ending Curse in Eastern Congo?' Blog. 11 June.
    <http://christophvogel.net/2013/06/11/the-fdlr-a-never-ending-curse-in-eastern-congo/>

—. 2014a. 'The FDLR Demobilization Gamble Reloaded.' Blog. 10 June.
    <http://christophvogel.net/2014/06/10/the-fdlr-demobilisation-gamble-reloaded/>

—. 2014b. 'Mapping Armed Groups in Eastern Congo.' Map. <http://christophvogel.net/mapping>

—. 2015. 'Why Was UN Sidelined in "Joint" DRC Operation against Rebels?–Analysis.' 26 February.
    <http://www.irinnews.org/report/101164/why-was-the-un-sidelined-in-joint-drc-operation-against-rebels>

Waldorf, Lars. 2009. *Transitional Justice and DDR: The Case of Rwanda*. New York: International Center for Transitional Justice. June.
    <http://www.ictj.org/sites/default/files/ICTJ-DDR-Rwanda-CaseStudy-2009-English.pdf>

Wood, Elisabeth. 2012. 'Rape during War Is not Inevitable: Variation in Wartime Sexual Violence.' In Morten Bergsmo, Alf Butenschøn Skre, and Elisabeth Wood, eds. *Understanding and Proving International Sex Crimes*. Forum for International Criminal and Humanitarian Law Publication Series No. 12. Beijing: Torkel Opsahl Academic EPublisher, pp. 389–420. <http://www.fichl.org/fileadmin/fichl/documents/FICHL_12_Web.pdf>

World Bank. 2009. *Disarmament, Demobilization and Reintegration*. Washington, DC: World Bank. February.
    <http://siteresources.worldbank.org/EXTSOCIALDEVELOPMENT/Resources/244362-1164107274725/DDRFinal3-print.pdf>

ACKNOWLEDGEMENTS

Principal authors

Raymond Debelle and Nicolas Florquin

Contributor

Marie Plamadiala (Conflict Armament Research)

Storage of weapons on board a floating armoury off Fujairah,
United Arab Emirates, 2014. © Anonymous

Stockpiles at Sea

FLOATING ARMOURIES IN THE INDIAN OCEAN

8

INTRODUCTION

Somali piracy has attracted considerable attention in recent years, including that of UN Secretary-General Ban-Ki Moon and British film director Paul Greengrass, whose *Captain Phillips* was inspired by an actual pirate hijacking of a US-registered vessel in the Indian Ocean in 2009 (UNSC, 2013, p. 4; *Captain Phillips*, 2013). Although the frequency of piracy attacks off the coast of Somalia began to decline in 2013, when Greengrass's film hit the cinemas, the shipping industry's demand for anti-piracy measures has remained high. Indeed, private armed guards were on board on roughly 35–40 per cent of the estimated 65,922 merchant vessels transiting across the Indian Ocean's 'high-risk area' (HRA) in 2013 (OBP, 2014, p. 18; see Box 8.1).

One of the major challenges for the armed guards on vessels in the HRA is moving arms and ammunition between coastal states that prohibit or have restrictions on vessels with arms on board. To overcome this challenge, many maritime private security companies (PSCs) have turned to floating armouries for the storage of arms and, in some cases, the accommodation of guards. Oceans Beyond Piracy estimates that one-quarter of HRA transit journeys with armed guards in January 2013 involved the use of a floating armoury for embarkation or disembarkation of personnel, arms, and equipment, and that the rate increased to more than one-third by September 2013 (OBP, 2014, p. 48).

The sudden appearance of ships full of weapons 'beyond the remit of any effective international regulatory authority' has sparked concerns among countries located around the HRA and among other international stakeholders (UNSC, 2012, para. 73; 2013, para. 9). In particular, it has been noted that there are no established standards for the storage of arms and ammunition on the floating armouries, a situation that could be exploited by 'unscrupulous and criminal actors', transforming the armouries from a maritime security solution into a 'threat to regional peace and security' (UNSC, 2012, para. 74; annexe 5.4, paras. 10, 15).

In an effort to bridge the knowledge gap on floating armouries, this chapter presents original research on maritime PSCs and other key stakeholders carried out during May–September 2014. Its key findings include the following:

- The number of registered maritime PSCs rose from 56 in 2010, the year the International Code of Conduct for Private Security Providers was officially established, to more than 400 in 2014, with the companies based in 65 countries.
- Floating armouries are lucrative businesses that have responded to diverse, often contradictory, legislative and administrative measures relating to the carriage of armed guards into territorial waters and ports.
- While there is no publicly available registry of floating armouries, this research indicates around 30 such vessels were operating in the HRA during 2014. Storage capacities vary, but some floating armouries can hold approximately 1,000 firearms, as well as ammunition.
- There are no international standards for floating armoury security or storage and armoury practices vary significantly. There is concern that new market entrants will seek to undercut existing operations by cutting costs and neglecting armoury security.

- Official government statements stress that no arms have been diverted from maritime PSCs or authorized floating armouries, but anecdotal evidence provided by maritime PSCs utilizing floating armouries reveals practices—such as transferring arms and ammunition from one maritime PSC to another—that violate the terms of arms export licensing provisions.
- While oversight is provided by some governments that authorize the supply of small arms to maritime PSCs (such as Germany and the UK) and by several flag states for vessels operating as floating armouries (such as Mongolia and Saint Kitts and Nevis), key stakeholders have not agreed common minimum standards for the safety and security of floating armouries that operate in international waters.

The chapter begins by presenting recent information on piracy off the eastern coast of Africa, along with the rationale for floating armouries, as provided by their supporters. It then examines the types of vessels, flag states, and maritime PSC services associated with floating armouries, reviews estimates of maritime PSC arms in the HRA, and considers some of the main security and safety concerns. This section includes a profile of the Sri Lankan government's approach to floating armouries. The chapter then outlines the nascent—and potential—approaches to regulating floating armouries to ensure safe and secure practices. The conclusion reflects on possible means of strengthening oversight of floating armouries and alternative measures for handling maritime PSC arms in the HRA. The chapter also reviews the potential for the use of floating armouries in other parts of the world.

ADDRESSING MARITIME INSECURITY: THE PSC SOLUTION

Piracy has been hampering international shipping off the eastern coast of Africa for almost a decade (see Box 8.1). The *Small Arms Survey 2012* reviews the root causes of Somali piracy, as well as the Somali pirate groups' 'business model', which involved the hijacking of merchant vessels, with ransom demands tied to the release of vessels and crews (Florquin, 2012). Figure 8.1 shows that the period 2009–11 witnessed a high point in piracy attacks on vessels,

Figure 8.1 **Pirate event statistics, as of September 2014**

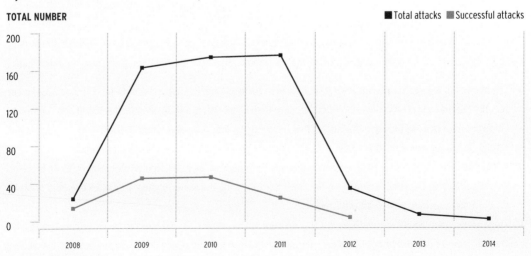

Source: EUNAVFOR-Somalia (2014)

followed by a dramatic decline in 2012. According to data available at the time of writing, there had not been a successful pirate attack since 2012. The decline in total attacks, and in successful attacks, correlates with the deployment of private armed guards on board vessels that are transiting the HRA and the increased presence of international naval forces in the region (OBP, 2014, p. 7). Moreover, there has not yet been a successful attack on a commercial vessel with an armed maritime PSC team on board in the HRA (OBP, 2014, p. 4).

Maritime PSCs have justified the use of private armed guards on board commercial vessels by highlighting this correlation (OBP, 2014, p. 44). At the same time, they argue that in view of the ongoing risk of a pirate or terrorist attack, the use of private armed guards on commercial vessels remains necessary. This section does not interrogate this causal argument. Rather, it outlines some of the main reasons offered for the existence of floating armouries in the HRA as well as their links to the increased number of maritime PSCs operating in the HRA. The private security industry is currently using similar arguments to promote the use of floating armouries in other parts of the world, most notably in the Gulf of Guinea, where piracy represents a major maritime security challenge (see Box 8.4).

According to the United Nations Convention on the Law of the Sea (UNCLOS), the sovereignty of coastal states extends into territorial waters (UN, 1958, art. 2; see Box 8.1). Therefore, coastal states' legislation determines whether, or under what conditions, commercial vessels are permitted to enter territorial waters with arms on board. UNCLOS makes no special provision for vessels carrying arms in international waters and thus the responsibility for and jurisdiction over these ships lies exclusively with the vessel's flag state. At the time of writing, however, no flag state had legislation governing the operation of floating armouries, such that their activities tend to be treated as legal grey areas.

The International Maritime Organization (IMO) has issued recommendations and guidance that address the issue of commercial vessels carrying private armed guards and arms in international and territorial waters (IMO, 2009a; 2009b; 2011; 2012). These call on private armed guards to ensure that the carriage and use of their weapons and equipment is in compliance with the legislation and policies of the vessel's flag state and of the countries with jurisdiction over the territorial waters and ports that the vessel is to enter (IMO, 2009a, para. 59; 2009b, para. 7).

Box 8.1 **Key definitions**

Floating armoury: A ship that is located in international waters and that provides services for maritime PSCs, in particular the storage of arms, ammunition, and other equipment belonging to private armed guards operating on board commercial vessels. Floating armouries are often referred to as logistical support vessels for anti-piracy operations.

High-risk area (HRA): The HRA boundaries are currently defined in the fourth version of the *Best Management Practices for Protection against Somalia Based Piracy* (UKMTO et al., 2011). Bounded by Port Suez and the Strait of Hormuz to the north, the HRA includes the Arabian Sea, the Gulf of Aden, and the Red Sea; it extends east to the Indian Ocean, up to the western coast of India, and southward into the Mozambique Channel (UKMTO et al., 2011, p. 4; see Map 8.1).

Maritime private security companies (PSCs): Private contractors employed to provide security personnel, both armed and unarmed, on board commercial vessels for protection against piracy.

Piracy: 'Any illegal acts of violence or detention, or any act of depredation, committed for private ends by the crew or the passengers of a private ship or a private aircraft, and directed:

(i) on the high seas, against another ship or aircraft, or against persons or property on board such ship or aircraft;

(ii) against a ship, aircraft, persons or property in a place outside the jurisdiction of any State' (UN, 1958, art. 101).

Territorial waters (or territorial seas): 'The sovereignty of a coastal State extends, beyond its land territory and internal waters and, in the case of an archipelagic State, its archipelagic waters, to an adjacent belt of sea, described as the territorial sea. [. . .] Every State has the right to establish the breadth of its territorial sea up to a limit not exceeding 12 nautical miles, measured from baselines determined in accordance with [the United Nations Convention on the Law of the Sea]' (UN, 1958, arts. 2.1, 3).

In 2011 the IMO issued recommendations calling on the coastal states bordering the Arabian Sea, Gulf of Aden, Indian Ocean, and Red Sea to establish policies and procedures that 'should facilitate the movement of [private armed guards] and of their firearms and security-related equipment and be made known to the shipping industry and to the [private armed security] service providers [. . .] and all [IMO] Member Governments' (IMO, 2011, para. 5). The IMO also provides good practice guidelines for ship owners, companies, ship operators, shipmasters, crews, and maritime PSCs regarding the carriage of private armed guards and arms (IMO, 2012, para. 5.12). Despite these various recommendations and guidelines, there are no common standards or practices agreed among flag states and coastal states regarding the carriage, embarkation, disembarkation, or storage of maritime PSC arms.

National laws and regulations relating to (a) arms exports and imports; (b) customs; and (c) the activities of private security companies in general can be utilized to regulate the carriage of private armed guards and their arms and ammunition in territorial waters and ports (Petrig, 2013, p. 675). The following list provides several examples of the different practices utilized by HRA coastal states:

There are no common standards or practices agreed among flag states and coastal states.

- All private armed guards and foreign-owned firearms are prohibited from entering territorial waters or ports, even temporarily, due to applicable national legislation (such as that of the United Arab Emirates, or UAE) or UN arms embargoes (such as those concerning Eritrea and Somalia) (UNSC, 2012, annexe 5.4, para. 9).
- The entry of private armed guards and foreign-owned firearms into territorial waters or ports is to be announced in advance of entry and the firearms are to be bonded and sealed on board any vessel for the duration of its time in territorial waters or ports (as stipulated by Saudi Arabian law) (McMahon, 2013a; Petrig, 2013, p. 685).
- The entry of private armed guards and foreign-owned firearms into territorial waters or ports is to be announced in advance of entry and the firearms disembarked from the vessel and stored under the supervision of national police or security forces for a fee (as in Kenya, Mauritius, and Oman) (McMahon, 2013a; Petrig, 2013, p. 685).

In addition, some states restrict the entrance into their territorial waters and ports to certain types of arms. For example, Oman only permits the carriage of semi-automatic firearms into its territorial waters and charges a fee for the storage of such firearms in a government-owned land-based armoury (Florquin, 2012, p. 209; Petrig, 2013, p. 685). Several Middle Eastern states have reportedly become particularly sensitive towards the storage of maritime PSC arms in land-based armouries as a result of internal instability following the 'Arab Spring' (AP, 2012). Although states that allow such storage earn revenue from it, the growing number of maritime PSCs transiting the HRA and their around-the-clock demands have put a strain on their land-based armouries. For these reasons, it has been argued that one of the biggest challenges for maritime PSCs today is 'a logistical one relating to the storage of controlled goods' (UKHC, 2014a, para. 372).

In the face of regulatory hurdles, including prohibitions on the entry of arms, and the often high cost of purchasing permits and paying for storage in government-owned land-based armouries, maritime PSCs have reportedly resorted to one of two options with regard to their arms. In the first case, a PSC buys weapons from states where purchasing firearms is relatively easy and dumps them overboard before entering territorial waters at the end of a particular operation (UNSC, 2012, annexe 5.4, para. 5).[1] In the second, increasingly popular, case, PSCs use floating armouries. Maritime PSCs that support the second option argue that floating armouries:[2]

- enable them to be armed in international waters, where they need to be, and keep arms out of ports, where they are not wanted;

- help them to avoid the problems of contending with a diverse range of national regulations;

- are less bureaucratic, easier to use, and cheaper than land-based armouries operated by governments; and

- are often more secure than a land-based armoury, where, depending on the country, physical security and stockpile management standards may be lax and weapons can go missing, posing a threat to fragile and conflict-affected states.

WHAT IS A FLOATING ARMOURY?

Floating armouries are owned and run by businesses that are usually connected to the private security industry. At present, governments in and around the HRA are not known to own or operate any floating armouries. All government-owned armouries that service the private security industry are land-based (such as in Djibouti).[3] Even the Galle floating armoury—which Sri Lanka authorizes, largely controls, and provides with access to a naval base—is actually run by a private company (see Box 8.3). Floating armouries are, in essence, commercial ventures, deriving their revenues from the services they offer maritime PSCs that operate in the HRA.

One of the main reasons behind concerns over the use of floating armouries in the HRA relates to the lack of information regarding their number, their use, the number of arms they store, and related physical security and stockpile management practices. At the time of writing, it was not possible to estimate with any certainty how many floating armouries were operating in the HRA. In 2012 and 2013, various sources placed the number anywhere between 10 and 20.[4] Research conducted for this chapter has identified some 30 vessels that serve as floating armouries or provide support for floating armouries in the HRA (see Map 8.1 and Table 8.1). Plans are also under way for the deployment of new floating armouries in the region.[5]

The market has remained dynamic, with private armed guards conducting an estimated 23,072–26,368 transit journeys in the HRA in 2013 (OBP, 2014, p. 18). Sovereign Global, a company that maintains a floating armoury in the Gulf of Oman and another in the Red Sea, reported in early 2014 that more than 1,000 private armed guards were transiting through the company's two floating armouries

Box 8.2 Research methodology

This chapter is based on two types of research carried out during May–September 2014. First, the authors undertook a thorough review of available open-source literature on floating armouries, including official documents and materials published by relevant states and international organizations, academic research centres, the media, and private maritime security industry associations. This review highlighted a paucity of material on floating armouries in general and on their development and operation in particular.

Second, semi-structured key informant interviews were conducted with maritime PSCs to fill this gap and to obtain the 'user's perspective' on floating armouries. The authors secured interviews with operations managers and managing directors of well-established maritime PSCs based in Greece, Sri Lanka, the UK, and the United Arab Emirates. The interviewees had been employed in the field for many years and had experience working on vessels as team leaders or making arrangements in relation to the use of floating armouries. In addition, the authors interviewed the managing director of a prominent floating armoury and an arms broker. The authors also corresponded with the Saint Kitts and Nevis registry and British and German licensing authorities. All interviewees provided informed, often candid, personal opinions on floating armouries, but they requested anonymity.

Due to the limited availability of open-source material on floating armouries, this chapter relies on information provided by a relatively small number of key informants. Yet it should be noted that different interviewees often provided the same information on the operation of floating armouries or presented similar options for strengthening standards and oversight. All of the chapter's main conclusions on the operation of floating armouries and options for strengthened standards and oversight are derived from two or more interviews. While the chapter provides new insight into an understudied topic, it also suggests areas for further study and analysis in this dynamic, fast-moving sector.

on a monthly basis (Sovereign Global, 2014). Avant Garde Maritime Services (AGMS), which runs the Sri Lankan floating armoury that enjoys a monopoly around the island country, reported '800–1,000 movements on and off' its floating armoury each month (Rickett, 2013). The following sections describe the types of vessels that were operating as floating armouries in 2014 and the services they were providing.

Map 8.1 **Floating armouries and the high-risk area, 2014**

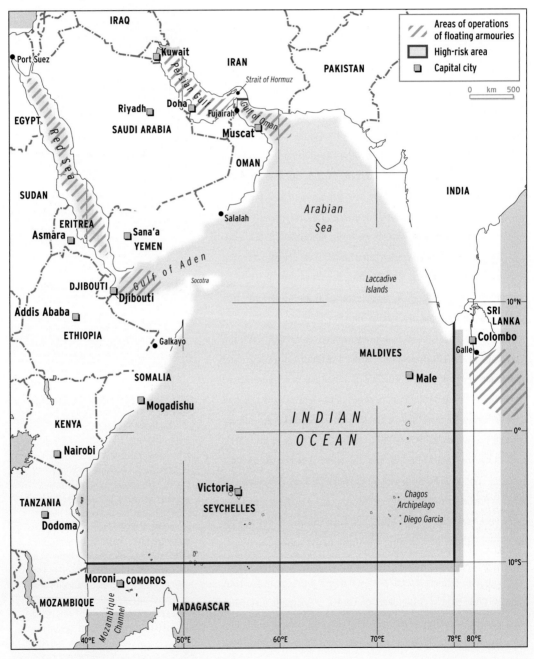

Table 8.1 List of known floating armouries and associated vessels, 2014

Ship name	IMO ship identification number	Flag state	Registered vessel type	Area
Abdallah	8112823	UAE	Supply tender	Gulf of Oman
Alladin	6524230	Djibouti	Research/survey vessel	Gulf of Oman
Al Nader	7027502	UAE	Supply ship	Gulf of Oman
Anchor 1	8965593	Cook Islands	Utility vessel	Red Sea
Antarctic Dream	5278432	Mongolia	Passenger ship	Gulf of Oman
Arina Dilber	8107713	Panama	Anchor handling vessel	Gulf of Oman
Avant Garde	n/a	New Zealand	Pleasure craft	Red Sea
Avant Garde	8107036	Sri Lanka	Supply ship	Red Sea
Deena	7313432	UAE	Supply ship	Gulf of Oman
Defiant	5427784	Panama	Pilot ship	Gulf of Oman
Deo Juvante	8701105	Cook Islands	Trawler	n/a
Dynamic Karim	8129084	Panama	Offshore supply ship	Gulf of Oman
Elishka	7406215	Liberia	Pipe carrier	Gulf of Oman
Express Opportune	9606194	Panama	Passenger	Persian Gulf
Home	8131386	Panama	Research vessel	Gulf of Oman
LG251	n/a	UK	n/a	Gulf of Oman
Maagen	n/a	Cook Islands	Pleasure craft	n/a
Mahanuwara	7412018	Mongolia and Sri Lanka	Anchor handling vessel	Sri Lanka
Milad	7624635	Comoros	Offshore supply ship	Gulf of Oman
MNG Resolution	8413174	Saint Kitts and Nevis	Supply ship	Gulf of Oman
Muru	n/a	Djibouti	Cargo ship	Gulf of Oman
Navis Star	7353432	Panama	Anchor handling vessel	Red Sea
Northern Queen	7709253	Tuvalu	Research vessel	Gulf of Oman
Samaritan	8206105	Mongolia	Utility vessel	Gulf of Oman
Samriyah	7911777	Mongolia	Offshore supply ship	Gulf of Oman
Sea Lion	7115567	Sierra Leone	Fishing vessel	Gulf of Oman
Sea Lion S	9050101	Panama	General cargo ship	Gulf of Oman
Sea Patrol	4908729	Saint Kitts and Nevis	Other cargo	Gulf of Oman
Seaman Guard Ohio	8410691	Sierra Leone	Patrol vessel	Gulf of Oman
Seapol One	8912572	Mongolia	Research vessel	Gulf of Oman
Selat Faith	8333283	UAE	Diving support vessel	Gulf of Oman
Selat Pisces	8301216	UAE	Offshore supply ship	Gulf of Oman
Sinbad	7932006	Sri Lanka	Fishery patrol vessel	Gulf of Oman
Soha Folk	8003175	UAE	Offshore supply ship	Gulf of Oman
Star Global	7319242	Palau	Offshore supply ship	Gulf of Oman
Sultan	7636339	Mongolia	Research/survey vessel	Red Sea
Suunta	7392854	Djibouti	Research vessel	Djibouti
Theresa	8333506	Mongolia	Tug	Gulf of Oman

Sources: MarineTraffic (n.d.); MIRIS International (n.d.); Moran Security Group (2013); Sovereign Global (2014); UK (2014a, pp. 54-55); VesselFinder (n.d.); author interviews with maritime PSCs, 20-22 May 2014

Types of vessels used as floating armouries

All ocean-going vessels must be certified as belonging to a particular category of vessel and must be maintained in line with minimum standards for this vessel type, to demonstrate safety and suitability for particular roles. Classification societies determine the main characteristics of each type of vessel, setting standards for their construction and maintenance. Every ocean-going vessel is then classified in accordance with these standards and its details are entered into a national registry. At present, classification societies have not designated any vessel as a 'floating armoury', nor have any flag states registered vessels as such. Although most floating armouries are converted tugs, a variety of other vessel types are also in operation, thus precluding the development of a specific typology. In 2014, that variety included offshore supply ships, patrol vessels, diving support vessels, anchor handling vessels, research or survey vessels, pleasure craft, trawlers, and general cargo ships (see Table 8.1 on previous page).

Complicating matters, some maritime PSCs operate armed escort vessels that could be misidentified as floating armouries. Moreover, changes in ship names, flag states, registered vessel types, and owners are frequent, although the constant IMO ship identification number—consisting of the letters IMO followed by a unique seven-digit number— can help to overcome related identification challenges. In 2013, for example, the Bahrain-flagged *Hadi XII* (IMO 8107713) was renamed *Arina Dilber* and reflagged to Panama, while in 2014 the 'supply ship' MV *Sea Lion* (IMO 7115567) reflagged from Panama to Sierra Leone, with the result that it was reregistered as a 'fishing vessel'.

Services provided by floating armouries

This section provides information on the services provided by floating armouries operating in the HRA, including the embarkation and disembarkation of PSC personnel, arms, and equipment between a commercial vessel or port and the floating armoury; storage, service, and maintenance, or rental of arms; and the provision of accommodation for private armed guard teams. Table 8.2 presents average prices in 2014 for the services provided by floating armouries in the HRA, based on interviews with several maritime PSCs.

Embarkation and disembarkation of maritime PSC personnel, arms, and equipment

Currently, there are no standardized practices for the embarkation or disembarkation of maritime PSC personnel or arms. Different floating armouries have a variety of procedures in place. One such procedure, which is utilized by well-established floating armouries for disembarkation, was characterized by several maritime PSC interviewees as an efficient, safe, and secure approach. It usually involves the signing of a contract by the PSC and the floating armoury before private armed guards, arms, ammunition, and equipment can be transferred from a commercial vessel to the floating armoury. As part of this process, the company that operates the floating armoury normally provides the maritime PSC with the following information and documentation: flag state approval, registry of shipping classification

Table 8.2	**Average prices for services provided by floating armouries, 2014**				
Offered service	Dis- and embarkation of arms and equipment and their storage	Dis- and embarkation of private armed guards	Visa arrangements	Arms service	Accommodation
Average price	USD 3,000-4,000	USD 500 per person	USD 50 per person	USD 100 per piece	USD 25-50 per person per day

Sources: Blue Palm Charters (n.d.); author interviews with maritime PSCs, 20–22 May 2014

status, pictures of the vessel, and details of the floating armoury's safety, security, and storage procedures for arms, ammunition, and equipment. In turn, the maritime PSC provides its registration details; documentary evidence that it is a well-established company that complies with relevant regulations and guidelines;[6] and arms export licences and end-user certificates for the arms, ammunition, and any controlled items being transferred to the floating armoury. If private armed guards are to be transferred to the floating armoury, it provides passports, seaman's discharge books, standards of training, certification, and watchkeeping endorsements, and other requested documentation.[7]

The actual process of disembarkation takes place when a commercial vessel carrying private armed guards reaches a pre-arranged point, where it is met by a launch that collects the private armed guards, arms, ammunition, and equipment for transfer to the floating armoury. During this process, the floating armoury requires the maritime PSC's team leader to ensure that the 'transfer application form', which contains information on the arms, ammunition, and equipment to be stored on board the floating armoury, is accurate (AGMS, n.d.c). Both the leader of the maritime PSC's team of armed guards and the floating armoury keep a copy of the 'Transfer Request Form'.

If the maritime PSC does not have another transit arranged shortly after the disembarkation or is reluctant to lodge the team on the floating armoury, the team is either transferred to accommodation ashore or transported to the local airport to fly back home. In such cases, the floating armoury can provide additional services, such as assisting with visa arrangements. In some cases the team disembarks only weapons and equipment onto the floating armoury. Other maritime PSC personnel on the same route collect the materiel, and the team stays with the commercial vessel and disembarks at the next port of call.[8]

Arms: storage, service, or rental

The primary service of a floating armoury is to store arms, ammunition, and equipment for maritime PSCs operating in international waters. As noted in Table 8.2, storage is usually included in the fee charged for disembarkation, although additional fees are incurred if the arms are kept on the floating armoury for a significant period of time. For example, maritime PSCs are charged a fee for storage on the MV *Sea Lion* after 90 days have passed (Blue Palm Charters, n.d.).

Since different types of vessels serve as floating armouries, their capacities vary (see Photo 8.2). The MV *Sea Patrol*, which is operated by MNG Maritime off the coast of Fujairah (UAE), can store up to 400 weapons, including semi-automatic and automatic assault weapons and rifles, bolt action rifles, semi-automatic pistols and shotguns, as well as ammunition and optics for these arms

A converted tug operating as a floating armoury. © Anonymous

(MV *Sea Patrol*, 2014). AGMS vessels have greater capacity, with the MV *Sinbad* located off the coast of the UAE reportedly able to hold up to 1,000 arms (AGMS, n.d.b; Shauketaly, 2012; see Box 8.3).

In addition to storing weapons, one well-established floating armoury carries a qualified armourer who services and repairs the arms stored on board, and issues the required certificates.[9] This service provision responds to clauses 4.2.5 and 4.6.2 of the ISO/PAS 28007 standard for maritime PSCs, which requires them to service and maintain their weapons regularly and keep records and certificates (ISO, 2013). As listed in Table 8.2, a fee of USD 100 is charged per weapon.

A typical rental package for a four-person team of private armed guards from AGMS floating armouries off the coasts of Mauritius, Muscat, and Sri Lanka consists of: 4 semi-automatic AK-47 84S rifles or fully automatic Chinese T-56 assault rifles and 480 rounds of 7.62 mm ammunition for 16 rifle magazines (AGMS, n.d.a; Florquin, 2012, pp. 210–11). Supplementary arms or ammunition can reportedly be rented at an additional cost (UNSC, 2012, annexe 5.4, para. 6). The arms are owned by the Sri Lankan government and accompanied not only by an end-user certificate issued by the Sri Lankan Ministry of Defence, but also by a sea marshal who is employed by the Sri Lankan government-owned company Rakna Arakshaka Lanka to safeguard the weapons and ensure their proper use. The weapons have to be returned to one of nine locations belonging to what AGMS refers to as its 'closed circuit network', accompanied by the sea marshal (AGMS, n.d.a).[10]

Box 8.3   MV Mahanuwara: Sri Lanka's monopoly floating armoury model

AGMS operates the MV *Mahanuwara*, a Mongolian- and Sri Lankan-registered anchor handling vessel, which is the only floating armoury authorized by the Sri Lankan government to operate in its territorial waters (AGMS, n.d.b). It can also operate in international waters, like the other floating armouries in and around the HRA, but tends to remain close to the Sri Lankan port of Galle. The Sri Lankan government has also granted AGMS permission for the floating armoury to be moored next to the Galle naval base, whenever necessary–for example, in order to avoid rough seas or replenish stocks (see Photo 8.3). This advantage is not enjoyed by floating armouries elsewhere in the HRA and is clearly linked to the fact that, to a great extent, the Sri Lankan government controls the floating armoury.

The MV *Mahanuwara* can store up to 1,000 weapons and associated ammunition in 'air-conditioned TEU containers with custom made racks for storage of weapons' (AGMS, n.d.b). Ammunition is usually stored separately from arms (AGMS, n.d.a). Night vision devices are also kept on board. All other maritime PSC equipment is stored on land in the Sri Lankan naval base's warehouses in Galle. The MV *Mahanuwara* operates strictly as a 'floating armoury' and does not provide accommodation for private armed guards. However, as the authors witnessed while conducting this research, many maritime PSCs using the MV *Mahanuwara* provide accommodation for their teams in Galle, which has transformed the town into a private maritime security hub.

One of the justifications provided for the monopoly model is the ongoing need for strict control and monitoring of arms in and around Sri Lanka following the recent civil war.[11] However, the fact that the Sri Lankan Ministry of Defence is willing to rent its arms to maritime PSCs suggests an economic motivation for the monopoly. While the MV *Mahanuwara* can resupply in the port of Galle and thus has lower operating costs than floating armouries in the Gulf of Oman, there are concerns that its monopoly status is leading to overcharging.[12] Moreover, several maritime PSCs have reportedly been told to use AGMS floating armouries in the Gulf of Oman and Red Sea if they want to use the MV *Mahanuwara*.[13]

8.3

The MV Mahanuwara alongside the naval base in Galle, Sri Lanka, 2014. © Ioannis Chapsos

Accommodation for armed guards

For an additional fee, many of the floating armouries referenced in Table 8.1 provide on-board meals and accommodation for private armed guards awaiting their next transit. Some floating armouries provide free meals and accommodation for private armed guards if their PSC has utilized the floating armoury for a specified number of transfers during a given month.[14]

ARMS CIRCULATING IN THE HIGH-RISK AREA

Due to limited transparency, questions persist regarding the control of arms supplies to maritime PSCs operating in the HRA, as well as the total number of arms that they use and store in floating armouries in the region. This section reviews some of the information that became available during 2013–14.

Few countries provide information regarding small arms transfers to maritime PSCs.

The UN Monitoring Group on Somalia and Eritrea reported in 2012 that maritime PSCs operating in the HRA held around 7,000 weapons, of which 90 per cent were semi-automatic rifles (UNSC, 2012, annexe 5.4, para. 4). James Brown of the Lowy Institute for International Policy estimated that there were 140 companies with at least 2,700 armed guards present on vessels transiting the Indian Ocean in 2011 (Brown, 2012, pp. 5–6). Since each of these guards is authorized to possess up to four small arms, the total number of PSC firearms may hover around 10,000. As of 2014, more than 400 maritime PSCs were signatories to the International Code of Conduct for Private Security Providers, a prerequisite for most shipping companies contracting PSC personnel (Chapsos, 2014, pp. 195–202; ICoC, 2010; UK, 2014d, p. 30). Since 2012, however, the average size of armed teams on board commercial vessels appears to be shrinking—from 4–6 to 1–3-member guard teams (OBP, 2014, pp. 16–17). It therefore remains difficult to arrive at an accurate estimate of the number of arms in the possession of maritime PSCs operating in the HRA.

Companies that supply or broker arms, ammunition, and other equipment for maritime PSCs are based in countries including Canada, Germany, Greece, Malta, South Africa, and the UK (ICoC, 2013). According to representatives of maritime PSCs interviewed for this chapter, their semi-automatic rifles are purchased primarily from companies based in Malta and the UK. The firearms used by maritime PSCs range in price from EUR 800 to EUR 1,500 (USD 900–1,750); among them are AR-15 semi-automatic rifles, Benelli semi-automatic shotguns, CZ 858 Tactical semi-automatic sporting rifles, FN-1A1 semi-automatic rifles, Izhmash Saiga semi-automatic hunting carbines, Zastava PAP semi-automatic sporting rifles, and Zastava M-2010 semi-automatic sporting rifles.[15]

Few countries provide information regarding small arms transfers to maritime PSCs. The Dutch government has publicly reported on its denials of authorizations for the transfer of small arms and ammunition to maritime PSCs when it considered the risk of diversion to be high and the requested transfer 'not in favour of the presence of armed guards on board seagoing vessels' (Netherlands, 2012, p. 12; van Ginkel, van der Putten, and Molenaar, 2013).[16] At the time of writing, the UK was the only country that had published information on authorizations and denials of exports of small arms and ammunition to maritime PSCs, including for use on floating armouries. Official UK data reveals that the UK issued various export and trade licences for the transfer of 181,708 items to maritime PSCs for counter-piracy purposes from April 2012 to September 2013 (UKHC, 2014a, para. 382).

Table 8.3 provides information on UK arms export licences for 61,992 small arms, broken down by type of weapon and destination.

Table 8.3 **UK arms exports licence approvals for goods for use in anti-piracy operations, April 2012–30 September 2013[17]**

Destination	Assault rifles	Combat shotguns	Machine guns	Pistols	Rifles	Sniper rifles	'Sporting guns' (shotguns)
Comoros	1,900	300	0	110	1,150	0	0
Djibouti	1,100	150	0	130	200	0	300
Egypt	700	150	0	60	0	200	700
Ghana	0	0	0	0	0	20	0
Kenya	300	100	0	50	101	0	200
Madagascar	4,900	750	0	490	1,000	204	300
Maldives	6,150	550	0	490	1,600	200	850
Mauritius	5,119	700	0	420	3,254	1	716
Oman	3,700	900	0	240	1,250	200	600
Russian Federation	17	0	0	0	0	19	0
Seychelles	12	0	22	0	0	0	0
South Africa	7,519	850	6	776	3,151	357	1,528
Sri Lanka	2,360	500	0	180	910	200	100
Tanzania	600	150	0	30	200	0	0
Total	34,377	5,100	28	2,976	12,816	1,401	5,294

Source: UKHC (2014a, para. 375)

Table 8.4 **Small arms authorized for export and delivered under UK-issued Open General Trade Control Licence (Maritime Anti-Piracy), April 2012–30 September 2013**

Small arms	Licences granted	Arms delivered
Assault rifles	34,377	2,332
Combat shotguns	5,100	83
Machine guns	28	6
Pistols	2,976	63
Rifles	12,816	623
Sniper rifles	1,401	0
'Sporting guns' (shotguns)	5,294	166
Total	61,992	3,273

Source: UKHC (2014a, para. 383-84)

In December 2013, the British parliament was informed that while the UK had authorized the transfer of 181,708 items for maritime PSCs, only 3,273 of these small arms had been delivered during the period April 2012–September 2013 (UKHC, 2014a, para. 382; see Table 8.4). The British business secretary, Vince Cable, explained that the difference between the number of items authorized for export and actual small arms deliveries was due to the fact that licence applicants were overestimating future demand; he emphasized that authorizations were not indicative of the 'eventual level of exports'. Yet he also highlighted the need for 'regular reporting of volumes exported to be included in the routine quarterly publication of export licensing data' (UKHC, 2014a, para. 382).

SAFE AND SECURE?

As noted above, one of the major concerns regarding floating armouries is that they may not be meeting minimum safety requirements for the storage of weapons and ammunition (Dutton, 2013, p. 155). Most maritime PSCs interviewed for this chapter were satisfied with the stockpile management and security standards on the floating armouries that they used. However, they also observed that each floating armoury had its own guidelines, standards, and procedures. One report notes that while some armouries are 'professionally run' and have secure storage and good records and security, 'there are concerns that others do not have proper storage for weapons, enough watchmen, or enough space' (Seacurus, 2012, p. 11). This section considers four areas critical to the safety and security of floating armouries in the HRA.

Each floating armoury had its own guidelines, standards, and procedures.

Vessel and armoury security

The physical security of a vessel depends on at least two factors. The first is whether the vessel complies with the International Convention for the Safety of Life at Sea's limitations on the number of passengers on board (IMO, 1974). Given that most floating armouries are converted tugs, which, by default, have limited capacity (see Photo 8.2), and that 3–6 armed guards are on board at any one time in addition to each vessel's crew members, these limitations may indeed be exceeded in some cases.[18] The second factor relates to the security provisions for the floating armoury. Some of these vessels maintain a sufficient number of armed guards to allow for a 24-hour security watch in shifts, as reportedly happens on the MV *Sinbad* (Badam, 2012). In some cases, PSC teams on board floating armouries have reportedly been expected to protect the vessels from attack. For such situations, there are no specific plans, procedures, or rules on the use of force, nor is there a designated commander.[19] These types of weaknesses spur fears that floating armouries could be captured by pirates or terrorists (PTI, 2013; Rickett, 2013).

Armoury management

Interviewees also raised concerns about the inadequate storage space allocated for weapons, ammunition, and equipment on some floating armouries operating in the HRA. Floating armouries are not designed to serve as armouries and demand can exceed storage capacity, especially on vessels that have converted existing compartments into storage units for arms and ammunition. As a result, pelican cases containing arms are sometimes simply tied to the deck of a floating armoury (see Photos 8.1 and 8.4). Among other problems, such poor storage conditions risk advertising the status of the vessel as a floating armoury and possibly attracting unwanted attention from pirates or terrorists.[20]

8.4

Storage on the deck of a floating armoury.
© Anonymous

Procedures to embark PSC arms, ammunition, and equipment onto a floating armoury can also be problematic (see Photo 8.5). Interviewees reported that documentation on the number, type, and other details of arms stored on board a floating armoury can easily be verified through a physical check, but that when it comes to ammunition, not all floating armoury personnel are willing or interested in checking declared volumes. In particular, interviewees noted that if another PSC team is due to embark or disembark, some floating armouries will save time and ask for verbal confirmation of the number of rounds to be stored. One informed interviewee attributed the discovery of one company's ammunition boxes on pirate skiffs to lax procedures of this kind.[21]

Potential for diversion

The UK says it is confident that arms delivered to PSCs have not been diverted, as evidence of diversion has not been presented to the government (UKHC, 2014a, para. 382). Without post-licensing checks, however, the government is not likely to find out about such incidents. The conditions of the Open General Trade Control Licence (Maritime Anti-piracy)—which authorizes vetted maritime PSCs to supply, deliver, and transfer particular types of small arms and ammunition

8.5

Loading equipment onto a floating armoury off Fujairah, United Arab Emirates, 2014.
© Anonymous

for use onto commercial vessels in the HRA—include a commitment not to transfer the materiel to any other entity (UK, 2014a).

Yet anecdotal evidence indicates that maritime PSCs do transfer arms to other maritime PSCs through the intermediary of floating armouries.[22] One interviewee stated that maritime PSCs increasingly share arms and equipment. For example, if maritime PSC X has stored arms on board a floating armoury and maritime PSC Z has a team in need of arms to conduct a transit, maritime PSC X will complete a 'transfer application form' and sign an employment contract with maritime PSC Z's team before formally transferring the arms to maritime PSC Z. The transfer can take place with or without the knowledge of the owners of the floating armoury, even though the arms were loaded onto the floating armoury as the property of maritime PSC X and removed by maritime PSC Z. Maritime PSCs interviewed for the chapter indicated that floating armouries do not question or stop such transfers of arms and ammunition.[23]

A second diversion risk can arise from the sudden cessation of maritime PSC activity. In July 2014, Gulf of Aden Group Transits, one of the world's top ten maritime PSCs in terms of employees and number of transits, ceased to exist (Gallagher and Owen, 2014). The company left private armed guards and their arms and ammunition on board vessels and floating armouries in and around the HRA. According to Steve Collins, operations manager of the well-established maritime PSC Sea Marshals:

> We've now taken responsibility for those that are on board vessels—they will be looked after by us. Additionally many of those onboard the floating armouries in the Gulf and Red Sea have been offered work by us or other [maritime PSCs], who are rallying around, and are therefore already covered for getting home (Gallagher and Owen, 2014).

There is no information concerning the arms and ammunition of Gulf of Aden Group Transits.

Floating into territorial waters

A final set of concerns revolves around floating armouries drifting or intentionally entering the territorial waters of a state bordering the HRA. As several episodes have shown, floating armouries can enter territorial waters by accident or because they need to resupply. Yet even innocent passage into territorial waters for resupply and refuelling may be regarded as problematic by HRA coastal states, due, for example, to fears that national security could be threatened if the weapons and ammunition on board were seized by terrorists, criminals, or insurgents.

The following three cases illustrate the kinds of problems that can arise in this regard. Sovereign Global utilizes the vessel *Muru* to serve as a supply ship for the floating armoury MV *Sultan*, ensuring that the floating armoury does not need to travel into territorial waters for resupply (Sovereign Global, 2013).

Case 1: Protection Vessels International's *Sea Scorpion*, 2010

The *Sea Scorpion* was a floating armoury used by Protection Vessels International for anti-piracy operations in the HRA. It entered Eritrean territorial waters in December 2010 to visit the port of Massawa for resupply and refuelling, having deposited its arms and ammunition on a small island in Eritrean waters before entering Massawa (UNSC, 2011, para. 355). The Eritrean government nevertheless detained the ship, holding four of the company's employees for six months on charges of 'organizing acts of terrorism and sabotage, as well as concealing [evidence]' (UNSC, 2011, annexe 6.5).

Case 2: AGMS's *Sinbad*, 2012

On 1 October 2012, the AGMS floating armoury *Sinbad* was seized by the UAE Coast Guard in international waters after the vessel was reportedly 'lured' into UAE territorial waters during a routine refuelling exercise. The vessel was released after a week. The seizure was reportedly connected with opposition to the vessel taking business from floating armouries established in the Gulf of Oman (Badam, 2012; Shauketaly, 2012).

Case 3: AdvantFort's *Seaman Guard Ohio*, 2013

In October 2013 AdvantFort's *Seaman Guard Ohio* was seized by government authorities while in Indian territorial waters (TNN, 2013). The 35 crew and guard members (12 Indians, 14 Estonians, 6 British nationals, and 3 Ukrainians), in possession of 35 firearms, well over 5,000 rounds of ammunition, and more than 100 magazines, were charged with illegally entering Indian territorial waters with arms and ammunition in violation of relevant national legislation (see Photo 8.6). A judge dismissed the case, however, deciding that the vessel had been in Indian waters

8.6

Indian policemen escort crew members of the MV Seaman Guard Ohio in Tuticorin, India, on 18 October 2013. © AP Photo

due to 'necessity' and had therefore been operating under the UN Convention on the Law of the Sea's principle of 'innocent passage'. He stated that the ship did not pose a threat to Indian national security, but was instead engaged in anti-piracy operations (Subramani, 2014).

REGULATING FLOATING ARMOURIES

A variety of approaches have been proposed for regulating floating armouries, to increase control and monitoring possibilities. The UN Monitoring Group on Somalia and Eritrea has called upon the UN Security Council to:

> consider options for the establishment of an international regulatory authority that regulates, monitors and inspects the activities of private maritime security companies operating floating armouries and providing armed protection to vessels in international waters (UNSC, 2012, para. 116(d)).

The Security Council has not followed up on this recommendation, but other proposals have been made for measures to be undertaken at the international level. Indian Admiral D.K. Joshi has called for the IMO to regulate floating armouries and ensure that all littoral states be aware of the location of floating armouries, and the number of private armed guards and arms on board (PTI, 2013). IMO guidelines, standards, and recommendations for floating armouries could, in fact, promote confidence and reassurance in the HRA without overburdening established operators. Such measures would, however, require that flag states pay greater attention to the issue of floating armouries. This section therefore begins by highlighting practices currently utilized by some flag states for registering vessels used as floating armouries. It also examines initiatives undertaken by arms-exporting states to authorize the use of floating armouries by maritime PSCs and the potential for moving away from the current self-regulatory approach towards international standards, such as those developed by the International Organization for Standardization.

Flag state regulation

Flag states are the only states that have jurisdiction over floating armouries operating in international waters. However, many of the floating armouries fly flags of convenience, such as those of Panama or Sierra Leone, which generally have lax regulations (AP, 2012). These open-registry flag states have shown limited interest in addressing the issue of floating armouries to date (ITF, 2012).

Djibouti, Mongolia, and Saint Kitts and Nevis all reportedly recognize the particularities of floating armouries when issuing flag state approval for this purpose, but none has introduced a vessel description for 'floating armouries'. Although the registry of Saint Kitts and Nevis claims that it has not yet defined or applied rules for floating armouries operating under its jurisdiction, the Security Association for the Maritime Industry reported that the two-island country's registry was the first to formulate such legislation (SAMI, 2014). The Saint Kitts and Nevis registry has elaborated the following set of minimum requirements for the registration of ships to be used as floating armouries:

> **Flag states are the only states that have jurisdiction over floating armouries.**

- The registered owners or time charterer operating the vessel must comply with due diligence requirements and identify the actual and beneficial owners.
- The ship must be assigned an IMO number that is marked on the vessel.
- The 'principals' of the vessel 'operators' must be interviewed at their offices by Saint Kitts and Nevis officials to ensure that the company is not merely a 'brass plate' operation (in other words, a firm that is duly registered, but that does not conduct any business or 'exist' beyond a nameplate at the declared address of operations).
- Evidence of appropriate insurance for the commercial activities of the vessel must be shown to Saint Kitts and Nevis officials.
- The vessel operators must hold a licence or permit to carry out storage, import and export, purchase, and use of arms and ammunition stored on the vessel (for example, an operator can hold a UK-issued Open Individual Trade Control Licence).
- The documentation provided to the government that issued the above-mentioned licence relating to arms and ammunition must be provided to Saint Kitts and Nevis officials.
- Minimum requirements for records on the use of the floating armoury must include: the number, type, serial numbers, and stocklist bar code for all arms, ammunition, and maritime PSC equipment held on the vessel as well as the names and details (passport and nationality) of personnel embarked and disembarked.
- Saint Kitts and Nevis officials must conduct an inspection of the vessel prior to its registration or its entering into operation to ensure the integrity of storage facilities, handling areas, and embarkation and disembarkation sites.
- The vessel must comply with all international conventions and national legislation applicable to its size and must have statutory certificates issued by a recognized organization authorized by the Saint Kitts and Nevis government (a classification society authorized by the government of Saint Kitts and Nevis according to the appropriate IMO resolution to inspect or survey registered ships to ensure compliance with national registry requirements).[24]

On 14 May 2014, Saint Kitts and Nevis granted flag state approval for MNG Maritime to operate the floating armoury MV *Sea Patrol*, registered as 'other vessel', near Fujairah in the UAE (SAMI, 2014, p. 15). As of September 2014, Saint Kitts and Nevis had received at least ten other enquiries to register floating armoury vessels and provided the above list as 'minimum requirements' in response to these enquiries. At the time of writing, it was processing a second application for the registration of a floating armoury,[25] yet the remainder of the applications had not progressed beyond the enquiry stage.

Arms exporters licensing the use of floating armouries

In 2013, the UK government recognized that floating armouries had become a fact of life for maritime PSCs operating in the HRA. It adopted a case-by-case approach to authorizing the use of floating armouries by maritime PSCs holding an Open General Trade Control Licence (Maritime Anti-piracy). In July 2013, the MV *Mahanuwara* was the first floating armoury to be authorized as an approved armoury for such a licence (UKHC, 2014a, para. 372).

By August 2013, the UK had reportedly issued 50 licences authorizing maritime PSCs to use specific floating armouries operating in and around the HRA (McMahon, 2013b). In 2014, the risk assessment criteria used by the UK for floating armouries were made publicly available:

- The name and International Maritime Organisation (IMO) number of the floating armoury.
- Details of the flag under which the vessel operates.
- Vessel size/class and description.
- The vessel's minimum and maximum crew complements.
- The location(s) where the vessel operates, including ports.
- Details of the operation and accessibility to the vessel's armoury.
- Details of which personnel, apart from the crew, will be allowed access to the vessel and under what circumstances.
- Details of vessel insurance.
- The maximum armoury capacity of the vessel and the types of weapons that will be stored on board.
- Details of plans for the disposal of surplus/abandoned equipment.
- Details of vessel protection measures.
- Details of legislation and regulations applicable to the vessel, including any inspections undertaken to date.
- Details of any circumstances under which the vessel may lease capacity to other organisations.
- Details about any circumstances under which weapons may be leased to other organisations (UKHC, 2014a, para. 372).

Some maritime PSCs operate their own floating armouries.

In addition, those holding a licence authorizing the use of particular floating armouries are required to keep records of all transactions carried out under the terms of the licence, provide quarterly reports on the use of the licence, and notify the licensing authorities of any changes in the status of the floating armoury with regard to the risk criteria outlined above. Further, UK export control organization officials conduct compliance audits of the licence holders' records. In July 2013 the UK government announced it was exploring the 'viability of conducting on-vessel inspections' (UKHC, 2014a, para. 372).

In contrast to the UK, Germany only authorizes the use of state-run floating armouries that operate in territorial waters for small arms and ammunition exported from Germany to maritime PSCs.[26] However, German maritime PSCs can utilize other floating armouries for the storage of arms and ammunition acquired from countries other than Germany and for transit on vessels that do not fly the German flag.

From self-regulation to an international standard?

During the early years of floating armouries, the only real form of regulation was self-regulation by the private maritime security industry. Maritime PSCs used floating armouries that they themselves owned or that they had come to trust over time. Some maritime PSCs operate their own floating armouries and reportedly do not make them available for use by other maritime PSCs (AP, 2012). British maritime PSCs have stressed that in controlling their arms and ammunition in accordance with UK licensing requirements, including on authorized floating armouries, they are able to exercise sufficient control and prevent diversion (McMahon, 2013b).

Yet some maritime PSCs express a desire for agreed international standards, especially given the variety of floating armouries' flag states and registries. These could be related to UK licensing requirements or based on the international ISO/PAS 28007 standard, which shipping companies use as one of their main criteria for the selection of maritime PSCs (ISO, 2013).[27] The ISO/PAS 28007 covers maritime PSC operations and guard training and qualifications, but not floating armouries.

It can be expensive and time-consuming for maritime PSCs to conduct due diligence, and in particular physical checks, of all the floating armouries that they might potentially use. Therefore, some maritime PSCs request their private armed guards to conduct checks and report back the first time that they use a floating armoury.[28] Reputation is an important factor in the selection of a floating armoury, as is the long-term use of the vessel. As a result, maritime PSCs may be reluctant to consider contracting newly established floating armouries.[29] Nevertheless, the market is competitive. In an attempt to entice customers, new floating armouries tend to offer lower prices than those charged

Box 8.4   Maritime security provision in the Gulf of Guinea

For more than three decades, the Gulf of Guinea has been a hot spot of maritime insecurity due to piracy and armed robbery at sea, but with key differences compared to the Indian Ocean's HRA. In this sub-region, heavily armed pirates mostly hijack oil tankers in order to offload the oil and other cargo for subsequent disposal via the black market (Chapsos, 2014, pp. 153–58). In 2013, an estimated 100 vessels were attacked in the Gulf of Guinea, with 56 of these attacks succeeding (OBP, 2014, p. 5).

As of October 2014, Nigeria, the key actor in the region, was still prohibiting commercial vessels from carrying arms into its territorial waters. However, Nigeria offers its armed forces personnel as vessel protection detachments on commercial vessels, with arrangements made via local PSCs and agents (Steffen, 2014a). Due to the lack of established and reliable mechanisms and procedures for the delivery of such services, there were nevertheless certain risks for

companies contracting Nigerian government security forces. These risks included: (a) discrepancies in the arrangements concluded between unauthorized agents and clients and the rules and policies set by security agencies; (b) insufficient training, which resulted in several fatalities and other problems; and (c) a lack of inter-agency coordination (Steffen, 2014b). Hence, the Round Table of International Shipping Industry Associations' revised guidelines for protection against piracy in the Gulf of Guinea indicate that:

- Care should be exercised when using private armed guards, as they are prevented by law from operating inside territorial waters of coastal states in the region, and authorities are known to enforce these regulations vigorously.
- Local or Government forces subcontracted by maritime PSCs should only be used if they are legitimate, and trusted [. . .]. For example it is illegal to use Nigerian Maritime Police beyond the fairway buoy (ICS, 2014, p. 7).

Several companies are reportedly exploring the option of deploying floating armouries in the region.[30] The application of the HRA model to the Gulf of Guinea seems unlikely, however. First, the risk of violent armed pirate groups attacking a floating armoury in the region is high and therefore other measures are preferred for addressing piracy. Second, in 2014 the UK stated it would reject applications for licences for armed anti-piracy operations and floating armouries in West Africa (UK, 2014b, p. 17); as of October 2014, UK maritime PSCs were not allowed to use floating armouries off the coast of Cape Verde (UK, 2014a, pp. 54–55). At the end of the day, a great deal will depend on the direction Nigeria takes with regard to permitting, or at least accommodating, armed private guards operating on commercial vessels in the region.

Map 8.2   Gulf of Guinea

by well-established counterparts. Competition on price is especially strong in the Gulf of Oman and in the Red Sea. Several maritime PSCs interviewed for this chapter expressed concerns that new entrants to the market could push down prices, with the result that floating armouries with good safety and security standards might begin to cut corners on security and safety to remain competitive.[31]

All maritime PSCs interviewed also stressed that they conduct due diligence when initially selecting and continuing to use a floating armoury, particularly in view of the responsibility they have for their equipment and personnel. They all reported having developed their own assessment criteria for floating armouries, which include the following elements:

- flag registration certificates;
- classification society inspections and documentation;
- health and safety certificates;
- crew manning documentation and health and vaccination reports;
- a security team that is available and qualified to provide physical security for the floating armoury;
- appropriate accommodation, good health, and sanitary conditions for the armed teams;
- good weapons and equipment storage conditions and physical security;
- communication and Internet access;
- operational procedures for embarkation and disembarkation;
- round-the-clock availability of disembarkation and embarkation services, as well as of storage and accommodation; and
- evidence of regular audits for all of the above.

There is scope for the development of international guidelines and standards based on the criteria that maritime PSCs are already using for floating armouries. In any case, whatever their source, international standards for floating armouries would undoubtedly help those that have good practices for stockpile management and security to maintain them, while encouraging those that do not have such practices to adopt them.

CONCLUSION

Several maritime PSCs have remarked that floating armouries would not be required if HRA coastal states followed relevant IMO recommendations and guidance.[32] They see state-controlled armouries ashore as a better alternative since they do not carry the same weapons diversion risks that unregulated and potentially substandard floating armouries do.[33] The onshore option would also address the needs of private armed guards for meals and accommodation between trips through the HRA. As the use of floating armouries has become commonplace among maritime PSCs transiting the HRA, its decline may require a dramatic drop in the use of the PSCs themselves. It is more likely that other areas at risk from piracy and armed robbery at sea will copy the HRA model, with the Gulf of Guinea, in particular, identified as a potential site for such activity.

To date, few flag states have shown interest in regulating or monitoring the 'fishing vessels' and 'cargo ships' in their registries that serve as floating armouries. This reluctance has fuelled concern for the security of maritime PSC arms and ammunition on board floating armouries. It has also limited efforts to determine the number of floating armouries in the HRA, map their location, and monitor their use. States and other stakeholders also exhibit low levels of interest in the development of standards, even industry standards, relating specifically to floating armouries, which could be modelled on the ISO/PAS 28007 for maritime PSCs.

Some flag states and governments that license maritime PSCs and PSC arms transfers have taken steps to monitor floating armouries. As part of this process, criteria are being elaborated to guide physical security and storage on board, record-keeping, documentation checks, and broader inspections. While such measures have no doubt also influenced the selection of floating armouries by maritime PSCs that take their own security and safety seriously, there are still no agreed international standards for floating armouries or evidence that flag states or other entities are shutting down those that are insecure. On the contrary, it appears that floating armouries currently respond primarily to market forces, striving in particular to offer their services at the lowest possible cost. This opens the door to the weakening, rather than strengthening, of on-board security. At present, it seems that only a catastrophic incident, such as a successful attack on a floating armoury, may prompt the international community to give the activity more attention and, most importantly, endeavour to regulate it. ◾

LIST OF ABBREVIATIONS

AGMS	Avant Garde Maritime Services
HRA	High-risk area
ICoC	International Code of Conduct
IMO	International Maritime Organization
ISO/PAS	International Organization for Standardization/Publicly Available Specification
PSC	Private security company
UAE	United Arab Emirates
UNCLOS	United Nations Convention on the Law of the Sea

ENDNOTES

1   Author telephone interview with a maritime PSC, 20 May 2014.

2   Author telephone interviews with maritime PSCs, 21–22 May 2014.

3   Author telephone interviews with maritime PSCs, 20–22 May 2014.

4   AP (2012); Houreld (2012); Rickett (2013); Shiptalk (2012); UNSC (2012, annexe 5.4, para. 9).

5   Author telephone interviews with maritime PSCs, 21–22 May 2014.

6   Such evidence may include proof that the PSC is a signatory to the International Code of Conduct for Private Security Service Providers (ICoC) and that it has received ISO/PAS 28007 certification. The International Organization for Standardization issued the standard as a Publicly Available Specification (ISO/PAS).

7   Author telephone interviews with maritime PSCs, 21 and 22 May 2014.

8   Author telephone interview with a maritime PSC, 21 May 2014.

9   Author telephone interview with a company operating a floating armoury, UK, 23 May 2014.

10   Besides Galle in Sri Lanka, the other eight locations for returning arms are: Dar es Salaam (Tanzania), Djibouti, Mauritius, Mombasa (Kenya), Port Suez (Egypt), the Seychelles, Zanzibar (Tanzania), and the floating armouries MV *Sinbad* (in the Gulf of Oman) and MV *Avant Garde* (in the Red Sea). See AGMS (n.d.).

11   Author telephone interview with a company operating a floating armoury, UK, 23 May 2014.

12   Author telephone interview with a company operating a floating armoury, UK, 23 May 2014.

13   Author telephone interview with a company operating a floating armoury, UK, 23 May 2014.

14   Author telephone interviews with maritime PSCs, 21–22 May 2014.

15   Author telephone interview with maritime PSCs, 20 and 22 May 2014.

16   The Netherlands only authorizes the use of Dutch military personnel—vessel protection detachments—on Dutch-flagged vessels. However, 12 Dutch maritime PSCs that are also signatories to the ICoC are licensed to provide security for vessels that do not fly the Dutch flag.

17   A representative of the British export control organization explained that the term 'sporting guns' referred to 'ordinary 12-bore shotguns', whereas a 'combat shotgun' was a semi-automatic shotgun (UKHC, 2014b, Q. 69).

18   Author telephone interview with a maritime PSC, 21 May 2014.

19   Author telephone interview with a company operating a floating armoury, UK, 23 May 2014.

20   Author telephone interview with a maritime PSC, 22 May 2014.

21   Author telephone interview with a maritime PSC, 21 May 2014.

22   Author telephone interview with a maritime PSC, 20 May 2014.

23   Author telephone interview with a Maritime PSC, 20 May 2014.

24   Author communication with Saint Kitts and Nevis International Ship Registry, 9 September 2014.

25   Author communication with Saint Kitts and Nevis International Ship Registry, 9 September 2014.

26   Author communiation with a representative of the German Federal Office for Economic Affairs and Export Control (Bundesamt für Wirtschaft und Ausfuhrkontrolle), 12 October 2014.

27   Author telephone interview with a company operating a floating armoury, UK, 23 May 2014.

28   Author telephone interview with a maritime PSC, 22 May 2014.

29   Author telephone interview with a maritime PSC, 22 May 2014.

30   Author telephone interview with a maritime PSC, 20 May 2014.

31   Author telephone interviews with maritime PSCs, 21–22 May 2014.

32   See IMO (2009a; 2009b; 2011; 2012).

33   Author telephone interviews with maritime PSCs, 21–22 May 2014.

BIBLIOGRAPHY

AGMS (Avant Garde Maritime Services). n.d.a. 'Weapons.' Accessed January 2015. <http://avantmaritime.com/weapons>

—. n.d.b. 'MV Mahanuwara.' Accessed January 2015.

    <http://avantmaritime.com/sites/default/files/FA%20off%20Galle%20Details%20updated%20-%2008Aug%2713.pdf>

—. n.d.c. 'Inward Transfer Application.' <http://avantmaritime.com/sites/default/files/New Air Transportation Forms - INWARD.pdf>

AP (Associated Press). 2012. 'Piracy Fighters Use Floating Armouries.' News24 (Cape Town). 23 March.

    <http://www.news24.com/Africa/News/Piracy-fighters-use-floating-armouries 20120322>

Badam, Ramola Talwar. 2012. 'UAE Coastguard Detains Floating Weapons Arsenal off Fujairah.' *National* (Abu Dhabi). 17 October.

    <http://www.thenational.ae/news/uae-news/uae-coastguard-detains-floating-weapons-arsenal-off-fujairah>

Blue Palm Charters. n.d. 'Logistics Platform Sea Lion.' <http://bluepalmcharters.es/onewebmedia/Sea%20Lion%20Flyer.pdf>

Brown, James. 2012. *Pirates and Privateers: Managing the Indian Ocean's Private Security Boom*. Sydney: Lowy Institute for International Policy. September.

Captain Phillips. 2013. Paul Greengrass, dir. Columbia Pictures.

Chapsos, Ioannis. 2014. 'The Privatisation of International Security: The Regulatory Framework for Private Maritime Security Companies, Using Operations off Somalia, 2005–13, as a Case Study'. Ph.D. thesis, Coventry University. May.

Dutton, Yvonne. 2013. 'Gunslingers on the High Seas: A Call for Regulation.' *Duke Journal of Comparative and International Law*, Vol. 24, Iss. 107, pp. 105–59.

EUNAVFOR (European Union Naval Force)–Somalia. 2014. 'Key Facts and Figures: EU Naval Force Somalia–Operation Atalanta.'

    <http://eunavfor.eu/key-facts-and-figures/>

Florquin, Nicolas. 2012. 'Escalation at Sea: Somali Piracy and Private Security Companies.' In Small Arms Survey. *Small Arms Survey 2012: Moving Targets*. Cambridge: Cambridge University Press, pp. 190–217.

Gallagher, Paul and Jonathan Owen. 2014. 'Exclusive: Anti-pirate Security Staff All at Sea after Major Firm Suddenly Goes Bust.' *Independent* (London). 29 July. <http://www.independent.co.uk/news/world/exclusive-antipirate-security-staff-all-at-sea-after-major-firm-suddenly-goes-bust-9636217.html>

Houreld, Katharine. 2012. 'Piracy Fighters Use Floating Armouries.' Associated Press. 22 March.

    <http://www.news24.com/Africa/News/Piracy-fighters-use-floating-armouries-20120322>

ICoC (International Code of Conduct for Private Security Service Providers). 2010. <http://www.icoc-psp.org/>

—. 2013. 'The International Code of Conduct for Private Security Service Providers: Signatory Companies—Complete List as of 1 August 2013: Version with Company Details.' <http://www.icoc-psp.org/uploads/Signatory_Companies_-_August_2013_-_Composite_List2.pdf>

ICS (International Chamber of Shipping). 2014. *Guidelines for Owners, Operators and Masters for Protection against Piracy in the Gulf of Guinea Region.* London: ICS. <http://www.ics-shipping.org/docs/default-source/Piracy-Docs/011014-gog-guidelines-revised-version-for-release-.pdf?sfvrsn=0>

IMO (International Maritime Organization). 1974. International Convention for the Safety of Life at Sea.

<http://www.imo.org/About/Conventions/ListOfConventions/Pages/International-Convention-for-the-Safety-of-Life-at-Sea-(SOLAS),-1974.aspx>

—. 2009a. *Annex: Guidance to Shipowners, Companies, Ship Operators, Shipmasters and Crews on Preventing and Suppressing Acts of Piracy and Armed Robbery against Ships.* MSC.1/Circ.1334. 23 June. London.

—. 2009b. *Annex: Recommendations to Governments for Preventing and Suppressing Piracy and Armed Robbery against Ships.* MSC.1/Circ.1333. 26 June. London.

—. 2011. *Annex: Interim Recommendations for Port and Coastal States Regarding the Use of Privately Contracted Armed Security Personnel on Board Ships in the High Risk Area.* MSC.1/Circ.1408. 16 September. London.

—. 2012. *Annex: Revised Interim Guidance to Shipowners, Ship Operators and Shipmasters on the Use of Privately Contracted Armed Security Personnel on Board Ships in the High Risk Area.* MSC.1/Circ.1405/Rev.2. 25 May. London.

ISO (International Organization for Standardization). 2013. 'ISO/PAS 28007:2012: Ships and Marine Technology—Guidelines for Private Maritime Security Companies (PMSC) Providing Privately Contracted Armed Security Personnel (PCASP) on Board Ships (and Pro Forma Contract).' 7 January. <http://www.iso.org/iso/catalogue_detail?csnumber=42146>

ITF (International Transport Workers' Federation). 2012. 'Flags of Convenience.'

<http://www.itfglobal.org/en/transport-sectors/seafarers/in-focus/flags-of-convenience-campaign/>

MarineTraffic. n.d. 'Vessels.' Accessed October 2014. <http://www.marinetraffic.com/>

McMahon, Liz. 2013a. 'Unwanted Weapons Pile up at Mombasa as Pirate Attacks Fall.' *Lloyds Loading List.* 17 July. <http://www.lloydsloadinglist.com/freight-directory/people/unwanted-weapons-pile-up-at-mombasa-as-pirate-attacks-fall/20018059533.htm#.U-9zePldVpE>

—. 2013b. 'UK Gives Go Ahead for Floating Armouries.' *Lloyds List.* 8 August. <http://www.lloydslist.com/ll/sector/regulation/article427433.ece>

MIRIS International. n.d. 'Global Maritime Security Operations: Areas of Operation.' Accessed January 2015.

<http://www.miris-int.com/about-us/where-we-work>

Moran Security Group. 2013. *Moran Security Group: Maritime Operations.* August. <http://moran-group.org/upload/file/47_130179929.pdf>

MV *Sea Patrol.* 2014. Copy of A3PFA Form. Signed 1 May 2014. <http://www.mngmaritime.com/docs/BIS-A3PFA.pdf>

Netherlands. 2012. *Annual Report on the Netherlands Arms Export Policy in 2011: Letter to Parliament.* 31 October.

<http://www.government.nl/issues/export-controls-of-strategic-goods>

OBP (Oceans Beyond Piracy). 2014. *The State of Maritime Piracy 2013.* Broomfield, CO: One Earth Future Foundation.

Petrig, Anna. 2013. 'The Use of Force and Firearms by Private Maritime Security Companies against Suspected Pirates.' *International and Comparative Law Quarterly,* Vol. 62, Iss. 3. July, pp. 667–701.

PTI (Press Trust of India). 2013. 'Floating Armouries Can Lead to 26/11-type Attack: Navy Chief.' *Times of India.* 3 December.

<http://timesofindia.indiatimes.com/india/Floating-armouries-can-lead-to-26/11-type-attack-Navy-chief/articleshow/26794932.cms>

Rickett, Oscar. 2013. 'Piracy Fears over Ships Laden with Weapons in International Waters.' *Guardian.* 10 January.

<http://www.theguardian.com/world/2013/jan/10/pirate-weapons-floating-armouries>

SAMI (Security Association for the Maritime Industry). 2014. 'Floating Armoury Approved by St Kitts and Nevis.' *Bridge,* Iss. 5, p. 15.

Seacurus. 2012. 'Floating Fortresses.' *Insurance Bulletin,* Iss. 13. March, pp. 11–12.

Shauketaly, Faraz. 2012. 'Arabian Sea Maritime Security Temporarily at Risk.' *Sunday Leader* (Sri Lanka). 14 October.

<http://www.thesundayleader.lk/2012/10/14/arabian-sea-maritime-security-temporarily-at-risk/>

Shiptalk. 2012. 'Floating Armoury Fuss.' 4 April. <http://www.shiptalk.com/floating-armoury-fuss/>

Sovereign Global. 2013. 'M/V *Muru* Operational in Red Sea!' 25 September. <https://gb.so-global.com/news/1237-mv-muru-operational-in-red-sea.html>

—. 2014. 'High Speed Internet on Board MV *Aladin* and MV *Sultan.*' 21 February. <https://gb.so-global.com/news.html?page=4>

Steffen, Dirk. 2014a. 'Troubled Waters? The Use of Nigerian Navy and Police in Private Maritime Security Roles.' Center for International Maritime Security. 1 July. <http://cimsec.org/troubled-waters-use-nigerian-navy-police-private-maritime-security-roles/11918>

—. 2014b. 'Risks in Contracting Government Security Forces in the Gulf of Guinea.' Center for International Maritime Security. 16 September. <http://cimsec.org/troubled-waters-2-risks-contracting-government-security-forces-gulf-guinea/13016>

Subramani, A. 2014. 'Madras High Court Quashes Criminal Case against Crew of US Ship.' *Times of India.* 10 July.

<http://timesofindia.indiatimes.com/india/Madras-high-court-quashes-criminal-case-against-crew-of-US-ship/articleshow/38147206.cms>

TNN (Times News Network). 2013. 'Court Reprieve for 35 Crew Members of US Floating Armoury.' *Times of India*. 27 December.
    <http://timesofindia.indiatimes.com/city/chennai/Court-reprieve-for-35-crew-members-of-US-floating-armoury/articleshow/27989717.cms>

UK (United Kingdom). 2014a. *Strategic Export Controls: Her Majesty's Government's Annual Report for 2012, Quarterly Reports for 2012 and 2013, and the Government's Policies on Arms Exports and International Arms Control Issues—Response of the Secretaries of State for Business, Innovation and Skills, Defence, Foreign and Commonwealth Affairs and International Development.* October.
    <http://www.parliament.uk/documents/commons-committees/Arms-export-controls/2014-15-Cm8935.pdf>

—. 2014b. 'Trade Licence: Open General Trade Control Licence (Maritime Anti-piracy).' 14 August.
    <https://www.gov.uk/government/uploads/system/uploads/attachment_data/file/343440/14-1048-ogtcl-maritime-anti-piracy.pdf>

—. 2014c. *United Kingdom Strategic Export Controls Annual Report 2013.*

—. 2014d. *The UK National Strategy for Maritime Security.* May.

UKHC (United Kingdom House of Commons—Committees on Arms Export Controls). 2014a. *Scrutiny of Arms Exports and Arms Controls: Scrutiny of the Government's UK Strategic Export Controls Annual Report 2012, the Government's Quarterly Reports from October 2012 to September 2013, and the Government's Policies on Arms Exports and International Arms Control Issues—First Joint Report of the Business, Innovation and Skills, Defence, Foreign Affairs and International Development Committees of Session 2014–15.* Vol. II. 23 July.
    <http://www.publications.parliament.uk/pa/cm201415/cmselect/cmquad/186/186ii.pdf>

—. 2014b. *Scrutiny of Arms Exports and Arms Controls. Scrutiny of the Government's UK Strategic Export Controls Annual Report 2012, the Government's Quarterly Reports from October 2012 to September 2013, and the Government's Policies on Arms Exports and International Arms Control Issues—First Joint Report of the Business, Innovation and Skills, Defence, Foreign Affairs and International Development Committees of Session 2014–15.* Vol. III. 23 July. <http://www.publications.parliament.uk/pa/cm201415/cmselect/cmquad/186/186iii.pdf>

UKMTO (United Kingdom Maritime Trade Operations) et al. 2011. *BMP4: Best Management Practices for Protection against Somalia Based Piracy.* Version 4. Edinburgh: Witherby Publishing Group. August.
    <http://www.mschoa.org/docs/public-documents/bmp4-low-res_sept_5_2011.pdf?sfvrsn=0>

UN (United Nations). 1958. United Nations Convention on Law of the Sea.

UNSC (United Nations Security Council). 2011. *Report of the Monitoring Group on Somalia and Eritrea Pursuant to Security Council Resolution 1916 (2010).* S/2011/433 of 18 July.

—. 2012. *Report of the Monitoring Group on Somalia and Eritrea Pursuant to Security Council Resolution 2002 (2011).* S/2012/544 of 13 July.

—. 2013. *Report of the Secretary-General: Small Arms.* S/2013/503 of 22 August.

van Ginkel, Bibi, Frans-Paul van der Putten, and Willem Molenaar. 2013. *State or Private Protection against Maritime Piracy? A Dutch Perspective.* Clingendael Report. February. The Hague: Netherlands Institute of International Relations.

VesselFinder. n.d. 'Vessels.' Accessed October 2014. <http://www.vesselfinder.com/>

ACKNOWLEDGEMENTS

Principal authors

Ioannis Chapsos and Paul Holtom

Burundian refugees, recently returned from Tanzania, look in at the doorway of a house in a resettlement camp in Musenyi, southern Burundi, November 2012.
© Tony Karumba/AFP Photo

Unprotected

YOUNG PEOPLE IN POST-CONFLICT BURUNDI

9

INTRODUCTION

Although civil war in Burundi ended more than a decade ago, the country remains deeply affected by insecurity. Many of the underlying conditions that led to the outbreak of armed conflict persist, including poverty, unemployment, a lack of access to basic social services, and a narrowing political space. While young people in Burundi demonstrate strength and resourcefulness in coping with these adversities, they face an uphill struggle.[1] Forced to 'live more in the present and to discount the future' (Wood, 2003), many young people in Burundi are coping with these adversities by adopting high-risk survival tactics. A history of conflict and its effects on their families fundamentally shape their understandings of their current lives, including conditions of poverty. As one youth summarized: 'The problems here are poverty and the war—they influence each other' (Seymour et al., 2014, p. 35).

This chapter reviews the circumstances and capacities of young people in Burundi and, in particular, the deleterious effects of years of violence and poverty on the protective factors that would otherwise have safeguarded them from involvement in violent activities. It examines the relationship between armed violence and material adversity and the ways in which young people experience and cope with the daily challenges of survival. Based on original fieldwork conducted with young Burundians between 2012 and 2014, the chapter builds on a literature review and previous research conducted by the Small Arms Survey in 2005 and by the Geneva Declaration in 2008 (Pézard and Florquin, 2007; Pézard and de Tessières, 2009).

The chapter's main findings include the following:

- The threats posed by young people's involvement in armed violence remain significant in Burundi, influenced by widespread poverty, land disputes, manipulation by political parties, and the availability of arms from the civil war era.
- Data on the use of firearms in Burundi is limited, but new monitoring mechanisms suggest that more than one-third of all incidents of armed violence involve the use of small arms and grenades.
- Banditry is perceived as the main security risk in Burundi, yet it is unclear to what extent banditry is politically or economically motivated.
- In the absence of family support, young Burundians adopt high-risk coping strategies, including those that lead to involvement in armed violence.
- Major international assistance projects in Burundi in the post-conflict period have tended to neglect the provision of support to young people, who are most at risk of becoming involved in violent activities.
- Local and national party-based politics play a significant role in provoking and sustaining youth violence in Burundi. Interviews show that for many young Burundians, joining youth wings of political parties represents one of the most easily accessible and effective short-term coping tactics, but one with long-term risks.
- Providing young people with opportunities to earn an income and ensure their own livelihood is likely to improve their prospects significantly, while also reducing their chances of adopting high-risk coping tactics.

This chapter is organized into four main sections. The first provides an overview of Burundi's legacy of conflict, describing both the conflict era and more recent violence. The second section highlights major internationally supported peace and security initiatives, including investments in disarmament, demobilization, and reintegration (DDR), peacebuilding, and security sector reform. It also describes how, despite significant international interventions, the structural causes of violence remain largely unaddressed. The third section presents young Burundians' perspectives on their everyday lives, the challenges they face, their coping mechanisms, and their understandings of the multiple types of violence affecting their lives. The fourth section considers the prevailing risks and protective factors for young Burundians within the ecological model of human development and suggests strategies for strengthening protective factors to support and protect Burundi's youths.

BURUNDI'S LEGACY OF CONFLICT AND VIOLENCE

Conflict and its aftermath

Burundi has long been afflicted by successive waves of extreme violence. Having gained its independence from Belgium in 1962, the country witnessed cyclical outbreaks of mass violence in 1965, 1972, 1988, 1991, and 1993, which resulted in the deaths of hundreds of thousands of people, the displacement of millions of others, and the perpetuation of a climate of distrust, fear, and extreme under-development (Lemarchand, 1996; Nindorera, 2012, pp. 33–34). All of these episodes were rooted in unresolved grievances and contestations for control of power and resources (Ngaruko and Nkurunziza, 2000, p. 379); they also reflected a political landscape in which deep ethnic divides pitted a Tutsi minority, whose elite controlled power, against a marginalized Hutu majority. Throughout this period, the political elite repeatedly fabricated suspicion and fear to mobilize the population to engage in extreme violence (Oketch and Polzer, 2002, pp. 123, 133).

The stage for violent transitions of power was set in 1961, even before independence, with the assassination of the leader of the

A Burundian soldier watches over a mass grave, subsequent to the massacre of more than 160 Congolese refugees, Gatumba, Burundi, August 2004. © Finbarr O'Reilly/Reuters

Union pour le Progrès National (Union for National Progress, UPRONA), Prince Louis Rwagasore, an event that coincided with the revolution in neighbouring Rwanda and contributed to the establishment of ethnic identity as the key driver for the violent contestation of power in the independence period. Four years later, the assassination of Prime Minister Pierre Ngendadumwe, a Hutu, further fomented ethnic-based distrust and resulted in mass killings of Tutsi and then Hutu civilians (Nindorera, 2012, p. 10). A military coup in 1966 initiated a period of Tutsi-led military rule that would last until the 1990s. During this period, multiple attempts by Hutu leaders to overthrow the Tutsi leadership were thwarted, only to be followed by further violent attacks on the Hutu population. A Hutu-led rebellion in 1972 in the southern part of the country involved the massacre of an estimated 1,000 Tutsi civilians and a brutal crackdown that eventually led to the killing of some 200,000 people and the flight of 300,000 others (Chrétien and Dupaquier, 2007; Ngaruko and Nkurunziza, 2000, pp. 375–76; Pézard and Florquin, 2007, p. 199).

As the successive military regimes tightened their hold on power, Hutu grievances grew, leading to popular revolts, killings of civilians, and further repression. An upsurge in violence in 1988 claimed the lives of several thousand people and eventually elicited concerted international pressure on the Burundian leadership to begin inter-ethnic dialogue. This process ushered in a political opening, the drafting of a new constitution, and the organization of the first multi-party elections in 1993. The Hutu Front pour la Démocratie au Burundi (Front for Democracy in Burundi, FRODEBU) earned 80 per cent of the vote in those elections (Nindorera, 2012, pp. 11–12). Yet, in line with historical precedent, antagonized elements in the national army assassinated the first democratically elected president of Burundi, Melchior Ndadaye, only three months after he took office, unleashing retaliatory massacres that progressively escalated into civil war. By 2003, the fighting had claimed some 300,000 lives and displaced at least 800,000 people (Vircoulon, 2014; Voors et al., 2012, p. 944). In 1996, former president Maj. Pierre Buyoya orchestrated a military coup, overthrew the interim head of state, and reassumed the presidency.[2] The main actors in the ongoing war included the military government and its locally mobilized militia—the Gardiens de la Paix (Guardians of the Peace), composed mainly of young people—which fought against the largely Hutu opposition actors, including:

- FRODEBU;
- the Conseil National Pour la Défense de la Démocratie (National Council for the Defence of Democracy, CNDD), a FRODEBU offshoot;
- the CNDD–Forces pour la Défense de la Démocratie (Forces for the Defence of Democracy, FDD), the CNDD's armed wing; and
- the Parti pour la Libération du Peuple Hutu–Forces Nationales de Libération (Party for the Liberation of the Hutu People–National Liberation Forces, Palipehutu–FNL), which had long organized outside of Burundi (Nindorera, 2012, pp. 14–15).

Although classified as a post-conflict country, Burundi still has high levels of armed violence.

In response to sustained rebellion and mounting international pressure on President Buyoya to address the conflict, peace negotiations were opened in Arusha, Tanzania, in 1998. These negotiations culminated in the Arusha Peace and Reconciliation Agreement of August 2000, which included provisions for reform of the security forces to ensure an ethnic balance, and assurances for the integration of members of the former rebel movements. Signatories included FRODEBU and UPRONA, as well as the political wings of the CNDD and Palipehutu, whose armed wings—the CNDD–FDD and Palipehutu–FNL—continued their rebellion.[3] In 2003, the CNDD–FDD signed the Comprehensive Ceasefire Agreement and the Pretoria Protocol on Political, Defence, and Security Power-Sharing, which set the conditions for the integration of the CNDD–FDD into the army, police, and government administration (ICG, 2004).

The CNDD–FDD subsequently entered the FRODEBU-led transitional government and began to prepare for the 2005 parliamentary and presidential elections, which it won easily, with Pierre Nkurunziza taking power. Although the 2005 elections technically brought Burundi into a post-conflict era, the Palipehutu–FNL rebellion continued for several more years (ICG, 2009). In September 2006 Palipehutu–FNL and the government signed a ceasefire, and a process of peace negotiations continued until the group declared an end to the armed struggle in 2008 and shortened its name to FNL. Legislative and presidential elections took place again in 2010 but were boycotted by the opposition. The CNDD–FDD won and Pierre Nkurunziza remained leader, although the lack of participation by the main opposition parties weakened the legitimacy of the process (UN, 2010). In the lead-up to the 2015 elections, numerous members of the international community expressed serious concerns about the free participation of the opposition and the threat of an upsurge in political violence (UN, 2014).

Recent violence

Although Burundi has been classified as a post-conflict country (RULAC, 2012), it has continued to experience high levels of armed violence. Documenting this unrest has proven challenging; in post-conflict and non-conflict settings, it is generally difficult to ascribe and disaggregate types and motivations of armed violence, which are often multiple and overlapping (De Martino and Dönges, 2012, p. 9). In Burundi, the act of reporting on violence can itself entail significant risks to personal security.

Despite such challenges, the Burundi Armed Violence Observatory is compiling and analysing national data on violent incidents.[4] Initial data collected by the observatory provides useful indications on current patterns of armed violence. For example, data collected in the first eight months of 2014 shows banditry to be the most prevalent form

Grenades removed from police armouries are prepared for destruction, Burundi, 2009. © MAG Burundi

of violence (BRAVO, 2014a, p. 15). Burundians have long perceived banditry as their main security threat (Pézard and de Tessières, 2009, pp. 56–57); yet in the current context of heightened political tensions, it is not clear whether such incidents are being perpetrated by 'simple bandits' who seek economic gain or by politically motivated youth militias that have allegedly been trained and armed to instigate violence ahead of the 2015 elections (RFI, 2014a; 2014b). According to the local media and interviews conducted in Burundi in November 2014, a surge in armed violence in Bujumbura was attributed to young men wielding machetes, who attacked homes and civilians walking in the streets at night. Although it was not possible to establish the perpetrators' identities or motivations—or indeed whether their acts were politically motivated, as interviewees contended—fear and perceptions of insecurity were notably higher at the end of 2014 than at any time in the 2012–14 research period (Seymour, 2014, p. 3).

The observatory also documents the types of arms used to perpetrate acts of violence. Data collected in the first eight months of 2014 suggests that bladed weapons—including machetes—are the most commonly used weapons, followed by rifles and grenades—arms that have been circulating since the civil war era (Pézard and Florquin, 2007, p. 198). Of the 966 weapons used in violent incidents recorded, more than one-third (37 per cent) involved rifles, grenades, or handguns. Due to incomplete reporting, information on the type of arm used was not available in 18 per cent of the cases (see Figure 9.1).[5]

Figure 9.1 **Distribution of 966 weapons used in violent incidents, by type, January–August 2014**

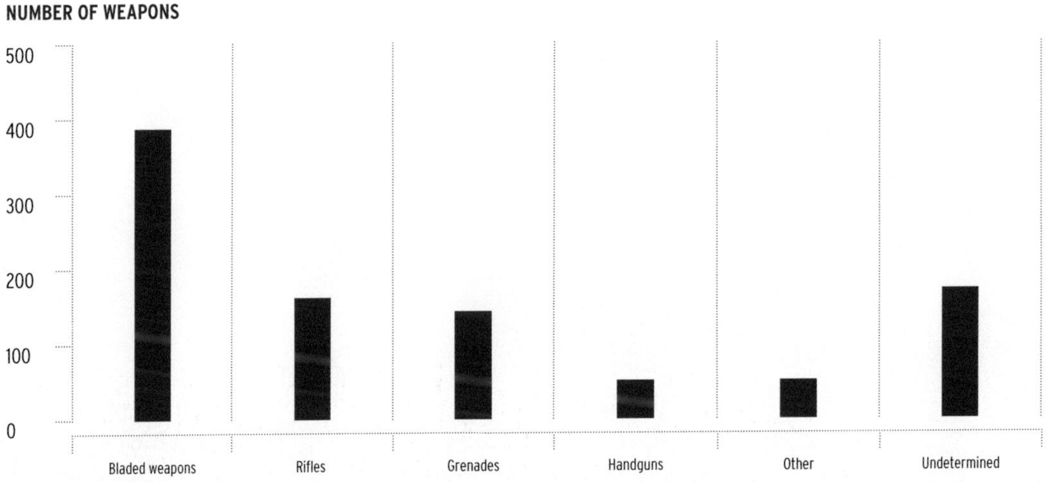

NUMBER OF WEAPONS

Sources: BRAVO (2014a, 2014b, 2014c)

In addition to banditry, the rise of youth wings of political parties is an important security concern in Burundi today (Seymour, 2014, p. 1). This is a particularly sensitive issue in the pre-electoral period, as political parties are reinforcing their youth wings to mobilize popular support throughout the country. In these contexts, the young people are especially vulnerable to becoming engaged in armed violence. In 2013 and 2014, multiple confrontations between government party and opposition groups were reported to have degenerated into violent confrontations (AI, 2014).

The mobilization of youth for political violence is not a new phenomenon in Burundi; historically, political elites have recruited youths to carry out acts of violence and intimidation (Berckmoes, 2014, p. 137). In 1972, for example, the Jeunesse Révolutionnaire Rwagasore (Rwagasore Revolutionary Youth)—a primarily Tutsi youth wing affiliated with the ruling party at the time—played an important role in reprisal attacks on the Hutu civilian population that left several thousand Tutsis and an estimated 200,000 Hutus dead (Ngaruko and Nkurunziza, 2000, p. 375). Subsequently, young people were widely mobilized for violence in the 1993 war: FRODEBU's youth wing—the Jeunesse Démocratique du Burundi (Democratic Youth of Burundi)—attacked Tutsi civilians following the assassination of the Hutu president, Melchior Ndadaye, as did the Jeunesse Patriotique Hutu (Patriotic Hutu Youth) of the Palipehutu–FNL. Meanwhile, Tutsi extremist groups such as Sans Échec (The Infallible) and Sans Défaite (The Undefeated) became notorious for acts of extreme violence and predation (Berckmoes, 2014, p. 141). As the war gained momentum in the second half of the 1990s, large numbers of young people enrolled in the fighting forces, including the national army (UN, 2003).

In Burundi's current political configuration, the youth wing of the ruling government party—the Imbonerakure ('Those Who See Far' in Kirundi)—presents specific concerns for armed violence. The group first drew the attention of international media and human rights actors in late 2008 in relation to reports of intimidation and demonstrations by youths who were wielding sticks and clubs while chanting slogans such as, 'Those that are not with us will be sent into exile or die' (Ghoshal, 2010, p. 16). In the first half of 2014, the UN reported on a range of politically motivated incidents involving the Imbonerakure, including the prevention or disruption of opposition party meetings, assaults on members of political parties, threats and intimidation against people accused of refusing to join the ruling party, and plain extortion and robbery (UN, 2014, p. 8).

The cascading effects of this violence include the mobilization of larger numbers of young people to opposition party youth wings. Increasingly, members of these groups are claiming that their only recourse is to defend themselves through violence. In the words of a 30-year-old leader in the Mouvement pour la Solidarité et la Démocratie (Movement for Solidarity and Democracy):

Violence has become inevitable. We youths are courageous, we need change. We cannot remain with our arms crossed [. . .]. We are ready to confront [the government] and the Imbonerakure. . . . We will use stones, batons against their guns if we need to. In 2010 we saw how the elections were stolen from us. This time we will not let it happen again [. . .]. The hope we used to have has run out (Seymour, 2014, p. 3).

Imbonerakure members march in the stadium of Gitega, Burundi, September 2014. © Damien Roulette

INTERNATIONAL INTERVENTIONS TO MITIGATE VIOLENCE

Investment in peacebuilding and security

In the past decade, international aid and development actors have invested heavily in Burundi's peace and security, including by supporting the Arusha peace process and by deploying various peacekeeping and peace support missions since then.[6]

Burundi was one of the first countries to be designated a recipient of the UN Peacebuilding Fund (PBF), the multi-year standing trust fund established in 2006 to support post-conflict peacebuilding (UNPBF, n.d.a). PBF interventions have included support for the implementation of peace agreements, political dialogue, and peaceful conflict resolution; economic revitalization and the creation of peace dividends; and the rebuilding of administrative services and capacities (UNPBF, n.d.b). By 2014, the PBF had allocated more than USD 49 million to peacebuilding projects in Burundi, including USD 35 million to the first Peacebuilding Priority Plan in 2007 (UNPBF, n.d.c). An independent evaluation of PBF support to Burundi between 2007 and 2013 deems the programme innovative and timely, particularly in its support for political negotiation processes that led to the transformation of the FNL into a political group, and for logistical preparations ahead of the 2010 elections (Campbell et al., 2014, pp. 5–6). At the same time, the evaluation concludes that some projects were not of consistently high quality and may even have produced negative effects, as plans for sustainability and follow-up were not sufficiently considered (Campbell et al., 2014, p. 6).

Another notable large-scale investment in Burundi's security was the Multi-Country Demobilization and Reintegration Programme (MDRP), a regionally focused, multi-donor framework managed by the World Bank to support the DDR of ex-combatants in the Great Lakes region.[7] In Burundi, the MDRP funded the executive secretariat of the National

A young man waits in a demobilization camp, in the province of Bubanza, north of Bujumbura, May 2009. © Jean Pierre Aimé Harerimana/Reuters

Box 9.1 DDR for children

The war that began in 1993 saw large numbers of children and young people engaged with all fighting forces. As documented in the November 2003 UN Secretary-General's report to the General Assembly, the Burundian armed groups that recruited and used young people under the age of 18 included the national army–the Forces Armées Burundaises–as well as the CNDD-FDD and the Palipehutu-FNL (UN, 2003, p. 20). Moreover, the Gardiens de la Paix were primarily made up of young people (Ntiyibagiruwayo, 2003), while less prominent rebel groups also included children in their ranks.

Two phases of children's DDR occurred in Burundi, the first between 2004 and 2006, and the second in 2009. The first phase witnessed the demobilization of more than 3,000 children, including those associated with the Gardiens de la Paix, the Forces Armées Burundaises, and the various rebel groups (Seymour, 2012). With the support of the World Bank MDRP programme, projects were implemented to assist communities and families; to enhance educational opportunities, provide psychosocial support, organize apprenticeships, and help to set up small businesses; and to make sports and cultural activities available to demobilized children and youths (World Bank, 2010, pp. 68–69). The second phase of the children's DDR occurred after the end of the FNL rebellion and led to the demobilization of more than 600 children. In total, between 2004 and 2009, well over 3,600 children were demobilized (see Table 9.1).

The children's DDR process in Burundi suffered from two notable weaknesses. First, the programme did not reach large numbers of young combatants. One reason was the highly bureaucratic listing process, as ex-combatant status could be validated only by local authorities and senior commanders, who often chose to exclude young people in their disfavour (Seymour, 2012, pp. 22-23). As these excluded young people could not formally enter the DDR process, they did not benefit from social and economic reintegration support, nor did they receive any psychosocial follow-up.[8]

Among those excluded were the many girls who had been affiliated with the armed groups. Although the precise number of girls who were involved as combatants, assistants, cooks, 'wives', dancers, singers, or informers is not known, interviews with local authorities, parents, NGOs, and young people indicate that many had been involved with the various armed groups. One NGO was working with 500 self-demobilized girls in two provinces alone, a striking contrast to the 53 girls who actually went through the formal national DDR process (Seymour, 2012, pp. 22-25). The challenges inherent in reaching girls in the context of other DDR processes have been well documented; they include girls' fear of social stigma, potential damage to the family honour, and a negative impact on future marriage possibilities (Verhey, 2004). These factors were foreseeable in Burundi, yet the children's DDR programme failed to integrate a community-based approach that would have provided girls with reintegration and psychosocial support while protecting them from stigmatization.

A second weakness was the lack of economic reintegration support. While the Paris Principles on children associated with armed groups hold that reintegration covers the acquisition of 'dignified livelihoods' (UNICEF, 2007), an evaluation of the first phase of the children's DDR programme finds that 'the economic situation of the child soldiers has reverted pretty much back to the situation they left years earlier' (Uvin, 2007, p. 13). A subsequent evaluation of the second phase shows that most of the ex-combatant youths were not gainfully employed but rather survived through daily wage labour, working on farms, carrying loads to markets, or digging for gold. They were generally angry, disillusioned by their experiences, and had little hope for improved prospects (Seymour, 2012, pp. 25-27).

Young men dig in a gold mine in the village of Rusoro, in the province of Cibitoke, Burundi, September 2010. © Abbie Trayler-Smith/Panos Pictures/Felix Features

Table 9.1 **Number of children demobilized in Burundi, by armed group and sex, 2004–06 and 2009**				
Phase	**Armed group affiliation**	**Boys**	**Girls**	**Number of children**
Phase 1 (2004–06)	Gardiens de la Paix			1,387
	Forces Armées Burundaises			891
	Other political parties and armed movements			644
	CNDD-FDD			106
	Total for phase 1	2,982	46	3,028
Phase 2 (2009)	Palipehutu-FNL	619	7	626
Totals for phases 1 and 2		**3,601**	**53**	**3,654**

Source: Seymour (2012, p. 18)

Commission for DDR with USD 74.8 million in 2004 to demobilize some 55,000 combatants—including the national army, the Gardiens de la Paix, and the various rebel movements—and to support their reintegration into civilian life (World Bank, 2010, p. 64). The DDR effort also included the demobilization of children (see Box 9.1 on previous page).

Although the continuing rebellion by the Palipehutu–FNL slowed the DDR process, the project reportedly demobilized well over 26,000 combatants between 2004 and 2008 (World Bank, 2010, p. 24). A second tranche of funding to the Burundi Emergency Demobilization and Transitional Reintegration Project after the closure of the MDRP allowed for the DDR of nearly 7,000 additional ex-combatants by the end of 2012 (World Bank, 2013). The World Bank judged the programme a success even though the demobilization of more than 35,000 combatants from all sides had yielded only 6,000 surrendered weapons by the end of 2007 (World Bank, 2010; GICHD, 2012, p. 19).

Significant international support has continued to flow into Burundi's security sector, primarily within the framework of the Burundi–Netherlands security sector development programme. Based on an eight-year memorandum of understanding signed by the two governments in April 2009, this programme is organized according to the three pillars of public security, defence, and governance. Its provisions include training, organization, and planning support; logistical support and equipment; building of infrastructure; financial management; internal and external control mechanisms; and forums for dialogue (DSS Burundi, n.d.). The programme's key priorities are to ensure political buy-in to the security sector reform process and to build trust among the various government security actors (Ball, 2014).[9] According to security sector actors in Burundi, this project represents a significant innovation in the way international donors engage with security sector reform in post-conflict countries, primarily in its acknowledgement of the extreme complexity of the work, the high political stakes, and the extended length of time needed to build trust and to begin effecting change (Seymour, 2014, p. 3).

Gaps in international approaches

As noted above, despite significant donor investments in peace and security programming, armed violence remains a serious threat in Burundi. While post-conflict peacebuilding is always challenging, there have been two noticeable shortcomings in Burundi: too weak a focus on the structural causes of violence, and too little attention paid to the needs and experiences of young people.

In the first instance, with the exception of the PBF, the international interventions described above have tended to ignore the structural causes of violence in Burundi. Anchored in historically entrenched inequalities and reinforced through violent, often identity-based politics, these causes include limited access to basic services such as health and education, and a lack of sustainable livelihood opportunities.[10] In 2013, Burundi ranked 180 of 187 countries for the indices of 'a long and healthy life', 'access to knowledge', and 'standard of living' (UNDP, 2014, p. 2);[11] the country's gross national income per capita stood below USD 750 (UNDP, n.d.b).

These socioeconomic challenges are aggravated by diminishing access to land, increasing fragmentation of land ownership, and over-exploitation of land. The consequent competition over land sparks frequent conflicts within families, between neighbours, and between communities and returning refugees (ICG, 2014).[12] Land-related conflict and declining resources are having an acutely negative effect on the prospects for political stability and peaceful development.

The second key gap in international peace and security interventions is a lack of focus on young people. PBF project interventions, for example, did not target youths affiliated with political parties—even though youth-related violence has long been identified as one of the greatest security threats in Burundi (Campbell et al., 2014). Moreover, 18–25-year-old combatants were not covered in the children's DDR process, which also failed to provide adequate reintegration support to child combatants once they turned 18 (Seymour, 2012, pp. 27–28). While young people in post-conflict contexts are often expected to contribute to the rebuilding of their societies, many young Burundians have not received the support they need to do so. Instead, they are forced to expend all their energies on basic survival.

VOICES OF YOUNG BURUNDIANS

Before effective steps can be taken to protect young Burundians, it is essential to hear their own opinions, ideas, and perspectives about the challenges and risks they face. The self-reported perceptions described in this section are drawn primarily from interviews and focus groups held in 2012–14 with almost 500 young people aged 10–25 in Bujumbura as well as in town centres and rural villages of six provinces (Bubanza, Bujumbura Rural, Bururi, Cibitoke, Kayanza, and Makamba) (see Map 9.1).[13] In 2013 and 2014, three young people formed an integral part of the core research team, while adolescent researchers were also trained and conducted interviews among their peers. In addition, more than 200 adults were interviewed during the fieldwork.

Map 9.1 **Field research locations in Burundi, 2012-14**

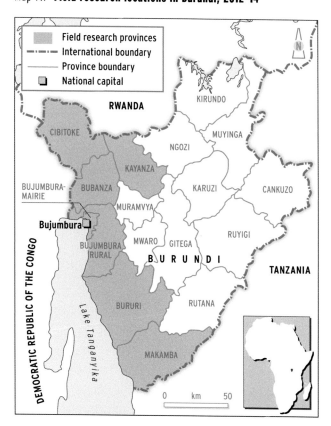

Surviving the everyday

In Burundi, young people's agency—their ability to act within and influence their situation (Bourdieu, 1977)—has been severely constrained by the hardships associated with war, and by the risks inherent in their everyday survival, including a lack of access to basic services. As in many contexts of violent conflict and entrenched poverty, young people's agency involves navigating the constraints on everyday life and seizing opportunities in a frequently changing environment (Vigh, 2006, pp. 10–11). For many young Burundians, meeting even basic needs presents profound challenges (Sommers, 2013); yet, despite these constraints, they are doing their best to make the most of their capacities and skills to improve their survival outcomes.

Many young people in Burundi today bear the heavy responsibility of ensuring their own livelihoods as well as those of their families. Most of the young people who participated in this research reported that they earn BIF 1,000–2,000 (USD 0.65–1.30) per day. Many of them are involved in cultivation, usually as day labourers, as transporters of goods and materials, as assistants in informal commercial activities, or as casual labourers in the construction industry. Although both young men and women reported doing all types of work, they tended to refer to cultivation as a 'girls' job', whereas work relating to transport and construction was perceived as more suited to boys. In almost all cases, young people reported being involved in more than one income-generating activity, taking advantage of any opportunity presented to them, and diversifying to increase chances of being able to afford food, medical care, and school fees and materials for themselves, their younger siblings, or their own children (Seymour et al., 2014, pp. 20–21).

Young women work in the fields, in the province of Cibitoke, northern Burundi, March 2010. © Thierry Bresillon/Godong/Corbis

Box 9.2 High-risk coping tactics

Why do Burundian youths let themselves be mobilized for violence? In part, their involvement should be seen as a form of coping, but one that comes with high risks. During the war, for example, large numbers of young people joined armed groups of their own volition, yet that 'volition' was deeply constrained. In their own words, young people who joined the army often did so for their physical safety, as army positions were thought to offer greater protection than one's home village (Ntirandekura, 2003; Uvin, 2007). Others joined the Gardiens de la Paix–a paramilitary force organized by local administrators–to protect local community interests (Ntiyibagiruwayo, 2003), or the CNDD-FDD or the Palipehutu-FNL for ideological reasons (Seymour, 2012). Often young people's choices were based on a combination of motivations that were at once economic and ideological, or based on a desire for revenge. As described by one 20-year-old:

> I joined the FNL in 2007 because I had no means of surviving. I thought that even if I died in combat it would be better than living in such misery. I wanted to fight against injustice, know freedom (Seymour, 2012, p. 17).[14]

Such mixed motivations for joining armed groups are consistent with findings from other conflict-affected contexts (HealthNet TPO, 2011).[15]

Even in the post-conflict period, young people's agency and attempts to improve their survival outcomes may lead them to make choices that increase their likelihood of becoming involved in violence. For example, young men who joined the Imbonerakure youth wing reported doing so for reasons linked to protecting their families–especially in cases where they or their family members were formerly affiliated with the FNL or other opposition political movements (Seymour, 2014). Other youths (of both sexes) reported joining the youth wing of a political party in order to increase their chances of securing patronage support (Berckmoes, 2014, pp. 154-55). In the lead-up to the 2015 elections, young people's main motivation for political involvement was to increase their chances of accessing money or material goods: 'We might be offered BIF 2,000 (USD 1.30) for being at an event. Why not go?' (Seymour et al., 2014, p. 38).

Although girls are also involved in political activities and thus also at risk of becoming involved in armed violence, some of them have adopted other high-risk coping tactics, largely because their options for meeting their survival needs, as well as the needs of their younger siblings and their own children, are severely limited. During the interviews conducted for this study, young women–as well as young men, parents, and other adult interviewees–repeatedly reported that girls were increasingly engaging in sexual activities in exchange for food, money, or other material support. According to one girl, material need is the main motivation:

> There is no money at home. We ask our parents for soap but they insult us: 'Are we a bank?' they ask us. But we need to wash our clothes so that we can look clean like the others. Then they tell us that we are wasting soap. Then a boy or a man comes to offer money for sex. . . . Girls will go to him. Girls might get 1,000 or 2,000 franbu [USD 0.65-1.30] each time. There is nowhere else to get the money (Seymour et al., 2014, p. 28).

While joining an armed group or a political youth wing may offer some young people a broader range of options–and thus facilitate their survival in the short term–it puts them at considerable long-term risk of becoming involved in armed violence. Similarly, for young women, the short-term benefits of engaging in transactional sex might include being able to pay school fees, buy food, or pay for medical care, but the long-term risks include not only contracting sexually transmitted infections or becoming pregnant, but also enduring psychosocial effects and poorer longer-term survival outcomes. Examining how young people cope with pervasive violence requires both short- and long-term perspectives, with an appreciation for the complexity of coping processes whose outcomes might not be measurable for many years.

Such efforts are extremely demanding. As one 17-year-old boy explained: 'Sometimes I'm just so tired, and I don't manage to earn enough so that I can eat enough [. . .] or even eat at all' (Seymour et al., 2014, p. 21). Many young women face the added responsibility of caring for younger siblings, their own children, and household tasks. A 19-year-old mother of two young children explained:

> I wake up in the morning and go to the fields to cultivate because that is my job. I work until 11:00. Then I return to prepare food for the children so that they have something to eat when they return from school. After that, around 15:00, I go to the roadside to sell tomatoes so that I might have the means to feed the family. I return home at 20:30 and do the necessary housework before going to bed (Seymour et al., 2014, p. 21).

In response to the question, 'What are the biggest worries you face?' young people's most common responses were variations on a theme: 'falling ill, being hungry, not being able to pay school fees or materials' (Seymour et al., 2014, p. 21).

With survival such a challenge, young people often have little hope of emerging from entrenched poverty. Young Burundians' 'low horizons' (Sommers, 2013, pp. 40–41) have a marked impact on their aspirations and contribute to feelings of humiliation and hopelessness, particularly among those unable to continue formal schooling or secure sustainable livelihoods. Consumed by the demands of the daily fight for survival, many have few reasons to aspire to a brighter future. This outlook can influence their adoption of high-risk coping tactics, such as joining armed groups or youth wings of political parties, or engaging in unsafe sexual activities (see Box 9.2 on previous page).

Breakdown in family support capacities

With survival such a challenge, youth have little hope of emerging from entrenched poverty.

Social support is a crucial aspect of young people's capacities for coping, yet, as recent studies have shown, 'young Burundians today are on their own, with less assistance from families and communities than ever before' (Sommers, 2013, p. 14, citing Uvin, 2009). This decline in support is largely attributable to factors associated with the long history of war and crippling macroeconomic conditions—which are not likely to be overcome in the near future.

In the absence of parental support, young people are left to find their own ways of meeting their basic needs. Asked whom they would turn to for support, many young people in group discussions initially replied, 'No one'. As one youth summarized: 'There is no one who can support us because mostly everyone is poor' (Seymour et al., 2014, p. 30). According to the research participants, the support needed by young people is above all material; as their families are not able to help them, they feel they have no one to turn to. Parents' inability to meet the basic needs of their children is mainly attributed to the war. In the words of one official: 'Since the war, poverty has prevented parents from caring for their children. As they don't give their children what they need, the children go astray.' Another local authority observed: 'Parents are too busy, they don't have the time to talk to their children, they are just overwhelmed with survival' (Seymour et al., 2014, p. 30).

Without adequate social support, young people are left to fend for themselves. One 15-year-old boy explained how, when he was younger, his parents would provide him with food and clothing; over time, however, they were no longer able to assure his basic needs. The inability of his family to provide this support led him to adopt alternate coping mechanisms:

Three years ago I still lived with my family. But because in my family we have nothing, I preferred to come and live on the streets. My family has a small parcel. We are eight children and my father would sideline me. I'm still in contact with my family, but I prefer to live on the streets. I am still close to them, I hear their news. If my mother is sick, I can go to be with her. My father too, I see him every now and then and if he has some money, he might give me something to eat. I left home because I wasn't satisfied. I worked so much without receiving something in return—you understand how hard that can be. They didn't even buy me underwear. Today, if I can earn a little bit of money, I can buy myself underwear, a shirt or something else. I can also have something to eat. My day is spent searching for money. I earn money carrying bags and merchandise to and from the market. This is what takes up my whole day. At night, I play cards with the others and wait for the day to end and to sleep. I don't set myself objectives because my first priority is right now: How will I get my food today? What will I cover myself with if there is rain tonight? (Seymour at el., 2014, p. 31).

This breakdown of families' capacities to support their children has important implications for potential youth pathways to violence. As the young man quoted above also noted, members of political parties frequently approached him and his peers who were living on the streets about participating in rallies and events. Payment in the form of food, clothes, or money of up to BIF 2,000 (USD 1.30) exceeds what they might have received from their families or earned from a day of labour. Political patronage is one of the main avenues for accessing material support or protection in Burundi, and thus one of the main channels for mobilizing young people for violence.

Cycles of violence and poverty

According to the young Burundians who participated in this research, armed violence both emerges from poverty and leads to poverty. For the majority of young people, the connection between past violence and present-day experiences of economic adversity is direct; the violence experienced by them in their childhood and by their parents lays the foundation for their current hardships. Certain young people related that the war that began in 1993 led to the death of one or both parents and thus the obligation to abandon school, which drastically narrowed future employment possibilities. One youth underscored the cyclical nature of this predicament: 'Violence happens because of poverty. Our parents died during the war. If they were alive today, we'd be okay. The war caused all this suffering' (Seymour et al., 2014, p. 35). One participant in a group of parents elaborated on the connections between contemporary material hardship and the legacy of the war:

> Children live with nothing. Growing up in a poor family, they will stay poor. Boys just spend their days drinking, they've lost their vision for the future. Young people today are only looking at the now—what can they gain now [. . .]. We are moving house all the time, unable to pay the rent and having to find somewhere more affordable. These changes are caused by the war. We left our land, lived in the forest, in refugee camps [. . .]. Before the war it wasn't like this. First it was the war, now it's the hunger (Seymour et al., 2014, p. 39).

Young people's narratives describe the extent to which past waves of armed violence have shaped their precarious present and restricted future possibilities. While people's memories of violence experienced in the past live on into the present, ongoing threats of armed violence are also directly linked to earlier waves of violence. One example concerns the rising levels of fear and uncertainty in relation to the return of hundreds of thousands of Hutu refugees who were displaced during the massacres of 1972. Another, related source of unease and growing mistrust revolves around land distribution, which has become increasingly politicized since the end of the conflict. Young people described how conflicts over land often involve the threat or use of machetes, batons, lances, and grenades to scare people off land. As one young person observed:

> Overpopulation is a problem, many displaced people are now returning. They are coming back with their children. The [government] will give them back the land, and we will be forced to leave, even if we show our papers to the authorities. If we go to the justice authorities, we will be threatened. We will be told that we will be killed or that we will have our teeth pulled out. [. . .] Now someone is living on my father's land. Because of this I now have hatred in my heart (Seymour et al., 2014, p. 36).

Based on young people's descriptions, past violence grew out of ethnic hatred, whereas ethnic identity no longer features as the principal explanation for ongoing violence. Indeed, young people identify the 1993 war—and the violence

Political patronage is one of the main avenues for accessing material support or protection.

preceding it—with hostilities 'between Hutu and Tutsi', as distinct from today's tensions and violence, which they link to 'politics'. According to many of the young people interviewed for this study, belonging to the current government party is a precondition for achieving or preserving their family's access to land, gaining employment, and assuring one's personal security (Seymour, 2014; Seymour et al., 2014). In fact, the threatened or explicit use of violence—a core element of Burundian politics—has been fully integrated into young people's processes of making sense of their experiences. For them, contemporary political violence is just one dimension of the violence affecting their everyday lives; it cannot be dissociated from long-standing inequalities and poverty. These perceptions have major implications for Burundi's prospects for long-term development and peace.

PROTECTING YOUNG PEOPLE FROM INVOLVEMENT IN ARMED VIOLENCE

Risks, protective factors, and the ecological model

Contemporary political violence cannot be dissociated from long-standing inequalities and poverty.

According to their own narratives, young people in Burundi are confronted by multiple risks on a daily basis. The risks that were associated with direct militarized violence during the war—including death, injury, and displacement—have been followed by the structural risks of a lack of access to basic social services, unemployment, and limited livelihood opportunities. Burundi is not unusual in this regard. In a wide range of war-affected contexts, chronic political, cultural, economic, and social stressors have been shown to have a significant effect on young people's coping capacities (Kostelny, 2006). In such places, the 'daily stressors' of material hardship and reduced access to social services often have a more detrimental impact on young people than the direct experience of militarized violence (Miller and Rasmussen, 2010, p. 7).

The narratives also indicate that traditional protective factors that were once core elements of their coping processes are no longer available or effective. Research in other war-affected contexts has shown that the role of the family is of singular importance in protecting young people's well-being (Panter-Brick and Eggerman, 2012, p. 374). In Afghanistan, Sierra Leone, Sri Lanka, and elsewhere, the death of a primary caregiver during violent conflict has been a key determinant in young people's developmental outcomes (Betancourt et al., 2013; Catani, Schauer, and Neuner, 2008), while the long-term impact of poverty on parental care capacities can be especially damaging (Catani, Schauer, and Neuner, 2008).

The ecological model of human development considers how a child's development is influenced by the multiple systems in which he or she is embedded (Bronfenbrenner, 1986); it is conceptually useful for analyses of the risks and protective factors influencing young people's coping processes and possibilities for well-being in highly complex and multifaceted contexts of violence.[16] In this multi-level model, the individual is situated within social networks made up of family, peers, teachers, and religious actors. Those community actors are embedded in a broader system influenced by socioeconomic and political dynamics. Each level fits within a macro-system that is rooted in culture and subject to change over time.

Child-focused research and humanitarian practice in war-affected contexts is increasingly adopting a socioecological perspective, influencing current thinking on young people's resilience to adversity (CPWG, 2012; Ungar, Ghazinour, and Richter, 2013; Wessells, 2009). Although this more holistic approach is gaining ground, further analysis is needed to determine how the various levels of the ecological system are affected and transformed by protracted violence, and what impact these transformations are having on young people's capacities for coping. According to young Burundians, the protective factors of their social and material environment have been completely eroded by violence. As discussed above, most families can no longer offer them support or protection, while educational, health, and employment opportunities are inaccessible for the majority of youths. In the near absence of protective factors, some young people migrate towards high-risk survival tactics, which may allow them to cope effectively in the short term; at the same time, the corresponding way of life significantly increases the risks to their well-being in the long term.[17]

The field research presented here suggests that the role of local and national party-based politics in Burundi requires specific attention in analyses of violence and young people's coping processes. Party-based politics currently permeate all levels of life—much as ethnic identity did until the end of the war. Youths' narratives indicate that it is only through political patronage that one might hope to access material resources, future livelihood opportunities, and enhanced physical security. As young people repeatedly stated, joining the youth wing of a political party is today considered the essential first step in increasing one's chances of gaining such patron support. Young people's engagement in politics is not necessarily problematic—indeed, their political engagement occasionally contributes to improved well-being and a sense of individual control (Barber, 2009; Blattman, 2009); in Burundi, however, party politics have a long history of manipulating young people to engage in violent activities.

Strategies for strengthening protective factors

Understanding the extreme challenges confronting young Burundians as well as their lack of protective factors is essential to developing more effective policies and interventions to respond to their needs and improve their prospects. Confirming findings from earlier research on the severe economic constraints facing young Burundians and the consequent lack of opportunities (Sommers and Uvin, 2011, p. 1), the narratives presented in this chapter demonstrate the extent to which young people are struggling to surmount adversities such as poverty, hunger, unemployment, and illness. While they exhibit great resourcefulness in coping with these challenges, their capacities to cope are not to be confused with resilience, which would require the availability of health-sustaining resources (Ungar, 2008; see Box 9.3).

Box 9.3 Resilience as a psychological construct

The field of psychology has led resilience research since the 1970s (Elder, 1974; Garmezy, 1985; Rutter and Madge, 1976). Early studies focused on children growing up at the margins of Western European or US society, or in families with parents who were mentally ill or dependent on drugs or alcohol. The general aim was to improve understandings of what characterizes individual coping mechanisms and responses among children living in high-risk social environments, and how treatment and prevention interventions could be more responsive to their needs (Luthar and Brown, 2007). Resilience studies were particularly helpful in moving the field from a focus on the traumatic and psychologically damaging impacts of adversity towards one that acknowledges the capacities of individuals to cope effectively in the face of extreme constraints. Resilience theory suggests that vulnerability can be reduced and relatively good outcomes experienced despite conditions of environmental risk (Rutter, 2012, p. 336).

Resilience researchers have more recently broadened their focus to examine the experiences of young people in a wider range of sociocultural contexts and, in particular, the social, political, cultural, and economic systems in which young people are embedded (Hazen, 2008, p. 250).[18] Building on Bronfenbrenner's conception of the ecological model of human development, a socioecological approach to resilience considers:

> both the capacity of individuals to navigate their way to health-sustaining resources, including opportunities to experience feelings of well-being, and a condition of the individual's family, community and culture to provide these health resources and experiences in culturally meaningful ways (Ungar, 2008, p. 225).

This conception of resilience as socially embedded has been especially relevant to the growing field of resilience studies in conflict settings and in places with limited access to the basic resources needed to sustain well-being. The socioecological approach to resilience allows for an understanding of well-being not only as an individual process, but also as social, economic, and political processes, open to multiple levels of analysis and intervention.

By considering the strengths and agency of young people, and by aiming to build protective factors, practitioners and policy-makers can develop interventions that enhance young people's ability to support themselves. Young Burundians report that they are most concerned about ensuring their survival and that of their families. Providing them

Supported by a micro-credit project, a 23-year-old woman runs a business selling fruit in Musaga market, Burundi, December 2010.
© Martina Bacigalupo/Keystone/Agence VU

with opportunities to earn an income and generate livelihoods is likely to improve their prospects significantly and reduce their chances of adopting high-risk coping tactics. According to Sommers and Uvin (2011, p. 11), generating employment opportunities and providing means to access credit would provide young people with the conditions they need to advance themselves.

Resilience theory suggests that encouraging youth participation in matters and processes that affect young people offers them an opportunity to express their individual agency in ways that can reduce their risks of engaging in violence. Approaches that place young people at the centre of interventions in Burundi include Search for Common Ground's *Intamenwa* ('Indivisibles') project to mobilize young people for peaceful elections in 2015 through conflict resolution skills development (SFCG, 2014); another such project is Action on Armed Violence's peer-based effort to reduce engagement in violence, accompanied by micro-credit loans (Madueno, 2014). These initiatives serve as positive examples of the kind of interventions that are needed to reinforce young people's capacities for resilience in the long term.

The socioecological model also suggests that young people's individual agency is not enough to ensure their well-being; as noted in Box 9.3, it is essential that interventions involve the wider systems in which young people are embedded. This means involving parents, teachers, religious actors, and other community members in the wide range of projects that currently target young people. One example of innovative programming is UNICEF Burundi's Peace-building, Education, and Advocacy Programme, which supports research and interventions to strengthen household caring practices, while at the same time engaging with communities and education service providers in improving life skills education for adolescents. UNICEF programmes currently under way include research on how violence may be transferred from one generation to the next, population-based household surveys on early childhood parenting practices, and resilience and social cohesion, as well as programmes to engage young people and cultivate their leadership skills.[19]

At the widest level of society, more effective polices are needed to respond to the needs of young people. Positive developments include the passage of a national child protection policy in 2013, the elaboration of Burundi's child protection code in May 2014,[20] and a national youth policy that prioritizes youths in employment, training, and access to micro-credit schemes (Mpfayokurera, 2014; Mukene et al., 2014; Peeters, Rees Smith, and Correia, 2012). Government policies of mandating free maternal and child health care[21] and free primary education send important political messages, but they remain far from being realized in practice. The considerable political will and financial resources needed to bring them to fruition remain elusive. Until this political impetus becomes a reality, it is difficult to imagine meaningful improvements in the lives of young Burundians.

CONCLUSION

The challenges facing young people in Burundi are profound. Having lived much of their lives in a situation of violent conflict, they have experienced extreme loss and hardships: the death of parents and other close family members, frequent displacement, loss of land and looting of property, illness, and disrupted access to school and other basic services. In the post-conflict period, young Burundians continue to suffer from a persistent lack of access to education and health care, food insecurity, and seemingly insurmountable challenges to obtaining gainful employment. In short, young people in Burundi remain highly vulnerable.

Despite the odds, young Burundians are doing their best to cope, with varying degrees of effectiveness. Understanding how they do so is important for developing positive support strategies. As this chapter has shown, young people use a variety of coping tactics to improve their access to resources and to ensure their immediate short-term survival. In the longer term, however, these strategies may increase the exposure to risks, as is the case when young people join youth wings of political parties for material gain, given Burundi's historical mobilization of young people for violent ends. While armed violence data is not yet refined enough to establish a link between such violence and political groups, it seems likely that some of the current violence is indeed linked to political party manipulation of young people. In this context, it is important to note that guns are used in more than one-third of all weapons-related violence, attesting to their ongoing availability despite post-conflict disarmament efforts.

The impacts of a situation in which so many young people are, as one young person said, 'busy just surviving' (Seymour, 2014, p. 3) are felt at all levels of society and have serious implications for Burundi's future. To avert, or at least mitigate, the potential damage, government leaders, policy-makers, and practitioners need to place a higher priority on improving the opportunities available to young people. Despite the profound challenges, advances can be—and, in some cases, are being—made. Yet to truly make a difference in the lives of young Burundians, concerted attention, political will, and an efficient use of existing funds are required. Burundi is not unique in its developmental challenges, but the country's particular history makes addressing the dire conditions of its youth particularly urgent. ◼

LIST OF ABBREVIATIONS

BIF	Burundi franc
CNDD	Conseil National Pour la Défense de la Démocratie
CNDD–FDD	Conseil National Pour la Défense de la Démocratie–Forces pour la Défense de la Démocratie
DDR	Disarmament, demobilization, and reintegration
FNL	Forces Nationales de Libération
FRODEBU	Front pour la Démocratie au Burundi
MDRP	Multi-Country Demobilization and Reintegration Programme
Palipehutu–FNL	Parti pour la Libération du Peuple Hutu–Forces Nationales de Libération
PBF	Peacebuilding Fund
UNICEF	United Nations Children's Fund
UPRONA	Union pour le Progrès National

ENDNOTES

1   For the purposes of this chapter a 'young person' is defined as anyone who falls between the ages of 10 and 25 years.

2   This interim president, Sylvestre Ntibantunganya, had been appointed in 1994, following the death of the first interim president, Cyprien Ntaryamira, who died in the April 1994 plane crash that also killed President Juvenal Habyarimana of Rwanda (Pézard and Florquin, 2007, p. 199).

3   See the Arusha Peace and Reconciliation Agreement (APRA, 2000).

4   Building on the work of an observatory that had previously operated with the support of the UN Development Programme, the Burundi Armed Violence Observatory was established to monitor and record events relating to armed violence at a national level. The project, led by the Burundian National Commission on Small Arms and Light Weapons in collaboration with the international NGO Action on Armed Violence, began a system-atic collection and analysis of reports of armed violence in Burundi in early 2014. Partners in the collection of data include the Burundian National Police, local administrations, human rights actors and other members of civil society, medical centres, and radio stations. The data collected by

the observatory is setting a long-needed baseline for analysing trends in armed violence throughout the country. The observatory documents information on each incident reported, including the sex of the victims and perpetrators, the type and number of arms used, the location of the incident, and the apparent motivation for the incident. For more information on the observatory, see CNAP (n.d.).

5 Pézard and Florquin (2007) document that of the almost 1,300 injuries treated at a Médecins sans Frontières–Belgium clinic in one Bujumbura neighbourhood, 58 per cent of the wounds were due to bullets, 21 per cent to grenades, 13 per cent to blunt objects, 5 per cent to bladed weapons, 2 per cent to landmines, and 1 per cent to mortar bombs. A number of factors may explain why these findings regarding the use of various weapons in violent incidents differ from those presented in this chapter, including the proximity to the conflict phase, the limited geographical scope of the reports documented in Pézard and Florquin (2007), and the international DDR and security sector reform interventions described above.

6 In 2003, the African Union established the African Mission in Burundi, which was replaced by the UN Operation in Burundi peacekeeping mission in 2004 (RULAC, 2010). The UN Integrated Office in Burundi was established in 2006; five years later, it was replaced by the UN Office in Burundi, which completed its mandate in December 2014, with UN responsibilities transferred to the UN Country Team (BNUB, n.d.).

7 Operating between 2002 and 2009, the MDRP supported the DDR processes in seven countries and reached an estimated 350,000 ex-combatants with a budget of about USD 500 million (World Bank, 2010, p. 1).

8 Having conducted a mental health diagnosis of more than 1,200 demobilized children in the provinces of Cancuzo, Kayanza, Ngozi, and Ruyigi, the NGO Trauma Healing and Reconciliation Services (THARS) recommended urgent psychotherapeutic interventions, which never took place (author correspondence with the THARS director, 20 October 2014).

9 Burundi has also received support from the German government to strengthen capacities of police structures and from the US Office of Weapons Removal and Abatement for weapons marking, the destruction of weapons and ammunition, and storage and management support (GIZ, n.d.; USDOS, 2009). International NGOs such as the Mines Advisory Group and Action on Armed Violence have also provided significant support for stockpile management, weapons destruction, and capacity building and training of national authorities to monitor and respond to acts of armed violence (AOAV, n.d.; GICHD, 2012).

10 Burundi's gross national income per capita decreased by 19 per cent between 1980 and 2013 (UNDP, 2014, p. 2). Counter to regional trends in sub-Saharan Africa, economic forecasts indicate worsening poverty in the future (World Bank, 2014).

11 In 2013, life expectancy at birth was 54.1 years, the mean years of schooling for the adult population over 25 was 2.7 years, and an estimated 82 per cent of the population was considered to live in 'multidimensional poverty', reflecting both economic hardship and 'overlapping deprivations suffered by people at the same time' (UNDP, 2014, p. 5; n.d.a).

12 With more than 350 people per square kilometre, Burundi is one of sub-Saharan Africa's most densely populated countries, yet also one of its most rural, with the majority of its population depending on subsistence farming (World Bank, 2012).

13 For more details on the methodologies used in this research, see Seymour (2012) and Seymour et al. (2014).

14 In many contexts of armed conflict, young people describe their mobilization by the fighting forces as a choice within severely limiting constraints; see, for example, Brett and Specht (2004) and Seymour (2013).

15 In a 2011 study funded by the International Labour Organization, 69 per cent of the 452 former child combatants interviewed indicated that their main reason for joining armed groups had been to gain material benefits, although they also cited fear, peer pressure, political ideology, and a desire for revenge. The study finds that the mean age of recruitment was 14.6 years and that the average length of involvement was 4.2 years. It also reports that 69 per cent of the young people had joined voluntarily, 16 per cent had been forcibly recruited, and another 8 per cent had been abducted. Once recruited, the youths were required to participate in active combat, help with transport, prepare food, and serve as guards and informers, among other tasks (HealthNet TPO, 2011, p. 21).

16 See Hazen (2008, pp. 250–51).

17 Similarly, qualitative research with former child combatants in the Democratic Republic of the Congo has shown how young people's voluntary enrolment in armed groups may have offered physical protection and a means of survival in the short term, even if such coping strategies left some of these young people with a strong sense of disillusionment and frustration years later (Seymour, 2013).

18 This approach has been taken by the Resilience Research Centre in Halifax, Canada. Since 2007, the Centre has led the International Pathways to Resilience project across five countries to examine the culturally specific strengths and capacities that young people use to cope with problems. See IPTR (n.d.).

19 Author correspondence with UNICEF Burundi, 12 January 2015.

20 Child protection is defined as 'the prevention of and response to abuse, neglect, exploitation and violence against children' (CPWG, 2012, p. 13). Current international best practice aims to strengthen the 'child protection system', defined as 'the people, processes, laws, institutions and behaviours that normally protect children' (p. 30), which effectively represents the outer level of Bronfenbrenner's ecological model.

21 Government policies stipulate that health care be provided free of charge for children five and under.

BIBLIOGRAPHY

AI (Amnesty International). 2014. *Locked Down: A Shrinking of Political Space*. London: AI.
    <http://www.amnesty.org/en/library/info/AFR16/002/2014/en>

AOAV (Action on Armed Violence). n.d. 'Our Work on the Ground: Burundi.'
    <https://aoav.org.uk/on-the-ground/burundi/>

APRA (Arusha Peace and Reconciliation Agreement for Burundi). 2000. Arusha, 28 August. <http://www.ucd.ie/ibis/filestore/Arusha (Burundi) .pdf>

Ball, Nicole. 2014. 'Putting Governance at the Heart of Security Sector Reform: Lessons from the Burundi–Netherlands Security Sector Development
    Programme.' The Hague: Netherlands Institute of International Relations Clingendael. April.
    <http://www.clingendael.nl/sites/default/files/Putting%20governance%20at%20the%20heart%20of%20SSR.pdf>

Barber, Brian. 2009. 'Glimpsing the Complexity of Youth and Political Violence.' In Brian Barber, ed. *Adolescents and War: How Youth Deal with
    Political Violence*. New York: Oxford University Press, pp. 3–32.

Berckmoes, Lidewyde. 2014. *Elusive Tactics: Urban Youth Navigating the Aftermath of War in Burundi*. Amsterdam: Vrije Universiteit.

Betancourt, Theresa, et al. 2013. 'Trajectories of Internalizing Problems in War-affected Sierra Leonean Youth: Examining Conflict and Postconflict Factors.'
    Child Development, Vol. 84, No. 2, pp. 455–70.

Blattman, Christopher. 2009. 'From Violence to Voting: War and Political Participation in Uganda.' *American Political Science Review*, Vol. 103, No. 2,
    pp. 231–47.

BNUB (United Nations Office in Burundi). n.d. Website. <http://bnub.unmissions.org>

Bourdieu, Pierre. 1977. *Outline of a Theory of Practice*. London: Cambridge University Press.

BRAVO (Burundi Armed Violence Observatory). 2014a. *Rapport de l'Observatoire de la Violence Armée au Burundi*. May.
    <http://aoav.org.uk/wp-content/uploads/2014/07/Rapport-OVA-Jan-Mai-2014-FINAL.pdf>

—. 2014b. *Rapport de l'Observatoire de la Violence Armée au Burundi*. June–July.
    <http://www.cnapburundi.bi/images/OVA_FINAL_REPORT_JUNE_JULY_2014.pdf>

—. 2014c. *Rapport de l'Observatoire de la Violence Armée au Burundi*. August.
    <http://www.cnapburundi.bi/images/OVA_FINAL_REPORT_AUGUST_2014.pdf>

Brett, Rachel and Irma Specht. 2004. *Young Soldiers: Why They Choose to Fight*. Geneva, London, and Boulder, CO: International Labour Office and
    Lynne Rienner Publishers.
    <http://www.quno.org/sites/default/files/resources/ENGLISH-Young_soldiers_why_they_choose_to_fight.pdf>

Bronfenbrenner, Urie. 1986. 'Ecology of the Family as a Context for Human Development: Research Perspectives.' *Development Psychology,* Vol. 22,
    No. 6, pp. 732–42.

Campbell, Susana, et al. 2014. 'Independent External Evaluation: UN Peacebuilding Fund Project Portfolio in Burundi 2007–2013.' 1 February.
    <http://www.unpbf.org/wp-content/uploads/FINAL-Independent-External-Evaluation-PBF-Burundi_English-version_March2014.pdf>

Catani, Claudia, Elisabeth Schauer, and Frank Neuner. 2008. 'Beyond Individual War Trauma: Domestic Violence against Children in Afghanistan and
    Sri Lanka.' *Journal of Marital and Family Therapy,* Vol. 34, No. 2, pp. 165–76.

Chrétien, Jean-Pierre and Jean-François Dupaquier. 2007. *Burundi 1972: au bord des génocides*. Paris: Editions Karthala.

CNAP (Commission Nationale Permanente de lutte contre la prolifération des armes légères et de petit calibre). n.d. 'Burundi Armed Violence
    Observatory: History.' <http://www.cnapburundi.bi/index.php/en/burundi-armed-violence-observatory>

CPWG (Child Protection Working Group). 2012. 'Minimum Standards for Child Protection in Humanitarian Action (CPMS).'
    <http://cpwg.net/wp-content/uploads/sites/2/2014/03/CP-Minimum-Standards-English-2013.pdf>

De Martino, Luigi and Hannah Dönges. 2012. 'Armed Conflicts: Defining the Concepts.' Unpublished background paper. Geneva: Small Arms Survey.

DSS (Programme de Développement du Secteur de la Sécurité) Burundi. n.d. 'Programme DSS.' <http://programmedss.bi/fr/about/programme>

Elder, Glen. 1974. *Children of the Great Depression: Social Change in Life Experience*. Chicago: University of Chicago Press.

Garmezy, Norman. 1985. 'Stress-resistant Children: The Search for Protective Factors.' In James Stevenson, ed. *Recent Research in Developmental
    Psychopathology*. Oxford: Pergamon Press, pp. 213–33.

Ghoshal, Neela. 2010. *'We'll Tie You Up and Shoot You': Lack of Accountability for Political Violence in Burundi*. New York: Human Rights Watch.
    <http://www.hrw.org/sites/default/files/reports/burundi0510webwcover_2.pdf>

GICHD (Geneva International Centre for Humanitarian Demining). 2012. *Programme de sécurité physique et gestion des stocks de Mines Advisory Group:
    Burundi Etude de Cas*. September.
    <http://www.gichd.org/fileadmin/pdf/other_languages/french/LMAD/AVR-Burundi-MAG-case-study-Sep2012-fr.pdf>

GIZ (Deutsche Gesellschaft für Internationale Zusammenarbeit). n.d. 'Strengthening the Capacities of the Police in Burundi.'

   <https://www.giz.de/en/worldwide/19207.html>

Hazen, Jennifer. 2008. 'Risk and Resilience: Understanding the Potential for Violence.' In Small Arms Survey. *Small Arms Survey 2008: Risk and Resilience*. Geneva: Small Arms Survey, pp. 245–73.

HealthNet TPO. 2011. 'Etude rétrospective de suivi des enfants associés aux forces ou aux groupes armés pour mesurer l'impact à long terme des programmes d'action ILO/IPEC au Burundi et en République Démocratique du Congo.' Bujumbura: HealthNet TPO.

ICG (International Crisis Group). 2004. *Fin de transition au Burundi: franchir le cap*. Rapport Afrique No. 81. Brussels: ICG. 5 July.

   <http://www.crisisgroup.org/fr/regions/afrique/afrique-centrale/burundi/081-end-of-the-transition-in-burundi-the-home-stretch.aspx>

—. 2009. 'Burundi: To Integrate the FNL Successfully.' African Briefing No. 63. Brussels: ICG. 30 July.

   <http://www.crisisgroup.org/en/regions/africa/central-africa/burundi/B063-burundi-to-integrate-the-fnl-successfully.aspx>

—. 2014. *Les terres de la discorde (II): restitution et réconciliation au Burundi*. Rapport Afrique No. 214. Brussels: ICG. ·17 February. <http://www. crisisgroup.org/en/regions/africa/central-africa/burundi/214-fields-of-bitterness-ii-restitution-and-reconciliation-in-burundi.aspx?alt_lang=fr>

IPTR (International Pathways to Resilience). n.d. 'About the Project.' <http://internationalresilience.org/about-the-project/>

Kostelny, Kathleen. 2006. 'A Culture-based, Integrative Approach: Helping War-affected Children.' In Neil Boothby, Alison Strang, and Michael Wessells, eds. *A World Turned Upside Down: Social Ecological Approaches to Children in War Zones*. Bloomfield, CT: Kumarian Press, pp. 19–37.

Lemarchand, René. 1996. *Burundi: Ethnic Conflict and Genocide*. Cambridge: Cambridge University Press.

Luthar, Suniya and Pamela Brown. 2007. 'Maximizing Resilience through Diverse Levels of Inquiry: Prevailing Paradigms, Possibilities, and Priorities for the Future.' *Development and Psychopathology*, Vol. 19, No. 3, pp. 931–55.

Madueno, Caroline. 2014. 'Preventing Election Violence in Burundi through Peer Support.' 25 July.

   <https://aoav.org.uk/2014/preventing-election-violence-burundi-peer-support/>

Miller, Kenneth and Andrew Rasmussen. 2010. 'War Exposure, Daily Stressors, and Mental Health in Conflict and Post-conflict Settings: Bridging the Divide between Trauma-focused and Psychosocial Frameworks.' *Social Science & Medicine,* Vol. 70, No. 1, pp. 7–16.

Mpfayokurera, Thierry. 2014. 'La première au Burundi: code de protection de l'enfant enfin!' Burundi Eco. 2 May. <http://www.burundi-eco.com/ index.php/societe/un-regard-aux-besoins-des-enfants-et-des-jeunes/301-la-premiere-au-burundi-code-de-protection-de-l-enfant-enfin>

Mukene, Pascal, et al. 2014. *Politique Nationale pour la Protection de l'Enfant au Burundi 2012– 2016*. Bujumbura: Ministère de la Solidarité Nationale, des Droits de la Personne Humaine et du Genre.

   <http://www.confemen.org/wp-content/uploads/2014/04/Burundi_A1_Qualit%C3%A9.pdf>

Ngaruko, Floribert and Janvier Nkurunziza. 2000. 'An Economic Interpretation of Conflict in Burundi.' *Journal of African Economies*, Vol. 9, No. 3, pp. 370–409.

Nindorera, Willy. 2012. *The CNDD-FDD in Burundi: The Path from Armed to Political Struggle*. Berghof Transitions Series No. 10. Berlin: Berghof Foundation.

Ntirandekura, Antoine. 2003. *Analyse de la situation des enfants en situation de violence au Burundi: Etude monographique sur les enfants officiellement recrutés dans les Forces Armées Burundaises (FAB) et les enfants associés avec les militaires*. Bujumbura: UNICEF Burundi. September.

Ntiyibagiruwayo, Firmin. 2003. *Analyse de la situation des enfants en situation de violence au Burundi: Etude monographique sur les enfants jeunes Gardiens de la Paix*. Bujumbura: UNICEF Burundi. September.

Oketch, Johnstone Summit and Tara Polzer. 2002. 'Conflict and Coffee in Burundi.' In Jeremy Lind and Karthryn Sturman, eds. *Scarcity and Surfeit: The Ecology of Africa's Conflicts*. Pretoria: Institute for Security Studies, pp. 84–156.

Panter-Brick, Catherine and Mark Eggerman. 2012. 'Understanding Culture, Resilience, and Mental Health: The Production of Hope.' In Michael Ungar, ed. *The Social Ecology of Resilience: A Handbook of Theory and Practice*. New York: Springer, pp. 369–86.

Peeters, Pia, Emilie Rees Smith, and Maria Correia. 2012. 'Voices of Youth in Post-conflict Burundi: Perspectives on Exclusion, Gender and Conflict.' Washington, DC: World Bank.

   <http://documents.worldbank.org/curated/en/2012/01/16274091/voices-youth-post-conflict-burundi-perspectives-exclusion-gender-conflict>

Pézard, Stéphanie and Nicolas Florquin. 2007. 'Conflict and Post-conflict Bujumbura.' In Small Arms Survey. *Small Arms Survey 2007: Guns and the City*. Geneva: Small Arms Survey, pp. 196–225.

— and Savannah de Tessières. 2009. *'Insecurity Is also a War': An Assessment of Armed Violence in Burundi*. Geneva: Geneva Declaration Secretariat.

RFI (Radio France International). 2014a. 'Retrait des soldats burundais de RDC: la discrétion des opposants.' 10 October.

   <http://www.rfi.fr/afrique/20141010-retrait-soldats-burundais-rdc-discretion-opposition-societe-civile/>

—. 2014b. 'Burundi: des bandes d'hommes armés de machettes sèment la terreur.' 9 November.

   <http://www.rfi.fr/afrique/20141109-burundi-bandes-hommes-armes-machettes-sement-terreur/>

RULAC (Rule of Law in Armed Conflicts Project). 2010. 'Burundi: Peace Operations.' Updated July.
    <http://www.geneva-academy.ch/RULAC/peace_operations.php?id_state=38>

—. 2012. 'Burundi: Applicable International Law.' Last updated 28 February.
    <http://www.geneva-academy.ch/RULAC/applicable_international_law.php?id_state=38>

Rutter, Michael. 2012. 'Resilience as a Dynamic Concept.' *Development and Psychopathology,* Vol. 24, No. 2, pp. 335–44.

— and Nicola Madge. 1976. *Cycles of Disadvantage: A Review of Research.* London: Heinemann.

Seymour, Claudia. 2012. *Leçons Apprises sur le Processus de Désarmement, Démobilisation et Réinsertion/Réintégration des Enfants Sortis des Forces
    et Groupes Armés au Burundi.* Bujumbura: UNICEF Burundi. July.

—. 2013. *Young People's Experiences of and Means of Coping with Violence in North and South Kivu Provinces, Democratic Republic of the Congo.*
    London: University of London. Ph.D. thesis.

—. 2014. *Young People's Experiences of Violence in Burundi: A Compilation of Narrative Testimonies.* Unpublished background paper. Geneva: Small
    Arms Survey.

—, et al. 2014. *Resilience Profiling and Capacities for Peace among Adolescents in Burundi.* Bujumbura: UNICEF. 1 May.

SFCG (Search for Common Ground). 2014. 'Intamenwa—"The Indivisibles"—Mobilizing Burundi's Youth for Peaceful Elections.' Internal document.
    October.

Sommers, Marc. 2013. *Low Horizons: Adolescents and Violence in Burundi.* Discussion Paper 2013.02. Antwerp: Institute of Development Policy and
    Management. <http://www.ineesite.org/uploads/files/resources/discussion_paper.pdf>

— and Peter Uvin. 2011. *Youth in Rwanda and Burundi: Contrasting Visions.* Washington, DC: United States Institute of Peace. October.
    <http://www.usip.org/sites/default/files/sr293.pdf>

UN (United Nations). 2003. *Children and Armed Conflict: Report of the Secretary-General.* A/58/546–S/2003/1053 of 10 November.
    <http://www.un.org/en/ga/search/view_doc.asp?symbol=S/2003/1053>

—. 2010. *Seventh Report of the Secretary-General on the United Nations Integrated Office in Burundi.* S/2010/608. 30 November.
    <http://www.un.org/en/ga/search/view_doc.asp?symbol=S/2010/608>

—. 2014. *Report of the Secretary-General on the United Nations Office in Burundi.* S/2014/550. 31 July.
    <http://www.un.org/en/sc/documents/sgreports/2014.shtml>

UNDP (United Nations Development Programme). 2014. 'Explanatory Note on the 2014 Human Development Report Composite Indices: Burundi.'
    <http://hdr.undp.org/sites/all/themes/hdr_theme/country-notes/BDI.pdf>

—. n.d.a. 'Multidimensional Poverty Index (MPI).' <http://hdr.undp.org/en/content/multidimensional-poverty-index-mpi>

—. n.d.b. 'Human Development Indicators.' <http://hdr.undp.org/en/countries/profiles/BDI>

Ungar, Michael. 2008. 'Resilience across Cultures.' *British Journal of Social Work,* Vol. 38, No. 2, pp 218–35.

—, Mehdi Ghazinour, and Jörg Richter. 2013. 'Annual Research Review: What Is Resilience within the Social Ecology of Human Development?' *Journal
    of Child Psychology and Psychiatry,* Vol. 54, No. 4, pp. 348–66.

UNICEF (United Nations Children's Fund). 2007. *The Paris Principles: The Principles and Guidelines on Children Associated with Armed Forces or
    Armed Groups.* New York: UNICEF. February. <http://www.unicef.org/emerg/files/ParisPrinciples310107English.pdf>

UNPBF (United Nations Peacebuilding Fund). n.d.a. 'Burundi.' <http://www.unpbf.org/countries/burundi/>

—. n.d.b. 'Who We Are.' <http://www.unpbf.org/who-we-are/>

—. n.d.c. 'What We Fund.' <http://www.unpbf.org/what-we-fund/>

USDOS (United States Department of State). 2009. *To Walk the Earth in Safety: The United States' Commitment to Humanitarian Mine Action and
    Conventional Weapons Destruction.* Washington, DC: Bureau of Political–Military Affairs. July.
    <http://www.state.gov/documents/organization/125873.pdf>

Uvin, Peter. 2007. 'Ex-combatants in Burundi: Why They Joined, Why They Left, How They Fared.' Multi-Country Demobilization and Reintegration
    Program Working Paper No 3. Washington, DC: World Bank. October.

—. 2009. *Life after Violence: A People's Story of Burundi.* London and New York: Zed Books.

Verhey, Beth. 2004. *Reaching the Girls: A Study on Girls Associated with Armed Forces and Groups in the Democratic Republic of Congo.* London: Save
    the Children UK. <http://resourcecentre.savethechildren.se/sites/default/files/documents/2600.pdf>

Vigh, Henrik. 2006. *Navigating Terrains of War: Youth and Soldiering in Guinea-Bissau.* New York: Berghahn Books.

Vircoulon, Thierry. 2014. 'Danger de rechute au Burundi: question foncière et consolidation de la paix.' *Afrique Décryptages.* 20 February.
    <https://afriquedecryptages.wordpress.com/2014/02/20/danger-de-rechute-au-burundi-question-fonciere-et-consolidation-de-la-paix/>

Voors, Maarten, et al. 2012. 'Violent Conflict and Behavior: A Field Experiment in Burundi.' *American Economic Review,* Vol. 102, No. 2, pp. 941–64.

Wessells, Michael. 2009. 'Do No Harm: Toward Contextually Appropriate Psychosocial Support in International Emergencies.' *American Psychologist*. November, pp. 842–54.

Wood, Geof. 2003. 'Staying Secure, Staying Poor: The "Faustian Bargain".' *World Development*, Vol. 31, No. 3, pp. 455–71.

World Bank. 2010. 'MDRP Final Report: Overview of Program Achievements.' Washington, DC: World Bank. July.

—. 2012. 'World Bank Country Data: Burundi.' <http://data.worldbank.org/country/burundi>

—. 2013. 'Emergency Demobilization and Transitional Reintegration in Burundi.' 31 January.
<http://www.worldbank.org/en/results/2013/01/31/emergency-demobilization-and-transitional-reintegration-in-burundi>

—. 2014. 'Country and Region Specific Forecasts and Data.'
<http://www.worldbank.org/en/publication/global-economic-prospects/data?variable=NYGDPMKTPKDZ&region=SST>

ACKNOWLEDGEMENTS

Principal author

Claudia Seymour

INDEX

tracing
    International Tracing Instrument 64–6
    modular weapons 70
    technological developments 65
trade embargoes *see* embargoes
traditional weapons, poachers' use of 21
trafficking
    Côte d'Ivoire 178–9
    jihadist groups 165
    Libya 175–6
    Mali 164–5
training
    donor-funding 145
    explosive ordnance disposal 143–4
    stockpile management 143–8
transfers
    anti-tank guided weapons 107
    authorized small arms transfers 86–111
    Chinese weapons, to Mali 166–70
    Eastern Bloc weapons, to Mali 166–70
    Libya 101–5
    maritime private security companies
        227–31
    regional reporting instruments 111–13
    Russian weapons, to Mali 166–70
    Syria 106–11
    transparency, regional reporting
        instruments 111–13
transit, control measures 110
transparency
    regional reporting instruments 111–13
    Small Arms Trade Transparency
        Barometer 87–8, 111
transport
    of ammunition 140–1
    extractive industries 45
tropical conflict areas 1
TRZ Kragujevac (Serbia) 137, 141–2
Tsavo National Park (Kenya) 21
Tsavo Trust (Kenya) 28
Tuareg, Mali 158–63, 164, 174
Tubu, Libya 175, 176
Tullow Oil (Kenya) 45
Tunisia, phosphate mining 37
Turkana county (Kenya) 45–6
Turkey
    exports
        Comtrade data 88, 90
        to Egypt 97, 100
        to Libya 103, 105
        to Syria 107, 109
    imports, Comtrade data 88

Tutsis
    Burundi 244, 245, 248
    Democratic Republic of the Congo, 194
    Rwanda 191

U

UAE *see* United Arab Emirates
UEMS *see* Unplanned Explosions at
    Munitions Sites
Uganda People's Defence Force (UPDF)
    16, 17
Uganda, poaching 16, 17, 27
Ukraine
    exports
        Comtrade data 88
        to Libya 103
ULP Mjekës (Albania) 137, 141–2, 143
'Umoja Wetu' operation (Democratic Republic
    of the Congo) 206, 208
UNCLOS *see* United Nations (UN),
    Convention on the Law of the Sea
unexploded ordnance (UXO),
    South-east Europe 128
UNICEF *see* United Nations
    Children's Fund
Unión Patriótica (UP) (Colombia) 43
United Arab Emirates (UAE)
    floating armoury seizure 232
    imports, Comtrade data 88
United Kingdom (UK)
    exports
        Comtrade data 88, 90
        to Egypt 101
        to Libya 103, 105
        to peshmerga 110
    floating armoury authorization 235
    imports, Comtrade data 88, 89, 91
    maritime private security companies,
        export licences 227–9
    Open General Trade Control Licence
        (Maritime Anti-Piracy) 228
United Nations (UN)
    Biennial Meetings of States (BMS)
        59–83
    Commodity Trade Statistics Database
        (Comtrade)
        2012 analysis 86–111
        global trends 2001–12 88–91
    Convention on the Law of the Sea
        219

Fifth Biennial Meeting of States (BMS5)
    59–83
        follow-up 67–8
        impact 75–6
        International Action Network on
        Small Arms 62
        outcome 62–9, 75
Guiding Principles on Business and
    Human Rights 42
Monitoring Group on Somalia and Eritrea
    227, 233
Open-ended Meeting of Government
    Experts (MGE) 2, 65, 67–8, 69–74, 76
Panel of Experts on Libya 104, 176, 177
Peacebuilding Fund (PBF) 250
Programme of Action to Prevent,
    Combat and Eradicate the Illicit Trade
    in Small Arms and Light Weapons in
    All Its Aspects (PoA) 59–83
        international cooperation 66–7
        International Tracing Instrument 64–6
        Review Conference, Second 60
        stockpile management 63–4
        women's involvement 64
Register of Conventional Arms
    93, 99, 103, 105, 107, 108
United Nations Children's Fund (UNICEF),
    Burundi Peacebuilding, Education, and
    Advocacy Programme 261
United Nations Multidimensional Integrated
    Stabilization Mission in Mali (MINUSMA)
    159, 166, 180
United Nations Organization Mission in the
    Democratic Republic of the Congo
    (MONUC) 203–4
United Nations Organization Stabilization
    Mission in the Democratic Republic of
    the Congo (MONUSCO) 208–9
United Nations Security Council (UNSC)
    arms embargoes 92, 102, 104–5
    Resolution 1973 104
    Resolution 2009 104
United States (US)
    Department of State, Weapons Removal
    and Abatement (WRA) 128
    exports
        Comtrade data 87–90
        to Egypt 97, 99, 101
    imports, Comtrade data 88, 89, 91
    military aid, to Egypt 99
    Syria policy 108–9
Unplanned Explosions at Munitions Sites
    (UEMS) 125, 127–8

Printed in the United States
by Baker & Taylor Publisher Services